The Streets of San Francisco

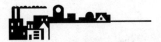

Also in the series:

Harlem: The Unmaking of a Ghetto
by Camilo José Vergara

Planning the Home Front: Building Bombers and Communities at Willow Run
by Sarah Jo Peterson

Purging the Poorest: Public Housing and the Design Politics of Twice-Cleared Communities
by Lawrence J. Vale

Brown in the Windy City: Mexicans and Puerto Ricans in Postwar Chicago
by Lilia Fernandez

Building a Market: The Rise of the Home Improvement Industry, 1914–1960
by Richard Harris

Segregation: A Global History of Divided Cities
by Carl H. Nightingale

Sundays at Sinai: A Jewish Congregation in Chicago
by Tobias Brinkmann

In the Watches of the Night: Life in the Nocturnal City, 1820–1930
by Peter C. Baldwin

Miss Cutler and the Case of the Resurrected Horse: Social Work and the Story of Poverty in America, Australia, and Britain
by Mark Peel

The Transatlantic Collapse of Urban Renewal: Postwar Urbanism from New York to Berlin
by Christopher Klemek

I've Got to Make My Livin': Black Women's Sex Work in Turn-of-the-Century Chicago
by Cynthia M. Blair

Additional series titles follow index

The Streets of San Francisco

POLICING AND THE CREATION
OF A COSMOPOLITAN LIBERAL
POLITICS, 1950-1972

Christopher Lowen Agee

The University of Chicago Press CHICAGO & LONDON

The University of Chicago Press, Chicago 60637
The University of Chicago Press, Ltd., London
© 2014 by The University of Chicago
All rights reserved. Published 2014.
Paperback edition 2016
Printed in the United States of America

25 24 23 22 21 20 19 18 17 16   2 3 4 5 6

ISBN-13: 978-0-226-12228-1 (cloth)
ISBN-13: 978-0-226-37808-4 (paper)
ISBN-13: 978-0-226-12231-1 (e-book)
DOI: 10.7208/chicago/9780226122311.001.0001

Library of Congress Cataloging-in-Publication Data

Agee, Christopher Lowen, author.
The streets of San Francisco : policing and the creation of a cosmopolitan liberal politics,
1950–1972 / Christopher Lowen Agee.
pages cm — (Historical studies of urban America)
ISBN 978-0-226-12228-1 (cloth : alk. paper) — ISBN 978-0-226-12231-1 (e-book) 1. San
Francisco (Calif.)—Politics and government—20th century. 2. San Francisco (Calif.)—
Social conditions—20th century. 3. Police—California—San Francisco. I. Title. II. Series:
Historical studies of urban America.
F869.S357A34 2014
979.4'61053—dc23   2013031039

For Mom and Dad

CONTENTS

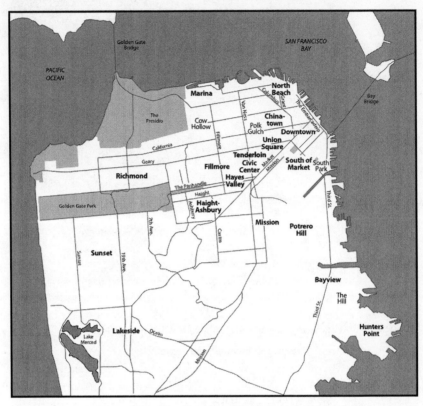

FIGURE 1. Map of San Francisco. (Credit: Peter Anthamatten.)

The protest songs echoing off of San Francisco City Hall's domed rotunda layered into a quaking, choral-like din. More than two hundred protesters packed the grand marble staircase that swept from City Hall's street-level lobby up toward the chambers of the San Francisco Board of Supervisors. Inside that oak-paneled hearing room, the House Committee on Un-American Activities (HUAC) was conducting a two-day investigation into suspected Communist activity. On this second afternoon, May 13, 1960, the congressional committee had dictated audience seating policies designed to deny the demonstrators access to the government proceedings. The protesters—mostly college students—now bellowed, "Break down the doors!"[1]

Inspector Michael "Iron Man" Maguire and a phalanx of helmeted officers assembled a line between those chants and the government hearings. Maguire was a member of the San Francisco Police Department (SFPD) intelligence squad, but he had no experience or special training in handling aggressive demonstrations. Still, the SFPD's command staff was content to leave the situation in the hands of the unprepared lieutenant; members of the department's top ranks remained conspicuously absent from the scene. It was thus Maguire who decided to act. He ordered his men to uncoil the fire hoses stored at the top of the stairs. They turned the nozzles on the protesters and unleashed a torrent of stinging water.[2]

The students held fast, and onlookers struggled to determine who controlled the situation. A young defense attorney later recalled rushing forward to stop the hosing: "I . . . asked a motorcycle policeman if I could speak with the officer in charge. As he did not answer, I repeated the question several times. While I was doing so, another hose was handed to the officer who I was addressing. He, smiling, turned the hose on me at a distance of 2 feet for 2 or 3 minutes. . . . I started to walk toward the stairs, the water was then directed toward my feet." The water splashing across the ground slickened the stone steps, and in minutes the staircase resembled a cascading waterfall. Losing their footing, students turned their backs on the police and sat down. The officers responded by cranking the spigots closed, drawing their batons, and splashing forward. "In a matter of seconds," one reporter commented, "the enormous stairway was alive with struggling groups in wild confusion." Another journalist added that "police were clubbing the demonstrators at will." After subduing the protesters, police slid and bounced the demonstrators' weakened bodies down the marble stairs and out into the police wagons now massed outside.[3]

Over the next decade, San Francisco's 1960 anti-HUAC protest and City Hall "police riot" served as touchstones in the nation's debates over law and order. These national law-and-order discussions divided over the question of whether the welfare regulatory state and increased pluralism in politics and behavior were responsible for the decade's frightening rise in violent crimes. In the aftermath of the San Francisco City Hall riot, HUAC quickly produced the film *Operation Abolition,* a misinformation piece providing a conservative explanation for the bedlam. Through deceptive editing and narration, the film blamed students for initiating the City Hall violence. The movie claimed that a college newspaper and a liberal politician had riled the young people with jeremiads against HUAC, and then "Communist agitators" had marched the impressionable students up the stairs of City Hall and into an assault on the police.[4]

Operation Abolition soon became a sensation among both the gathering New Right and the nascent New Left. When civic groups and conservative clubs screened the film, audience members nodded approvingly at the concluding footage of police beating the "air of defiance" out of the students. When the film played on university campuses, by contrast, college students frequently disregarded the film narrator's insistence that Communist puppet masters lurked off camera and instead focused their attention on the SFPD violence in plain sight. The film became a "camp favorite" among young people who saw in the police response evidence that the government opposed political pluralism. From this perspective, the City Hall police riot "gave the student left its first martyrs."[5]

In their responses to the City Hall clash, both conservatives and college students took aim at the failures they perceived in the liberal state. From the vantage point of conservatives, liberal institutional tolerance for youthful insubordination had created "confused" students easily swayed to mayhem. Conservatives demanded that the state allow law enforcement to crack down on disobedience before it swelled into mob bloodshed. New Left activists regarded the state as hypocritical. College students pointed out that while the government claimed to value free expression, it deployed violent police against boisterous speech. With their respective references to the "thin blue line" and the "pigs of the state," the New Right and New Left both assumed that the police served as a reliable arm of the state and differed over whether that state should offer stricter or more permissive governance.[6]

The 1960 City Hall protest and police riot also drew the attention of such liberals as San Francisco journalists Wes Willoughby and Hadley Roff. Eight months after the protest, the duo published a five-part series recounting the clash and its political fallout. They identified three reactions to the violence: "Supporters of the [HUAC] committee say the police weren't firm enough at City Hall. . . . Objectors to the committee say the police were brutal." The reporters emphasized the third interpretation: "Others say the police were inept."[7]

Willoughby and Roff were part of a growing cadre of young liberals who, during the 1950s and 1960s, repeatedly uncovered evidence of what they regarded as mismanaged law enforcement. Liberals particularly questioned the operational independence of police officers like Inspector Maguire. When San Francisco mayor George Christopher blamed Communist organizers for the City Hall bedlam, a local columnist responded by drawing attention to Christopher's lack of supervision over the scene. The mayor, the columnist ribbed, "tells all about exactly how the student riot started and how the students were 'Communists.' And it's a very dramatic eyewitness account. Mainly because Our Mayor was in Burlingame at the time. Making a luncheon speech. But that just proves how far-seeing he is." Another liberal journalist stressed that "although a riot call had been sounded," the "police brass," like Christopher, "arrived during the aftermath of the riots." With both city and police leadership absent from the scene, liberals emphasized, Inspector Maguire had enjoyed tremendous discretion. One liberal lawyer characterized Maguire as "maniacal," "sadistic," and "stupid," saying he was "solely and singly" responsible for the melee.[8]

As the New Left and New Right responded to police-resident clashes by rejecting the liberal state, urban liberals endeavored to make the state more effective. They began moderately, insisting that simple administrative reforms could ensure democratic law enforcement. Over the course of the 1960s and 1970s, however, this modest managerial reform project exploded in unexpected directions. Through debates over police arrangements—and particularly fights

FIGURE 2. Police seize a demonstrator on the interior steps of City Hall during the 1960 anti-HUAC demonstration and subsequent police riot. Behind them, a woman still drenched from the earlier police hosing attempts to descend the slick marble steps. May 13, 1960. (Reprinted with permission, Bancroft Library, BANC PIC 1959.010—NEG PT III 05-13-60.10: 2.)

over police discretion—a new wave of cosmopolitan liberals reconceived the liberal definitions of crime, citizenship, and democratic governance, insisting that cities could promote physical security by expanding pluralist debate. San Francisco was at the forefront of this liberal transformation. In 1967, at the height of the New Left and New Right assaults on Democrats, San Franciscans elected Joseph Alioto mayor on the basis of his cosmopolitan liberal promise that inclusiveness could produce tough policing. By the 1970s and 1980s, liberals in cities across the nation—including Cleveland, Los Angeles, Atlanta, Boston, Seattle, and Chicago—were using the politics of policing to draw similar arguments over the relationship between democracy and order.[9]

San Francisco was both emblematic of and a mainspring for this transformation in postwar liberalism.

CITIZENSHIP AND GOVERNANCE IN THE POST-WORLD WAR II CITY

The national law-and-order debates of the 1960s had roots in the epochal demographic and economic transformations of the 1940s and 1950s. After World War II, city leaders across the North and West faced an influx of working-class families of color and an exodus of white families and manufacturing jobs. In San Francisco and other cities, urban elites scrambled to develop governing arrangements with which to reestablish their own sense of social and economic stability.

San Francisco is a peninsular metropolis whose front door opens on its eastern, bay side. Prior to World War II, this edge bustled with boat and automobile traffic as old piers drew cargo ships in through the Golden Gate and the new Bay Bridge tied the city to its East Bay neighbors. Newcomers arriving through these bayside entrances were greeted by an expanse of diminutive pastel buildings and a rarely wavering street grid. These two features accentuated both the pitch of the rolling hills stretching between the city's northern and southern borders and the flatness of the reclaimed sand dunes extending west to the Pacific Ocean.

San Francisco's population before World War II had been marked by its racial homogeneity. Although the city was popularly associated with Chinese immigrants, the 1940 Census catalogued the city's population—at just under 635,000 residents—as 95 percent white and less than 3 percent ethnic Chinese. The city's heterogeneity existed within its white population; in 1940, 20 percent of all San Franciscans were foreign-born whites. This demographic makeup was transformed during World War II when the military remade San Francisco's waterfront into an industrial shipbuilding center and a way station for service personnel. New military-oriented jobs attracted a rush of migrants, and by 1950 San Francisco was the eleventh most populous city in the nation, with 775,000 residents.[10]

The feature of that growth that drew the most mainstream attention was the arrival of black southerners. San Francisco's African-American population, totaling less than 5,000 on the eve of the war, rocketed upward by more than 900 percent during the 1940s. Chain migration and the return of military jobs during the Korean War continued to propel the black population's expansion through the 1950s. At the start of that decade, blacks outnumbered the city's ethnic Chinese population by nearly two to one, and by 1960 over 74,000 black residents called San Francisco home. In 1970 African Americans made up 13.4 percent of the city's total population.[11]

Post–World War II suburbanization spurred a simultaneous out-migration of white San Franciscans. During the 1950s federal and local agencies stimulated the construction of factories and homes in the suburbs and enacted racially discriminatory lending and zoning policies that ensured that the new occupational and residential opportunities would be open to whites only. Young white San Francisco families rushed into the spreading suburban developments to the east and south, so while San Francisco's black population climbed upward during the 1950s, the city's overall population during that decade declined by 4.5 percent.[12]

Political elites in San Francisco, like leaders in the nation's other cities, grappled over how to respond to the city's fast-changing economic and demographic makeup. In these debates, public officials argued over how to conceive of the citizenry and how to organize government so it could identify and attend to the citizens' interests. Between 1948 and 1967, San Franciscans elected three mayors with three different understandings of democracy. Mayor Elmer Robinson led San Francisco between 1948 and 1955 as a machine politician; Mayor George Christopher administered the city between 1956 and 1963 as a managerial growth advocate; and Mayor Jack Shelley governed San Francisco between 1964 and 1967 as a traditional liberal.

Mayors Robinson, Christopher, and Shelley all clung to definitions of citizenship that idealized and served the needs of the city's dominant prewar population. On the one hand, the three mayors accepted limited class, religious, and ethnic pluralism—tolerating, for example, the legitimacy of explicitly working-class viewpoints when laborers channeled their class consciousness through union representatives at the collective bargaining table. On the other hand, Robinson, Christopher, and Shelley responded to the growing population of African Americans and the declining number of white families by defensively defining citizenship around putatively color-blind and traditional family values. Following a national pattern identified by the historian Robert Self, the three leaders conceived of the model rights-bearing citizen as a white, breadwinning, heterosexual husband and father. The mayors rejected the notion that San Franciscans could claim rights that were based on a race-conscious identity or a cultural or sexual identity that did not fit within the norm of the nuclear family, with its breadwinning father and homemaking mother. Indeed, the city's leaders did not even imagine gender and sex as political categories.[13]

The three mayors shared common understandings of the citizenry, but they differed over how to organize democratic governance. Mayor Robinson's machine provided contracts and services to various constituencies of white laborers and small-business owners in exchange for votes and graft. In 1956 Mayor Christopher, as part of a national reform wave, replaced Robinson's system with a managerial growth politics. This new governing philosophy responded to suburbanization and the increased racial diversity of cities by embracing empiricism and centralizing policy-making power in the hands of appointed experts. In San Francisco, New Haven, Philadelphia, Boston, Pittsburgh, New York City, and elsewhere, managerial growth advocates used these technocratic arrangements to stimulate the urban economy by redeveloping downtowns.[14]

By the 1960s traditional liberals were critiquing the managerial growth agenda as a power grab by corporate executives and wealthy landowners. Mayor Jack Shelley entered City Hall insisting that traditional liberal politics provided for more equitable growth. Urban liberalism was hardly a fixed and unambiguous philosophy when Shelley took office. For decades urban residents had confronted each other with competing understandings of liberalism. Nevertheless, during the 1950s and early 1960s, traditional liberals generally accepted three major principles. First, they encouraged citizens to enter civic debates as individuals rather than members of a class. Traditional liberals defended this individualist orientation through an avowed commitment to civil liberties. Second, traditional liberals trusted that all citizens maintained a shared interest in economic growth. Men in particular had a duty to contribute to this common good by breadwinning for their families and providing their fellow citizens with equal economic opportunities. Third, during the 1960s, traditional liberals recognized that greedy or prejudiced individuals and structural impediments denied some potential breadwinners their full economic rights. They advocated for overcoming these obstacles through regulatory welfare state action.[15]

As urban machine politicians, managerial growth proponents, and traditional liberals debated over the appropriate government response to urban America's demographic and economic transformations, crime increasingly claimed their attention. At the end of the 1950s and the beginning of the 1960s, policy makers began to see a worrying rise in rates of homicide and robbery. Urban black residents, officials further noted, accounted for a disproportionate number of those involved in these criminal activities. Then during the 1960s, rates of violent crime exploded. According to the federal Uniform Crime Reports surveys from 1960 and 1971, the number of recorded murders in metropolitan areas increased from 5,211 to 13,675, and recorded robberies jumped from 76,184 to 370,643. In the latter year, moreover, African Americans, who constituted less than 10 percent of the total United States population, accounted for more than two-thirds of all robbery arrests and almost two-thirds of all homicide arrests. Policy makers debated the veracity of these figures, but issues of crime now screamed to the fore of urban political debates. City leaders were forced to explain how police departments fit into their democratic visions.[16]

MACHINE-ERA POLICING IN SAN FRANCISCO

Urban police departments stepped into the post–World War II period as products of an earlier machine-politics era. Police reformers had attempted to introduce military models to law enforcement during the early twentieth century, but the urban police departments of the late 1940s retained many of the principles and functions of the first municipal police forces of the mid-nineteenth century. Those machine-era values and roles placed police departments in a paradoxical position vis-à-vis City Hall. Over the course of a term in office, machine politicians looked at the police as servants of government officials. They did not accept police officers' voices in civic debates, nor did they encourage police officers to work cooperatively with the community. Instead, officials expected the department to act as an electioneering arm of the machine. Political elites appointed and promoted loyal police officers, then relied on those officers to fill their campaign coffers with graft collected from the local underworld. City officials found their appointees among existing pools of loyal constituencies; in San Francisco, the white, male, heavily Catholic city leadership maintained a nearly all-white, all-male, and all-Catholic police force.[17]

On a day-to-day basis, by contrast, machine politicians encouraged police to maintain their autonomy from City Hall. Machine leaders wished to maximize the value of their appointments within the department while also minimizing their personal role in graft-related decisions. As a result, officials cultivated a decentralized bureaucratic police arrangement in which authority over policy (and with it the authority to make decisions regarding graft) resided with district station captains and the chief of inspectors, not with the chief of police. At the same time, city officials often allowed patrol officers to determine for themselves how to enforce laws and when to employ force. Autonomous police discretion was a signature feature of day-to-day, street-level law enforcement.

The machine-era policing system thus provided policy makers in City Hall with access to payola but very little influence over the policing practices of the officers on the beat. The SFPD's high brass rarely bothered to give officers detailed explanations of what city leaders wanted. At police academies, recruits received only skills training, basic instruction on state and municipal codes, and a rules and procedures manual. This instruction booklet was largely an abstract statement of duties, and department leaders seldom explained to recruits how they were to apply the city's codes in real-life circumstances. When the SFPD introduced the chemical agent Mace to its arsenal in June 1967, for instance, the city's rules and procedures guide simply advised that Mace "will be used in situations such as serious resistings of arrest." A 1967 federal survey of police department handbooks found San Francisco's manual to be typical. The study warned:

> What such manuals almost never discuss are the hard choices policemen must make every day: whether or not to break up a sidewalk gathering, whether or not to intervene in a domestic dispute, whether or not to silence a street-corner speaker, whether or not to stop and frisk, whether or not to arrest. Yet these decisions are the heart of police work.[18]

The SFPD leadership delivered specific instructions to the department's rank and file but did little to ensure that officers ever read or heard these directives. Through the early 1970s, the SFPD lacked any regular procedure for disseminating orders through the department's various district stations. In some districts new directives were read at roll call, at other stations they were posted on a wall, and in other districts the commands were simply filed away. When a permanent order was issued, the SFPD had no regular method for incorporating it into its manual, and the department lacked a policy for removing orders. Keeping track of which permanent orders in the manual had been overridden by subsequent edicts was further complicated by the fact that the department published the orders by chronological number and failed to provide an index listing the dictates by topic. Within this crazy-quilt system, a police chief's declaration seldom translated into a change in day-to-day law enforcement.[19]

As the SFPD's approximately 1,500 patrolmen and sergeants took to the streets without clear and coherent directions from above, their daily activities presented them with wide-ranging and often unpredictable situations.[20] As a result, officers frequently formulated and enacted their own policing policies when encountering questionable activities. John Mindermann, a San Francisco patrolman during the late 1950s, explained:

To be regarded as an effective police officer in the SFPD, the bottom-line . . . criteria was that you had to be able to handle anything that came up. Okay? That was it. If you had to call for help, if you had to call for assistance, if you couldn't figure it out, "What? Why did we hire you? We hired you specifically because we're going to send you into situations, and you have to do what's right. So don't call us." So you had to figure it out.[21]

Tasked with the nebulous mandate of maintaining order, patrol officers enjoyed the discretion to use broad formal charges like common vagrancy and the freedom to employ informal strategies such as negotiation or harassment. These choices transformed a beat officer into a "curbstone judge." Mindermann explained, "There were a lot of ad-hoc, spontaneous, without form, but highly effective resolutions to things that guys did. . . . And there wasn't anything out there. I mean, you were it. Which was one of the great attractions to the work."[22]

Historians examining the 1960s (and much of the twentieth century more generally) have frequently downplayed discretion and have focused on those moments when police "served as the protective arm of the economic and political interests of the capital system." The postwar urban historiography draws attention to well-publicized police responses to riots and demonstrations, major police sweeps and raids, and the law-and-order declarations of powerful mayors, such as Chicago's Richard J. Daley, and celebrity law enforcement officials, including Police Chief William Parker of the Los Angeles Police Department (LAPD). When historians have turned their attention to less conspicuous moments of day-to-day policing, they have often emphasized patterns of harassment and brutality attributable to a "police culture" or to a police leadership that developed statistical rationales for deploying police in communities of color. Studies by Edward Escobar and Mike Davis have identified how the twentieth-century LAPD possessed its own institutional interests independent from City Hall. By emphasizing the LAPD's trendsetting "metamorphosis into a technopolice," however, these histories have often presented police department interests in singular terms.[23]

When police officers like Patrolman Mindermann decided how they intended to use their discretion, they often considered their own personal interests within the police department. Recently, historians studying the modern state from the bottom up have begun revealing that when low-level government functionaries—including immigration agents, Veterans Administration bureaucrats, and border patrol officers—employed discretion, they rarely served as simple extensions of either lawmakers or the political movements motivating those legislators.[24] Instead, they often based their decisions on their own values and workplace considerations.

Urban police officers followed this trend. Law enforcement officials some-times approached street-level decisions with an interest in serving the goals of lawmakers, but they also considered their own sense of right and wrong, their interest in winning—or compelling—respect from the community, and their desire to achieve their goals in the easiest, least time- and energy-consuming manner. At the same time, police officers took into account their relations with other officers and remained cognizant of how their decisions would affect interdepartmental alliances and rifts based on rank, bureau, age, religion, race, and gender. The politics within police departments thus sometimes failed to fit neatly into the various political categories driving debates in City Hall.

TRADITIONAL LIBERALISM AND
LAW-AND-ORDER CONSERVATISM

During the late 1950s and early 1960s, managerial growth advocates and tradi-tional liberals confronted the problem of crime with police departments that maintained a host of principles and arrangements stretching back to the machine-politics era. As mayors Christopher and Shelley formulated responses to law-breaking and perceived disorder, each needed to determine the role discretion would play in their agenda. Christopher celebrated technocratic governance, but he appreciated how discretion provided police officers with the power to punish residents for crossing cultural, sexual, and racial lines not specifically proscribed by law. For instance, one San Francisco patrol officer defended traditional cultural norms by arresting a male bohemian who did not shave. Another officer maintained traditional sexual boundaries by booking a gay man who stroked another man's hair. Yet another upheld traditional racial mores by detaining a black man and a white woman caught driving together in a car.[25] In all instances, the city's managerial growth proponents trusted that police officers were defending the citizenry's shared interests.

Traditional liberals found themselves in a bind in the debates over discre-tion. Facing climbing and disproportionate rates of black violence, liberals like Shelley understood black crime as a problem of black alienation. They propounded two solutions. First, liberals would defend civil liberties by bring-ing police officers under "the rule of law."[26] On the federal level, this cam-paign produced the Supreme Court's landmark *Escobedo* (1964) and *Miranda* (1966) decisions dictating rules of arrest. Second, liberals trained their faith in compensatory state welfare on the employment and residential obstacles confronting urban America's young black men. On the national stage, this effort reached its apogee when President Lyndon B. Johnson initiated the War on Poverty (an early component of his Great Society) and sold the uplift campaign as a "war on crime."[27] As they pursued these root-cause measures, however, traditional liberals like Mayor Shelley retained their commitment to the old definition of citizenship and continued to rely on police discretion to contain behaviors they believed evinced an untraditional racial, cultural, or sexual perspective.

The confused traditional liberal response was met by an eruption of public, pluralist expression. Throughout the North and West, civil rights activists staged large-scale, downtown demonstrations against racial discrimination. The media, meanwhile, made spectacles of the new bohemian scenes arising around the homosexual populations drawn into cities by World War II and the urban art schools packed with returning veterans. At the same time, erotic commercial entertainment sites became regular features of the urban core.[28]

A gathering conservative movement capitalized on these developments with a law-and-order message, arguing that traditional liberals had set off a moral crisis resulting in expanded pluralism and heightened crime when they began "handcuffing" law enforcement and rewarding criminals with welfare. The 1971 film *Dirty Harry* singled out San Francisco for this conservative smear. In the film, liberal officials reduce San Francisco to a Sodom by the sea by irrationally restraining police and defending the immoral. Plagued by black radical bank robbers and a deranged hippie murderer, the city is saved only when the film's hero, Inspector Harry Callahan, reclaims his discretion, unholsters his .45 Magnum, and reimposes traditional mores.

Outside the box office and in the voting booth, law-and-order conservatives effected a dramatic political realignment. Conservatives pulled together working-class urban whites and middle-class suburban whites with an internally consistent and emotionally satisfying message: conservatives would unleash the police to enforce traditional standards of citizenship in the street and would exclude untraditional perspectives from government debate. After Arizona senator Barry Goldwater first employed the law-and-order formula in his failed 1964 bid for the presidency, conservatives used their new urban-suburban coalition to score state- and federal-level victories. Ronald Reagan capitalized on the platform to win the California governorship, and in 1968 Richard Nixon's law-and-order message earned him the White House.[29] From these state and federal perches, law-and-order conservatives legislated a philosophic sea change in sentencing law as they made incarceration rather than rehabilitation the key to public order.[30]

Scholars seeking to explain urban America's current police politics have traditionally followed this narrative of conservative ascent. Local studies have given little attention to interdepartmental police politics and have instead focused on civic debates over the boundaries of citizenship. From this perspective, the police have appeared to be reliable representatives of law-and-order conservatism. During the late 1960s and early 1970s, after all, police were some of the most vociferous opponents of expanded pluralism. Historians examining law-and-order politics on the state and national levels have noted that Democrats, tired of being trounced as soft and seeking to recapture the coveted white suburban voting bloc, eventually embraced the new mania for imprisonment. On the basis of these narratives, historians have intimated that when urban Democrats made peace with their police departments they simply grafted conservative, law-and-order institutions onto their Democratic governing coalitions.[31] An examination of local police politics both within and outside police departments, however, reveals a different story. Urban liberals and police together used the law enforcement debates of the postwar period to effect an enduring realignment in liberal politics and liberal coalitions.

THE RISE OF COSMOPOLITAN LIBERALISM

Postwar police politics produced a new cosmopolitan liberal philosophy and coalition. Marginalized urban residents catalyzed this liberal turn during the late 1950s. In cities across the nation, groups that had traditionally faced discriminatory policing discovered that public discussions over police discretion afforded them new paths of resistance. In San Francisco, for instance, Chinatown business owners, North Beach beats, gay-bar owners, producers of sexually explicit art, and black activists all achieved a voice in mainstream politics by framing their encounters with discriminatory police discretion as problems of police organization. In particular, these groups capitalized on contradictions that arose when rank-and-file police officers used their discretion in ways that conflicted with the avowed governing principles and goals of managerial growth proponents and traditional liberals. By offering administrative critiques of police discretion, each marginalized group could enter mainstream debates without offending elites with culturally, sexually, and racially pluralist perspectives.

These protests coincided with a swelling back-to-the-city movement among young white professionals. The new office- and apartment-tower skylines built by the managerial growth advocates attracted thousands of white-collar workers. In San Francisco the number of clerical employees living in the city climbed

26.5 percent between 1950 and 1970, while the number of city-dwelling professionals jumped 55.6 percent.[32] Many of the young downtown workers arrived
without domestic attachments, and they were more interested in creating a safe
but exciting urban scene than in upholding rigid boundaries of citizenship.
By the late 1950s, the interests of these young white-collar workers were being
aired in civic debates by a new generation of white liberal journalists.

The young journalists and the spokespersons for the city's marginalized
groups crafted a cosmopolitan liberal message around the notion that the city
could create a secure but entertaining environment by addressing the marginalized groups' calls for police reform. To make this case, marginalized residents
and young reporters used administrative protests against police discretion as a
stalking horse for a harm-principle approach to crime and pluralism. Rooted
in John Stuart Mill's nineteenth-century philosophy, the post–World War II
harm principle insisted that the state was justified in policing only activities
that physically or materially harmed others. Some private acts, proponents of
the harm principle averred, do not affect public order. These arguments received international attention in 1957 when the British government–sponsored
Wolfenden Report employed the harm principle to recommend decriminalization of homosexual acts between consenting adults.[33]

In San Francisco, the arising cosmopolitan liberal coalition used the harm
principle to question discretionary policing against untraditional cultural,
sexual, and racial perspectives. Cosmopolitan liberals argued that subjective
policing distracted police from crimes of violence and stifled economic growth
by producing a simultaneously dull and dangerous city. In other words, they
used the harm principle not only to express tolerance for expanded pluralism
but to underscore the citizenry's common interest in reducing violence.

By critiquing police discretion in this way, cosmopolitan liberals advanced
new understandings of citizenship. The young white-collar members of the
new liberal coalition argued that citizens who served the civic good by encouraging growth and eschewing violence could make rights-based claims on the
state with perspectives that fell outside the civic sphere's traditional cultural,
sexual, and racial boundaries. Many of those same young white professionals,
however, presumed that different groups contributed to economic development and crime abatement in different ways. As a result, the cosmopolitan
liberal coalition's expansion of pluralism stopped short of extending the same
civic rights and responsibilities to all San Franciscans.

In 1968 Mayor Joseph Alioto ushered cosmopolitan liberal politics into San
Francisco's City Hall. With this new power, cosmopolitan liberals took their
turn in attempting to reform the SFPD to serve their conception of the citi-

zenry's pluralist and shared interests. The police reforms that arose from the interaction between the SFPD's interdepartmental politics and the politics of managerial growth proponents, traditional liberals, and cosmopolitan liberals obliterated many core features of the machine-era police department.

Between 1950 and 1975, in the space of just one generation, the machine-era policing system that had operated for over a century was replaced with a new, cosmopolitan liberal policing arrangement. In the cosmopolitan police force, rank-and-file officers no longer served as bagmen. Policy making and political power shifted away from district station captains and bureau chiefs and into the hands of the police chief and the Police Commission. The department accepted large-scale racial integration (and later, integration along lines of gender and sexuality), and the rank and file lost its unquestioned autonomous discretion both to employ force and to dictate the city's cultural, sexual, and racial boundaries. At the same time, cosmopolitan liberals accepted the rank and file's participation in politics and granted the police new discretionary powers based on cooperation. Indeed, by the early 1970s, cosmopolitan liberals in San Francisco saw police officers—the supposed guardians of law and order—as neither automatons nor free agents, but as partners with whom they could encourage democracy and fight violence. From this position, police officers influenced not only their own role in the cosmopolitan liberal city but liberal principles themselves.

"I Will Never Degrade the Spirit of Unity": Managerial Growth Politics and Police Professionalism

"I am going to warn you I am not accustomed to mincing words," Mayor George Christopher thundered. Standing on the stage of the Commerce High School auditorium, San Francisco's chief executive looked down upon hundreds of seated San Francisco police officers. Five days earlier, on January 8, 1954, Christopher had taken the oath of office on the heels of yet another SFPD scandal. In this latest embarrassment, federal Treasury officials had raided a bar offering open gambling just one block from the Hall of Justice. Christopher entered City Hall aiming to assert the authority of his office with a department-wide assembly. "I do not intend to have anybody tell me or the [Police] Commission that something has been under their noses and they don't know anything about it," he lectured. "Very frankly, if something is going on under your nose or under ours it means we are either blind or incompetent. And it means we are not fit to hold our jobs."[1]

With Christopher's election, San Francisco joined a growing wave of cities turning to managerial growth mayors committed to clean-government reforms and downtown redevelopment. These mayors—including New York City's Robert Wagner, St. Louis's Raymond Tucker, Philadelphia's Joseph Clark, and Boston's John Hynes—presumed that downtown growth served the interest of all citizens. Those citizens, Mayor Christopher believed, maintained a host of preexisting shared values. He accepted nominal class and religious pluralism in civic debate, but asserted that the primary purpose of government was to never "degrade the spirit of unity."[2] The mayor believed that poor management produced factional rifts, and he proposed to avoid that pitfall by consolidating power in the hands of administrative experts from the business community. Christopher's new Police Commission, for instance, consisted of a corporate lawyer and two former presidents of the city's Chamber of Commerce. These new officials, he promised, would institute a system in which police officers were "promoted on merit, not by a mayor calling up someone and using his influence." Christopher vowed that he himself would "administer the big business of San Francisco . . . on a sound, constructive, business-like basis."[3]

Christopher's technocratic pledges thrilled the reporters crammed along the wings of the Commerce High School auditorium. The following morning, the *San Francisco Chronicle*'s front-page, top-of-the-fold coverage heralded Christopher's fight against "inefficiency and corruption" as a generational sea change. When the assembly ended and the mayor and his police commissioners "invited" officers to shake their hands, the *Chronicle* reported, "younger officers in the department . . . went out of their way to stand in line and meet the officials."[4]

In truth, many of the young officers seethed. Thomas Cahill, who subsequently served as Mayor Christopher's police chief, recalled that officers who considered themselves honest felt that Christopher "was casting reflections on them." Sol Weiner, a three-wheeled-motorcycle officer, later characterized the speech as "rotten," and Patrolman Elliot Blackstone remembered:

> So Christopher got up, and he accused us all of being a bunch of thieves and crooks and everything else. But he said, "You know I'd be glad to work with you." . . . And he made us all so mad. Then after he got done talking, we were all invited to come up on stage to shake hands with him. Well, I and two or three hundred of us at least turned around and walked out of there. We wanted nothing to do with this guy.[5]

It likely never occurred to either Christopher or the journalists to survey the rank and file for their perspectives. The mayor and his supporters all trusted that the city's common interests could be met through administrative, top-down reforms. Indeed, Christopher and his backers assumed that more than any other clean-government changes, police reform would convince the electorate of the efficacy and righteousness of managerial growth politics.

THE DOWNTOWN LEADERSHIP AND POLICE PROFESSIONALISM

Mayor Christopher's efforts at police reform during the mid-1950s represented the culmination of a decades-old battle between San Francisco's downtown business leaders and the city's traditional machine politicians. Similar downtown-versus-machine struggles had been roiling in American cities since the turn of the century, as large-scale business interests sought greater influence in urban affairs and machine politicians struggled to retain their political and financial independence from downtown elites. In cities like San Francisco, machine officials employed their licensing powers to collect favors and graft from small-business owners, and they used their appointment powers—over institutions including schools, fire departments, and public works departments—to earn the votes of working-class residents.[6]

Through the first half of the twentieth century, downtown representatives attempted to bring their local governments to heel with clean-government reforms. In 1932 a group of San Francisco entrepreneurs, financial officers, and corporate executives—serving such economic behemoths as Bank of America, Standard Oil of California, Pacific Gas and Electric, and the Bechtel Corporation—scored a major victory in their city when they shepherded through a new city charter ending mayoral appointments to the public works department and transferring licensing authority out of the San Francisco Board of Supervisors and into the hands of various appointees. (San Francisco's city and county lines are identical, so the board functions as a city council.) Because the 1932 charter retained the city's at-large election format, candidates for supervisor now saw little choice but to turn to downtown elites for help in funding their expensive citywide campaigns. For the next forty years, the Board of Supervisors rarely wavered as a representative of the downtown leadership's agenda.[7]

During the late 1940s, new potential crises and windfalls motivated San Francisco corporate elites to press for further influence in local politics. San Francisco's big-business leadership emerged from World War II alarmed that a downturn in local military spending and a concomitant rise in suburban and Sun Belt manufacturing threatened to drain San Francisco of its economic vitality. Through groups like the Chamber of Commerce, San Francisco's corporate representatives responded to this threat with a regional plan that called for City Hall to remake San Francisco into a financial and administrative center—what one scholar termed the "brains and heart"—for a Bay Area–wide manufacturing economy.[8]

The federal Housing Act of 1949 opened the possibility for just this sort of transformation. Under the new law, the federal government offered to cover two-thirds of the costs associated with purchasing areas pegged for redevelopment. Moreover, it permitted cities to sell or lease the lands to private developers at below-market values.[9] In order to tap the Housing Act subsidies, the city government simply had to prove that an area under consideration for redevelopment was blighted and that the government had plans to renew the land with projects serving the civic interest.

The managerial growth advocates' desire for new federal redevelopment dollars steered them into a final showdown with San Francisco's traditional machine politicians. In 1947 San Franciscans elected Elmer Robinson, a former member of the judiciary and a committed practitioner of machine politics. When Congress passed the Housing Act two years later, downtown officials implored Robinson to install a competent director for the new San Francisco Redevelopment Agency (SFRA). Instead, Robinson tapped a political hatchet man who filled the SFRA's staff positions with other political cronies. Robinson's SFRA planners possessed neither the motivation nor the competence required to craft and submit redevelopment studies and plans. The various downtown redevelopment schemes thus floundered in what one scholar described as a web of "obstructionism and venality."[10]

Managerial growth proponents recognized that although charter reform had created an obedient Board of Supervisors, one final unreformed institution—the San Francisco Police Department—allowed the mayor to maintain his independence. Police departments like the SFPD had been sustaining machine politics since their creation in the mid-19th century. Machine politicians doled out important positions in their police departments with the expectation that beholden officers would get out the vote and collect payoffs for the machine's campaign war chest. A 1937 inquiry into SFPD corruption—dubbed the Atherton investigation—found that San Francisco's police served as "an organized and powerful electioneering force" that would solicit votes and "aid materially in raising campaign funds." Indeed, the probe unearthed a vast network of payoffs linking officers of all ranks to the city's gambling, prostitution, and bail bond industries.[11] The Atherton investigation estimated that the SFPD collected on average over one million dollars per year.[12]

Managerial growth advocates confronted this corruption with the concept of police professionalism. A product of the Progressive era, police professionalism followed the principles that reformers had already used to restructure other institutions underpinning the machine, such as schools. Professionalism advocates proposed to funnel police authority upward into the hands of an expert, nonpartisan police chief. This honest police leader, reformers assumed, would then use his autonomy to select and train officers dedicated to serving citywide interests through a vigorous campaign against crime. Police professionalizers were primarily concerned with the venal links between city officials and police department commanders, and they thus rarely offered specifics on what a professionalized police chief would do other than reject payoffs. Police professionalism, the legal scholar David Sklansky explains, was more of a "governing mindset" than a policy prescription.[13]

Following the Atherton scandal, San Francisco's Chamber of Commerce suc-cessfully lobbied for two charter amendments aimed at transferring power from district station captains to the chief of police. First, San Francisco increased the chief's oversight over district captains by joining a wave of cities (eventu-ally including Cleveland, Pittsburgh, Rochester, Cincinnati, and New Orleans) consolidating police districts, reducing San Francisco's fourteen district stations to nine. Second, it followed the lead of other municipalities by transferring re-sponsibility for so-called vice crimes (a formal SFPD category that included gambling, narcotics, and sex offenses) out of the district stations and into a new Bureau of Special Services. The twelve officers of Special Services operated as part of the Inspectors Bureau but answered directly to the chief of police.[14]

The Atherton reforms proved fleeting. The attempt to concentrate respon-sibility within the SFPD via the charter amendments meant little if the police chief did not then use his consolidated authority to crack down on payola. One observer noted that the centralization of authority over vice policing served simply to "centralize collections." Reformers understood that corruption per-sisted with the consent of the mayor: the 1932 city charter had granted the three-member, civilian Police Commission authority over SFPD policies, ap-pointments, and disciplinary decisions, but the commissioners served at the mayor's will and thus attended to his interests reliably.[15]

When Mayor Robinson took office in 1948, his Police Commission set out to create an SFPD arrangement conducive to the flow of favors and graft. The new administration appointed Michael Mitchell police chief, then immediately treated the SFPD leader as a straw boss. Robinson recognized that he could collect far more favors by bypassing Mitchell and personally doling out posi-tions and authority along the two main branches of power extending from under Chief Mitchell. First and foremost, the police commissioners distrib-uted prized positions within the Inspectors Bureau. The SFPD's plainclothes inspectors enjoyed status and authority over uniformed patrol officers, and once inspectors were appointed, their positions were protected by their bu-reau's tenure rules and Byzantine disciplinary procedures. As a result, the less motivated inspectors could spend their workdays thumbing through pa-perwork and keeping what one reporter charitably labeled "bankers' hours." Police commissioners racked up a multitude of favors for Robinson by trans-ferring well-connected police officers to the bureau. Commenting on the active hand Robinson's commissioners played in inspector appointments, the chief of inspectors explained, "I work on the theory that if the Police Commission will give me even one man I've picked out myself for every two men who are assigned to me, I'll get along fairly well."[16]

Robinson's Police Commission cultivated a second line of influence through key appointments within the district stations. Police commanders usually desired positions atop the Northern, Central, Southern, and Mission Stations because these stations covered neighborhoods (such as the waterfront, the Tenderloin, the Fillmore, and North Beach) with high-profile crimes and high-reward payola. Police commissioners usually limited themselves to command-rank appointments and then allowed police captains to run their districts as their own personal fiefdoms. On occasion, however, commissioners meddled with patrol posts along payola-rich beats. One of the Robinson Police Commission's first acts was to replace a long-tenured patrolman assigned to the Broadway Street nightlife scene. Noting that Robinson's Police Commission was "usurp[ing]" Mitchell's "function as Chief" "down to the placement and transfer of ordinary patrolmen," the *San Francisco Chronicle* pondered, "What's behind all this manipulation in the Police Department?"[17]

By abetting police payola practices, Robinson's machine ran afoul of state and federal police agencies warring against organized crime. Outside law enforcement officials repeatedly targeted San Francisco gambling houses that they feared might become footholds for East Coast gangsters. To the consternation of state and federal officials, SFPD officers on the take withheld assistance from and actively interfered with external investigations. Following one bookmaking sting by state agents, a local newspaper jeered, "The San Francisco Police Department was not informed of plans for the raid. Why? Apparently because the raiders wanted to succeed by surprise." Mayor Robinson shrugged off these scandals and worked to roll back the meager post–Atherton investigation reforms. The mayor's Police Commission sidelined the Bureau of Special Services by slashing the positions of all but three inspectors and returning vice policing back to the district stations.[18]

CHINATOWN ENTREPRENEURS AND POLICE PROFESSIONALISM

During the early postwar period, business leaders did not press their professionalization campaign any further than was necessary for cutting off payola to City Hall and consolidating their power over the SFRA. San Francisco's managerial growth proponents railed against the corrupt connections Robinson's administration maintained with the SFPD leadership, but the police reformers rarely explained how an independent, professional police chief would set policies serving the citizenry's shared values. This imprecision carried political benefits for professionalism advocates. By allowing various groups of San

Franciscans to independently imagine how professionalized police reforms might serve their needs, the downtown reformers gathered a wide range of constituencies under their clean-government banner.

In Chinatown a new generation of Chinese-American businessmen joined the police professionalism movement in a broader campaign for full citizenship rights. Chinatown's young entrepreneurs hoped that once managerial growth advocates achieved power, they would use professionalism's emphasis on consolidated, color-blind police authority to grant Chinese Americans honest and equal law enforcement.

During the machine-politics era, the SFPD's approach to Chinatown diverged further from the principles of police professionalism than its policies in any other area of the city. The department had created the Chinatown detail sometime around 1878 in response to neighborhood tong wars, but large-scale Chinatown gang violence had long since abated. Still, after World War II, the fifteen-member detail remained the SFPD's only police presence in the neighborhood. An archetype for the core principles and practices of machine-era policing, the Chinatown detail was race conscious, free from day-to-day oversight, disconnected from the residents it policed, and an integral component of the machine's payola networks.[19]

The Chinatown detail operated without any formal physical or functional connections to the regular police. Although the neighborhood was mere blocks from the SFPD's Central Station, the Chinatown detail did not operate out of this district station. Instead, the detail was based in a small, secret Chinatown hideout. The office had a private phone line, but the desk was rarely staffed, so the detail maintained little daily contact with the Hall of Justice. At the same time, official SFPD policy forbade Bureau of Special Services inspectors or Central Station patrol officers from stepping foot into the neighborhood. Chinatown was thus the only residential neighborhood in the entire city not supervised by a district station and the Hall of Justice's Inspectors Bureau.[20]

The detail's operational autonomy reflected the SFPD leadership's bigoted attitudes toward Chinese Americans. The high brass articulated that prejudice when explaining why they allowed the Chinatown detail to forgo standard blue uniforms for stylish suits that made the officers look like "movie detectives." One official suggested that Chinatown residents were too backward to associate blue uniforms with anything other than the "tyrannical officials of the courts of China." Another SFPD leader stressed neighborhood insularity and criminality, warning, "In Chinatown the uniform tips your hand. That star shines up very nicely. They can see you coming blocks away. . . . In many cases, such as gambling houses, a lookout or 'look-see' is posted outside. Police wearing a uniform would have a hard time gaining evidence."[21]

SFPD leaders further evinced their dim views toward Chinatown residents by discouraging dialogue between the Chinatown detail and Chinese Americans. During the 1940s and early 1950s, the police force did not require members of the Chinatown detail to possess any facility in Chinese languages and did not include any Chinese-American officers. (The SFPD as a whole did not employ a Chinese-American patrolman until 1964.) Moreover, the department made it impossible for neighborhood residents to contact officers by phone. In the days before two-way radios, San Franciscans living outside of Chinatown called a central communications hub, which then contacted the appropriate district station to arrange an officer response. Chinatown residents could not reach police in this manner because their detail was not attached to a station. The SFPD expected Chinatown residents to stand and wait for the detail to pass by the intersection of Washington and Grant streets or to leave a message at Red's Bar at the corner of Jackson Street and Beckett Alley. These old-world arrangements enhanced the squad's cachet with the nation's true crime magazines, but the Chinese Chamber of Commerce complained that merchants often could not locate police when robberies occurred.[22]

Although machine politicians gave negligible consideration to crime fighting in Chinatown, they did value the neighborhood as a well of graft. Postwar observers estimated that under the Chinatown detail's watch, the neighborhood gambling industry generated six to seven million dollars in proceeds a year.[23] Wide-eyed machine officials looking to tap into these proceeds jostled with one another for influence over Chinatown detail appointments.

It took Mayor Elmer Robinson nearly his entire first term to gain full control over the Chinatown detail. Shortly before he took office in 1948, the previous administration's Police Commission tried to curtail the incoming mayor's access to payola by abolishing the detail. Robinson had no trouble reactivating the squad, but he then found himself wrestling with his police chief, Michael Mitchell. Police details comprised short-term appointments set by the officers' immediate supervisor, not the mayor's Police Commission. The Chinatown detail officially reported to the police chief, and thus as soon as Mitchell became chief, he assigned a Chinatown detail leader loyal to himself. Indignant, Robinson attempted to replace Mitchell's pick with his own police ally, but the chief went to the press and exposed Robinson's meddling. Noting that authority over Chinatown appointments had "always been a sore spot," Mitchell charged that Chinatown residents were "in league with the mayor" to "relax" Mitchell's supposed demand that the neighborhood "stay closed."[24]

FIGURE 3. Officer Leo Osuna, a member of the Chinatown squad, overlooks a street in Chinatown. Chinatown squad members wore well-tailored suits rather than the SFPD's standard blue uniforms. This sartorial choice allowed squad members to strike photogenic poses, but Chinese-American business leaders complained that the suits made it harder for neighborhood residents and visiting tourists to find and communicate with police. August 18, 1955. (Reprinted with permission, Bancroft Library, BANC PIC 2006.029: 138946.0208.)

Ultimately, Mitchell and Robinson established a truce in which detail officers under Mitchell and members of the Bureau of Special Services answering to Robinson's Police Commission allegedly both exacted concessions from Chinatown gamblers. When Chief Mitchell retired at the end of 1950, Mayor Robinson streamlined the lines of loyalty. His new police chief took power announcing only a single transfer: a Robinson-approved officer at the head of the Chinatown detail.[25]

Since the opening decades of the twentieth century, Chinatown's entrepreneurs had hoped to earn more equal government services in housing, law enforcement, and host of other areas by reforming their neighborhood's reputation. San Francisco's traditional leadership conceived of family men as ideal citizens, but, as Nayan Shah has shown, these same city officials regarded Chinatown as "an immoral and disease-infested slum" occupied by working-class bachelors and female prostitutes. Through the first half of the century, Shah illustrates, Chinatown business owners attempted to overcome this impediment to integration by remaking their neighborhood's image as a "family society of independent family households."[26]

Following World War II, Chinatown entrepreneurs found that their public relations efforts were being stymied by mainstream press reports on Chinatown gambling. These articles referred to illegal gaming as both an active Chinatown tradition and a threat (via roving lottery ticket sellers) to the rest of the city. When H. L. Wong, president of the Chinese Chamber of Commerce, later explained his motivation for developing the family-oriented Chinese New Year Festival, he emphasized his desire to rid the neighborhood of its gambling reputation. "I always saw the newspaper headlines 'Chinatown Gambling Raid' . . . in the pre–Chinese New Year Festival days," Wong recalled. "I always grumbled, 'What's the matter with them? There are so many good things about Chinese and our Chinatown. Why do they play up this gambling?'"[27]

These business leaders recognized that wiping away Chinatown's gambling reputation and securing a family-oriented image for their neighborhood was not simply a project of reforming Chinatown residents and culture. The mission also required that Chinese Americans help clean up the white government in City Hall. Chinese-American spokespersons who wished to decouple Chinatown and gambling in the mainstream's perception understood that "Chinatown Gambling Raid" headlines persisted because the SFPD refused to professionalize its policing of the neighborhood.

This public relations problem was worsening during the late 1940s as a new generation of local politicians curried downtown support with campaigns against police payola. Repeatedly, these reform efforts against police venality implicated Chinatown. In 1950, for instance, San Francisco district attorney Thomas Lynch took on the machine by recording testimony accusing Chinatown detail officers and Mayor Robinson's Chinatown campaign organizer of receiving monthly extortion payments amounting to $35,000 from Chinatown gambling operations. That same year Sacramento legislators pursuing a similar clean-government agenda accused members of the Bureau of Special Services—which operated under the influence of the Police Commission and thus the mayor—of collecting Chinatown payoffs as well. One informant for this state inquiry claimed that Inspector George "Paddy" Wafer spent so much time inside a Chinatown gambling house that other customers mistook the detective for the establishment's owner.[28]

Chinatown's business elites groused over the negative press, and they saw in police professionalism an opportunity to establish themselves as partners with managerial growth proponents. Young entrepreneurs and professionals in the neighborhood fumed over the fact that "of all the many racial groups in San Francisco the Chinese alone require a special police squad." However, neighborhood spokespersons did not want to ruffle the feathers of those city officials empowered to abolish the detail with charges of race-conscious discrimination.[29]

Spokespersons found a color-blind language of protest in growth-oriented police professionalism. In 1949, for instance, the president of the Chinatown Chamber of Commerce responded to a gambling raid conducted by state agents with the careful suggestion that the SFPD could provide white tourists visiting their neighborhood with a better sense of security if it replaced the Chinatown detail with recognizable uniformed police. During the mid-1950s, Dai-Ming Lee, an editor and English-language columnist for the *Chinese World,* insisted that it was the detail's autonomous nature—the fact that it was "supreme unto itself"—that led to its "abuse of authority." The "plain-clothes sinecures in the Chinatown detail," Lee stormed, were an anachronism from "the dim, distant past." Lee noted that two studies—including an "efficiency survey" sponsored by downtown-friendly politicians on the Board of Supervisors—had recommended abolition of the Chinatown detail, and he suggested that Mayor Robinson's refusal to accept modern management principles stifled broad-based economic growth. "In spite of its lack of advocates," Lee wrote, "the Chinatown squad continues in existence. We wonder what unseen power makes this possible and what benefits accrue thereby, and to whom. Some day these facts may be revealed, and if and when they are, they should make interesting reading."[30]

Lee's insinuations of police corruption and improper management captured the attention of the city's mainstream press. The same day Lee levied this oblique accusation in the *Chinese World,* the afternoon-printed *San Francisco Examiner* included Lee's quote in its own call for the detail's elimination.[31]

THE *SAN FRANCISCO CHRONICLE* AND POLICE PROFESSIONALISM

Chinatown's young entrepreneurs championed police professionalism on the assumption that a professionalized police chief would initiate top-down reforms serving the color-blind interests of the city's families. However, the professionalism campaign's vague approach to law enforcement strategies also enabled it to attract constituencies less invested in the city's traditional family values. During the early 1950s, a collection of young, white *San Francisco Chronicle* journalists who frequently reveled in the city's bawdy reputation emerged as the local professionalism campaign's most public proponents.

The *Chronicle* entered the 1950s as a third-place afterthought among the city's four major newspapers. In terms of both circulation and political influence, the *San Francisco Examiner* towered over the local media landscape. Proclaiming itself the "Monarch of the Dailies," the *Examiner* attracted the favor of select politicians by boosting the officials' public image and supplying them with information critical for the policy-making process. As the political scientist Frederick Wirt explained, passing a single policy item through San Francisco's convoluted government (the city maintained 65 separate elective offices and 29 boards and commissions) often required local politicians to broker deals with an array of boards, commissions, and departments. Politicians could maximize their powers of persuasion in these negotiations if they understood the interests motivating each of these government bodies. Local journalists, Wirt observed, often possessed just this sort of knowledge, and political elites thus respected reporters as important policy-making allies.[32]

The *Examiner* used its dominant circulation and news-gathering abilities to win influence in City Hall, then employed that leverage to affect appointments within the SFPD. During the late 1940s and early 1950s, for instance, the mayor's Police Commission always appointed the chief of police nominated by Bill Wren, the *Examiner*'s managing editor. In a self-reinforcing fashion, the newspaper then used the loyalty of police officers, who gave the *Examiner* scoops on newsworthy crimes, to expand its news-gathering prowess over its competitors. "The good old *Ex*," a *Chronicle* editor later grumbled, "owned, body and soul, the police department and the mayor's office."[33]

During the early 1950s, a small cluster of ambitious journalists and editors at the *San Francisco Chronicle* saw an opportunity to challenge the *Examiner*'s favored position by advocating police professionalism. This campaign took off in earnest in 1952 when the *Chronicle*'s owners promoted Scott Newhall to the editor's chair. Newhall had joined the newspaper in 1935 as a photographer and quickly climbed his way into the supervisorial ranks. Between 1952 and 1970, Newhall oversaw the *Chronicle*'s day-to-day operations and controlled the newspaper's editorial voice. In a spectacular run, the *Chronicle* gained ground on the *Examiner* until it surpassed it in circulation by 1960.[34]

Newhall cut into the *Examiner*'s sales and political clout with two interrelated strategies. First, the young editor attracted San Francisco readers by developing a reporting style that he felt reflected the readership's culture. Describing the *Chronicle*'s editorial approach during the late 1960s, two media scholars wrote, "It is unlikely that there is another group of newspaper executives anywhere in the country—with the possible exception of those running the New York *Times*—that is so conscious of its audience, and of the effect of its newspaper on that audience." Monopolizing and unleashing the Bay Area's best writing talents (including, for most of this period, Herb Caen, the dean of local columnists), Newhall encouraged his writers to convey their own reactions to events in their stories. This approach produced what one *Chronicle* editor described as a "cult of personality" within the newspaper's pages.[35]

Newhall undercut the *Examiner*'s power from a second direction by exposing corruption within the SFPD and advocating for police professionalism via exposés on the "Blue Gang" atop the police force. Newhall hoped these reforms would "liberate the mayor and the police department" from the *Examiner*'s machinations. The scandal reports also served Newhall's first goal of projecting his vision of the city's culture. In the newspaper's various corruption investigations, the *Chronicle* repeatedly characterized police payola, rather than the criminal activities permitted by the payoffs, as the true threat to the city's welfare. The newspaper often portrayed the exposed underworld operations as exciting sources of entertainment. In 1953 the *Chronicle* series "Tenderloin: The Secret City" spent a week and a half railing against police extortion while introducing its readership to the city's red-light district with amused winks and nods. Each report came with a boxed glossary defining catchy underworld terms and phrases such as *three striper* and *drop the junk*. Like the Chinatown entrepreneurs, the *Chronicle* hoped to use police professionalism against the city's traditional machine. But while Chinatown's entrepreneurs assumed that centralized policing would reinforce the traditional leadership's avowed mores, some of the *Chronicle*'s professionalization advocates appeared unconcerned by the prospect of more relaxed cultural codes.[36]

MANAGERIAL GROWTH ADVOCATES AND THE POLICE PROFESSIONALISM COALITION

During the late 1940s and early 1950s, San Francisco supervisor George Christopher drew together Chinatown's entrepreneurs, the *Chronicle*'s young staff, and a range of other constituencies to form a broad and powerful political coalition around the issue of police professionalism. The son of Greek immigrants and a product of San Francisco's working-class South of Market neighborhood, Christopher amassed a small fortune in the dairy industry prior to World War II. In 1945 the "wavy-haired dairyman" stepped into the political arena with a run for the Board of Supervisors. Because he lacked strong connections within the city's patronage networks, he found it easy to campaign against them. Christopher's clean-government message won him a seat on the board, and from there Christopher played, according to one supporter, "the role of the young Turk, charging headlong at every municipal sin he could unearth."[37]

Christopher aimed most of his fire at the venal ties binding the underground economy, the SFPD, and the Robinson administration. Similar to Lee, he insisted that corrupt policing failed to serve either the citizenry's financial interests or its social mores. When machine-politics defenders claimed that tolerance for gambling and prostitution benefited San Franciscans by luring convention dollars into the city, Christopher scoffed, "Some people say . . . that an open town would create prosperity. But . . . prosperity doesn't mean prosperity for a half-dozen gamblers and racketeers. It is only prosperity when all the men, women and children of San Francisco are in it." Machine politics, Christopher further intimated, threatened the family. "All these so-called open town elements care about," Christopher warned, "is the fast buck. They don't care where they get it—whether it's from your daughter or the kid next door."[38]

Through police professionalism Christopher hoped both to illustrate the efficacy of his managerial governing style and to take the first steps toward downtown redevelopment. An honest chief with the authority to end the unscrupulous relationship between the mayor's office and the Hall of Justice, Christopher vowed, would free city officials to serve the citizenry's supposed common interests. He promised that these new circumstances would allow expert planners in City Hall to lower tax rates, clear slums, revivify the port, and draw Major League baseball into the city.[39] By contrast, Christopher said very little about what the police chief would do with his newfound freedom from payola. Voters were unbothered by this haziness; in 1949 and 1953, Christopher received more votes for supervisor than any other candidate (an astounding 73 percent of the electorate voted for him in the latter election), and the young politician served as the board's president for the first half of the 1950s.[40]

In 1955 Christopher ran for mayor against George Reilly, a union-friendly machine Democrat whom one Christopher supporter labeled "an old-time fixture of the city's political trough." (Because San Francisco maintained a nonpartisan election format, Christopher could avoid compromising his common-good posturing with a party identification. He finally introduced himself as a Republican in 1958 when he ran for United States Senate.) Christopher placed police reform at the top of his campaign platform, and with the backing of downtown business leaders, the *Chronicle,* and Chinatown's young entrepreneurs, he won the 1955 election by a greater margin than any candidate in San Francisco history. Understanding police reform as the key to his growth agenda, the mayor-elect anticipated, "The success of my administration depends a great deal on the success of the Police Department."[41]

Christopher looked to consolidate police power in the hands of an honest police chief, and an outside raid by federal Treasury agents against six bookmaking establishments, conveniently conducted three days before his inauguration, provided him with his opportunity. After inveighing against corruption in the department-wide assembly at Commerce High School, Christopher brought together representatives from the *Examiner* and, for the first time, the *Chronicle* for a meeting to choose a new police chief. Christopher and his advisors emerged from the gathering with a selection that thundered through the SFPD's command ranks. Traditionally, the chief was chosen from among the SFPD's pool of captains, but Christopher's Police Commission now selected Inspector Francis "Frank" Ahern, an officer with a patrolman's civil service rank. Chief Ahern then doubled down on this break with custom by tapping Thomas Cahill, another patrolman-ranked inspector, as his deputy chief.[42]

Ahern was the San Francisco police officer most associated with professionalism. During the early 1950s, politically savvy officers across America were reaching out to up-and-coming managerial growth advocates through vigorous campaigns against potential sources of graft. In Philadelphia, for instance, Frank Rizzo won a name for himself among professionalizers through his drives against prostitution and gambling rackets. In 1967 he was appointed Philadelphia's police commissioner.[43] In San Francisco, Ahern earned his professionalism bona fides in a similar manner. During the late 1940s, District Attorney Edmund "Pat" Brown was busy establishing himself as a friend of managerial growth advocates through a drive against abortion clinics operating under the sanction of corrupt police officers. Brown needed a police officer willing to break ranks and conduct his raids, and he found an eager ally in Inspector Ahern. Ahern then captured the imagination of the press when, during his bust of the city's largest abortion clinic, he turned down an offer for a $280,000 payoff.[44]

Following the clinic crackdown, Ahern continued burnishing his reputation in the SFPD's elite homicide squad. He hand-selected the young and promising Cahill as his partner, and the duo made headlines with their investigations of gangland murders. In 1950 they earned national attention for their testimony before Senator Estes Kefauver's Committee to Investigate Organized Crime in Interstate Commerce. The senators were so impressed with Ahern's and

Cahill's grasp of national organized crime networks, criminal enterprises with little presence in San Francisco, that the committee borrowed the two officers for the next six months as it continued touring other parts of the country.[45]

San Francisco's machine officials attempted to use and contain Ahern during the early 1950s. When the SFPD's police chiefs needed to respond to corruption scandals with short-term drives, they turned Ahern and Cahill loose. In November 1955, however, Ahern recognized in Mayor Christopher's election a chance to vault over his commanders. He thus accepted a secret invitation from federal Treasury agents to participate in their January 1956 gambling house raids. After Ahern then received his appointment as chief, he quickly established his authority over his former commanding officers with a massive shake-up. Most dramatically, Ahern transferred his politically formidable former supervisor, the chief of inspectors, to a sleepy "fog belt" posting as captain of Taraval Station.[46]

Regarding police professionalism as a two-man arrangement involving himself and the chief, Christopher reaffirmed his own personal incorruptibility. "I was in office only a short while," the mayor later advertised, "when a man came into my office and with hardly more than a hello, hinted he'd pay me $150,000 for gambling concessions. I booted him right out the door." Christopher also claimed that he had turned away a police captain who approached him and offered, "I can play it any way you want. I can keep things opened up, or I can close them down—whatever you say." Christopher assured the public that his personal determination to stay out of police affairs would allow his honest police leader to create "a streamlined, efficient department whose integrity was unquestioned." Confident in Ahern's power to impose his will on the police force beneath him, Mayor Christopher trumpeted, "We're in business."[47]

MANAGERIAL GROWTH POLITICS
AND THE COMMON GOOD

For managerial growth mayors like Christopher, police professionalism served a double purpose. On one hand, clean-government officials used police reforms to eliminate the graft hindering their redevelopment agenda. On the other hand, elites like Christopher exploited professionalism to present themselves as guardians of the public good. Managerial growth administrations across the country—in cities as wide-ranging as Los Angeles, Chicago, Denver, Oakland, Boston, and Atlanta—made police professionalism the dominant police model of the 1950s.[48]

As managerial growth advocates achieved power and instituted police professionalism, their faith in top-down administrative reform freed police depart-

F I G U R E 4 . Homicide bureau inspectors pose with evidence seized during a gambling raid. During the early 1950s, politically savvy police officers raised their status among managerial growth advocates by cracking down on gambling houses and other sources of police payola. Evidence for how clean-government law enforcement served as a launching pad for a generation of police officials, this photograph includes the SFPD's next three police chiefs: Frank Ahern (second from left), Thomas Cahill (far left), and Al Nelder (far right). Michael Maguire, the commanding officer at the 1960 anti-HUAC demonstration at City Hall, is also present (fifth from right). April 23, 1955. (Reprinted with permission, Bancroft Library, BANC PIC 1959.010—NEG PT III 04–23–55.7: 6.)

ments to enact a wide range of seemingly contradictory law enforcement strategies. In San Francisco, for instance, Christopher and his new police leaders proved comfortable operating machine-era and professional policing strategies side-by-side. Officers participating in either approach, Christopher, Ahern, and Cahill agreed, would reliably follow the will of the clean-government leadership.

The new administration's willingness to maintain machine-era policing strategies came as a rude shock to the young entrepreneurs in Chinatown. When Christopher took office in 1956, both he and Chinatown's business leaders sought to make Chinatown a demonstration project for the democratic potential of managerial growth politics. The mayor and the entrepreneurs agreed to integrate Chinatown into the growth agenda by transforming the neighborhood into a tourist destination for white families. Within the first thirty days of his administration, the mayor appointed Chinese-American entrepreneurs and landowners to various Chinatown development and tourism advisory committees, set plans for a new Chinatown parking garage, and approved the construction of a Grant Avenue archway marking the tourist entrance into the neighborhood. Chinatown's development, Christopher and the neighborhood entrepreneurs hoped, would illustrate that citizens who accepted a development strategy reinforcing the city's color-blind, family-oriented values could expect to enjoy a civic voice and personal enrichment.[49]

Chinatown's young business elites assumed that Mayor Christopher's avowed commitments to color-blindness and consolidated authority in the upper ranks of government would lead to a final abolition of the Chinatown detail in their community. Months before Christopher took office, Mayor Robinson's administration had cheered Chinatown entrepreneurs when its SFPD command staff, like the SFPD leadership under the previous administration, eliminated the Chinatown detail. Robinson's police chief was likely hoping to either ingratiate himself with Christopher or deny the new mayor payola, but he explained the detail's abolition by equating equal citizenship with uniform law enforcement. Chinatown's residents, the Robinson's chief declared, were "Americans of Chinese ancestry [who] should be treated as Americans." When Christopher entered office, Chinatown spokespersons expressed their hope that the detail would remain demobilized. After all, Lee reminded his English-reading audience, the detail's "corrupt practices" had worked against the interests of "the majority of law-abiding citizens."[50]

A month and a half into Christopher's first term, the mayor and Chief Ahern encouraged white residents and tourists to attend Chinatown's Chinese New Year Festival by banning gambling and fireworks and promising, in the *Chronicle*'s words, a "safe" and "honest" celebration. Chinatown business leaders swallowed these proscriptions, but other Chinatown residents proved less interested in remaking their neighborhood into a playground for white parents and their children. During the New Year parade, locals brazenly ignited fireworks and rained verbal abuse down on Chief Ahern's parade car.[51]

Christopher and Ahern immediately reactivated the Chinatown detail. The mayor assumed that Ahern would be able to direct all units under his command—even decentralized and formerly corrupt details—toward honest and color-blind law enforcement policies. The reconstituted squad quickly engaged in a series of raids against neighborhood gambling sites, and, as City Hall and SFPD officials predicted, the detail remained committed to this drive against open gaming. Indeed, by the end of the 1950s, the mainstream press used pictures of Chinatown detail officers to underscore the neighborhood's new, law-abiding image. An extended *San Francisco Examiner* series on local policing, for instance, limited its depiction of the Chinatown detail to a single photograph of two squad members calmly supervising a legal game of mah-jongg. Chinatown entrepreneurs accepted the trade-off of dissimilar state services for economic gain. Recognizing that detail officers now served the neighborhood business community's financial interests by rejecting payola, the *Chinese World* dropped its half-decade–long campaign against the detail and instead offered approving coverage of the Chinatown detail's gambling house busts.[52]

Ahern relied on machine-era policing approaches because he was confident of the transformative power of his personal honesty, but also because he lacked the creativity to devise modern, professional strategies. In 1958, while attending a Labor Day home game of the newly arrived San Francisco Giants, and during a dramatic play at the home plate, Ahern suffered a fatal heart attack. For his replacement, Christopher turned to Cahill.[53] The new chief possessed Ahern's willingness to turn down graft, but he also brought a keener tactical and administrative mind to the office. Under Cahill, the SFPD leapt into the van of the nation's police professionalism movement.

Cahill was born in Chicago, but he spent his first seventeen years in Ireland with his mother. After she passed away in 1929, Cahill returned to the United States to settle close to relatives in the Bay Area. He worked for the next thirteen years as a farmhand, a cement hauler, an elevator operator, and an ice deliveryman. In this final position, Cahill's leadership potential emerged, and he was elected to serve as the Ice Wagon Drivers Union representative to the powerful San Francisco Labor Council. By now, Cahill had grown into a striking and magnetic figure. Tall and broad-shouldered, Cahill charmed with his blue eyes, red hair, and Irish brogue. In 1942 the thirty-two-year-old Cahill entered San Francisco's Police Academy, where his final class yearbook identified him as "most likely to become Chief of Police." Cahill not only made good on that prediction but went on to serve as the longest-tenured SFPD chief in San Francisco history.[54]

Elsewhere in the country, police professionalism advocates were arguing that the nation's newly reformed police departments could now serve the common good through preventive policing. Criminology scholars, such as the University of California's O. W. Wilson, and prominent police leaders, including Police Chief William Parker in Los Angeles, urged police departments to begin seeking out criminals rather than waiting for citizen complaints. Just weeks after his appointment, Chief Cahill introduced Operation S as a novel preventive approach to violent crime. Cahill explained that the *S* stood for *saturation*, and he promised a professional program based on centralized personnel authority and putatively color-blind, scientific data sets. Operation S leaders at the Hall of Justice used crime statistics to identify criminal "hot-spot" neighborhoods, and then, twice a week, they flooded these hot spots with roughly fifty police officers handpicked from the district stations.[55]

In December 1958 a *Chronicle* feature offered a typically effusive description of Operation S's top-down arrangement. The report began by explaining how Deputy Chief Al Nelder personally briefed the participating Operation S officers. These meetings rarely included concrete information beyond a hot sheet enumerating the licenses of stolen automobiles, but the wowed *Chronicle* compared the orientations to "an evening in night school." After officers received this preparation, the newspaper continued, the police headed out as "shock troops" to not only solve crimes but prevent them. When police encountered citizens on the street, the article explained, officers employed vagrancy charges against those whom police believed were ready to break the law and compelled the remainder to fill out identification cards. These identity cards, the *Chronicle* concluded, then became "tactical weapons" by providing police with a ready list of suspects for any nearby crimes.[56]

Operation S served managerial growth advocates by establishing rationales for large-scale redevelopment. Christopher's opposition to government welfare had initially made the new mayor wary of large redevelopment projects necessitating federal aid. He had therefore initially pursued small, privately funded projects, such as the construction of the Chinatown tourist-entrance archway. By 1958, however, the mayor was considering an upcoming reelection race alongside the continued demands of his downtown backers for access to federal redevelopment funds.[57] Christopher thus relented, and Operation S now helpfully taught citizens to identify planned zones of redevelopment as crime hot spots in need of rescuing.

From the start, Operation S commanders and the SFRA's large-scale planners both set their sites on the Fillmore District, a predominantly black neighborhood bordering City Hall. In December 1959, Ernest Lenn, a *San Francisco Examiner* journalist, recounted an evening he spent shadowing two Operation S officers through "the neon-lit, trouble-spot Fillmore area." Beginning his feature with a stock description of Deputy Chief Nelder's orientation, Lenn recounted how the officers' patrol car rolled into the Fillmore, where "slum clearance" had "leveled a swath of drab, ancient buildings." The city had replaced the former neighborhood with "many-storied housing projects" that looked to Lenn like passing "hospital ships in wartime." However, the redevelopment campaign remained incomplete: other "slum buildings still stand, waiting patiently for the end." Lenn believed that until the clearance was finished, Operation S officers were necessary guardians against violence. His article recounted how, over the course of the evening, the two patrol officers prevented a rape, issued a vagrancy arrest to an armed former convict "lurking" behind tall bushes, and questioned a variety of other men.[58]

Both Operation S and redevelopment, managerial growth proponents averred, represented clear examples of the city leadership's ability to promote a color-blind common good. This service to broader shared interests, downtown growth advocates concluded, allowed the city to look past questions of individual civil liberties. "The respectable citizen," District Attorney Thomas Lynch explained, "shouldn't object to being stopped and questioned politely if he realizes it's for his own protection."[59]

Operation S established San Francisco as a national leader in police professionalism. Television shows ranging from *The Lineup* during the 1950s to *The Streets of San Francisco* two decades later celebrated the SFPD for its combination of technical proficiency, academic expertise, and tough-fisted policing. Meanwhile, managerial growth administrations in other cities began recognizing that they too could employ putatively centrally orchestrated policing arrangements to rationalize increased police pressure. In 1960 the Chicago Police Department used Operation S as a point of inspiration when it launched stop-and-frisk policing. Over the next decade, growth-oriented cities across the nation followed San Francisco's and Chicago's lead with their own programs of "aggressive preventive patrol."[60]

THE DISCOVERY OF DISCRETION

Mayor Christopher's broad electoral coalition and the SFPD's mixture of machine-era and professional policing strategies all rested on the assumption that state institutions served as reliable extensions of the city leadership's will. But just as Mayor Christopher achieved power through police professionalism, criminologists made a startling discovery with the potential to undercut Christopher's conception of governance. Policing scholars who observed officers on the street slowly recognized that even professional police did not act as simple automatons of the department and city leadership; instead, officers used and enjoyed tremendous amounts of discretion.

The discovery of discretion began with a 1956 American Bar Association (ABA) study of urban police activities. The ABA initiated this national investigation into day-to-day law enforcement to better understand the police corruption garnering attention from managerial growth advocates. From the start, ABA investigators uncovered widespread evidence of police misbehavior. One field report, for instance, recounted an incident in which police interrogated a suspect with a fake polygraph machine fashioned from a kitchen colander.[61] Revelations of police wrongdoing were nothing new; a range of studies during the 1930s—including San Francisco's Atherton investigation and the congressional Wickersham Report—found endemic police criminality in urban police departments. These earlier inquiries, however, assumed that police malfeasance arose from feeble leadership and partisan outside interests corrupting officers who suffered from weak morals. The notion of police discretion played little role in this story. O. W. Wilson's *Police Administration* (1950), the so-called bible of professionalism, advocated top-down reforms without employing the term *discretion* once.[62]

The ABA researchers, however, viewed instances of police criminality in the context of all the officers' day-to-day activities. In this new light, the surveyors recognized that the practice of law enforcement in the United States usually rested on the subjective decision making of individual officers.[63] Law enforcement officials, the study found, then sometimes used that discretion to pursue their own institutional interests. Managerial growth proponents were soon forced to confront the fact that the administration of law enforcement did not parallel the governance of redevelopment. Whereas redevelopment officials in San Francisco plotted out neighborhood razings and construction projects with relative exactitude from SFRA board rooms, the Hall of Justice's police policies were always mediated through an array of considerations made by the department's 1,800 officers. This realization raised the question of whether police professionalization necessitated more than a consolidation of power at the upper ranks.

By the late 1950s, the survey's new interpretation of discretion filtered into the public through articles and conferences. California scholars played a prominent role in the ABA research, and thus an awareness of police discretion hit the Golden State early.[64] For careful observers of the SFPD, it became clear that officers involved in policing programs like the Chinatown detail and Operation S relied on their own subjective determinations. In Chinatown, a new generation of activists began asserting that some Chinatown detail officers used their autonomy to disregard intraneighborhood violence. These community spokespersons believed that City Hall leaders and Chinatown businesspeople tolerated the squad's discretionary underenforcement of the law because reports of resident-on-resident violence hurt the area's reputation as a "safe and clean" tourist spot for white families.[65]

Operation S, by contrast, created institutional incentives encouraging officers to use their discretion to engage in aggressive law enforcement. The twice-a-week program offered uniformed officers the thrilling opportunity to play the role of inspectors. "We weren't hemmed in by boundaries," Patrolman John Mindermann recalled. "We were thrown into the whole environment of the city to do whatever the hell we wanted." Patrol officers understood, moreover, that distinguished work on this special assignment could earn them a transfer into the vaunted Inspectors Bureau. Thus, as participating police pursued arrests, one patrolman recalled, the sense of competition among officers was "open and raw."[66]

Mayor Christopher and the managerial growth proponents ultimately appreciated the subjective policing encouraged by Operation S. Autonomous discretion strengthened the participating police officers' ability to maintain San Francisco's traditional boundaries of citizenship. Managerial growth advocates gave little public consideration to the workplace motivations of police officers but assumed that white male patrol officers would follow the city leadership's color-blind family values. Christopher and Cahill therefore trusted these officers to use their discretion to enforce the city's cultural, sexual, and racial norms.

The *Examiner*'s Lenn illustrated these assumptions in his report on his night shadowing two Operation S officers. The two patrol officers, Lenn related, spent the evening sizing up people on the street but then came to a stop when they encountered "two Negroes." The two Fillmore residents made themselves suspicious to the officers, Lenn explained, by wearing "windbreakers and dungarees" and "loitering" in the entryway of a residence. To Lenn and the officers it was obvious that these black men were exhibiting dangerous intentions through their clothes and behavior. Thus for Lenn it went without saying that the officers had used their discretion to serve the common good when they compelled the two men—and eight other residents before the night was over—to show their identification papers and "fill out Operation S interrogation cards." The fact that the officers eventually dismissed all ten of those men without charge did not dissuade Lenn from presuming that the patrol officers' discretion served "to bolster the thin blue line" between order and chaos.[67]

CONCLUSION

During the mid-twentieth century, downtown elites in cities across the country wrested power from traditional machines through managerial growth politics. Seeking to sideline working-class voters, big-business representatives argued that the city could protect the traditional standards of citizenship and promote widespread economic growth by consolidating governing power into the hands of supposedly dispassionate experts like themselves. Police professionalism served a double purpose in this campaign: the reforms squelched the machine's payola, and the program's abstract promises of top-down, common-good governance won support from an array of constituencies maintaining different understandings of the city's interests.

As Mayor Christopher and the SFPD's new leadership entered office promising law enforcement reform from above, scholars discovered that much of police policy was made on the beat. Recognizing how discretion-oriented programs like the Chinatown detail and Operation S served the redevelopment agenda, managerial growth advocates scrambled to rationalize the rank and file's broad prerogatives. Managerial growth proponents ultimately justified discretion by insisting that the city's officers could be trusted to use their powers in the service of the citizenry's shared color-blind, traditional family values.

CHAPTER 2

North Beach Beat: Bohemians, Patrol Officers, and Cultural Pluralism

Wendy Murphy's troubles began just before 2 a.m. on October 21, 1958, when the thong to her cheap rubber sandals snapped. A twenty-year-old former college student, Murphy had traveled in from Berkeley with two male companions for a night of socializing in North Beach's bohemian entertainment scene. The trio were heading toward the Co-Existence Bagel Shop for a final drink. Undeterred by her broken shoe, Murphy ditched the footwear and pressed on.[1]

Standing outside the Bagel Shop's Dutch doors, Patrolman William "Bill" Bigarani monitored North Beach's late-night crowds. Over the previous year, the publication of Allen Ginsberg's *Howl and Other Poems* and Jack Kerouac's *On the Road* had identified North Beach as an epicenter of the beat movement. The works rejected many of the racial, sexual, and gender mores of mainstream culture, and now each evening young people streamed into North Beach to flout these boundaries themselves. Patrolman Bigarani, a member of what he termed "the beatnik patrol," was the young officer tasked with maintaining order over this scene.[2] Bigarani interpreted the directive as a mandate to uphold the city's traditional behavioral standards. In possession of those assumed powers, the officer now saw a diminutive blonde woman with bare feet coming his way.

Bigarani stepped between Murphy and the Bagel Shop's entrance, demanded to see the young woman's identification, and then ordered her to return to Berkeley. Nervous, Murphy's male companions urged their friend to retreat, but Murphy threw her arms around a pole and, according to Bigarani, protested, "No **** cop is going to intimidate me." Incensed by her temerity,

Bigarani grabbed Murphy and announced that she was under arrest for vagrancy. When the young officer attempted to drag Murphy to a nearby police wagon, the young woman, in the officer's words, "fought like a tiger," and her thrashing sent the two of them to the pavement. Bigarani eventually regained control and tagged Murphy with an additional charge of resisting arrest.[3]

When the press learned of Bigarani's run-in with Murphy, local newspapers wove together two law-and-order storylines that were achieving prominence at the close of the 1950s. On the one hand, journalists used the episode to draw attention to the violations of assumed community standards within beat bohemias. During the late 1950s, beat scenes were emerging in urban enclaves like New York City's Greenwich Village and southern California's Venice Beach, as well as San Francisco's North Beach. The beat art and literary movements revolved around painting, theater, music (mostly jazz), and writing—poetry, fiction, and spoken word.[4]

The national media's discussions of the beats often brushed over their professional artistic work. Instead, national magazines, Hollywood films, television series, and local newspapers fixated on the beats' social relationships inside beat bars, coffeehouses, and apartment "pads." These mass-market depictions of bohemia created beatnik caricatures: black-clad, bereted, goateed men and similarly dressed, waifish women. The dark clothes allegedly evinced dark moods, and the ubiquitous references to the beats' "vacant stares" suggested a nihilistic rejection of work, political engagement, color-blind ideology, and family-oriented traditional gender roles. These violations of traditional citizenship standards, some national observers believed, made beats "fugitives of the great American middle class" and a threat to law and order.[5]

The media also used the confrontation between Bigarani and Murphy to consider the justness of police discretion. At the end of the decade, the nation's policy makers, scholars, journalists, and attorneys were slowly coming to terms with the broad prerogatives enjoyed by officers on the beat. The vagrancy law under which Bigarani arrested Murphy, for instance, was a sweeping statute empowering officers to arrest "every person who roams from place to place without any lawful business" and "every person who wanders about the streets at late or unusual hours without any visible or lawful business." The law allowed officers to make an arrest on the basis of their subjective interpretation of a suspect's status. Now criminologists were realizing the degree to which urban police relied on such laws. Indeed, during the mid-1950s, conservative estimates claimed that "vagrancy-type" charges accounted for one-third of all the nation's arrests.[6] Coverage of North Beach police confrontations, such as the incident involving Murphy and Bigarani, illustrated to newspaper readers how autonomous police discretion served as a cornerstone of San Francisco's traditional policing system. North Beach stories further revealed that officers used their discretion to rein in residents who did not break specific laws but had nevertheless stepped outside the city's traditional gender, sexual, and racial mores.

North Beach beats and their defenders exploited the new recognition of discretion to reorient discussions of North Beach policing from arguments over community-wide mores toward debates about individual prerogatives. At Murphy's trial, she and her lawyers emphasized the one-on-one nature of the young woman's confrontation with Bigarani. Highlighting Bigarani's individual sanction, Murphy testified, "I asked him what right he had to tell me to go home." Murphy's lawyers, meanwhile, argued that because there was no "law against going into the Bagel Shop," Bigarani's personal decision to arrest Murphy "as a beatnik" had violated the young woman's rights. In their challenges to the discretion of SFPD patrol officers, beats and their supporters were discovering an opportunity to introduce culturally pluralist conceptions of citizenship.[7]

THE EMERGENCE OF THE NORTH BEACH BEAT SCENE

Tucked between Telegraph Hill and Russian Hill, the financial district and the bay, San Francisco's North Beach carried deep immigrant, bohemian, and nightlife traditions. The neighborhood bordered the old, well-known Chinatown and Barbary Coast entertainment areas. It had long supported its own assortment of bars, cafes, and restaurants, and the area had a reputation for permissiveness. North Beach was the most densely peopled neighborhood of the city and housed an ethnically diverse population that included significant numbers of Irish-, Chinese-, Basque-, and Mexican-Americans. Italian-Americans, however, had held cultural sway over the neighborhood since the turn of the twentieth century. Some Italian-Americans had cultivated the neighborhood's laissez-faire image by making homemade wine during Prohibition and establishing a small-scale sex-entertainment industry after Prohibition ended.[8]

North Beach's tolerant bar and cafe scene, ethnic heterogeneity, and physical isolation from the rest of the city, combined with the area's low rents, attracted artists to the neighborhood's southern edge at the end of the nineteenth century. Its bohemian scene flourished through World War II around poets such as Kenneth Rexroth, Philip Lamantia, and William Everson. The postwar growth of the California School of Fine Arts (renamed the San Francisco Art

Institute in 1960) on Russian Hill, along with the migration to North Beach of a group of poets trained at the University of California, Berkeley (including Robert Duncan, Jack Spicer, and Robin Blaser), injected vitality into the area's creative circles during the early 1950s. A new beat movement began coalescing in 1953 and 1954 when writers and poets such as Kerouac, Ginsberg, and Gary Snyder arrived on North Beach's already thriving literary scene.[9]

Many beat artists felt that the North Beach community supported their creative work and bohemian lifestyle. David Meltzer, a beat poet, later explained that during the mid-1950s:

> North Beach . . . was a much more of a European atmosphere, because primarily most of the real estate was managed by Italians and often first-generation Italians, so there was more than one language spoken. And the Italians never felt uncomfortable with the idea of somebody being an artist or a poet. They thought it was a legitimate job—the same as being a plumber. And in fact they had a high regard for this. So rents were low and the atmosphere was conducive to productive work.[10]

The beats living and working in North Beach also socialized in the neighborhood. The commercial hub of the district's bohemia shifted north during the postwar period, away from the city's expanding financial district and deeper into the Italian-American neighborhood. In 1949 Henri Lenoir started this migration by opening Vesuvio Cafe on Columbus Avenue, just south of Broadway Street, and in 1953 Lawrence Ferlinghetti and Peter Martin launched City Lights Pocket Book Shop (renamed City Lights Bookstore a year later) next door to Lenoir's bar. That same year Knute Stiles and Leo Krikorian helped push bohemia's commercial hub still farther into residential North Beach by opening The Place, a bar and art gallery, on upper Grant Avenue. The oldest street in San Francisco, Grant Avenue terminated with a narrow, four-block commercial corridor crowded with bars, galleries, art shops, bookstores, Chinese dressmaking factories, and Italian bakeries. Two popular establishments at the corner of Grant Avenue and Green Street—the Co-Existence Bagel Shop and the Coffee Gallery, a dilapidated bar and art space—made that intersection the symbolic epicenter of the neighborhood's burgeoning beat scene.[11]

These beat commercial establishments were launched during a period when the North Beach's Italian-American merchants and longtime residents were locked in a fight over neighborhood development. Managerial growth advocates argued that they could serve North Beach's interests by integrating the neighborhood into the city's mainstream tourist and entertainment economy. North Beach businesspeople encouraged this agenda through the Chinatown–North Beach Development Committee. Residents who did not own businesses, by contrast, regarded these plans as a threat to the neighborhood's small-scale, family-oriented arrangement. These locals successfully blocked efforts to construct neighborhood parking garages and apartment towers.[12]

Initially, neither side in this debate over development and the residents' interests could come to a clear consensus on whether the beats represented a boon or danger to its respective neighborhood vision. Older North Beach entrepreneurs often viewed the new beat commercial establishments as invasive competition, while neighborhood consumers appeared appreciative of some of the bohemian businesses. Krikorian, owner of The Place, experienced this divided reception. On the one hand, a neighboring business owner reported to police that Krikorian's bohemian bar bootlegged hard liquor. This was an accurate accusation, but Krikorian later defended the practice, saying that "the Italians in the neighborhood, not the beats," purchased this alcohol.[13] As the 1950s continued, even traditional business and property owners learned to appreciate beat consumers and renters as sources of profit. Indeed, the beat scene attracted an influx of young white professionals into the neighborhood, and rents rocketed upward by 92 percent during the 1950s in the northern, central, and eastern sections of the neighborhood.[14]

Thus there was no broad-based neighborhood antipathy toward the beats when, in the summer of 1957, a small group of culturally conservative North Beach residents demanded a crackdown. The protesters submitted a petition to city leaders complaining that when beats roiled the night air with their fights, obscenities, singing, and musical instruments, "regular policemen" did "nothing to stop this disturbance." A "great many of the mal-adjusted and anti-social individuals [*sic*] of our city," the appeal continued, "have learned that they can come to this small area and demonstrate their contempt for law and order."[15] Police countered that community indifference enabled the beat scene to grow. In September 1959, for instance, Charles de Caro, a sixty-six-year-old Italian-American butcher, enraged Patrolman Joseph Galik when he refused to help the officer arrest a beat book salesperson. Absurdly, Galik took de Caro in on a posse comitatus charge, invoking a code that had not been used in San Francisco since the nineteenth century. One North Beach booster who objected to the beats' presence had to admit that the scene flourished along upper Grant Avenue "because the people of this community don't give a damn."[16]

THE DANGEROUS BEAT

During the fall of 1958, the beat scene's growing literary reputation drew new mainstream attention to North Beach's bohemian colony. In late August, San Francisco's district attorney prosecuted Ferlinghetti, the beat bookstore owner, for the sale of obscene material, and in September, Jack Kerouac's *On the Road* hit the nation's bookstands. Together, these two events unleashed a torrent of national media attention on San Francisco's North Beach scene. *Look, The Nation, Harper's Magazine, Time,* and *Playboy* all ran features covering beats in the neighborhood. Entranced by the notion of an alternative to traditional family values, most of these early national reports painted a pathetic picture of the North Beach denizens.[17] Nevertheless, the attention generated new waves of visitors and migrants. By early 1958 the neighborhood's thronging bars were drawing local columnists in search of a good story and free drinks, and the beat social world entered the pages of the San Francisco press.[18]

In the late spring of 1958, the *San Francisco Examiner*'s June Muller and the *San Francisco Chronicle*'s Allen Brown each responded to North Beach's increased notoriety with an investigative series into the beat social world. Neither Muller, a socially active woman, nor Brown, a closeted gay man, was a teetotaler, but each characterized the North Beach scene as an embarrassing underworld of drugs, sex, and fake bohemianism.[19] Their two series reflected and reinforced the narrative framework within which the city's future beat policy discussions took place.

In their reports, Muller and Brown limited the conceptual borders of the beat bohemia to North Beach. The bars and cafes along Grant Avenue did provide a social hub for the beat bohemia, but the beat professional and social world extended into the San Francisco Art Institute, the San Francisco State College Poetry Center, areas of the Fillmore District, and locations elsewhere in the Bay Area, including Berkeley and Stinson Beach. Even the beat scene's famous coming out event, Ginsberg's reading of *Howl* at the Six Gallery, occurred away from North Beach, in the Cow Hollow neighborhood. Within this tightly bound commercial scene of North Beach, Muller and Brown drew attention to the male beats' disdain for breadwinning manhood. Muller lamented that the industrious and creative poets and authors who had sparked the beat movement (Ginsberg, Kerouac, and Gregory Corso) no longer belonged to the North Beach scene. She cast the new male beats, by contrast, as unproductive, childish poseurs. Muller quoted North Beach's "oldtimers"—including both "the Bohemians and the businessmen"—who scoffed at male beats as: "'The motorcycle crowd without motorcycles.' 'Little children from the country.' 'Juvenile delinquents a little bit grown up.'"[20]

The local and national media's repeated characterizations of the beats as children refusing to mature appeared at the same time that suburbanization and downtown growth efforts were transforming the household composition of many American cities. San Francisco entered the 1950s with a population solidly made up of families. As in Chicago, where boosters touted their metropolis as a "city of family men," postwar leaders in San Francisco prided themselves in their city's family orientation. Managerial growth experts assumed that they would reinforce their cities' family character with redevelopment policies expanding employment related to finance, insurance, and real estate (FIRE); by 1960 San Francisco's FIRE economy was the city's second largest job-providing sector. In cities like San Francisco, Chicago, and New York City, these white-collar jobs attracted young white college graduates who were either single or married without children. By 1960 more than half of San Francisco men in their twenties were unmarried, and between 1950 and 1960 the percentage of women in their twenties who were single jumped 9 points to 29 percent. This expanding corps of young downtown employees enjoyed an off-work life largely free of many forms of traditional adult control. Within the context of these demographic and social changes, cultural conservatives worried over the beats' public rejection of the traditional markers of adulthood.[21]

None of the beats' deviations from traditional models provoked more concern in San Francisco than the bohemians' abandonment of the city's supposedly color-blind perspective. Muller explained that beats communicated in "the frantic paced parlance of jazz," and Brown condemned white beat women for using their sexual freedom to associate with black men. For both reporters, black people entered the beat scene only as objects of white obsession rather than as active contributors to the North Beach bohemia. Brown, a proponent of color-blind liberalism, based his understanding of the beats' relationship with blacks on Norman Podhoretz's nationally renowned beat critique, "The Know-Nothing Bohemians." Both Brown and Podhoretz characterized the white beats' interest in blackness as an expression of the bohemians' paternalistic "desire for the primitive." Traditional liberals continued to voice this sort of critique through the decline of the beat scene. In 1960 a jazz publicist remarked to the *Chronicle*'s music critic that when the beat scene was "really swinging," "you saw a tremendous number of young Caucasian girls escorting Negro males. These girls were making a determined effort to prove they had no racial inhibitions and no prejudice." Not until the naive beat "girls" had "grown up," the publicist continued, would they "realize . . . that true racial tolerance only comes when the color of a man's skin is disregarded completely."[22]

Liberals initially warned that this bohemian race mixing would result in violence. The *Chronicle*'s Brown quoted one poet explaining that the white beats' supposed interest in black men was "all tied up with the [beat] death-wish, of course." Journalists located evidence for this racially oriented "death-wish" during their coverage of the Connie Sublette murder. On the evening of June 17, 1958, Sublette, a white North Beach habitué, was killed only hours after attending the North Beach memorial service of Paul Swanson, her fiancé. Days earlier Swanson had seemingly demonstrated the beats' proclivity for self-destruction by tumbling off the roof of a North Beach apartment building. Following the funeral, the grief-stricken Sublette left upper Grant Avenue to visit her estranged husband, Albert Sublette, in the interracial Haight-Ashbury neighborhood. Not far from Albert's home, however, Sublette encountered Frank Harris, a black civilian launderer on leave from a docked Navy supply ship. Harris later claimed that Sublette willingly accompanied him into a nearby alley for a sexual liaison but that the young woman had started screaming after he undressed her. Harris asserted that he was only attempting to silence Sublette when he suffocated her to death. The following morning police discovered Sublette's disrobed, lifeless body, and by that evening authorities traced the trail of evidence back to Harris aboard his ship.[23]

In their coverage of the murder, the city's three major dailies eschewed the traditional tale of white female honor ravaged by violent black male sexuality. Instead, the local press focused on Sublette's history in North Beach and suggested that her beat lifestyle—and particularly her sexual appetite—led to her homicide. In the following days, the press tagged the young woman as an "obscene, drunken," "flamboyant" "playgirl" who had "engaged in several shoddy sexual liaisons," had once streaked along Broadway "stark naked," and was wearing a "sleazy" dress on the night she was murdered.[24]

Downtown journalists further asserted that while young women required authoritative, masculine supervision, the beat world had allowed Sublette to live a dangerously untethered, independent life. The young woman, one journalist melodramatically noted, wore "a St. Christopher's medal—guardian of travelers—around her neck." This pretention at independence, the press continued, masked a hunger for male guidance. Prior to Sublette's murder, Muller reported, Sublette had been witnessed striking Swanson and hysterically sobbing, "You can't leave me," "I can't go on alone." But Swanson, Muller reminded her readers, had abandoned Sublette when his beat nihilism took him over the ledge of the North Beach rooftop. (By the time of Sublette's murder, police had determined that Swanson's fall had been accidental and not a suicide, but journalists continued to attribute his death to a beat penchant for self-destruction.) Sublette's whirlwind of North Beach recklessness and criminality, the press made clear, was facilitated by the failures of the weak white men in the North Beach bohemia.[25]

Through the Sublette story, the downtown media illustrated that the beat women's sexual cravings were especially dangerous because female beats spurned the mainstream's supposedly color-blind outlook and turned to black men for satisfaction. White reporters readily accepted Harris's assertion that Sublette consented to his initial advances, and the *News*, *Chronicle*, and *Examiner* all used photographs to communicate to readers that Sublette's estranged husband was dark-skinned.[26] Ultimately Sublette's unrooted, desperate life had brought North Beach bohemia; the city's working-class waterfront; and the interracial, centrally located Panhandle neighborhood into combustible contact.

The journalists covering the story all looked to the SFPD to reestablish its authority over the chaotic mixture of races and urban spaces that a lifestyle like Sublette's had created. The *Examiner* juxtaposed its descriptions of Sublette's wild life with a steady narrative of the Homicide Bureau's gumshoe investigation. Describing the bureau's deliberate and rational work, the *Examiner* reported: "From Harris' story of his whereabouts the night before, from habitués of the juke box joints and the gin mills, the clubs and the taverns and such places as the Co-Existence Bagel Shop, which members of the 'Beat Generation' frequent, and from backtracking on the last night of Connie Sublette, the police put together the jigsaw of death."[27] Traditional liberals and conservatives alike regarded police officers as the public servants best equipped to address the alleged racial disorder set loose by the beats.

COSMOPOLITAN LIBERALISM, HARM, AND THE PROFITABLE BEAT SCENE

The press highlighted narratives like the Sublette tragedy to raise the alarm over the beats' suicidal tendencies, but the Sublette storyline also reinforced popular perceptions of the North Beach bohemia as white. Sublette had incited interracial violence when she left the confines of North Beach and naively consorted with black men in another neighborhood. Within the bounds of North Beach, the San Francisco press uncovered evidence only of beats bringing violence upon themselves.

The various articles on beat self-destruction thus carried the possible subtext that for mature people, North Beach could be an exciting but safe environment in which they could find a release from traditional cultural strictures. Following these conclusions, a new generation of white journalists used their coverage of the North Beach beat scene to begin questioning the city leadership's commitment to traditional family values. Introducing a new, cosmopolitan liberal posture, these young journalists characterized the beats' rejection of old gender boundaries as harmless and even a boon to the city's economy.

The tourists streaming into North Beach, Venice Beach, and Greenwich Village revealed that a sizeable segment of the white middle class found beats more entertaining than terrifying. In San Francisco, Gray Line added a bus-tour route for upper Grant Avenue to satisfy the new rush of sightseers pouring into the neighborhood. The nation's mass culture makers, meanwhile, scrambled to cash in on the fast-spreading beat phenomenon. Some beat-themed productions, such as the film *The Beatniks* (1960), traded in violence and sexual degradation, but Atlantic Records associated the scene with fun and excitement when it proclaimed itself "the label in tune with the beat generation." Similarly, television shows such as *The Many Loves of Dobie Gillis* and films like *The Subterraneans* (1960) relayed comedic or sympathetic representations of beat culture.[28]

The effusion of national interest inspired some liberals to suggest that the beats buttressed the neighborhood's reputation as cosmopolitan and economically productive. One North Beach resident rejoiced that the beats provided his neighborhood with a "prestige" similar to that of New York's Greenwich Village, and he noted that very few of the patrons flowing into "Grant Street [*sic*] establishments could be called bums." A San Francisco film critic lauded *The Subterraneans*—an otherwise almost universally panned movie—as "a visually exciting picture" that offered "jeweled night views" of the bustling city.[29] This excitement over the economic possibilities of beat neighborhoods extended beyond major beat centers like San Francisco and New York City. In St. Louis, for instance, the *Globe-Democrat* and the *Post-Dispatch* celebrated their city's bohemian Gaslight District under the headlines "Homeland of the Individualists" and "Rehabilitation in Gaslight."[30]

In San Francisco the emerging cosmopolitan liberal appreciation for North Beach was clearest in the press's reports on Eric Nord, a North Beach entertainment entrepreneur. Charismatic, red-bearded, and "gargantuan," Nord had worked on and off in the North Beach nightlife scene since the late 1940s. He was a master of gossip-column self-promotion, and Herb Caen proclaimed him "The King of North Beach." In January 1958, Nord began promoting a beat Party Pad and established himself as a beat scene spokesperson in the press. Recalling Nord's celebrity, the poet Meltzer described the entrepreneur:

> Eric was, you know, a very larger-than-life figure and was getting just a lot of publicity for being this big, Falstafian guy with babes on each knee looking, you know, looking like stuff on a car, you know like hood ornaments. Because he was large: tall and wide, and just generally like a very avuncular sort of guy. And he was cashing in too.[31]

Through Nord, cosmopolitan liberals illustrated how North Beach's rejection of family values opened sexual and entrepreneurial possibilities for white, heterosexual men. That message paralleled the urban-oriented challenges to traditional family values being mounted in national publications like *Playboy*. During the 1950s, *Playboy* became a sensation by encouraging men to abandon the family responsibilities of suburbia for a life of sexual and consumerist hedonism in the city. However, the magazine's editors regarded the beats as pathetic because, in their estimation, the bohemians had unchained themselves from the supposed shackles of marriage only to waste that freedom in sexless poverty. Nord's entrepreneurial promiscuous lifestyle served as a sharp counterpoint to *Playboy*'s stereotype of the beats. As Nord proved he could use the beat scene to rake in tourist dollars and young white women, local cosmopolitan liberal reporters began using Nord's legal transgressions to offer amused and unworried descriptions of beat gender-role bending. In the late summer of 1958, for instance, Nord was caught absconding out of town with two white, high school–aged girls. Even before the girls resurfaced—apparently unharmed—cosmopolitan liberal journalists reported on Nord's actions as a titillating but harmless joke. Through their reports on Nord's various run-ins with police, sometimes presented in the newspapers' entertainment sections, cosmopolitan liberal reporters raised the possibility that the beat scene offered enterprising white men financial profit and heterosexual excitement.[32]

From the start, the cosmopolitan liberal perspective on North Beach assumed that one could be in the scene without being of it. The new brand of liberals drew this distinction by differentiating between "hardcore beats" and "weekend beats." Cynthia Grey, advice columnist for the *San Francisco News*, referenced these two categories in July 1958 when a mother identified as "Upset" wrote her anxiously, "I think my daughter is becoming a beatnik." Upset's daughter had refused to join the family on vacation and had instead spent her college break associating with bearded men. Grey was unruffled.

"For one," the columnist chided, "stop worrying. Chances are your daughter is merely a 'Sunday Beatnik' which is quite different from a full-time Beatnik who is a permanent parasite rejecting life's responsibilities." Grey suggested that the daughter would leave the beats behind once the school year began, but that Upset could accelerate this process by withholding the daughter's car and allowance.[33]

Cosmopolitan liberals often delivered their unperturbed reactions to the beats as jokes, but their new approach to cultural pluralism represented the early stages of a seismic shift in liberal conceptions of crime. During the mid- and late 1950s, liberals in the United States and Western Europe began breaking away from old definitions of law by turning to the so-called harm principle. The postwar harm principle, based on the mid-nineteenth-century writings of John Stuart Mill, viewed the state as justified in policing only activities that physically or materially injured others.[34]

Across the country, cosmopolitan liberals used the policing of beats to issue harm-principle critiques of moralistic law enforcement. In 1959, Philadelphia's *Evening Bulletin* mocked Captain Frank Rizzo's raid of a beat bar by pointing out that the police raid had been motivated by "Beards! Turtle neck sweaters! Tights! People sitting around and talking." *Evening Bulletin* readers then flooded the newspaper with letters to the editor charging that Rizzo's policing of culture distracted law enforcement from harmful crimes that merited police attention. Separate letters decried the policing of the beats by pointing to the "muggings," the "cut-throat hoods," the "crimes of violence," and "all the murders, holdups and rackets in the City."[35]

Regarding beat behavior as harmless, other cosmopolitan liberals suggested that police repression of the beats warranted defiance. In the spring of 1958, Caen began patronizing the Coffee Gallery, and his columns soon addressed SFPD harassment. One Caen dispatch began:

> Fri., two cops stalked into the Bagel Shop on Grant Ave. and announced to the assembled Beatniks: "Awright, we're gonna vag (charge with vagrancy) anybody who can't prove employment." This was greeted with such a roar of laughter that the cops wavered, fell back, broke ranks, fled in vagrant confusion. Having sniffed along Beat Blvd. recently. . . . I think fragrancy might be a more reasonable charge.

Caen denigrated the beats as smelly, ridiculous "Beatniks," but then used this characterization to describe the beat rejection of police authority as innocuous and even funny.[36]

AUTONOMOUS POLICE DISCRETION
AND CULTURAL PLURALISM

The growing attention toward the beats made it clear that the SFPD leadership relied on discretionary policing by patrol officers to maintain order in North Beach. Following the *Chronicle*'s and *Examiner*'s North Beach exposés in the late spring and early summer of 1958, the SFPD leadership initiated a short, centrally orchestrated crackdown on the beat scene. After this brief campaign, Central Station turned to overlapping foot patrols to maintain order in North Beach.[37] This strategy, coupled with broad charges like vagrancy, allowed individual rank-and-file officers to set North Beach's behavioral boundaries.

During the 1950s and 1960s, the SFPD officers patrolling San Francisco's streets were predominantly Catholic and white and exclusively male. SFPD leaders cultivated the department's Catholic composition by prioritizing Catholics for promotion. Indeed, between 1907 and 1971, the Police Commission selected only Catholics for the position of police chief.[38] Meanwhile, the SFPD high brass initially capped its female membership at eight. Police leaders forbade these women from wearing uniforms and relegated them to the sex detail and the Juvenile Bureau. In those capacities, female officers interviewed children and dictated recordings off high-tech snooping devices to male inspectors. Police commanders regarded female officers as unqualified to interact with adult residents; the high brass even excluded female officers from interviews with adult female rape victims. SFPD leaders did permit black officers to wear uniforms and trusted them to interact with adult San Franciscans, but they similarly limited black membership to a few token hires. By 1959 the department had only seventeen black police officers.[39]

As SFPD leaders maintained a patrol corps that was relatively homogenous in its racial, religious, and gender composition, the high brass felt comfortable making personnel decisions broadening the rank and file's discretionary powers. Most notably, the department expanded its patrol and sergeant corps by about 30 percent in the six years after World War II but chose not to match this growth with a comparable increase in the number of lieutenants until 1967. The SFPD's district stations thus maintained bottom-heavy organizational structures. At the top each station had a single captain, who, of course, could not work twenty-four-hour shifts, so police stations went without a top commander during the busy nighttime hours. Under the captain, three deskbound lieutenants (one for each of the department's three shifts) were expected to monitor an average total of sixteen sergeants on the street. Those district sergeants, in turn, supervised an average total of eighty-four patrol officers. During a period before two-way radios (officers checked in on widely dispersed police call boxes), the SFPD's pyramid-like arrangement precluded steady supervision.[40]

Police and city leaders resisted reforms to the SFPD's structure for a variety of reasons. More supervisor positions would dilute the policing and political power of the officers who had already reached lofty positions. Department leaders also valued the weak lines of supervision for the political insulation they provided when the police made controversial decisions. At the 1960 anti-HUAC City Hall protest, for instance, the high brass left Inspector Michael Maguire in charge of the scene and responded slowly to the riot alarm he sounded. When Maguire was subsequently pilloried in the courts and press for ordering an attack on the student protesters, the SFPD leadership refused to address its own culpability for the police violence. "They left the troops . . . out there to try to come up with something," Patrolman John Mindermann later recalled. "You were expected to take the proper police action but you were given no direction. Yet you were accountable." Discretion thus served a policy function by providing police with the means to maintain order and a political function by shielding top officials from culpability for that activity.[41]

In North Beach, the SFPD's reliance on patrol officers allowed Mayor Christopher to remove himself from an issue of which he clearly wanted no part. When interracial murders like Sublette's suffocation necessitated a reaction from the mayor, Christopher suggested that "girls" like Sublette needed "psychiatric treatment." Still, Christopher hedged and insisted that productive "true artists" were respectable citizens. After the Sublette murder, Christopher largely withdrew himself from the North Beach beat debate.[42]

Patrol officers had their own institutional motivations for remaining self-sufficient. Often they wished to live up to the departmental culture of independence cultivated by their superiors. "If you had to ask for help with regard to evaluating or handling a situation, other than physical help to overcome resistance," Mindermann explained, "you were regarded as an ineffective officer, and you wouldn't be on the street very long." Patrolmen recognized, moreover, that any requests for assistance would likely attract sergeants and inspectors who would take not only control of the scene but credit for any arrest. Thus, in North Beach, although the Hall of Justice sat on the neighborhood's northeastern border and the department's high brass often lunched along Columbus Avenue, neighborhood patrolmen sought to solve problems themselves.[43]

The nighttime, two-man "beatnik patrol" along upper Grant Avenue and western Broadway Street shouldered the primary responsibility for policing the beat scene. In the latter half of 1958, Central Station commanders assigned

Patrolman Bigarani, a young rising star, to this high-profile post. Although new officers typically spent years in the department before obtaining their own foot patrols, Bigarani was well positioned as both the son of a Painter's Union official and a graduate of the University of San Francisco (a Jesuit university that was a traditional incubator for the city's political elite). These advantages enabled the "highly articulate" officer to achieve his important position only one year out of the Police Academy.[44]

Professionally ambitious and naturally self-reliant, Bigarani adapted easily to the SFPD's decentralized policing regime. Indeed, he evinced a crusader's zeal while working to defend what he regarded as North Beach's traditional family values. As the Murphy incident illustrated, Bigarani was willing to employ force to impose his sense of order. North Beach beats frequently accused his partners of brutality, but the reputations of these officers paled in comparison to Bigarani's. The Northern California American Civil Liberties Union (ACLU) received so many complaints against Bigarani during his first year assigned to North Beach that the local director of the ACLU personally implored Police Chief Thomas Cahill to discipline the officer. The SFPD leader dismissed the request.[45]

Bigarani took his fight against the bohemians beyond the streets and into the beats' commercial establishments and private residences. He frequently stationed himself in the doorways of both the Bagel Shop and the Coffee Gallery, intimidating would-be patrons and closely monitoring the number of customers to be sure the establishments did not exceed their mandated capacity limits (a statute rarely enforced in bars and clubs in other parts of the city). The young patrol officer also spent time inspecting the single-room-occupancy lodgings along the Broadway corridor. In October 1959, for instance, Bigarani and three other officers allegedly entered a residential hotel room to search for drugs, then administered a compulsory physical examination of both the female renter and the man with whom she was living. (The man was under indictment for possession of narcotics.) When Bigarani spotted an infection on the woman's leg, he forced her, on pain of arrest, to seek treatment at a nearby clinic.[46]

When Bigarani wished to issue an arrest, he often employed drunkenness charges or the broad vagrancy accusation he applied to Murphy. The officer understood that local judges would throw out most of his nuisance arrests, so he sometimes failed to attend the subsequent court hearings.[47] His absence from the courtroom spared most arrestees serious jail sentences or fines but also denied beats the opportunity to confront him over his tactics in front of a judge. Moreover, Bigarani's nighttime arrests forced detained beats to endure at least one night in San Francisco's notoriously grim city jail. If a police officer arrested a suspect on a Friday, the accused had to remain in jail until Monday morning, when a judge could dismiss the charges.[48]

The unwritten codes and procedures with which officers like Bigarani maintained order had concerned traditional liberals for decades. Even before the recognition of police discretion, the traditional liberal emphasis on top-down regulations as a key to equal opportunity had inspired liberal campaigns to bring police departments under "the rule of law." In 1954 the California State Supreme Court case *People v. Cahan* attempted to limit police prerogatives by establishing an exclusionary rule forbidding courts from accepting evidence collected by the police without a warrant. The discovery of police discretion had raised the stakes on these debates, as activists came to realize how much police policy was set on the beat. During the late 1950s, as political power in Sacramento see-sawed back and forth between Democrats and Republicans, the state legislature alternately expanded and constricted regulations over police procedures.[49]

At the end of the 1950s, liberals and conservatives oriented the rule-of-law debate around vagrancy law. Since the 1930s, traditional liberals had highlighted the police department's use of vagrancy law against men looking for work and men protesting for better wages and working conditions. Vagrancy law arrests, according to these liberal critiques, impeded men's ability to fulfill their civic duties as breadwinners. Conservatives countered that vagrancy law served as an invaluable "preventative measure" against disorder. In particular, cultural conservatives argued that vagrancy law buttressed the family-oriented social order by empowering police to punish men who refused to accept their wage-earning responsibility. One police officer in Hutchinson, Kansas, for instance, defined a beatnik as a person who "doesn't like work" and promised, "Any man who doesn't like work is a vagrant and a vagrant goes to jail around here."[50]

In San Francisco, Police Chief Cahill charged that the beats' threat to the family-oriented citizenship model extended beyond financial considerations. Explaining to a New York City newspaper that the SFPD did not keep separate crime rate statistics for North Beach, Cahill retorted, "Anyway, what do you mean by crime? Don't you consider leading juveniles into a life like that a crime? That's the greatest crime you can commit." Cahill warned that beats were exposing children to "sacrilegious" "quotations" ("The way they talked about Christ!" he exclaimed) and to a bacchanal belief that "anything went" "as far as sex was concerned." The police, he concluded, had a responsibility "to protect our young people from that."[51]

A growing number of liberals, however, began using the beats to question whether police might make mistakes with their autonomous discretion. In 1958 Democrats retook the state Senate and Assembly, and Jack O'Connell, a Democrat elected to San Francisco's liberal twenty-first Assembly district, secured positions atop the Assembly's Judiciary and Criminal Procedures Subcommittees. From these perches he interrogated the subjective powers of patrol officers in the 1958 Constitutional Rights hearings and the 1960 Laws of Arrest inquiries.[52]

When O'Connell brought the Constitutional Rights subcommittee to San Francisco, he agreed to accept Nord as a witness. Nord edified both O'Connell and the liberal reporters covering the hearing on the primacy of discretion in North Beach policing.[53] Hadley Roff, the liberal *News* reporter who later commentated on the SFPD's rule-of-law violations at the 1960 anti-HUAC demonstration, opened his coverage of the O'Connell hearings by quoting Nord's charge that police violated civil liberties when they "act as jury and judge over a segment of society without knowing how that segment thinks." The following spring Wes Willoughby, later the coauthor of Roff's anti-HUAC protest report, ran a *News* feature that similarly described how North Beach police officers employed their autonomous discretion in error. According to a Congregationalist minister interviewed by Willoughby, police officers regularly subjected local denizens to harassment, false arrests, and obscenities and had recently intimidated a nonbohemian woman they misjudged as a beat. "We're not out to get the police," the religious leader concluded, "just encourage proper law enforcement."[54]

Beyond making procedural arguments that discretion raised the chances of police miscalculations, some cosmopolitan liberals used vagrancy debates to promote a culturally pluralist vision of the citizenry. In Philadelphia, the criminologist Caleb Foote used his critiques of vagrancy law to insist that men who chose bohemian lifestyles "like Thoreau in *Walden*" did not represent criminals. Roff's coverage of O'Connell's San Francisco hearings offered a similar message when he quoted Nord pronouncing, "So-called eccentricity is a sign of a healthy society."[55] Scott Newhall, the *Chronicle*'s editor in chief, responded to Nord's testimony with his own editorial, titled "Are Beatniks Being Pushed around Because They Are Nonconformists?" Pounding the "supersensitive and unduly hostile" police, Newhall commented, "If this little group of North Beach residents is singled out for special treatment because its members wear whiskers on their chins, and read avant-garde verse aloud, and don't feel like working a 9-to-5 shift in a pants factory—because they are different and nonconforming—then these police scurryings become obnoxious." Eliding the substantial break that beat behavior represented with earlier bohemian traditions, the *Chronicle* argued that policing in North Beach violated the "unwritten traditions that this city has long favored."[56]

As cosmopolitan liberals questioned discretionary policing of activities they deemed harmless, some began to assert that individual beats had rights in the face of an individual patrol officer's moralizing. In 1958 the ACLU introduced this argument into the civic sphere through its defense of Murphy.[57] The ACLU, the prosecution, and the press all characterized Murphy's encounter with Patrolman Bigarani as a one-on-one confrontation, and thus the trial and the trial coverage revolved around Bigarani's and Murphy's individual prerogatives. Supporters for both sides portrayed Murphy and Bigarani in similar terms, juxtaposing the former college student as a "petite," "baby-faced," "small and fragile" weekend beat against the patrolman's "burly," "husky" frame. Cultural conservatives writing for the *Examiner* used the childlike image of Murphy to suggest that Bigarani was reasserting appropriate family hierarchies when he used fatherly physical powers to punish the young woman's childish immorality. The San Francisco Police Officers' Association's newspaper applauded this sort of reasoning when it rhymed that beats were "lads / who never were bathed or spanked / by their dads." Murphy's jury ultimately endorsed this reasoning as well, coming to quick guilty verdicts for both the vagrancy and resisting arrest charges.[58]

The *Chronicle*'s cosmopolitan liberal coverage of the trial, by contrast, used Murphy's juvenile image to depict the young woman as physically unthreatening. The *Chronicle*'s Donovan McClure, later the press secretary for Eugene McCarthy's presidential campaign, described Murphy's walk to the bar as a neighborhood "stroll," and the newspaper's copy editors mocked the notion that Murphy had presented a physical challenge by captioning Bigarani's photograph: "He was embattled." Within this context, McClure casually quipped that the trial would answer an explosive question: "Does a pretty young thing have to go home when a policeman tells her to?" McClure did not provide an explicit answer, but the article's wisecracking tone made his sympathies toward Murphy clear. McClure's reporting suggested that Murphy had rights "as a beatnik" not to be harassed by the police. In McClure's eyes, Bigarani had failed to serve the city's shared interests in his discretionary policing of North Beach culture.[59]

By 1960 the beats had become a touchstone for both defenders and opponents of vagrancy law. Assembly member O'Connell used both rule-of-law and harm-principle rationales to submit a bill rewriting the state's vagrancy code. Donald Grunsky, a Republican from Watsonville (a city ninety miles south of San Francisco), derided O'Connell's proposed revision as "the Beatnik's bill of rights," but conservatives failed to prevent the bill's passage through the Assembly and the Senate. Governor Edmund "Pat" Brown pocket vetoed O'Connell's 1960 measure after receiving protests from the state's local police departments, but in the next general session, O'Connell introduced and passed a second vagrancy revision bill with the stipulation that officers could continue to force citizens to identify themselves. This addendum placated police, but O'Connell correctly predicted that the courts would strike out the identification provision as unconstitutional. On May 31, 1961, Governor Brown signed O'Connell's new bill into law. San Francisco's cosmopolitan liberals, in a two-pronged campaign to legitimize cultural pluralism and professionalize rank-and-file policing, made California only the second state in the nation without a common vagrancy statute.[60]

AUTONOMOUS POLICE DISCRETION
AND RACIAL PLURALISM

San Francisco's emerging cadres of white cosmopolitan liberals cheered the demise of the common vagrancy code, but few protested when in their dealings with black San Franciscans, patrol officers simply replaced vagrancy charges with broad and subjective "drunkenness" and "suspicion of felony" charges.[61] The *San Francisco Chronicle* had already adopted this double standard during the height of the anti-vagrancy law campaign; as the newspaper's news and editorial pages ridiculed the vagrancy arrests of the beats, the *Chronicle* praised the vagrancy charge–driven Operation S for its policing of San Francisco's black and indigent populations. Indeed, the media's coverage of Murphy and Nord obscured the fact that even in North Beach black bohemians found themselves the targets of harassment and arrest far more frequently than did their white compatriots.

Harassment by North Beach police officers followed identifiable racial and gender patterns. North Beach patrol officers sometimes targeted white men in North Beach with abuse or arrest when the men bore visible bohemian markers like beards, when they operated a beat commercial establishment, or when they provided legal services to beats. Police also subjected white male beats to unequal policing by denying them protection from outside "hoodlums" who entered the neighborhood looking to cause trouble. In general, however, white men in North Beach needed to be openly antagonistic toward the police in order to provoke an arrest.[62]

Police officers' relatively dismissive attitude toward white men extended to white gays, unless they displayed their affections publicly. One local newspaper feature on Bigarani's "beatnik patrol" described the young officer warning off a bar patron doing "peculiar things" (presumably activities regarded as gay). On other occasions, however, Bigarani and the other North Beach officers paid little heed to white gay men. Some officers avoided antigay policing because of the discomfort they felt toward homosexuality. Krikorian recalled how an Italian-American business owner once tried to close down Krikorian's beat bar, The Place, by reporting his establishment as a gay bar to the police. "A guy from the vice squad came by and checked me out," Krikorian remembered. "He says, 'You know you can't run a gay joint here.' I said, 'I don't know what gay is.' First he was tough, then he softened up. I didn't look gay, nobody in the place looked or acted gay. I said, 'How do I find out what a gay guy is?' He turned red in the face, then walked out."[63]

Bigarani and his fellow North Beach officers policed white beat women with more vigor. Jacqueline Hoyt, a poet, experienced an unusual amount of harassment and later recalled, "Everytime I'd walk down the street with a male person, black or white, even if just in casual conversation, if that officer [Bigarani] saw us, he'd stop us for vagrancy. I couldn't walk down the street with any male without being patted down." Bigarani frequently referred to beat women as "prostitutes," a rhetorical association that carried important legal ramifications. Whereas he employed common vagrancy charges when detaining men, he often used "lewd vagrancy" for his arrests of beat women, and a lewd vagrancy charge compelled the female arrestee to undergo a venereal disease examination before she saw a judge. Beats stated that Bigarani was especially quick to tag white beat women as prostitutes if the women associated with black men. Jerry Kamstra, a white North Beach bookstore owner, later asserted that Bigarani's "favorite targets" were "black dudes with white chicks." "When Big B saw black and white he couldn't contain himself," Kamstra continued. "He'd stop the couple, accuse the chick of being a hustler and the dude of being a pimp and threaten to run them in the next time he saw them on the street."[64]

Many police pursued these interracial couples because they feared that the beats served as shock troops for the neighborhood's racial integration. North Beach was bifurcating into gentrifying and deteriorating sectors during the late 1950s, and the black population was growing in the "blighted" southern and western ends of the neighborhood.[65] "There is no question that the police department of the City and County of San Francisco is actively deterring integration," a frequent lawyer for the beats declared in early 1960. "They, particularly through Officer Bigarani, make it a policy to interrogate any mixed situation." These police efforts targeted private residences as well as the streets. In May

FIGURE 5 . Police arrest Christopher Coker, a participant in the North Beach beat scene. Coker is pointing to his car, which he wants to lock up before he heads off to jail. The photographer capturing this scene likely appreciated the contrast between the race- and gender-boundary–crossing lifestyle of beats like Coker and the traditional family values represented on the bus stand advertisement. Local newspapers, however, consistently downplayed the active role people of color played in the beat scene, and this image was never published. August 11, 1958. (Reprinted with permission, Bancroft Library, BANC PIC 1959.010 — NEG PT III 08-11-58.3: 10.)

1959, an interracial married couple reported that six officers illegally searched their North Beach residential hotel room and then terrorized the black husband by driving him around in a patrol car for fifteen minutes before releasing him onto the curb without a charge.[66]

Police also harassed white business owners who they believed fostered hetero- or homosocial interracial mixing. For instance, when the police first informed Jay Hoppe that they would be badgering the Bagel Shop because of its appearance in Muller's May 1958 *Examiner* series, the local sergeant added that the department was tired of Hoppe allowing "so many Commies and jigs to patronize" his establishment. Although the rising rents engendered by Grant Avenue establishments like the Bagel Shop helped stifle residential integration, officers nevertheless fretted that the beat businesses' presence threatened to turn North Beach "into a little Fillmore," a small-scale replica of the social and cultural hub of San Francisco's black population. "We're going to stop it," an officer promised Hoppe, "before it goes too far."[67]

Bigarani's racial motivations were clear to many North Beach beats and their neighborhood sympathizers, but a variety of factors prevented the white media from addressing the SFPD's harassment of black people in North Beach. The structural relationship between the police and the press left newspapers ignorant of most encounters between the police and black residents. The city's police beat reporters generally gathered stories by sitting in a Hall of Justice radio room and responding to the calls coming in from inspectors. Patrol officers, however, were expected to personally handle all situations that did not require an investigation, and thus Bigarani and the other North Beach officers seldom radioed in their on-street encounters.[68]

The mainstream media's own bigoted disinterest further stifled the white press's attention to antiblack police violence. Warren Hinckle, a reporter covering traffic accidents and crime in the *San Francisco Chronicle*'s Oakland bureau during the early 1960s, explained his newspaper's approach to stories of black victimization:

> To get a late story in the final editions required making changes, and by tradition only white traffic deaths were considered worth submitting. The exception to this rule was in the area of quantity: If two black persons died in a late evening auto crash, that event had a fair chance of making the news columns. Three dead was considered a safe number by everyone except those reporters who were known to be viciously anti-Negro.

Black reporters would likely have been more attuned to and interested in examples of antiblack brutality, but none of the major dailies hired a full-time black reporter until the *San Francisco Examiner* crossed that color line in 1962. For the rest of the decade, the *Chronicle* lagged far behind the *Examiner* in its efforts to recruit and train journalists of color.[69]

The white press's understanding of the beats as a white issue further restricted the mainstream media's discussions of police and North Beach's black denizens. When white journalists learned about clashes between North Beach police and blacks, they reported on these incidents as either racial-rather-than-cultural citywide events or cultural-rather-than-racial North Beach incidents. An example of the former occurred in May 1958 when North Beach police falsely arrested and then beat Otis Rauls, a black insurance agent from San Francisco's Hunters Point neighborhood. Rauls was leaving the Jazz Workshop, a Broadway Street jazz club that overlapped with the beat scene, when police set upon him. The ACLU represented Rauls and used the victim's middle-class status to bring mainstream media attention to this example of police racism. But because the white press viewed beat bohemia as a white scene, the *Examiner*'s and *Chronicle*'s coverage of the Rauls assault did not connect the attack with the ongoing SFPD crackdown that had been initiated in response to Muller's exposé. The newspapers instead wrote up the incident as a story that was not specific to any neighborhood.[70]

One year later, the white press reported on a police attack of a black beat but presented the conflict as a nonracial, bohemian issue. In June 1959, the ACLU alerted the media that Bigarani and his partner had brutalized Aaron Miller, a thirty-three-year-old black muralist, then falsely arrested William "Bill" Margolis, a white poet, when Margolis attempted to intercede. The *Sun-Reporter*, San Francisco's leading black newspaper, did not suggest that Miller's effeminate and openly gay behavior might have incited the police violence, but the newspaper had received enough reports of the beatnik patrol's racial obsessions to assail Bigarani's "persecution of beatniks" as largely an indication that he was a "racial bigot." The *Chronicle* and the *Examiner*, on the other hand, did not reveal Miller's skin color, and although Miller's attorneys explicitly identified racism as the driving motivation in North Beach policing, both mainstream newspapers reported on Miller's trial as a cultural, rather than racial, case. San Francisco's white journalists and editors clung to a color-blind perspective that allowed them to downplay racial conflict. The Miller episode communicated to Bigarani that in their coverage of his upper Grant Avenue law enforcement, San Francisco's white newspapers would never question whether he was driven by race-conscious motivations.[71]

The San Francisco white press's obfuscation of North Beach racial tensions was most evident in its coverage of Robert Kaufman, the SFPD's favorite North Beach target. A black New Orleans native, Kaufman arrived in North Beach in 1954, and he soon became locally famous for delivering seemingly spontaneous oral poems. In a hoarse baritone, Kaufman wove original verses together with quotes from others' work, creating, his wife later remembered, "a long vine of poetry, which continually erupts into flowers." In 1959 City Lights Books published Kaufman's *Abomunist Manifesto,* a poem that Bay Area beats ranked with Ginsberg's *Howl* as a clarion call of the movement.[72]

Although Kaufman was well recognized for his poetic talent, his celebrity in the North Beach social scene rested nearly as much on his run-ins with the police. He had an explosive personality that sometimes resulted in bloody and destructive clashes with area beats and entrepreneurs, but his encounters with police arose from more political motivations. Kaufman often claimed to be the most arrested man in San Francisco, and he was jailed with enough regularity—at least two dozen times over one two-year period—that several North Beach bars collected weekly donations for the poet's bail money. In addition to being frequent, Kaufman's detentions were violent. "The cops," a friend of Kaufman's recalled, "would beat him up and beat him up, again and again." A North Beach bookstore owner later explained that the stories of Kaufman's beatings on Grant Avenue and within the Hall of Justice's elevator circulated widely as "a sick joke on The Beach."[73]

An assortment of SFPD officers arrested and manhandled Kaufman, but local beats claimed that Patrolman Bigarani exhibited the greatest mania. Kaufman and Bigarani both advertised their conflicts, making their relationship the most notorious police-beat rivalry in North Beach. Bigarani showed little interest in Kaufman's connections to the neighborhood's gay habitués (Kaufman flirted with and had sexual relations with the white gay painter Russell Fitzgerald in 1957), but the black poet's associations with white women—including his wife, Eileen Kaufman—rankled the young officer. Understanding that the press would not challenge his treatment of black people, Bigarani felt free to assault Kaufman out in the open. Meltzer saw Kaufman's role in these confrontations as "overtly political" and emphasized that Kaufman baited the police, "antagonizing them to the point where they'd beat the shit out of him and take him to jail. Then he'd come back and do it again."[74]

Through most of the late 1950s, downtown journalists gave no attention to Kaufman's physical clashes with Bigarani. But finally Kaufman managed to rouse local reporters when he orchestrated a confrontation with Bigarani that white journalists could view in terms of censorship toward poets rather than violence against blacks. As Eileen Kaufman later noted, her husband was "more frank than a lot of people about the police," and he had long tested free speech limits with his verbal and written condemnations of law enforcement.[75] In the summer of 1959, Kaufman caught the mainstream press's notice when he posted an anti-police poem on the wall of the Co-Existence Bagel Shop.

The catalyst for Kaufman's poem was a series of arrests by Bigarani and Patrolman John Cuneo during the first week and a half of August. In one arrest Cuneo crushed Kaufman's toe, and in another incident Bigarani charged several painters at a private party for disturbing the peace, including one bohemian who was reportedly asleep. The beats struck back, first by hanging an effigy of Bigarani from a telephone pole outside the Bagel Shop. The effigy was down in minutes, but then, days later, Kaufman and Margolis posted two crude and vitriolic poems on the wall of the Bagel Shop. Kaufman's poem compared Bigarani to Adolf Hitler, while Margolis wished of the police: "May their eyes bulge / from their paperbag heads / may their rotting souls / disintegrate among their / rancid foetid nightstick bones." An enraged Bigarani quickly tore the broadsides down. The beats reported this censorship to the ACLU, and with the civil liberties group promising to defend anyone arrested for posting the offending poems, the walls and telephone poles of North Beach erupted with copies of the screeds.[76]

The ACLU informed local newspapers of the incident, and this new turn in the Bigarani-Kaufman saga captured the press's attention. In their coverage of the story, white reporters used the color-blind issue of artistic censorship to cover over the history of antiblack violence that prompted Kaufman's vulgar words. Culturally conservative journalists and many police representatives they interviewed defended Bigarani's individual decision to censor the poems. Kaufman's and Margolis's poetry marked a new level of police defamation, and Arthur Hoppe, a traditional liberal and *Chronicle* journalist (of no relation to the Bagel Shop owner), quoted Bigarani to illustrate how the language hurt Bigarani individually. "What do they think a police officer is, a robot?" Bigarani plaintively asked. "After all, I do have feelings." Hoppe then quoted Central Station captain Charles Borland arguing that patrol officers were stand-ins for the community at large and that slurs against individual patrol officers were thus "offensive to the public."[77]

Other young journalists used the debate to advance a cosmopolitan liberal understanding of the city's cultural interests. Ignoring Bigarani's history of force against Kaufman, a *Chronicle* editorial gently scolded Bigarani for confiscating the poem. The editorial employed the stereotypical image of childish beats to present their vitriolic and personal "free verse lampoons" as harmless, and suggested that Bigarani should have embraced this cultural pluralism; met the beats on their level; and penned his own poetic, schoolyard, sticks-and-stones-will-break-my-bones retort.[78]

Recognizing that further censorship attempts would fail to stand in court, Chief Cahill directed the police force to allow the newly posted poems to remain. The SFPD's rank and file, meanwhile, accepted this command with little lasting concern. Members of the department understood that the speech protections Kaufman and Margolis received in the poetry incident would have little effect on police prerogatives over black people. The *Chronicle*'s editorial defense of the poems, after all, had addressed censorship and cultural behavior and had skirted the catalyst for the poems—Kaufman's belief that Bigarani's violence was racially motivated. The putatively color-blind newspaper had refused to consider whether the poetry constituted a race-conscious protest.[79]

FIGURE 6. Officers Ray Yazzolino and H. Winkler take down an effigy of Patrolman William "Bill" Bigarani, which local beats hung at the corner of Grant Avenue and Green Street. This intersection was a frequent flashpoint for Bigarani and beats. A year before, Bigarani had arrested Wendy Murphy for vagrancy on this spot, and later in 1959 beats taunted the "beatnik patrol" officer again by adorning the police call box with a swastika. August 8, 1959. (Reprinted with permission, Bancroft Library, BANC PIC 2006.029: 135955.03.04.)

Through the late 1950s, all of San Francisco's downtown dailies avoided reporting on black challenges to law enforcement. For instance, two weeks before the Kaufman-Margolis episode, the *Chronicle* downplayed the false arrest of Carlton Goodlett, the wealthy, well-connected black editor of the *Sun-Reporter*. The arrest set off a small firestorm of political activity involving both local and state officials, and Goodlett not only forced the SFPD to drop the charges against him, but also compelled Chief Cahill to create a position for a minority relations representative and institute a course in community relations at the SFPD Police Academy. White city leaders did not publicize these concessions, and the local white press gave the story cursory treatment. Later that year the downtown newspapers continued to dodge the issue of black antipolice protests, failing to comment on a well-attended anti-SFPD meeting in the Fillmore District. This avoidance, along with the refusal of cosmopolitan liberal journalists to address the issue of race in the Kaufman-Margolis episode, left North Beach officers confident that their prerogatives over black people remained intact.[80]

BIGARANI'S REVENGE

On January 22, 1960, state agents, with the support of local police, exacted what they called Bigarani's Revenge. Over two days the joint mission swept the beat bohemia for drugs. Five months before, authorities had received a break when Robert Estes, a private booking agent, approached state narcotics agents and claimed to have extensive knowledge about drug use in the beat scene. Bureau officials made Estes a part of their undercover team, and the culminating January sweep netted twenty-three arrests, most for marijuana dealing and suspicion of marijuana possession.[81]

The officers participating in Bigarani's Revenge, the *Examiner* explained, viewed the arrests "as a measure of retribution for the beleaguered patrolman." Indeed, the sweep addressed not only Bigarani's concern for drug use, but also his purported dread of racial mixing. Agents targeted white people in the integrating areas of North Beach, and Bigarani himself concluded the first evening of the sting by entering the Co-Existence Bagel Shop and arresting a group of three black couples who were first-time visitors to upper Grant Avenue.[82]

In its reporting on the sweep, the *Chronicle* ignored the issue of North Beach integration and instead used the incident to convey what the writers considered the comedy of cultural pluralism inside North Beach and the chilling dangers of racial pluralism elsewhere in the city. The *Chronicle*'s cosmopolitan liberal reporting on the undercover policing inside North Beach included quotes from snickering beats who jeered that the state agents had blown their own cover early in the investigation with their unhip behavior. One state agent, a beat related, "looked real corn-ball. He was too Beat to be real. He used to walk around the Beach with a black puppy called Weedhead."[83]

By contrast, the *Chronicle*'s coverage of the investigators' attempts to protect white beat women from black violence "far from 'the Beach'" presented the police as courageous public servants. Rehashing old narratives from the Sublette episode, the *Chronicle* scorned the white female beats who attended parties in the city's Fillmore District. The *Chronicle* quoted Estes recalling one marijuana-filled Fillmore fete:

> In the bedroom there was six guys and one girl. We were in a hell of a fix, we were undercover, yet this girl was being raped. Finally we persuaded two of the other girls to help her. They started putting her clothes back on, but the hostess shouldered them aside. She took the girl to her car and drove her to a hotel. She sold the room key to a man and he stayed the night.

White female North Beach beats, the anecdote illustrated, courted sexual violence with their disregard for racial, sexual, and geographic boundaries. Racial mixing, in other words, threatened the white populace's physical security, not its family values.[84]

One week after Bigarani's Revenge, a group of North Beach beats responded to the sting and its targeting of black people with an antipolice protest in North Beach's Washington Square Park that attracted three hundred to four hundred demonstrators. The beats who organized the rally attempted to confront outside liberals with two new arguments. First, they framed police repression in North Beach as a racial issue. A white beat bookstore owner and friend of Kaufman declared, "I admit that if Officer Bigerani [*sic*] is whacking a 'nigger' over the head, he isn't whacking me—but that 'nigger's' head is much akin to mine—and, too, the 'nigger' might be innocent of whatever it is Officer Bigerani [*sic*] is whacking him for." Second, the beats rejected police professionalism's emphasis on removing the public from police decision making and advocated community supervision of the police. Chester Anderson, a beat journal editor, urged beats to begin suing police for false arrests, and the *Chronicle* quoted him calling on beats to hire detectives to follow and monitor police officers on and off duty.[85]

In the minds of the *Chronicle*'s news and editorial writers, the beat protest violated the terms on which cosmopolitan liberals were willing to defend the bohemians. On the one hand, the beats' public charges of police racism breached the newspaper's color-blind partitions. The newspaper's coverage of the protest handled this transgression by reducing the beats' various declarations against police racism to a single and buried paraphrase. Neither the *Examiner* nor the *News-Call Bulletin,* which both quoted the protest speakers liberally, mentioned the charge of racism at all.[86]

On the other hand, Anderson's calls for community surveillance over the police contravened the *Chronicle*'s commitment to police professionalism and centralized expert governance. Anderson claimed that the *Chronicle* misquoted him; he insisted that he had only suggested monitoring police while they were on duty and not in their private lives. (The other downtown newspapers covering the protest did not quote Anderson calling for surveillance of police officers when they were off duty.) Nevertheless, the *Chronicle*'s furious reaction to the supposed statement revealed the limits of its democratic vision. The newspaper had defended cultural pluralism in civic debate, even when it exposed the city to crude, disrespectful language. However, the editors had hoped to protect these perspectives by consolidating policing power in the Hall of Justice and City Hall, not by devolving government functions to the citizenry. The *Chronicle* no longer found the beats useful for its reform agenda. Dismissing the bohemian scene, the *Chronicle* opined scornfully, "Speaking and acting almost entirely in the cliches and outworn attitudes of rebelliousness, the beatniks have become frankly boring."[87]

As newspapers began abandoning the beats as political actors, Chief Cahill did his best not to stifle the neighborhood tourist economy. In March 1960, for instance, the SFPD leader warned his North Beach officers not to harass a group of bearded Calaveras County reenactors coming to San Francisco to celebrate their county's centennial. However, the police did continue to harass the beats themselves, and an expanding drug economy coupled with rivalries between beat cliques hindered the beats' ability to organize an effective defense. All the while, the unceasing stream of tourists into the neighborhood inflated land values and rents and priced beats out of the very neighborhood they had made famous. Beat entrepreneurs, including Nord, and beat bohemians, like Kaufman, responded to these sundry challenges by deserting the North Beach scene.[88]

Cosmopolitan liberal reporters began eulogizing the dwindling bohemia. The local press had long understood the beats in commercial terms, defining the scene around the bars and galleries of upper Grant Avenue. Now, as they took stock, they ruminated on the relationship between cultural pluralism and economic growth. Ralph Gleason, the *Chronicle*'s music critic, celebrated San Francisco's willingness to tolerate the North Beach's edgy beat scene, but he lamented that the neighborhood's exciting cultural innovation had been overrun by hordes of "camera-bearing little old ladies from Des Moines, Dubuque and Hartford." These uncosmopolitan women, Gleason intimated, had swept aside the true cultural transgressions of the "Original Beatniks" (whom the press understood to be all male) in search for kitsch. Feminine commercial forces, Gleason concluded, had transformed upper Grant Avenue into a middlebrow "Boardwalk at Atlantic City." Other cosmopolitan liberals, however, cheered the economic potential of cultural pluralism. As the Grant Avenue beat scene fell into decline, a new, large-scale North Beach club scene arose along Broadway Street. In the fall of 1963 Ron Fimrite—a young liberal *Chronicle* journalist and North Beach resident—cheerfully reported that North Beach had become "about as Italianesque as Oslo, as Bohemian as Las Vegas." Whether liberals opposed or supported the neighborhood's commercialization, none doubted that cultural pluralism had served as an engine of development.[89]

As the press began bidding the North Beach beat scene farewell, the SFPD leadership recognized an opportunity to hasten the beats' demise. The press, the SFPD leadership understood, had always regarded clashes between the beatnik patrol and the beats as a defining feature of the scene. Now that the media was content to imagine the bohemia away, Officer Bigarani's notoriety became a liability; his confrontations with beats breathed new life into a dying storyline. In August 1960 Bigarani disrupted a poetry reading, and the *Chronicle* responded with the mocking headline: "Poets' Orgy: 'Beat' Verse Overwhelms Raiding Cop." Two weeks later, the SFPD transferred Bigarani to the Mission District, and Chief Cahill insisted that Bigarani's new posting symbolized the department's victory over the beats: "I wanted to wait until things quieted down before I moved him. I didn't want the beatniks thinking they had persuaded me to move him."[90]

The downtown newspapers concluded their beat narratives on October 12, 1960, when Bigarani's commercial nemesis, the Co-Existence Bagel Shop, closed its doors. Earlier in the spring of that year, police had arrested Jay Hoppe after a woman hit him in the chest with a brick, and then in the fall, the state's Alcoholic Beverage Control Board had ordered a hearing to review his beer license. "I am tired of having to deal with a sick city administration and a psychopathic police department," Hoppe spat. "I am tired of San Francisco and I never want to see it again." The central characters of the press's North Beach narratives—Nord, Kaufman, Hoppe, and Bigarani—had now all left the neighborhood. San Francisco journalists continued to debate the city's proper cultural arrangement, but they ceased looking to upper Grant Avenue as a source for their allegories.[91]

CONCLUSION

During the late 1950s, the broad-based coalition dedicated to police professionalism fractured around issues of police discretion and the cultural boundaries of citizenship. A new generation of politicians and journalists used the police-bohemian encounters in North Beach to introduce a cosmopolitan liberal approach to law enforcement and democracy. Cosmopolitan liberals charged that the SFPD's discretionary enforcement of traditional family values in North Beach violated the procedural principles of professionalism and hindered San Francisco's transformation into a safe, exciting, and economically vital city. They suggested that although male beats failed to perform the role of the family breadwinner, the bohemians nevertheless fulfilled a responsibility of citizenship by promoting civic growth. On these terms, cosmopolitan liberals defended the beats' rights against the moralizing of autonomous police officers.

Cosmopolitan liberals attempted to create a governing arrangement that protected these rights through a campaign against vagrancy codes. Vagrancy laws had long served as a cornerstone of the city's traditional policing system, allowing patrol officers to extend their autonomous discretion over the city's cultural, sexual, and racial boundaries. The new liberals thus hoped for a significant expansion in civil liberties when they successfully repealed California's common vagrancy code.

However, the abolition of the state's common vagrancy law failed to dramatically affect North Beach law enforcement. The cosmopolitan liberals' limited interest in and understanding of the way bohemia was policed contributed to the lack of reform. The liberals imagined the beats as harmless by characterizing them as white and ignored the race-conscious abuse North Beach police piled upon area denizens of color. Furthermore, cosmopolitan liberals failed to appreciate the challenges of top-down police reform. They circumscribed vagrancy law but neglected to place any positive influences or controls over patrol officers, so the officers replaced vagrancy arrests with a host of discretionary strategies. Liberals elsewhere later learned this lesson when procedural and legal restraints established as a result of the U.S. Supreme Court rulings failed to tether police discretion.[92] In San Francisco, cosmopolitan liberals emerged from the North Beach debates with growing confidence in their culturally pluralist understanding of the city but still searching for the reforms that would allow them to implement that vision on the street.

CHAPTER 3

Gayola: Gay-Bar Politics, Police Corruption, and Sexual Pluralism

Bob Ross, a bartender at the 5A5 Club during the late 1950s, knew something was amiss when a lieutenant for the San Francisco Police Department strode into his workplace. The officer, Ross later recounted, was there to introduce the downtown drinking establishment to Central Station's policy of police payoffs:

"Hi Bob, are you the manager?"

And I'd say, "Why yes."

"Hi, I'm Lieutenant So-and-so."

"You don't say, Lieutenant So-and-so."

"Yes, the San Francisco Police Department."

And right away you'd go *Oh shit.* You know, *What are we up to now?*

And the first time he came in he was soliciting for the . . . Police Athletic League. And I said, "Oh." I said, "I just sent them $25 or something."

And he said, "Oh." He said, "This is actually the Police Officer's Retirement League section of the Police Athletic League."

I said, "I never heard of that."

He said, "You will; let me assure you."

And I said, "What do you need, $100?"

He says, "No, it's gonna be $500 a month." And he says, "The captain'll be by to collect it next Tuesday at 7:30." That's how brazen they were. The captain walked in at 7:30 to collect his money.

In addition to making the monthly payment to the police captain, Ross claimed, he was expected to purchase the captain a dinner and supply him with a female prostitute.[1]

This payola arrangement between Ross and the district captain fit within a broader postwar policing strategy that sought to hide and constrain, but not eradicate, San Francisco's gay and lesbian population. Extortion was one of several informal means San Francisco police officers employed in their regulation of the city's gay and lesbian bars.

During the 1950s San Francisco's leadership—traditional machine politicians and managerial growth advocates alike—reflexively assumed that gay men like Ross did not deserve full citizenship rights. Across the nation post–World War II politicians associated gay men with poor morals and weak wills and thus characterized homosexual perspectives as anathema in policy making.[2] Urban elites took for granted that citizens maintained heterosexual identities; they could not, during the 1950s, conceive of a sexual citizenship based on other sexual perspectives. Political elites thus felt comfortable denying gay men the citizenry's rights to privacy, association, and public expression. At the same time, urban officials trusted that individual police officers would defend the citizenry's common interests when policing gay men like Ross. On these terms, managerial growth advocates like Mayor George Christopher allowed police officers to use their autonomous discretion to maintain the city's traditional boundaries of sexual behavior.

Over time, dramatic cultural shifts among liberals opened new opportunities for gay protest across the urban United States. By the late 1950s, cosmopolitan liberals were issuing harm-principle defenses of the beats' untraditional gender behaviors, and, historian John D'Emilio argues, gay and lesbian activists capitalized on this broadening tolerance to fashion and then advertise a positive collective homosexual identity. Homophile groups like the Mattachine Society and Daughters of Bilitis—organizations dedicated to winning homosexual rights through interest-group politics—spearheaded this effort by promoting a middle-class, sexually restrained homosexual image that historian Martin Meeker has termed the "mask of respectability."[3]

Both Meeker and Elizabeth Armstrong show how gay and lesbian activists spread this public, professional collective identity by organizing gay and lesbian people and developing relationships with social service providers and liberal journalists. In cities throughout the United States, homosexual bars— one of the few relatively stable and sheltered urban gathering spots available to gays and lesbians—emerged as a primary site for gay male activism. When police conducted media-attracting raids against these establishments during the

1960s, D'Emilio, Nan Boyd, and Marc Stein all note, the law enforcement officials unwittingly played into the homophile activists' larger political agenda. The raids provided gay men with visibility and opportunities to advertise their "mask of respectability" in ongoing civic discussions over sexual boundaries.[4]

Attention to police politics within City Hall and the SFPD reveals that San Francisco's gay bars also maintained a frontline position in the debates over government organization. Managerial growth politicians like Mayor Christopher had distinguished themselves from their machine predecessors with promises of clean governance. Honest leadership in City Hall, growth politicians insisted, would allow the government to eliminate corruption and technocratically set policies to serve the citizenry. Yet when the mayor encouraged police to employ their autonomous discretion over the city's sexual boundaries, officers like the lieutenant supervising the 5A5 Club used those prerogatives to pursue their own financial interests. In other words, police officers exploited Mayor Christopher's commitment to traditional citizenship standards to violate the managerial growth advocates' governing principles. This contradiction opened an opportunity for gay-bar owners and workers, who seized on the technocratic politics of the managerial growth proponents to introduce a sexually pluralist understanding of citizenship and achieve new political leverage over the San Francisco Police Department.

THE SFPD'S REGULATION OF HOMOSEXUALITY

During the 1950s mainstream political leaders at the local, state, and federal levels scorned gay males. From the perspective of these political elites, gay men preyed on children, lacked emotional and mental stability, and failed to financially support women. In other words, gay men did not fulfill the basic, traditional responsibilities of male citizenry. Postwar officials at all levels thus vigilantly enforced the boundaries of political debate to ensure that gay male interests remained excluded from government policy making.[5]

However, urban leaders approached the policing of street-level homosexual behavior with a more complicated set of considerations than did legislators in the state and federal capitols. In California most state lawmakers represented districts without sizeable gay and lesbian social worlds and thus faced few personal implications when they enacted rabid antigay legislation. In cities like San Francisco, by contrast, drives against homosexuals had the potential to advertise the city's existing gay and lesbian scenes and thereby attract more homosexual migrants. With this concern in mind, San Francisco's antigay media figures and government officials avoided spotlighting gay people during the 1950s. When local homicides made the topic of homosexuality unavoidable, the *San Francisco Examiner* and SFPD readily employed sensational images of psychopathic gay men to draw an ill-defined connection between gay men and the city's murder rate. But during a period when the California legislature was crafting the most explicitly antihomosexual legislation of any state in the country, San Francisco's officials and journalists were often content to simply cordon off homosexual behavior in hopes that it would remain out of the public eye.[6]

When managerial growth politicians rose to power in San Francisco and other major American cities, they vowed to break the venal connections binding their police departments to the criminal underworld by consolidating police authority and waging war against so-called vice crimes. In San Francisco, Mayor Christopher's police chief, Francis "Frank" Ahern, boosted the SFPD's centralized pressure against gambling and sex crimes by expanding the Bureau of Special Services from five to twenty-four officers. However, Ahern remained committed to the SFPD's closeting approach. When state liquor agents initiated a drive against homosexual bars, Ahern publicly worried that these efforts would simply push gays into harder-to-police areas.[7]

The gradual shift from machine policing to professional policing led to an uptick in gay-related policing but not a change in SFPD philosophy. First, the department continued to rely on the autonomous discretion of street-level police officers to make arrests. Catching or entrapping gay men in illegal sexual acts was often difficult, so SFPD officers, like metropolitan police officers across the country, often detained gay men with broad, subjective vagrancy and lewd vagrancy codes. Second, the SFPD's Bureau of Special Services followed a precedent set in the machine-politics period by calibrating its sex-code enforcement to match the local leadership's interests in concealing gay people. On a day-to-day basis, the so-called sex detail waged its harassment program by targeting those areas of the city with the greatest potential for public observation (parks, public bathrooms, and bus terminals, for example). Although the sex detail's physical presence was thus limited, the inspectors' psychological reach extended much further. "The Morals Squad was everywhere," Robert Duncan, a gay poet, remembered, "and the entrapment of gay males in the streets, the parks and in the numerous public places was a constant fear and common occurrence."[8]

The sex detail paid relatively little attention to homosexual bars because most homosexual drinking establishments remained discreet. Remembering the secrecy of gay bars, George Mendenhall, a gay rights activist and journal editor, explained:

There were no signs outside with the names on them. [The bars] were in base-ments. Some of them were on second story lofts. You didn't have bars on street level. . . . They were in doorways, and alleyways. You would walk by a Gay bar 50 times and not know it was a Gay bar . . . and they did that because they didn't want the general public. They wanted to make sure that only Gay people came in. They didn't want any trouble with the general public.

If heterosexuals did find their way into a homosexual bar, the bar staff and homosexual patrons often harassed the interlopers until they left. The sex detail disregarded homosexual bars that remained inconspicuous and did not violate a host of other unwritten dicta—rules that shifted according to time and location. Responsibility over these drinking establishments thus passed to the district stations.[9]

Patrol officers bore the lion's share of responsibility for policing San Francisco's homosexual bars. When describing their interactions with ho-mosexuals, officers rarely invoked the sexual psychopath image popular in mass culture. Instead, they often discussed their policing of gay residents in comic tones. For instance, a 1959 account in the San Francisco Police Of-ficers' Association journal read, "JASPER STARKIE and JIM KRUEGER, Northern, were embarrassed when they happened upon a pretty young thing, her satin skirt lifted, relieving herself between two autos parked on Fillmore St. But shucks, it was only gay Willie-Boy Bell. The boys at City Prison were delighted with his new Maidenform." As this quote illustrates with both its emphasis on the officers' embarrassment and its insistence that the two officers had only "happened upon" their victim, many patrol officers did not regard the policing of gay people as real law enforcement. Police proved their worth to one another through their investigative skills and their ability to subdue physically imposing threats. The broad vagrancy charges officers employed against gay men offered police little opportunity to prove their analytical skills, and few police would ever want to admit that a gay man had posed a physical challenge.[10]

Many police could approach the antigay exploits of sex detail inspectors and patrol officers with humor, but most found close contact with gay people unsettling. Discussing temporary transfers to the sex detail, Chief Thomas Cahill later admitted, "Now I know that my officers who were on those as-signments, vice assignments, resented it very much. They wanted no part of it. They'd rather get out and do regular police work than to be working un-dercover to entrap people like those." In 1953 Don Lucas and Hal Call, leaders of the local Mattachine Society, invited a sex detail inspector to Call's apartment so they could introduce their organization and reassure the officer that they posed no threat to the police. The inspector appeared to worry that the encounter placed him in a compromising position, and he therefore arrived with a female officer, who was presumably there to shield him from any sexual advances.[11]

The officers' apprehension stemmed in part from their ignorance about and confusion over homosexual people. Former patrol officer Richard Hongisto described officers' attitudes in the early 1960s:

> I think the basic attitudes of rank and file police officers then were . . . no real understanding, there was a feeling first that all homosexual men were limp wrested [*sic*], effeminate, what is sometimes called swishy, and so on. There was an extreme degree of stereotyping of homosexual males. . . . There was no recognition that a masculine appearing male might be a homosexual.

Lesbian women, Hongisto added, baffled police officers even further. "I think there was virtually no recognition that Lesbian women existed except in books," the former officer claimed. Indeed, the SFPD's antihomosexual crackdowns generally disregarded lesbian women, although cross-dressing considerably increased a woman's chances of being harassed by police or arrested.[12]

When officers encountered gay and lesbian bars on their patrols, they approached the establishments with a mixture of amusement, foreboding, and uncertainty. Patrolman John Mindermann remembered experiencing this welter of feelings on his first encounter with a gay bar—the Cable Car Village—when he was a rookie substitute patrol officer in the Polk Gulch neighborhood:

> I walk into the Cable Car Village on the north side of California above Hyde, there, and I stopped as I go inside the front door. And I'm shocked because I see nothing but men down the bar and in the back there's a jukebox, and there's, I guess, a small dance floor, because I never quite got back that way. It's maybe 40 feet. And I see men dancing with each other back there—and whoa!—and I stopped. [Laughing] I've never seen anything like this. I was twenty-two years, I've been going on the street car to San Francisco State and living at home. . . . I look in there and I go, *Wha—?* Could this be a-a-a—in the parlance of SFPD, could this be a fruit joint? Well, maybe it is, . . . and everything stops when they see, when they see me. Everybody's apprehensive. They've never seen this guy before, you know. I look in, and I go, *I better not do anything because there's so many of them, and there's just me, and I have no radio.* But I think it's a fruit joint, so I back out and I go about my diligent business.[13]

Despite the obvious bewilderment many young officers like Mindermann felt toward homosexual people, the high brass provided the patrol officers with very little street-level guidance on how to handle gay and lesbian bars. The SF-PD's command ranks influenced policing of gay and lesbian people when they ordered individual raids and sweeps, but the day-to-day police-homosexual relations were often determined by the patrol officers and gay and lesbian people themselves.

Left to their own devices, San Francisco police officers chose from a number of strategies when approaching gay and lesbian bars. One alternative was to simply follow the department's official vice policy: report evidence of wrongdoing to the Bureau of Special Services and assist the inspectors in enforcing the state's legal codes. This option, however, was often unattractive because it required patrol officers to turn over control of their police work to an inspector and because the harsh penalties the state delivered for so-called morals crimes within a homosexual bar required lengthy hearings and considerable amounts of time and effort on the part of the arresting officers. In the absence of pressure from either the public or City Hall for a crackdown, patrol officers had good reason to develop informal gay-bar policing strategies that were both less work intensive and less reliant on outside inspectors.

In some cases officers simply turned a blind eye. Sergeant John Lehane described the attitude of many officers in Central Station toward gay bars:

> It was just another bar. It's like it was down the street from the station. There were all gays in there so you . . . would only go down there when you get called. And they had the same problems as straight bars, see. And . . . they didn't want the police around the place, see. And when you got there they usually took care of their beefs themselves, or if you did, they wanted you [out] as fast as they could get you out of there. And the police didn't want to go near them, anyway. It was like a Mexican standoff.

In the case of lesbian bars, the police disengagement often became its own form of discriminatory law enforcement. Male locals and tourists frequently intruded on lesbian bars seeking to inflict terror and violence, and the department made little effort to address this abuse.[14]

Acting on their own and without the direction of the sex detail, patrol officers commonly arrested men exiting homosexual bars using broad and subjective misdemeanors, such as public drunkenness, disturbing the peace, or vagrancy. Regardless of where the arrest took place, police photographed and fingerprinted the detained patrons; locked them in jail for one night; and, like other police departments in the nation, frequently forwarded their names and occupations to local newspapers. Sometimes the police phoned their employers directly. Thus, after being released the next morning, the arrested bar-goers often went home to find themselves in the press and out of a job.[15]

A number of police officers harassed homosexual bars. They did so for a variety of reasons: to express antigay animus, to encourage the bars to remain discreet, to keep the gay nightlife circumscribed within specific geographic boundaries, or to encourage protection payments. Police officers who chose to harass a gay or lesbian bar set their strategy according to the amount of physical contact they wished to have with the patrons. For instance, officers could enter a bar and, instead of pressing charges against the bar owner, simply arrest gay and lesbian people who were touching one another. The sex detail occasionally recruited undercover officers from out of the regular force to employ this sort of harassment.[16]

Some police officers, however, found that detaining gay and lesbian people required too much intimacy. As a result, most officers who harassed homosexual bars employed methods that did not involve a booking. Officers often used their mere presence to intimidate gay and lesbian bar-goers, walking repeatedly in front of the bar or passing through among its patrons. They sometimes took photographs of patrons entering and exiting the bar, parked a patrol wagon in front of the door, and occasionally even called in a fake bomb scare to clear out the premises.[17]

Another police strategy for disciplining homosexual bars was to demand extortion payments. Throughout the 1950s police officers across urban America exploited the gulf between draconian "antivice" laws and the public's ignorance of (or relative tolerance for) hidden gambling houses, brothels, and homosexual bars to engage in extortion.[18] Nearly every establishment in San Francisco that offered illegal activities made payoffs. Bars catering to homosexual patrons, however, operated in a gray area. Because serving alcohol to homosexuals was not by itself an illegal act in California in the 1950s, homosexual bars could decide to refuse police extortion attempts.[19] By rejecting payoff requests, however, owners of homosexual bars were forced to conduct their own rigid self-policing, eliminating all other forms of illegal behavior, including same-sex touching and dancing. Moreover, bar owners who refused payoff demands made themselves more susceptible to other forms of police harassment.

Decisions to demand payola stemmed from bigotry, greed, and pressure from supervising officers. The culture of the SFPD through at least the late 1960s condoned payoffs, and officers could collect payola without losing standing among their peers. Explaining how police involved in extortion could still be respected by their fellow officers, Mindermann recalled:

> You can be a very good cop and still take advantage with respect to money, drinking, so forth. SFPD, the culture allowed for certain of these discretionary activities that were illegal. . . . I saw many, many excellent officers who worked diligently making very high-quality officers and worked very, very hard who were involved in these kinds of petty activities.

Beat officers could rationalize their shakedowns with a long list of working-condition grievances. The department's bottom-heavy organizational structure created a glass ceiling that kept most patrolmen trapped in a career on the beat. Meanwhile, uniformed police often watched with resentment as City Hall politicians passed over qualified applicants and handed out choice departmental positions to other, more politically connected officers.[20]

Any police officer in the Inspectors Bureau or any district officer with the rank of sergeant on up could decide to extort money from a homosexual bar. But while captains or lieutenants could easily demand that their officers collect payments for them, thwarting extortion in the lower ranks was a more difficult proposition. The department's pyramid-like organizational structure prevented lieutenants from knowing what activities the districts' patrolmen were doing on their sergeants' behalf. As the only officers who regularly left their desks and monitored the patrolmen on the streets, the department's two hundred sergeants held the most policing power in the SFPD, and they maintained tremendous discretion over whether their patrolmen took protection payments.

San Francisco police primarily extorted money from homosexual bars in the downtown, lower Market, and Embarcadero areas (neighborhoods covered by Central Station). It was easier for police to squeeze bars in those districts because the establishments often permitted overt homosexual activity or other crimes, like drug use and gambling. Ross explained:

> You've got to understand that a lot of these people operating these bars were very shady to start with, and they were looking for quick money—and the cops knew that. And they were serving rot-gut booze in many cases, and the cops knew that also. So their prices were based according to that.[21]

During the late 1940s and early 1950s, Mayor Elmer Robinson's traditional machine demanded graft collection, and the burgeoning extortion networks allowed homosexual bars to proliferate. By the end of Robinson's first term, San Francisco contained at least thirty-four gay and lesbian drinking establishments. Most of the city's homosexual bars catered to a predominantly male clientele, although San Francisco had a concentrated lesbian bar scene in North Beach. San Francisco's gay male bars were also found in North Beach, as well as the Embarcadero and Tenderloin areas. At the conclusion of Robinson's second term in 1955, an estimated fifty homosexual bars operated within the city.[22]

As downtown elites fought Robinson's machine with the politics of police professionalization, Robinson's allies in the SFPD were occasionally forced to initiate short-term crackdowns. These sweeps insulated the SFPD from real reform, but the busts exposed the police force to a new set of public relations pitfalls. In particular, the sweeps raised the expectations of local cultural and sexual conservatives. If a gambling house, brothel, or homosexual bar unexpectedly reappeared in the press after a crackdown, the department suddenly had to answer to disappointed conservatives frustrated over the department's inability to finish a drive. This scenario materialized in the late spring and early summer of 1954 when Police Chief Michael Gaffey tried to quiet criticisms from federal tax agents by unleashing raids against Chinatown betting parlors, "breakfast clubs" (bars that stayed open past the 1 a.m. curfew), and bars with illegal pinball machines. At District Attorney Thomas Lynch's urging, the chief then expanded this drive to include gay and lesbian bars. (Lynch, a political moderate with statewide ambitions, was responding to a recent state legislative study into "sexual deviance.") In a single weekend sweep, the department detained scores of men and women and charged fourteen people for homosexual activity.[23]

Following a short run of positive *Examiner* coverage, Chief Gaffey dialed down the police pressure on gay San Franciscans. Two months later, however, the Juvenile Bureau, acting independently from the chief, raided Tommy's Place, a North Beach lesbian night spot. The exception that proved the rule, the Tommy's Place raid revealed the apathetic attitude of the city's police department and newspaper readers toward prosecuting gay and lesbian bars. The Juvenile Bureau historically paid little attention to gay and lesbian issues, and Tommy's Place had only piqued its interest when the bar became entangled in an ongoing investigation revolving around a group of white, high school–aged girls who allegedly used narcotics and consorted with Jesse Winston, a forty-one-year old black man. The inspectors began monitoring Tommy's Place after a parent informed them that these young women "dressed in mannish apparel and frequented bars notorious as homosexual hangouts." Even at this stage in the investigation, however, the bureau remained focused on the drugs and possible interracial relations. Thus when the officers raided Tommy's Place, they planted narcotics paraphernalia, arrested the bar owners, and allowed the bar's patrons to leave without further incident.[24]

The local press initially adopted the Juvenile Bureau's prioritization, concentrating on Winston rather than the issue of homosexuality. The day after the Tommy's Place bust, the *Chronicle*'s subheadline proclaimed, "Man Held as Corrupter of Youths." Repeatedly emphasizing how Winston transgressed racial and class boundaries by living "beyond his means" in "sybaritic" surroundings, the *Chronicle* averred that it was the black man, not Tommy's Place patrons, who taught the girls "sexual rebellion." Similarly, the *Examiner* initially explained that the danger of Tommy's Place lay in the fact that Winston used the bar to recruit girls for parties back at his apartment. In light of Chief Gaffey and District Attorney Lynch's recent drive against homosexual bars, however, the *Examiner*'s second report upbraided Gaffey for his earlier "lackadaisical" effort, and the newspaper pointed out that even though the military had placed Tommy's Place on its off-limits posting over a year before, neither the department's sex detail nor the district's patrol officers had busted the establishment. An *Examiner* editorial then wondered over Gaffey's commitment to his new antigay crackdown. "Will he get results?" the newspaper asked. "An aroused city will be watching."[25]

Notwithstanding the *Examiner* editorial's suggestive sign-off, the citizenry appeared content to move to other issues. The *Chronicle* replaced headlines on Tommy's Place with stories of gang violence and police brutality toward innocent white women. Later in the month, when the U.S. Senate Subcommittee on Juvenile Delinquency came to San Francisco and revisited the issue of Tommy's Place, the superintendent of schools, the chief probation officer, and the head of the SFPD Juvenile Bureau issued a joint statement claiming that politicians and the press were exaggerating the city's juvenile crime problem. The *Chronicle* seconded this point through editorials and letters to the editor. Chastened by his earlier experience in gay-baiting, Gaffey took advantage of these public dismissals and insisted that increased policing of homosexual people was unnecessary. The Tommy's Place raid, Gaffey dissembled, had "frightened" gay and lesbian people "away from their usual haunts." The police department's interest in maintaining the city's machine politics thus encouraged officials like Gaffey to restrain their antigay hostility.[26]

STATE-LEVEL PROFESSIONALISM AND
THE THREAT TO HOMOSEXUAL BARS

When Chief Gaffey announced that the SFPD would refrain from following its 1954 Tommy's Place raid with additional crackdowns, he also passed the buck and claimed that homosexual behavior in bars fell under the purview of the state's Board of Equalization, not the local police. That board, however, was already drawing fire from managerial growth advocates who charged that the state agency's entire leadership was "wet-nursed" by the liquor lobby. In 1934 the California liquor lobby had convinced the state legislature to transfer liquor control responsibilities to the Board of Equalization. Liquor lobbyists were attracted to the board's decentralized bureaucratic arrangement. Splintering the state into myriad districts and subdistricts, it maintained far too many jurisdictions and offices for top supervisors to monitor on a daily basis. As a result, most alcohol enforcement power resided at the local level where liquor industry representatives subverted Sacramento's reform attempts with bribes.[27]

The Board of Equalization's interest in homosexuality emerged during the late 1940s. In 1949 state legislators responded to fears of juvenile delinquency by pressing the board to begin enforcing the state's morals in California's drinking establishments. Shortly thereafter the board's San Francisco office became embroiled in a labor dispute involving the Black Cat Café. Sol Stoumen, an Austrian Holocaust survivor and self-proclaimed libertarian, had purchased the Black Cat in 1945, and as the owner he cultivated the bar's existing bohemian reputation. Earl McGrath, a gay artist, described the bar as "a real drinking establishment" during the early 1950s. "Sailors and hookers and just everything in there. Intellectuals; painters; it was very 'modern,' in that sense, because you had everything from transvestites to businessmen to girls out on dates with young boys."[28]

Stoumen's trouble with local law enforcement began in 1949 when he rejected the local culinary workers union's insistence that he sign a closed-shop agreement. The labor group retaliated by requesting assistance from George Reilly, the chair and San Francisco district supervisor of the Board of Equalization. Reilly, a prolabor Democrat, instructed his agents to warn Stoumen that the board would revoke Stoumen's license if he continued denying his workers their rights. Stoumen proved difficult to intimidate, and when Reilly observed no change, he angrily ordered San Francisco's liquor control administrator to develop a case against the bar. Armed with the state's new morals mandate, the board's San Francisco office focused on one segment of the bar's bohemian clientele and proposed that it could revoke a bar's license if the establishment functioned as a "homosexual hangout." Thus, by way of a local labor dispute, the state Board of Equalization entered the new territory of homosexual repression.[29]

The Board of Equalization's disciplinary process operated almost wholly outside the regular justice system. The board maintained its own prosecutors, hearing officers, and supervisors, and the same board supervisors who demanded that prosecutors file charges against the Black Cat then accepted the hearing officers' recommendation for a license revocation. Most revocation cases ended here; appeals were expensive and often unfruitful.[30]

Stoumen, however, possessed both money and determination, and he hired Morris Lowenthal to move his case into the state's judicial system. In 1951 Lowenthal brought *Stoumen v. Reilly* before the California Supreme Court, and to the shock of many observers, the moderately liberal court unanimously sided with Stoumen, declaring that "mere proof of patronage by homosexuals" was insufficient cause for a license revocation. The court left open the door for a legislative overruling by basing its decision on technicalities in California's alcohol statutes and the state constitution's mandate for the Board of Equalization; nevertheless, the decision was momentous. As California's legislature was busy codifying the most explicitly antihomosexual laws in the United States, its highest court had made it the only state in the nation to legalize gay and lesbian bars.[31] The high court's decision embarrassed the Board of Equalization and enraged officials in Sacramento, but board officials refrained from waging a full counterattack against homosexual bars. This listless response appeared to be one more piece of evidence that corruption undermined the board's enforcement of the law.

In 1952 a new champion in the fight to reform the state's liquor law enforcement emerged when San Franciscans living in the twenty-first Assembly district elected Caspar Weinberger as their representative to the California State Assembly. Weinberger was a fast-rising Republican ally of San Francisco's redevelopment proponents. He and his downtown supporters understood that Artie Samish, the liquor industry's chief lobbyist, controlled the state's liquor law enforcement agency and oversaw a massive payola network of drinking establishments and state alcohol agents. Samish's corruption had drawn the ire of downtown elites when Mayor Robinson dealt a local airport parking concession to one of Samish's cronies. With alcohol-industry graft impeding San Francisco's growth agenda, Weinberger arrived in Sacramento committed to professionalizing liquor law enforcement.[32]

Weinberger launched his clean-government effort through a bipartisan legislative inquiry into the Board of Equalization's operation. The investigation quickly unearthed widespread board corruption, particularly within the Southern California district. Weinberger and his allies capitalized on the resulting public disgust by placing Proposition 3 on the 1954 state ballot. A state constitutional amendment transferring liquor law power to a new Department of Alcoholic Beverage Control (ABC), it consolidated liquor law power in the hands of a single ABC director. Confident in the ability of experts to determine and defend the state's shared values, the framers of Proposition 3 also named the ABC a protector of the state's morals and welfare. Voters embraced the proposition's vision of top-down governance, approving it in a landslide.[33]

Stoumen's lawyer charged that the ABC's new director used the sweeping powers vested in his position to demand automatic license revocations for all bars in which agents witnessed gay and lesbian behavior. Indeed, between the time when the ABC was established and the early 1960s, ABC hearing officers adjudicating homosexual bar cases never ruled for anything less. One hearing officer displayed this single-mindedness in 1955 when he ruled against the Black Cat Café for serving a minor even though the youth failed to remember many of the bar's distinguishing features and twice identified his server as a waiter who had not worked at the bar during the night in question. After the establishment of the ABC, San Francisco's homosexual bars could expect to hold their liquor licenses for no more than two years.[34]

To aid the ABC in its push against homosexual drinking establishments, the state legislature equipped the agency with Section 24200(e) of the Business and Professions Code. Section 24200(e) sought to negate *Stoumen v. Reilly* by prohibiting bars from acting "as a resort for illegal possessors or users of narcotics, prostitutes, pimps, panderers, or sexual perverts" and allowing ABC agents to consider as evidence "the general reputation" of the premises as a resort for "sexual perverts." The ABC understood that this statute breached *Stoumen v. Reilly* and was thus susceptible to a constitutional challenge. ABC agents therefore attached an additional charge of "keeping a disorderly house" to every gay-bar case. The disorderly house charge applied to behaviors deemed immoral by local custom. Because moral standards varied between communities, the disorderly house statute did not stipulate which specific actions were illegal. Thus the disorderly house code empowered ABC agents with the discretion to indict bar owners for violation of unwritten laws.[35]

For a variety of reasons, most owners of homosexual bars chose not to dispute the constitutionality of Section 24200(e). It was pointless for the gay and lesbian bars that permitted gambling or prostitution or allowed explicitly homosexual acts to take place (ranging from hand holding to sexual intercourse) to contest the statute, because the ABC would still win a license revocation with

the disorderly house accusation. The state legislature also dissuaded bar owners from fighting the statute by designing a lengthy appeals process that enabled
the ABC to exhaust the financial resources of the accused bar owners. The ABC
further hindered challenges to 24200(e) by loosening evidentiary standards for
ABC agents building disorderly house cases against homosexual bars.[36]

ABC officials sent young plainclothes agents to monitor a homosexual bar
as soon as they learned of its existence. In addition to recording any activities
that might be construed as homosexual, these agents flirted with patrons to
prompt sexual advances. Sometimes, officers even solicited a drunk patron
and then arrested the patron if he or she accepted. But ABC officials cautioned
their agents never to make arrests inside a bar, lest they alert the bar owner that
infractions were being committed on the grounds of the establishment. ABC
agents issued warnings to other types of bars so they could conform to ABC
standards without a formal hearing, but agents concealed their investigations
from homosexual bars. Recounting his investigation of the Black Cat Café, one
ABC agent explained, "The instructions which I received were not to make
any arrests in the [Black Cat], but make the arrest outside the place, to sew up
a tight case against the premises."[37]

While establishing a bar's pattern of transgressions, state agents only recorded the type of illegal act committed and withheld information about the
persons involved in the infraction. "In alleging disorderly premises," ABC
chiefs informed local prosecutors and agents, "general allegations should be
made to avoid the necessity of findings on a number of unproved items." Thus,
after eighteen months of investigation, the ABC would present a bar owner
with a list of incidents, some well over a year old, in which an unspecified
number of faceless, unnamed persons were said to have committed specific
illegal acts.[38]

When bar owners appealed ABC decisions to the city's superior courts,
San Francisco jurists proved amenable to these investigative tactics. Although
one judge admitted that ABC agents rehearsed testimony that often sounded
"strikingly similar" from case to case, courts rarely took a bar owner's word
over a liquor agent's. In a 1961 Black Cat case, for instance, a judge dismissed
as immaterial the fact that one of the agents who filed a charge had previously been expelled from the Black Cat for drunkenness. The judge then accepted the testimony of an agent who documented a sexual solicitation even
though the agent had consumed drinks at four bars in five hours on the night
in question and despite the fact that the agent's partner, who had been standing no more than ten feet away from the place where the alleged incident had
occurred, could not corroborate any part of the accusation. In another case

Judge Phil Gibson went so far as to defend the ABC hearing officers' apparent prejudging of gay and lesbian bar cases. Preconceived determinations, Gibson reasoned, were "inherent in a commendable and zealous effort" to discipline those businesses that were "inimical to public welfare and morals."[39] With the local bench confident that homosexuality violated the citizenry's shared values, the ABC maintained a perfect track record against homosexual bars through the early 1960s.

Though owners of gay and lesbian bars faced certain defeat in the courts, they could employ several strategies to delay the liquor agency's charges. A bar owner could declare the establishment a no-touch bar and expel patrons who engaged in amorous contact. A bartender could give a marked glass (for example, an unchilled mug or a glass with a gold ring around the lip) to anyone suspected of being an undercover officer. On threat of expulsion, no one was to talk to a person with a marked glass until the bartender checked out the newcomer and cleared the patron with a regular glass. Owners of gay bars in the downtown, lower Market Street, and Embarcadero areas could also pay off dishonest ABC agents. According to Frank Fullenwider, the ABC's Northern Coast area director, low morale among ABC agents had created a "snowballing" turnover rate.[40] As in the SFPD, job dissatisfaction stirred with homophobia and greed to facilitate corruption.

No-touch rules, marked glasses, and payoffs served as little more than stop-gap measures to delay the inevitable license revocation. The ABC's drive against gay bars froze the number of homosexual bars in San Francisco. Although an estimated five thousand people joined the San Francisco gay and lesbian social world between 1955 and 1960, the number of gay bars climbed only from fifty to fifty-three during the same period.[41] Still, the ABC's Sacramento leaders wanted an actual rollback in the number of bars, and they understood that the first step toward eradication was a reversal of *Stoumen v. Reilly.*

In the winter of 1959, the ABC decided to pursue this agenda through its prosecution of Albert Vallerga and Mary Azar's primarily lesbian bar in Oakland, Mary's First and Last Chance. In *Vallerga v. Munro* the state charged the bar owners with Section 24200(e) but not disorderly house. The ABC chose *Vallerga* as its test case precisely because its evidence against the bar was so weak; Vallerga and Azar had not permitted any touching within their bar, and the only persistent objectionable behavior uncovered by agents was that women wore "mannish" clothing and that members of the same sex paired off with one another. Under these conditions, the ABC hoped to force the California Supreme Court to choose between Section 24200(e) and the *Stoumen* precedent.[42]

The high court's *Vallerga* ruling shocked both the ABC and supporters of homosexual bars. It first reaffirmed *Stoumen v. Reilly* and declared Section 24200(e) unconstitutional; bars could legally serve as sites of homosexual association. But the court then declared that the female patrons' cross-dressing legitimized the ABC's decision to revoke Vallerga's liquor license. "Any public display which manifests sexual desires and urges" and appeared in the bar "as a continuing course of conduct," the court ruled, could be considered harmful to the society's shared interests.[43]

The vague meaning of "continuing course of conduct" and the potentially all-encompassing definition of "sexual desires and urges" suddenly placed all gay bars at risk. "The Vallerga obiter dicta," Lowenthal lamented, "will become known as 'Oh, bitter dicta!'" He called the dicta "discrimination against homosexuals *as a class*—not because of what they *do,* but because of what they *are.*" In *Stoumen v. Reilly* the high court had struck a powerful blow against homosexual status crimes, but the state's high court now broke into a full retreat by conflating homosexual status and actions.[44]

Charlotte Coleman described how the ABC built up a "course of conduct" case regarding moral violations in her lesbian bar, the Golden Cask, following the *Vallerga* ruling:

> I had an anniversary party, and one guy came in. It was a little bit of a costume party; it was a lot of funny costumes; it wasn't really drag. And one guy was seen to wear slippers, silver slippers. That was a morals charge. And I had a funny bartender from, ah, he was from New Orleans, little, a funny little guy. Somebody had given me a great big bottle of Tabu perfume, which I couldn't stand, and I left it at the bar, and he'd take a little dab and he'd go behind the ears of customers like that, just for kicks—he was sort of a kicky guy. That was a morals charge. So they had about fifty things like that and no one, they never got the names of anybody. You couldn't call those people in; there were just frames, descriptions.[45]

Such an array of petty and vague accusations made a guilty verdict unavoidable.

Most ABC officials understood the potential of *Vallerga* and were thus elated by the decision. The ABC area administrator, still undefeated in gay-bar cases (he handled all of the Northern Coast area prosecutions), predicted that the *Vallerga* dicta "probably" made the closure of all gay bars "inevitable."[46] As the 1960s began, the San Francisco ABC office prepared to complete its march against homosexual bars.

CITY-LEVEL PROFESSIONALISM AND THE
OPPORTUNITY FOR HOMOSEXUAL BARS

As Weinberger carried the banner for police professionalism at the state level, San Francisco's managerial growth advocates turned to Mayor Christopher to wage the campaign in San Francisco's City Hall. Christopher presumed that if he broke the lines of corruption binding the police force to City Hall, the SFPD would dedicate itself to serving the citizenry's shared interests. Chief Ahern thus challenged corruption in the upper ranks through a well-publicized shakeup, but he did not check the autonomy of officers on the beat. By the end of Christopher's first term, however, the mayor was finding it increasingly difficult to avoid the intertwined issues of police discretion over sexuality and persisting police payola.[47]

Mayor Christopher was first confronted with matters of corruption and homosexuality during his 1959 mayoral reelection campaign against Russell L. Wolden, the city assessor. Wolden enjoyed support from small-business owners, but he was otherwise a weak candidate from the start. He had recently switched over from the Republican Party in an unsubtle attempt to catch California's Democratic wave, but tardy, half-hearted endorsements from labor and the Democratic Party had done little to boost his flagging numbers. With a little less than a month remaining before election day, Wolden attempted to jump-start his campaign by charging that Mayor Christopher had allowed the city to become the nation's headquarters for "sex deviates." He further claimed that Christopher and Chief Cahill had been praised for their tolerance of homosexuals at a Mattachine Society convention in Denver.[48] These sorts of accusations were unprecedented; Wolden's attacks introduced homosexuality as a campaign issue in a major-city election for the first time in American history.

Wolden had reason to believe that his allegations might scuttle Christopher's campaign. The Republican national leadership had slung gay-baiting charges at Christopher the previous year when the mayor refused to concede to their candidate, Goodwin Knight, in the Senate primary race. Then only months before the mayoral election, the Young Republicans Club in San Francisco's 24th Assembly district had illustrated its hostility toward gay people by unanimously and permanently expelling its own chairman after it was learned that he had been arrested for a gay-related lewd vagrancy charge.[49]

Wolden's accusations, however, detonated in his face. The downtown press was thrilled with Christopher's and Cahill's Operation S, and embarrassed local journalists excoriated Wolden for "giving the city a bad name" with his public association of San Francisco and homosexuals. Among the "many" San Franciscans who "wished the tight-pants boys would go away," argued one Christopher supporter, "there was the resentful feeling. . . . that there must be a more circumspect way to deal with the situation." An *Examiner* editorial sputtered that San Francisco did not have a worse homosexual problem than "any large city of like size and makeup"; the red-faced daily hoped to make the issue go away by eschewing calls for a crackdown.[50]

The mainstream press not only refrained from an attack on homosexuality but suggested that when it came to issues of clean governance even gay residents enjoyed certain rights. Immediately after Wolden levied his accusation against Christopher, the Mattachine Society boldly revealed that a Wolden operative had planted the pro-Christopher statement at their convention. The society further announced that it planned to hit Wolden with a slander suit for over a million dollars. Remarkably, the downtown newspapers remained composed as they reported on the Mattachine's assertiveness. The press accepted that gay people had a positive right to state protection from those seeking to corrupt the government.[51]

Press reactions further revealed that some liberal observers prioritized the city's commitment to clean governance over its maintenance of traditional sexual boundaries. Hadley Roff, a journalist for the *News-Call Bulletin,* followed Wolden's accusation with a seven-part series extolling Mayor Christopher's and Chief Cahill's professionalization of the SFPD. The series approvingly quoted Cahill's assurances that the SFPD made "sex deviates" feel "not wanted" in the city, but the *News-Call Bulletin*'s editorial board then suggested a new definition of decency by heralding the supposed elimination of police corruption as evidence of a true "moral revolution in the city."[52]

In succession, the *News-Call Bulletin* and the *Chronicle* called on Wolden to withdraw from the race, while the *Examiner* encouraged him to remain a candidate so voters could thrash him at the polls. The assessor chose the latter path, and his violations of the gay closet, his dirty politicking, and Christopher's own popularity buried Wolden in a crushing 145,009-to-92,252 defeat.[53]

The press's coverage of both Wolden's accusations and the Mattachine's lawsuit revealed a new potential path of resistance to owners of gay bars. They could achieve civic legitimacy and earn the right to make positive claims for state service by attaching themselves to the managerial growth advocates' campaign for clean government. Bar owners were learning this lesson during a recession year when declining bar profits made police payoffs more onerous. In early 1960 William "Uncle Billy" Morrell, the owner of the 5A5 Club, organized a group of gay-bar owners from the downtown and waterfront areas to confront Chief Cahill with the payoff demands of the department's Central and Northern Station officers.[54]

Morrell had opened the 5A5 Club in 1952 and had gone on to develop an unusually broad network of predominantly white gay-bar owners. Whereas most owners of homosexual drinking establishments knew, at most, one or two other such owners, Morrell was acquainted with gay-bar operators throughout the city. When he decided to resist police payoff demands in 1960, he capitalized on these connections and invited over a small group of bar owners from the Embarcadero and lower Market Street areas. Morrell "had a meeting at the bar of all his staff," recalled Ross, a former employee of Morrell. "And he had four or five other bar owners there; and of the four or five, . . . three were terrified that it would be found out that they were gay-bar owners; and the other two were very friendly bar people. And they decided that they would all stick together and that we would blow the whistle."[55]

The Black Cat's Stoumen then helped arrange a meeting between this group of bar owners and both Chief Cahill and the ABC area administrator. During the first two meetings, bar owners tagged ABC supervisory agent Lawrence Cardellini, a veteran of the Black Cat cases, and Sergeant Waldo Reesink Jr. with extortion. Cahill harbored little sympathy for the bar owners, but the Wolden scandal had served as a reminder that much of the chief's favor in the press hinged on his ability to eliminate extortion through police professionalism. Some downtown supporters, he could now recognize, regarded corruption as a greater threat to the managerial growth agenda than homosexuality.[56]

Mayor Christopher, meanwhile, was more committed than ever to pushing San Francisco away from payola-based machine governance and toward managerial growth politicking. Historically, urban reform politicians like Christopher had abandoned their clean-government principles once they took office. Police payola was simply too lucrative to let pass. In San Francisco, observers estimated that if Mayor Christopher chose to tolerate police payola, the SFPD could collect two million to three million dollars a year. This impressive potential haul, however, was dwarfed by the federal subsidies offered for large-scale redevelopment. Over the course of the 1960s, San Francisco's redevelopment projects drew a third of a billion federal dollars into the city. As downtown growth politicians like Christopher gave up the police payola patronage system, they could now call on engorged developers, landowners, and corporate leaders for campaign contributions. Christopher embraced this transition and staked his political legitimacy on a clean SFPD. "You can't have graft without the mayor knowing about it," Mayor Christopher declared in his race against Wolden. "It has to seep right through the Police Department."[57]

Mayor Christopher and Chief Cahill understood that they could use high-profile prosecutions to maintain downtown leaders' perception that they were committed to clean government. Chief Cahill therefore aligned himself with the gay-bar owners and set traps for the accused police officers. The first sting occurred in late February, when police investigators caught Sergeant Reesink leaving The Handlebar with $120 in marked bills. Two weeks later, the owner of The Handlebar implicated another patrol officer, and although Cahill lacked enough evidence for an indictment, he promptly transferred the officer to a desk job. A local columnist reported that uniformed officers were grumbling that they were drawing prosecutions for crimes that would only earn inspectors a transfer, and then one day after the column ran, Cahill and the Police Commission suspended two inspectors for taking payoffs from the 5A5 Club and Have One Bar on Bush Street. As these accusations mounted, the press applauded Cahill for his tough stance against corruption, and rank-and-file police gave the scandal its name when they coined the term *gayola*.[58]

In early May the ABC joined the sting and, with the help of the SFPD, caught ABC agent Cardellini leaving Castaway Bar with $150 in marked bills. The final arrests revolved around Edward George Bauman's drinking establishment, Jack's Waterfront Hangout. Unlike most owners of gay bars during the 1950s and 1960s, Bauman was himself gay. He reported that in the fall of 1958 he informed Officer Edward Bigarani (of no relation to the beatnik patrol's Bill Bigarani) that he wished to run the Waterfront Hangout as a gay bar. Bauman claimed that the officer approved of the conversion as long as Bauman made sure the police were "taken care of." The payoffs increased as business improved, and by the time the scandal broke, Bauman stated, he had paid Bigarani, two sergeants, and a second patrolman a total of $2,900.[59]

Although one bar manager speculated that the payoffs from Jack's Waterfront Hangout flowed all the way to Central Station captain Charles Borland, both the captain and his lieutenants avoided prosecution. Nevertheless, in fewer than four months, a grand jury had indicted five of the eight accused police officers and one ABC agent for gay-bar payoffs. Cahill was "mad—and a little sad" over the gayola scandal and felt confident that the police officers were guilty. "I will stand behind any policeman doing his job," he told reporters, "or who makes an honest mistake in judgment. But this does not involve an honest mistake in judgment." Mayor Christopher endorsed the prosecutions as a strike against machine politics. "If you let them get away with a little bit," he warned, "the next thing you know we'll be like Chicago, where automatically police expect payoffs." As Chief Cahill and District Attorney Lynch moved forward, convictions appeared likely. Cahill and Lynch earned

FIGURE 7. Bryan Ray (left), a gay bartender at a gay drinking establishment, and Norman L. Tullis (right), the gay owner of two gay bars, wait to deliver grand jury testimony during the gayola trials. Tullis levied extortion charges against Sergeant Alfred Cecchi and Inspectors Telfred O. Slettvedt and Donald J. Murphy. Tullis also participated in a sting against ABC supervisory agent Lawrence Cardellini. Like the other gay prosecution witnesses in the gayola trials, Ray and Tullis projected professional images by wearing suits and ties. (Reprinted with permission, Bancroft Library, BANC PIC 2006.029: 136383.07 3B-4.)

their first court victory early in July, when Sergeant Reesink, the police officer caught taking $120 from The Handlebar, accepted a plea bargain and received a one-year prison sentence. The other four indicted San Francisco police officers (two patrolmen and two sergeants), however, maintained their innocence and began a joint trial in late July 1960.[60]

The defense team in the month-long gayola trial walked a homophobic tightrope. The accused officers needed to discredit the accusers, and they thus attacked the credibility of the bar owners with scandalous descriptions of the gay-bar world. At the same time, the four police officers had to then justify why they had not chosen to book these allegedly dangerous bar owners. The defense claimed that the city's security rested on the maintenance of a single sexual standard and that the preservation of these boundaries required subjective decision making. The accused patrol officers' unimpeachable masculine credentials, the defense continued, made these officers ideal wielders of such autonomous discretion.

The defense presented gay men as a moral, rather than physical, threat to the community. Predictably, the officers warned that gay people posed a danger to the city's youth, but the defense also obliquely depicted gay men as a menace to the city's women. Martha Sugrue, pregnant and wearing a maternity dress, told jurors that she once convinced her husband, Patrolman Michael Sugrue, to take her to Jack's Waterfront Hangout so she could experience a gay bar. Officer Sugrue, she related, had grudgingly consented, but as soon as she entered the bar, "I felt very uneasy, and we left without having a drink."[61] This anecdote summed up the defense's case. On the one hand, the accused police officers acceded to the public's interest in tolerating the gay bars as part of the city's exciting sexual color. On the other hand, naive San Franciscans (particularly women and children) needed the officers as protectors when they were confronted with the unnamed dangers of the closet.

The citizenry's increasing sexual tolerance, the defense continued, prevented the police from eradicating the drinking establishments' sexual threats. In particular, the defense emphasized that recent censorship trials, such as the city's *Howl and Other Poems* case in 1957, had circumscribed their ability to label art obscene. Patrolman Edward Bigarani testified that the paintings of unclothed men hanging in Jack's Waterfront Hangout had always worried him. Bauman, the bar's owner, countered that Bigarani had never objected to the pictures lining the walls and had even brought in his wife to view them. Bigarani assured the court that he was no cosmopolitan liberal—"I'm not a regular customer of the Palace of Fine Arts," Bigarani smirked—and claimed that he had asked his supervising officer for permission to issue obscenity charges against Bauman's artwork. Unfortunately, Bigarani claimed, his lieutenant denied his request because "the public," like Martha Sugrue, did not "realize— the way police know now—what a problem" homoerotic paintings presented. Handcuffed by the liberal strain of police professionalism, permissive courts, and an ignorant society, Bigarani had no choice but to let the pictures be. He claimed that with few formal legal options he had instead regulated the Waterfront Hangout by subjecting Bauman and his customers to a steady stream of verbal ridicule. The defense attorney mimicked this approach by gay-baiting the various accusers, particularly Bauman, on the stand.[62]

The assistant district attorney's failure to focus the case on corruption rather than homosexuality contributed to the prosecution's defeat. In late August the juries entered not-guilty verdicts for all four police officers.[63] Three

FIGURE 8. Following the announcement of their not-guilty verdicts in the gayola trials, Edward Bigarani, Robert McFarland, and Alfred Cecchi (pictured from right to left) celebrate with their respective wives and girlfriend. The defense used the testimony of accused officers' spouses to illustrate how the defendants employed their discretion to defend traditional family values from the ill-defined moral and physical dangers of gay bars. (Reprinted with permission, Bancroft Library, BANC PIC 2006.029: 136383.29.4F6.)

months later ABC agent Cardellini avoided a felony extortion conviction and only received a three-year probationary sentence for the misdemeanor of accepting a gratuity. Cardellini's defense attorneys built their entire case around the character-witness statements from nineteen local ABC agents and San Francisco ABC administrator Norbert Falvey. The assistant district attorney suspected that these twenty witnesses, many of whom had allegedly donated their own bribery earnings to the agents' defense fund, testified less out of friendship than out of a fear that their own criminality would be exposed.[64] Nevertheless, jurors in both cases accepted the defense's argument that law enforcement officials needed discretion to properly police homosexual behavior.

The gayola trial jurors approved of the accused officers' supposed use of discretion, but the trial itself centralized subjective powers away from the beat. This consolidation of policing authority transformed the relationship between the SFPD and San Francisco's gay and lesbian bars. Cahill's entrapment and prosecution of the gayola officers, coupled with a simultaneous extortion scandal in Hunters Point involving a lieutenant and a weekly poker game, made it clear to members of the police force and the ABC that the chief intended to deal seriously with extortion. While petty theft and graft continued, organized, large-scale payoff networks ceased operation in the mid-1960s.[65]

Through their public accusations and testimony, the gay-bar owners involved in the gayola scandal created an opportunity for liberals to begin integrating a tolerance toward homosexual perspectives into the emerging cosmopolitan liberal ideology. Cosmopolitan liberal journalists used the discussions over discretion to forward unthreatening gay images and to defend gay bars with harm-principle arguments. The local press calmly reported on Bauman and the other prosecution witnesses, and the cosmopolitan liberal *Chronicle* journalists went so far as to mock police for regulating gay art and stifling commerce. When Sergeant Cecchi testified that he had forbidden a gay-bar performance that was "one of the lewdest I believe I've ever seen," the *Chronicle* ran the headline, "Cop Says He 'Censored' Gay Bars." Ribbing Cecchi as a "husky, solemn-faced" officer, the newspaper questioned his discretion by emphasizing "he alone decided when the shows got too rough for the customers." The article reported neutrally on the SFPD's harassment of gay people, but characterized Cecchi as a prude for governing the leisure of adult customers. On issues of commercial entertainment, the *Chronicle* suggested, police lost their prerogative to subjectively police gay bars.[66]

Cosmopolitan liberals eventually used the gayola trial to contend that gay people possessed citizenship rights. Allen Brown, the liberal and closeted gay journalist for the *Chronicle,* capitalized on his position as the newspaper's "Question Man" to advance the perception that San Franciscans had reached a consensus on the basic rights of gay people to associate and on the value of a protective closet. Brown posed questions such as "Should We Discourage Gay Bars?" and "What is San Francisco's Worst Vice?," and he selected answers presenting gay people either as wholly unthreatening or as acceptable when hidden. The only published respondent who characterized gay people as a danger was a comically naive young sailor who related how he had once been shocked that a male stranger made a pass at him after he agreed to go into the stranger's apartment for a drink. The *Chronicle*'s editors, meanwhile, printed a letter to the editor comparing Edward Bigarani's attitude toward the Waterfront Hangout to bigotry against blacks and Jews.[67] Thus, as the gayola scandal centralized policing of gay bars, cosmopolitan liberals signaled their desire for an end to the SFPD's antigay repression.

THE PROFESSIONALIZED
HOMOSEXUAL-BAR CRACKDOWN

San Francisco's gayola scandal occurred alongside similar professionalization-driven police scandals in other cities where downtown growth advocates were attempting to centralize power within their police departments. In cities like Chicago and, later, Seattle, professionalized police leaders used their newly consolidated authority to increase pressure on homosexual bars. San Francisco followed this pattern. Payoffs had been demeaning and financially burdensome, but they had also offered gay and lesbian bars a modicum of protection from the antihomosexual whims of government officials. After gay-bar policing was professionalized, police officers no longer had a financial stake in safeguarding gay bars and were thus more responsive when outside agencies like the ABC pushed officers to make the elimination of gay bars a priority.[68]

In City Hall, Mayor Christopher could now see how homosexual bars might threaten his administration with two types of scandals. Gay and lesbian bars offered spaces for sexual activity that violated the mayor's traditional, family-oriented conception of the citizenry and also provided tempting shakedown targets for disreputable police who threatened his promises of clean governance. At a June 28, 1960, meeting—after the gayola accusations, but before the trials—Mayor Christopher called for a crackdown, and Chief Cahill, District Attorney Lynch, and ABC deputy director Malcolm Harris promised "complete cooperation and close coordination." Chief Cahill waged this centralized campaign against gay bars by deploying the Bureau of Special Services sex detail for an "attack on San Francisco's homosexual 'problem'" and pressing for raids against homosexual and disreputable bars in the lower Market, downtown, and Embarcadero areas.[69]

In Sacramento politicians could see how police officers were using their autonomy to violate the interests of managerial growth advocates, but they continued to view rank-and-file discretion as a crucial component of the government's antigay repression. In August 1961 the state legislature rewrote the state's vagrancy code, eliminating common vagrancy but strengthening lewd vagrancy. The revised statute allowed police to make vagrants of all persons who loitered at a public toilet or who loitered around "any school or public place which children attend or normally congregate." The code further empowered police to make a vagrant of anyone who solicited another to engage in "lewd or dissolute conduct in any public place or in any place open to the public or exposed to public view"—an extended definition of space that addressed the semipublic, semiprivate nature of bars. With these laws from the capitol and the pressure from City Hall, the SFPD's reported arrests for sex offenses, not including rape and prostitution, rose from 406 in 1959, to 778 in 1960, to 967 in 1961.[70]

The gayola scandal also reenergized the San Francisco ABC's drive against homosexual bars. Furious over the charges leveled against Cardellini, ABC agents swiftly prosecuted the fifteen gay-bar cases they had opened before the gayola scandal. By October 1961, the ABC had closed twelve of the city's thirty identified homosexual bars, including all of the bars involved in gayola. To move against the remaining, unindicted establishments, however, the ABC required the SFPD's assistance.[71]

During the late 1950s, homosexual-bar owners and their employees began staking out the ABC's San Francisco headquarters, photographing ABC agents entering and leaving the office. As a result, the ABC needed more undercover agents who were not recognizable to bartenders at gay and lesbian drinking establishments. Falvey looked to the SFPD for new faces, and Cahill obliged, supplying the ABC administrator with young patrol officers. The state courts, meanwhile, continued to assist the ABC by accepting the *Vallerga* precedent and upholding all disorderly house convictions, no matter how subtle the supposedly homosexual behavior. Thus, with the police department's backing and the court system's approval, the ABC shuttered twenty-four gay and lesbian drinking establishments in San Francisco in the year and a half after gayola.[72] The ABC bagged its most coveted quarry in 1963, when the California Supreme Court denied the final appeal of the Black Cat Café and Stoumen was forced to close his doors for good.[73]

The newly centralized policing arrangements allowed city and police officials to drive more aggressively against homosexual bars, but the post-gayola raids also drew increased media attention to the issue of homosexuality. Police officials hoped such notice would allow them to warn of the carnal transgressions occurring inside the city's homosexual drinking establishments. In the summer of 1961, for instance, police raided the Tay-Bush Inn, and after arresting eighty-nine men and fourteen women, authorities emphasized to local reporters that same-sex dancing occurred inside the downtown bar.[74]

Homophile activists and cosmopolitan liberals in the press, however, exploited the post-gayola raids to continue promoting an unthreatening, middle-class characterization of gays and lesbians. During the gayola trial, the Daughters of Bilitis had advertised a professional homosexual image by inviting a cosmopolitan liberal *Chronicle* journalist to a conference at which an ABC official and a civil rights lawyer explained the state's code for bars. After the raid on the Tay-Bush Inn a year later, the *Chronicle* portrayed the arrested patrons in a sympathetic light. The newspaper described the arrestees as white, middle-class, passive victims, noting that the police "herded" them like "sheep" into the patrol wagons—a portrayal that contrasted with the article's own description of patrons escaping the scene. The newspaper similarly characterized Bob Johnson, the white, gay, twenty-seven-year-old owner of the Tay-Bush Inn, as a martyr who "seemed more concerned about his patrons than himself." Johnson, however, took the opportunity to mock the SFPD. While the *Chronicle* had initially placed the raid in the context of a desexualized, teetotaling tradition—"The raid," the newspaper stated, "was . . . reminiscent of the old speakeasy days of prohibition"—Johnson characterized the policing of sexuality as parochial, prudish, and emotional. He insisted that "show people and others" liked his bar's "New York atmosphere," and he ripped the police for being "very sassy" toward his patrons.[75]

That gay-bar owners and the cosmopolitan liberal reporters covering them were changing the terms of mainstream debate was evident in the reactions of the city's moderates. Moderate journalists continued to express homophobia, but they also began regarding an avowed tolerance for gay bars as a necessary component of a modern, urbane image. Two months before the Tay-Bush raid, Guy Wright, a San Francisco newspaper columnist, stated that while he was neither "tolerant" nor "even broadminded" on the subject of male homosexuality, he believed local law enforcement should ease its pressure on gay bars and return to its earlier closeting strategy. Wright argued that the closures of gay bars simply drove gay men into heterosexual drinking establishments and led to intimate contacts with gay men that he found disgusting. He also suggested, however, that the city's acceptance of closeted gay bars was a sign of its modern self-assuredness. Remarking on the newly aggressive law enforcement regime, Wright mocked the ABC agents and quoted an attorney for gay bars remarking, "None of the customers is shocked by anything that goes on, only the tourists from the liquor board."[76]

Police professionalization had directly involved Mayor Christopher in the city's now-centralized policing of gay bars, and he thus found himself implicated in this emerging chorus of media criticism. Christopher ultimately proved more committed to clean-government reforms than to the city's traditional standards of citizenship; he pulled away from a direct fight over sexual pluralism. When commenting on the Tay-Bush Inn raid, the mayor disregarded the bar's same-sex dancing and, as the *Examiner* reported, "was mainly interested in finding out why so many people were allowed to congregate in one small cafe." This less aggressive rhetoric was mirrored by a change in SFPD policy. After the Tay-Bush Inn bust, Chief Cahill ended the

SFPD's attention-grabbing, centrally directed raids and thus helped distance the mayor from the SFPD's activities against gay and lesbian bars.[77]

THE TAVERN GUILD, COSMOPOLITAN LIBERALS, AND SEXUAL PLURALISM

The SFPD and ABC continued working together to pull alcohol licenses from owners of homosexual bars, but as they closed gay and lesbian drinking establishments, more continued to open. In 1962 an estimated twenty-five gay and lesbian bars operated in the city. The owners of the new gay and lesbian establishments, moreover, were far more likely to resist license revocations than the bar owners of the previous decade. This increased resilience largely stemmed from the fact that a growing number of owners were homosexual themselves. Although these gay and lesbian entrepreneurs remained dedicated to the bottom line, many viewed their bars as more than business ventures. They often saw the community-building potential in their establishments and thus displayed a greater tenacity in their conflicts with law enforcement. When the ABC revoked the licenses of bar owners who were gay or lesbian, the entrepreneurs often did not abandon the idea of operating a bar but instead quickly reopened, using friends, lovers, or relatives as front-persons for their license applications. These individual acts of persistence hindered the ABC's drive.[78]

The upswing in homosexuals' ownership of bars also facilitated the development of networks among the bars. These relationships took concrete shape in August 1961 when Morrell and a group of white gay owners and bartenders from the Tenderloin and Polk Street areas convened for the first meeting of the San Francisco Tavern Guild. These men initially conceived of the group as a social organization, but Guild organizers—a collection that quickly came to include a handful of lesbian owners of bars—soon recognized that the Guild's lines of communication could abet resistance to the police. Guild members, for instance, alerted one another when they were involved with the SFPD or ABC so other owners and bartenders could come to the hearings and view the complaining officers. Members then began distributing photographs of undercover agents among themselves and within local gay and lesbian publications, such as *LCE News*. Guild participants also defended their patrons from both police abuse and discriminatory underpolicing by retaining lawyers and providers of bail bonds to work with those arrested at their bars and by enlisting street violence–prevention groups to protect their patrons from vigilantes.[79]

As the Guild strengthened the bonds between the city's homosexual entrepreneurs and the patrons of their bars, the organization's members continued to fight stereotypes in the press. In 1963, for instance, a bartender responded to a column by Merla Zellerbach, a *Chronicle* columnist and frequent celebrant of the city's cosmopolitan liberal reputation. In an article in which Zellerbach criticized the ABC's infringement of homosexuals' "civil rights and liberties," she portrayed gay men as vulnerable, effeminate, cross-dressing victims. The assertive gay bartender read past Zellerbach's stereotyping and recognized in the columnist a potential ally. The bartender sent her a letter in which he argued, "Lots of the most masculine men, are as gay as Christmas." Many of his patrons, he continued, wore "western" and "motorcycle" outfits, and none were "dressing up as girls." The bartender's letter appeared in Zellerbach's column, and the her subsequent writings on gay men replaced descriptions of weakness with an emphasis on self-confidence.[80]

By the mid-1960s, owners of San Francisco's gay and lesbian bars were ready to build bridges with cosmopolitan liberal politicians. By this time, the bar owners had crafted images that were sexually acceptable to cosmopolitan liberals and had proven their desire to serve as partners in the city's clean-government reforms. Now they began teaching liberal politicians to conceive of a gay electoral bloc and to see gay and lesbian drinking establishments as access points to that constituency.[81] Bar owners and bartenders were uniquely positioned to register voters, disseminate information, and collect funds. In 1964 the Guild created a political committee to arrange meetings with city officials, and stumping liberals soon stopped by Guild gatherings to enlist financial and electoral support. In a city where local political candidates could not count on a political machine and often faced closely contested citywide elections, San Francisco office seekers frequently attached great import to group endorsements. Within this environment, Ross later recalled, the Guild very quickly established itself as "the sounding board for the [white gay and lesbian] community on politicians."[82]

The Tavern Guild's willingness to protect its members and its ability to draw links with mainstream politicians motivated increased participation. Indeed, the San Francisco gay rights movement captured more broad-based, grassroots support than any other homophile movement in the nation. In the latter half of 1964, the ebb and flow of the Tavern Guild's active membership gave way to a sustained rise, and by November the Guild's minutes were trumpeting that attendance "seems to get larger at every meeting."[83] With gathering energy and increasing funds, the Tavern Guild now stood securely at the center of the city's gay rights movement. These gay entrepreneurs had centralized the policing of homosexual bars and fostered a public image that restrained moderate homophobes in City Hall. Still, Tavern Guild members had not translated that growing public tolerance into leverage over Chief Cahill, who quietly continued to supply the ABC with officers for its ongoing drive against homosexual bars.

THE NEW YEAR'S DAY BALL AND GAY LIBERATION

When gay and lesbian homophile activists began integrating themselves into the cosmopolitan liberal coalition, they made a particular effort to forge alliances with the city's liberal clergy. By the summer of 1964, the leaders of the city's various homophile groups—including the Daughters of Bilitis, the Mattachine Society, the Society for Individual Rights (SIR), *Citizens News,* and the Tavern Guild—were ready to hold a retreat with twenty San Francisco ministers representing Episcopal, Methodist, Lutheran, and United Church of Christ denominations. Many of these religious figures received their funding through national or state organizations as part of special assignments—to do missionary work, for example. These clergy members therefore did not have to answer to congregations for their public positions on issues of sexuality. At the three-day conference, the religious and homosexual spokespersons formalized an alliance by establishing a permanent organization, the Council on Religion and the Homosexual (CRH). Traditionally, San Francisco's gay and lesbian groups had chosen obscure and unrevealing names in order to shield themselves from public scrutiny. But with the legitimizing presence of the clergy and their increased confidence in their own professional image, the gay and lesbian organizers felt secure in establishing the first organization in the United States to use the word "homosexual" in its name.[84]

Within half a year, the CRH became incorporated. To celebrate this accomplishment, the ministers suggested renting out California Hall for a New Year's Day Mardi Gras dance. The religious leaders recognized that a drag ball would likely attract police attention, and the ministers therefore met with the SFPD's Bureau of Special Services to obtain the department's approval. After a tense meeting, the religious leaders elicited grudging consent from Inspector Rudolph Nieto, the head of the SFPD's sex detail. The gay and lesbian activists approached the event with cautious optimism. The Tavern Guild predicted, "The ball, it seems, may become another important milestone in the 'movement.'"[85]

The ball proved momentous, but not peaceful. On the night of the dance, CRH organizers opened the doors to California Hall and found Inspector Nieto, seventeen uniformed officers, two patrol wagons, and (by CRH's estimation) thirty plainclothes police officers waiting outside on the street. Phyllis

Lyon, a founder of the Daughters of Bilitis, recalled that the police officers formed a line leading up to the hall's front door. They "had floodlights lighting the entrance," Lyon explained, "and police photographers taking moving pictures and still photographs of everybody who came in or went out." The scare tactics succeeded in sending a majority of the 1,500 prospective attendees back home, but five hundred or six hundred braved the intimidation and passed by the bursting camera bulbs.[86]

Once the dance was under way, sex detail officers entered the building and demanded to check the interior ballroom for code violations. The CRH organizers, however, had already received clean bills of health from police and fire code inspectors, and two CRH lawyers, Herb Donaldson and Evander Smith, informed the police that they would need a search warrant if they wished to proceed any further. The police quickly handcuffed the two attorneys. "I thought my career was over," Donaldson later reported. The SFPD tried to realize his fear by calling the American Bar Association and informing the organization of Donaldson and Smith's arrest. The lawyer group disregarded the defamation attempt.[87]

Police then broke their way through a crowd of ministers and searched for potential arrestees on the dance floor. Officers spotted two men standing on folding chairs. One of the men's chairs started to collapse, and in bracing himself, the man touched the other's buttocks. Within seconds, the police arrested the pair for public lewdness. Officers then arrested attorney Elliot Leighton and SIR member Nancy May when the two organizers blocked another police attempt to enter the ballroom. Unable to find more violations inside the building, the police gathered outside the hall and endeavored to incite a riot with slurs and taunts. CRH organizers managed to restrain the increasingly agitated dancers, and eventually the police left the event without making mass arrests.[88] The SFPD probably concluded the evening believing their operation was a success. The officers had humiliated and frightened the partygoers and inhibited the gays' and lesbians' attempt to socialize on a mass scale. In addition, the police had photographed over five hundred cross-dressing men and women and could now employ these pictures in future slandering.

The subsequent joint trial of Donaldson, Smith, Leighton, and May, however, demolished the SFPD's institutional insulation from gay and lesbian activists. Marshall Krause, an attorney with the Northern California American Civil Liberties Union (ACLU), readily agreed to defend the four in court. During his cross-examination of the accusing officers, Krause repeatedly caught the police lying on the stand. But much of the interrogation of police witnesses came from the exasperated judge, Leo Friedman. A seventy-five-year-old former San Francisco defense attorney long familiar with the SFPD's shadier courtroom tactics, Judge Friedman grilled Inspector Nieto: "Do you mean to tell me that you went there with 13 policemen and two cameramen and did not intend to make an arrest?" Nieto fell back on the common Cold War connection between homosexuality and Communism, insisting that he had brought photographers not to harass the dancers but because he "wanted pictures" of those attendees who were "connected to national security." Nobody in the courtroom took such a link seriously, and Krause did not bother pursuing the remark.[89]

Like many other gay and lesbian activists in the court's audience, Ross was stunned by the proceedings. Judge Friedman, Ross remembered, turned to the prosecution and shouted, "You're cops! You're spending all of this time in the hallways, and you're not even rehearsing your lines here." Once the prosecutor had finished presenting his case, Friedman accepted a motion to dismiss the charges and directed the jury to deliver a not-guilty verdict. The SFPD had charged the defendants with obstructing the police's entrance into California Hall, Friedman explained, but the officers had then testified that the accused had allowed the police to enter the building and not the ballroom. "You can't charge people with one thing," Friedman lectured, "and prove another." Friedman then demanded that police bring him the photographs and negatives taken of the dancers so that he could have them destroyed. The police in the courtroom, the *Chronicle* reported, listened to Friedman's ruling with their "mouths agape." The SFPD had suffered losses in cases concerning homosexually themed art, but it never had received such a serious judicial rebuke in a case regarding gay and lesbian people.[90]

The SFPD's incompetence ultimately limited the gravity of the not-guilty verdict. Members of the mainstream press contended that the CRH had won on a "technicality," and Evander Smith lamented that the defense was unable to argue that the police had violated citizenship rights by breaching the CRH members' privacy. Nor could gay and lesbian people safely interpret the directed jury verdict as evidence of a shift in the attitude of the public at large. Weeks later another San Francisco jury convicted the two men standing on folding chairs for lewd and indecent acts. The men were fined $200 each and registered by the state as sex offenders for the next two years.[91]

Despite these shortcomings the trial proved to be a pivotal moment in the relationship between the police and gays and lesbians in San Francisco. First, the proceedings advertised to gay and lesbian San Franciscans that they now enjoyed sizeable support among local members of the bar. A long list of heterosexual criminal attorneys had signaled their willingness to represent gays and lesbians in future cases by signing on as "of council" with the ACLU for the CRH trial. Second, Friedman's ruling influenced local jurists in subsequent trials of gays and lesbians. Krause later explained:

> Judge Friedman was courageous in that he incurred the wrath of the police department and subjected himself to criticism as favoring gays. But when he did it, it seemed to inspire more backbone to the other judges, and they began to realize this gross discrimination against sexual minorities was not to be tolerated in the law. And we began to get a lot more favorable decisions.[92]

Finally, the CRH trial opened the possibility of a wrongful arrest lawsuit. At the conclusion of the trial, Friedman turned to the defendants and explained that he would accept countercharges for their illegal arrests. Gay and lesbian activists now held, for the first time in history, a legal weapon against the SFPD. The gayola scandal had consolidated the responsibility over gay bars into the hands of the police chief, and the CRH now confronted Chief Cahill with a potential $1.5 million lawsuit. Eventually settling the matter out of court for $50, Donaldson and the CRH used the false-arrest suit to cool centrally orchestrated police pressures against gay and lesbian bars and large-scale gatherings. "The cops," Ross explained, "always dreaded the fact that we were going to come after them."[93]

The SFPD responded to this defeat with a brief, knee-jerk wave of repression. The day after Friedman threw out the case, police arrested fifty-six people in the Tenderloin neighborhood's homosexual bars. Cahill derided homosexual San Franciscans as "a segment of the population that requires constant policing," and Inspector Nieto attempted to reignite public dread by associating homosexual residents with murder, threats to the government, and lewd acts in public places. The Tenderloin sweep and the antigay rhetoric, however, represented the last gasp in the SFPD's large-scale, centrally orchestrated oppression of gay bars. Facing a potential lawsuit and a newly revealed contingent of homosexual-friendly lawyers, Chief Cahill ended the raids on gay dances and bars. Tavern Guild leaders noted that at their next large dance the police appeared only briefly and concentrated their efforts on controlling the crowd outside. "The police department representatives present were friendly," Guild members reported, "and some of the inspectors expressed a friendly attitude toward the affair."[94]

Later in the decade, Del Martin, a founder of the Daughters of Bilitis, happily noted that homophile activists "could not cite recent cases of police harassment, brutality or raids of gay bars." Furthermore, after the CRH ball, there was no evidence of the SFPD supplying plainclothes officers to the ABC. The ABC remained committed to revoking the licenses of the city's gay bars, but without SFPD officers the ABC was understaffed, and state liquor agents were quickly overwhelmed by an upswing in new gay and lesbian drinking establishments.[95]

Finally, the CRH defeat convinced Chief Cahill to seek political cover with a new gay community liaison position in the SFPD's police-community relations (PCR) unit. First formed to salve tensions between black San Franciscans and the police, the PCR had not initially promoted a brand of liberalism supportive of gay people. In a Fillmore community meeting, for instance, one black PCR officer identified "narcotic addiction, alcoholism, and homosexuality" as "conditions that indicate mental problems" and that "invariably result in police problems." Cahill now appointed to the new position Patrolman Elliot Blackstone, a heterosexual officer who had requested to serve as a liaison with gay San Franciscans. This connection to the PCR, coupled with the networks facilitated by the CRH, allowed homophile activists to build contacts with spokespersons from other marginalized communities. Through these intergroup alliances, gay and lesbian activists turned their attention to street-level police harassment and discriminatory police neglect, particularly regarding vigilantes in the city's parks and public restrooms. Gay and lesbian leaders recognized that although gay-bar activism had centralized policing over homosexual drinking establishments, policing power on the beat remained diffuse.[96]

San Francisco's gay-bar activists' political success during the mid-1960s was unusual, but by the end of that decade and into the early 1970s, activists in Los Angeles, Seattle, Philadelphia, Chicago, and Washington, DC, exploited contradictions between the economic desires of downtown growth proponents and the discretionary activities of police officers to follow the political pattern set in San Francisco. In each of these cities, gay activists mobilized a gay vote around issues of police repression, then integrated themselves into cosmopolitan liberal coalitions through campaigns against police discretion. In Chicago gay activists exploited a 1972 police payola scandal involving gay bars to unite with the city's growing population of young white professionals. Like the cosmopolitan liberals in San Francisco, these white-collar Chicagoans regarded government corruption as more threatening to their interests than gay and lesbian socializing. In Los Angeles cosmopolitan liberal politicians found common ground with economically productive gay bars during the late 1960s and early 1970s through their common opposition to California's subjective lewd vagrancy code. Like San Francisco's cosmopolitan liberals, they used debates over procedural regularity to promote sexual pluralism as harmless and potentially profitable.[97] The nation's fights over police discretion thus enabled urban liberals to promote broadened understandings of citizenship.

CONCLUSION

During the 1960s owners of gay bars in San Francisco pressed the city's emerging cosmopolitan liberal coalition toward an acceptance of sexual pluralism by striking at the foundation of the city's machine-era policing practices. Machine politicians had accepted the rank and file's discretionary policing over gay and lesbian residents, and police had used that autonomy to closet gay people in payola-rich bars. When managerial growth advocates like Mayor Christopher usurped the machine, their simultaneous desire to maintain the old definitions of citizenship and to introduce new governing arrangements created contradictions. Christopher promised to eradicate payola practices, but his desire to police the city's sexual boundaries with subjective or unwritten law prevented him from cracking down on the sort of discretion that facilitated police corruption. The mayor assumed that police officers would use their discretion to serve the interests of their professional police chief, but corrupt officers rejected the chief's clean-government dictums and used their autonomy to continue shaking down gay bars.

Owners of gay and lesbian bars recognized an opportunity in this incongruity. These entrepreneurs watched through the late 1940s, the 1950s, and the early 1960s as clean-government reformers across the nation exposed police corruption to put themselves forward as representatives of the common good.[98] In 1960, San Francisco's gay-bar owners introduced themselves as potential partners in this clean-government crusade by challenging payola in the courts. Once they had centralized law enforcement over their establishments, gay-bar owners then used the centrally orchestrated police raids to advertise their businesses as safe-but-exciting features of the city's nightlife. On these terms, gay-bar activists worked themselves into the emerging cosmopolitan liberal coalition. Together with white liberal journalists and politicians, the bartenders and bar owners circumscribed the SFPD's purview over sexual behavior and championed a sexually pluralist understanding of the citizenry.

CHAPTER 4

"The Most Powerful Force in Man": Sexually Explicit Art, Police Censorship, and the Cosmopolitan Liberal Ascent

to fuck with love—to know the tremor of your flesh within my own—
  feeling of thick sweet juices running wild
  sweat bodies tight and tongue to tongue

I am all those ladies of antiquity enamored of the sun
my cunt is a honeycomb we are covered with come and honey we are
covered with each other my skin is the taste of you

  fuck—the fuck of love-fuck—the yes entire—
  love out of ours—the cock in the cunt fuck—
  the fuck of pore into pore—the smell of fuck
  taste it—love dripping from skin to skin—
  tongue at the doorways—cock god in heaven—
  love blooms entire universe—I / you

reflected in the golden mirror we are avatars of Krishna and Radha
  pure love-lust of godhead   beauty unbearable
    carnal incarnate

I am the god-animal, the mindless cuntdeity   the hegod-animal is
over me, through me   we are become one total angel united in fire
united in semen and sweat   united in lovescream

  sacred our acts and our actions
  sacred our parts and our persons

sacred the sacred cunt!
sacred the sacred cock!
miracle!   miracle!   sacred the primal miracle!

  sacred the god-animal, twisting and wailing

  sacred the beautiful fuck

  LENORE KANDEL, "To Fuck With Love Phase II," *The Love Book* (1966)[1]

On November 15, 1966, Inspectors Peter Maloney and Sol Weiner entered the Psychedelic Shop, a Haight-Ashbury store that the *Chronicle* matter-of-factly described as "the Bay Area's No. 1 center for young persons seeking far-out information on new emotional and philosophical experiences." Maloney and Weiner had arrived searching for baser expressions. As the only two members of the San Francisco Police Department's obscenity detail, the pair had read *The Love Book* and had found in its five pages of poetry a dangerous fusion of lesbian imagery, religious invocations, and—in the *Chronicle*'s description— "earthy, four-letter words customarily employed only in places like male locker rooms." Maloney and Weiner confiscated Lenore Kandel's slender volume and arrested Allen Cohen, the store's proprietor, for distributing obscene materials.[2]

Maloney and Weiner's arrest of Cohen quickly attracted a gaggle of reporters eager to resurrect old story lines. "The controversy," the *Chronicle* reminisced, "recalled the 1950s . . . police actions against the CoExistence Bagel Shop, a beatnik bistro in North Beach." But as journalists interviewed the principal actors, the press narrative veered in new directions. Local journalists characterized *The Love Book* bust as a thoroughly professional police action. Inspector Weiner possessed a college education, Maloney had an intimate knowledge of the state's obscenity laws and judicial precedents, and both had raided the Psychedelic Shop with the express consent of both the chief of inspectors and the district attorney.[3]

When journalists were introduced to Kandel, press reports on *The Love Book* bust turned further from old beat narratives. Identifying herself as a Buddhist, Kandel related that she and her husband regarded all things as holy and that the two honored each other's blessedness through sex. *The Love Book* was an extension of that coupling, simultaneously an affirmation of her own holiness and a devotional to the "divinity" of her husband. Kandel also touted her poetry as useful to modern men. A man working in advertising in San Francisco's fast-expanding downtown, Kandel averred, lived an inauthentic existence and thus did not "feel very much of a man." The poet thought that her work might help release these white-collar men from their own feelings of enervation and alienation. Coverage of *The Love Book* controversy therefore turned on the question of whether broadening the speech rights of a "poet-housewife" would serve male interests.[4]

As a field of law enforcement that was centralized and linked to issues of male interests, obscenity policing provided San Francisco's male politicians an opportunity to illustrate their understanding of masculine leadership. Between the end of World War II and the expansion of second-wave feminism during the early 1970s, conservative and liberal male politicians and commentators insisted that proper expressions of manliness were a prerequisite for political leadership.[5] Conservative men promoted a heterosexual, family-oriented male model and charged that liberals tolerated cultural and sexual pluralism because they were too weak to maintain traditional boundaries. Traditional liberals similarly emphasized traditional family values through their celebration of the male breadwinner, but they also provided the legal groundwork for the so-called permissive society through their support for civil liberties. As Whitney Strub has illustrated, liberals on the national stage promoted speech and privacy rights that then cleared the way for forms of sexually explicit art and entertainment that those same liberals had no practical rationale for defending. Republicans hammered Democrats over this contradiction in their national competition for white suburban voters.[6]

The postwar politics of obscenity at the city level diverged from this national drama. In metropolitan centers like San Francisco, the young professionals streaming into the city expected their politicians to reduce violent crime and spur economic growth. Beginning in Mayor George Christopher's first term and running through the battle over *The Love Book,* male officials thus debated over how their approaches to sexually explicit expressions addressed the citizenry's desire for physical and economic security. The fights over the policing of sexually explicit works ultimately provided cosmopolitan liberals with an opportunity to argue that their qualified tolerance for cultural and sexual expressions provided a manly path to peace and prosperity.

HOWL AND OTHER POEMS AND THE PROFESSIONALIZATION OF OBSCENITY POLICING

During the first half of the twentieth century, censorship campaigns against sexually explicit works were predicated on understandings of a common good. Traditionally the nation's jurists agreed that materials were obscene and thus not eligible for First Amendment protections when they threatened to "deprave and corrupt" the minds and morals of readers. Judges were less settled, however, over whose minds and morals deserved protection. Prior to the 1930s, justices drew an obscenity line that shielded children, but beginning with the New York Supreme Court's 1934 *Ulysses* ruling, some magistrates began delineating obscenity standards with the mores of the "average person" in mind. In its 1957 *Roth v. United States* decision, the United States Supreme Court weighed in on the side of this average-person standard.[7]

The SFPD rarely employed the term *average person,* but the police leadership emphasized that officers' status as god-fearing fathers gave them the prerogative to censor sexually explicit materials they deemed objectionable. Although the department's high brass never elucidated official boundaries for sexual expression, police generally permitted the enjoyment of female eroticism as an adult male prerogative and censored works that displayed male sexuality of any sort or that presented female sexuality in a way not clearly designed to gratify heterosexual adult men. In practice, this meant that while police cracked down on sunbathing magazines with depictions of male nudity and intimidated gallery owners whose sexually explicit paintings might be seen by children, officers adopted a comparatively lax policy toward *Playboy* magazine. The SFPD's legal advisor spoke for much of the department in 1959 when he testified that the subjective policing of sexually explicit materials— those that were not "outwardly so obviously pornographic that no question is involved"—was "a field that shouldn't belong to us."[8]

The rank and file's ambivalent attitude toward sexually explicit expressions produced a relatively centralized law enforcement regime. Most beat officers ceded responsibility of obscenity policing to the Juvenile Bureau, the SFPD section formally mandated to enforce obscenity laws. The inspectors in the Juvenile Bureau concerned themselves primarily with works that might endanger the minds and morals of white, culturally mainstream San Franciscans. Inspectors recognized that formal obscenity charges against the purveyors of sexually explicit works would potentially bring the objectionable material to the attention of curious but naive mainstream whites. Thus, when the Juvenile Bureau confronted works that circulated outside the mainstream marketplace or among people of color and the avant-garde, they frequently disregarded the material or employed informal law enforcement tactics. On occasion, the Juvenile Bureau conducted well-publicized sweeps against distributors selling lowbrow sexual material to white adults, but even among these purveyors bureau officers preferred to use harassment and threats.[9]

By the mid-1950s the SFPD's closeting approach to obscenity policing was drawing criticism from a handful of lay Catholic activists outside the police department. Many of these lay Catholics had entered politics through a Catholic Action movement dating back to the Great Depression. During the 1930s the Vatican initiated an international Catholic Action movement that aimed to draw battling industrialists and workers into Catholic-brokered negotiations. By overseeing these dialogues, church leaders anticipated, the Catholic Action movement could lead the warring factions away from the polarized extremes of fascism and communism and toward the conclusion that industrialists and workers shared common human interests—interests that reflected Catholic principles. Indeed, Catholic Action encouraged lay Catholics to serve the common good by introducing Catholic principles into all areas of policy making. In San Francisco, church leaders promoted Catholic Action politicking in manly, martial terms. Mobilizing male Catholics in all-male organizations, such as Catholic Men of San Francisco, church leaders urged their followers to "fight courageously under the banner of Christ their King."[10]

Catholic Action participants had played a pivotal role in brokering a relative peace between business and labor in San Francisco, and they entered the 1950s searching for other areas of policy making where they could apply their religious mores. Some Catholic Action activists saw the city's print and visual cultures as the next field of battle. The courts' single-standard justifications for censorship, coupled with the established humanist rhetoric of Catholic Action, allowed San Francisco's male clean-culture proponents to wage this religious fight in the secular language of family values, and they ultimately expressed far more commitment to stamping out sexually transgressive materials than they did to cracking down on bohemians and gays and lesbians. The police could confine the latter groups to certain streets and neighborhoods, but sexually explicit materials had the ability to invade Catholic homes anywhere in the city.

Managerial growth politics similarly claimed to serve the city's preexisting shared family-oriented interests in redevelopment, and it was thus unsurprising that some clean-culture activists brought Catholic Action and managerial growth politics together for a single campaign against cultural and sexual transgressions. During the late 1940s and early 1950s, Chester MacPhee illustrated how politicians could integrate clean-government reform, progrowth politics, and Catholic Action principles into a winning electoral combination. A realtor and publicly devout Catholic, MacPhee was elected to the San Francisco Board of Supervisors in 1945 as part of the same clean-government wave that George Christopher rode into office. Reform advocates celebrated MacPhee as "a sincere, courageous fighter for the municipal good" and praised his support for clean government, urban renewal, and policies serving the city's children.[11]

During the mid-1950s, MacPhee continued defending traditional family values through his work as the chief customs collector for the Port of San Francisco. MacPhee initially concentrated his obscenity-fighting energies on low-culture materials, confiscating popular publications that contained dirty words or pictures of nude men and women on the same page. (He permitted material with nude male and female images on separate pages.) MacPhee publicly framed these efforts in humanist terms, but he organized weekly office prayer sessions that reminded his subordinates of the religious impulses firing his policy objectives.[12]

In late 1956 and early 1957, MacPhee placed his office on the alert for sexually explicit materials in the aftermath of a series of local scandals involving male youth and reputedly gay men.[13] MacPhee's heightened fears of child predation inspired him to widen his net to catch sexually explicit highbrow literature. His office impounded a shipment containing both *Miscellaneous Man,* an obscure literary quarterly with a short story including four-letter words, and *Howl and Other Poems,* a bound collection of Allen Ginsberg's work.

Although the confiscated version of *Howl and Other Poems* included ellipses in lieu of the poems' most scandalous words, the homosexually themed title piece rattled MacPhee's conscience. "Howl" begins with the famous declaration "I saw the best minds of my generation destroyed by madness/ starving hysterical naked" and later continues:

> who bit detectives in the neck and shrieked with delight in
> police cars for committing no crime but their own wild
> cooking pederasty and intoxication,
> who howled on their knees in the subway and were dragged off
> the roof waving genitals and manuscripts,
> who let themselves be . . . . . . in the . . . by saintly motor-
> cyclists, and screamed with joy.[14]

MacPhee was confident that the works violated accepted speech standards, but the customs collector was sensitive to the possibility that publicity over the seizure would pique the public's curiosity. Thus when reporters inquired into his censorship of *Howl and Other Poems,* MacPhee kept his answer curt: "You wouldn't want your children to come across it."[15]

The confiscation backfired in multiple ways. Most important, MacPhee had grossly underestimated the outcry that his censorship would trigger. Ernest Besig, the energetic director of the San Francisco–based Northern California American Civil Liberties Union (ACLU), led the counterattack against MacPhee's impoundments. Besig's office was more committed to defending sexually explicit speech than the nation's other ACLU branches, and Lawrence Ferlinghetti, the owner of City Lights Bookstore and publisher of *Howl and Other Poems,* had already secured Besig's pledge to defend "Howl" prior to the poem's confiscation. Now Besig initiated his defense by alerting the press to the customs officer's action.[16]

Besig found his strongest public relations support on free speech issues among the liberal journalists at the *San Francisco Chronicle.* In defending *Howl and Other Poems,* the *Chronicle*'s staff ignored Ginsberg and his homosexuality and never addressed the gay themes in "Howl." Instead, the newspaper covered the controversy as a question of professionalism. Abe Mellinkoff, a *Chronicle* columnist whom a colleague later described as a "conservative, Brooks Brothers Democrat," stressed that he had not read "Howl" (a common disclaimer among the *Chronicle*'s early defenders of the work), but insisted that if the city required a wall against sexually explicit material, local leaders should turn to experts, whom he defined as "professors of literature," to operate the gates.[17]

Two weeks later Michael Harris, a young general-assignment writer for the *Chronicle,* emphasized the lack of professionalism within the Customs Office. In his feature on the office, Harris described an agency that afforded tremendous power to poorly educated translators and agents. (The supervisory translator had told Harris that he held an accountant's degree from Golden Gate College and had learned "what is the truth and what is not the truth" "by reading current publications of the world events.") More sympathetic to labor politics than Mellinkoff, Harris mentioned the confiscation of *Miscellaneous Man* and *Howl and Other Poems* only in the final three paragraphs and instead focused his article on the Customs Office's vigorous fight against communist magazines. Harris knew that among the *Chronicle*'s labor-supporting readers, the descriptions of thorough political censorship amounted to damnation with faint praise.[18]

In May 1957 the U.S. Attorney's office abruptly derailed MacPhee's crusade against avant-garde art by reversing his decision and clearing *Howl and Other Poems* and *Miscellaneous Man.* North Beach's City Lights Bookstore began selling both publications, moving them into the jurisdiction of the SFPD. Mayor Christopher's Police Commission president was an established leader of San Francisco's Catholic Action movement, and in early 1957, the SFPD leadership elevated Captain William Hanrahan, a devout Catholic, to the head of the Juvenile Bureau. Hanrahan received no public pressure from the downtown press or even North Beach neighborhood newspapers to continue MacPhee's prosecution, but he worried that a problem had been created by the "publicity given the Collector of Customs when he tried to keep the books out of this country." Indeed, when Hanrahan saw a local student newspaper reporting on Ferlinghetti's intention to resume selling *Howl and Other Poems* at City Lights Bookstore, the police captain recognized that the works now had the potential to reach mainstream white youth.[19]

When Hanrahan moved against City Lights Bookstore, he adhered to the city's formal process for policing sexually explicit works. Hanrahan first notified the district attorney's office that he wished to issue a ban against both

Man and *Howl and Other Poems.* Using their understanding of
determine whether an arrest could be made, the prosecutors
an to publicly prohibit the city's stores from selling the book.
store disregarded this proscription, and on June 3, 1957, a
SFPD officer arrested Shig Murao, the salesclerk, for selling him
the two works. A day later the district attorney's office filed charges against
Ferlinghetti. Hanrahan insisted that he had no intention of initiating a larger
campaign, but he claimed that both *Miscellaneous Man* and *Howl and Other
Poems* were "obscene and unfit for children to read."[20]

In a petition demanding that Mayor George Christopher reverse the con-
fiscations by the Juvenile Bureau, the Democratic League of the 21st Assembly
District and twenty-one booksellers, including large-scale, downtown empori-
ums such as Macy's Bookstore, suggested that the censorship would hamper
the city's economy by causing "harm" to San Francisco's "reputation as a
center of culture and enlightenment." Christopher refused to intervene and
instead exited the debate though diversion. The mayor responded that he
was "certainly opposed to censorship" but was also against "lewd shows."[21]

As the case moved into municipal court, Besig assembled a high-powered
defense team, including Jacob "Jake" Ehrlich, a nationally renowned trial lawyer and locally prominent Democrat, and Albert Bendich, the ACLU's new
twenty-eight-year-old staff attorney. Ehrlich's involvement in the case immediately attracted national interest. Known as "Never Plead Guilty" Ehrlich and
as "the Master," Ehrlich had achieved fame as a murder trial lawyer and a civil
case attorney for celebrities. His career was later fictionalized in the popular
Sam Benedict television series.[22]

The defense team waived a jury trial, and the case's outcome thus landed
in the hands of Judge Clayton Horn. Ehrlich later described Horn as "a close
friend of mine," but few observers at the time could guess on which side the
judge's sympathies would fall. Horn, local lawyers noted, was a "dapper" intellectual, proud of his literary knowledge. However, he was also a Sunday school
teacher who believed that traditional religious mores sometimes trumped concerns over individual rights. Only weeks before the *Howl* trial, Horn had sen-
tenced a group of young women convicted of misdemeanor shoplifting to view
the film *The Ten Commandments* then write essays on it. Ferlinghetti, for one,
approached the trial pessimistically. "I really felt that we'd probably be found
guilty," the bookstore owner later recalled.[23]

When the trial got under way in June 1957, Assistant District Attorney
Ralph McIntosh had no case against either Shig Murao or the sale of *Miscellaneous Man.* Familiarity with the content was a necessary element of a Califor-

nia obscenity conviction, and the prosecutor lacked proof that Murao knew of the work's contents or that Ferlinghetti was familiar with *Miscellaneous Man*. The prosecutor thus concentrated on Ferlinghetti and *Howl and Other Poems*. Because the Supreme Court had invalidated the youth-corruption rationale for censorship, McIntosh assailed *Howl and Other Poems* as a threat to the traditional citizenry's moral compass. Ferlinghetti's defense responded with sporadic attempts at sacralizing Ginsberg's poems (two defense witnesses referred to "Howl" as "biblical" and "resurrective in quality"), but the free-speech attorneys primarily curried Horn's favor with scholarly arguments. As the historian Richard Cándida Smith shows, Ferlinghetti's lawyers profession-alized Ginsberg's poetry and the obscenity trial itself by introducing the expert testimony of university scholars and professional writers.[24]

Prior to the *Howl* case, California courts had forbidden scholarly testimony in obscenity trials. Bendich, however, submitted to Horn pretrial briefs argu-ing that the U.S. Supreme Court's 1957 *Roth* ruling now legitimated scholarly testimony. *Roth* represented the High Court's first ever attempt to define ob-scenity, and the *Howl* trial was the first major test of the *Roth* decision. In *Roth* the High Court had rejected both free speech absolutism and a strict harm-principle rationale that would have required for censorship convictions proof of a "clear and present danger." Instead, the U.S. Supreme Court followed the New York Supreme Court's *Ulysses* precedent and declared that a work could be found obscene if "the average person, applying contemporary community standards, [found that] the dominant theme of the material, taken as a whole, appeals to prurient interest." The decision also described an obscene work as being "utterly without redeeming social importance."[25]

Bendich's pretrial briefs provided a novel and expansive interpretation of the Supreme Court's ambiguous decision. Arguing that the "social impor-tance" clause was a test in itself, Bendich insisted that the defense could render the "prurient interests" of the "common person" moot by proving a work's social value. This legal argument circumvented the question of moral corrup-tion with a new conception of the citizenry. Bendich's briefs maintained that San Francisco residents maintained pluralist cultural values and that scholars and artists constituted a separate social group with interests deserving state protection.[26]

Horn agreed to Bendich's interpretation of *Roth* and his culturally plural-ist understanding of the city. The judge thus permitted Ehrlich to draw on the local constellation of colleges and universities, and the defense called to the stand six Bay Area professors, one newspaper book critic, and two au-thors—all of whom were white and male—to prove the work's importance for intellectuals and artists. Meanwhile, Horn refused to hear from psychiatrists or sociologists who could discuss whether Ginsberg's poetry undermined the moral fiber of the entire community. McIntosh tried to counter with his own experts, but could muster only two grossly underqualified witnesses. In humiliating fashion, Ehrlich dismissed the professionalism of Gail Potter, the second scholar for the prosecution, by declining to even cross-examine her.[27]

Without support from the local academy, McIntosh was unprepared to engage the poetry on technical grounds. "The man was very, very unsophisticated about literature, about art, about history," Bendich later recalled. "He was kind of a low-level bureaucrat." McIntosh was thus at the mercy of defense witnesses when they began misrepresenting academic thought. For instance, Mark Schorer, a University of California, Berkeley, English professor and the defense team's star witness, insisted that it was impossible to translate the poem's sex-laden stanzas into understandable prose. Few contemporary poetry experts, the scholar Victor Tulli notes, would have accepted such an extreme proscription of paraphrasing, but this prohibition confounded McIntosh's attempts to identify the deviant themes of "Howl."[28]

Similarly, McIntosh lacked advisors who could alert him when defense witnesses were distorting the message of Ginsberg's poetry. Ferlinghetti's published version of "Howl" had replaced the most explicit terms with suggestive ellipses, and the assistant district attorney was therefore forced to focus on more ambiguous lines. McIntosh raised his eyebrows over, "Who blew and were blown by those human seraphim, the sailors, caresses of Atlantic and Caribbean love," but Schorer defused the line's message by arguing, "The essence of this poem is the impression of a world in which all sexuality is confused and corrupted. These words indicated a corrupt sexual act." As Tulli points out, Schorer disingenuously omitted the sections of the volume in which Ginsberg celebrates homosexuality, and the professor suggested that Ginsberg simply used homosexually themed language to portray "modern life as a state of hell."[29]

The defense's closeting of the volume's homosexual perspectives required that Erhlich and his witnesses also closet Ginsberg's homosexuality. Ginsberg had moved out of the Bay Area a year before and was touring Europe during the trial. Neither the attorneys in the courtroom nor the journalists in the press paid any attention to the poet's bohemian or homosexual identity. Instead, the defense characterized *Howl and Other Poems* simply as the work of a professional male poet who did not wish to "temper his feelings" by expressing them "more softly."[30]

On October 3 Judge Horn exonerated Ferlinghetti and *Howl and Other Poems*. Drawing heavily on Bendich's briefs, Horn's thirty-nine-page decision expounded on the "utterly without redeeming social importance" clause with such force that his ruling helped establish the foundation for a new national standard.[31] Locally an ebullient *Chronicle* praised Horn's ruling. The newspaper's coverage of the verdict presented color-blind cultural pluralism as a modern alternative to the backward racial consciousness of southern conservatives. "The Judge's decision," the *Chronicle* rejoiced, "was hailed with applause and cheers from a packed audience that offered the most fantastic collection of beards, turtle-necked shirts and Italian hair-dos ever to grace the grimy precincts of the Hall of Justice." The newspaper did not address whether San Francisco's white cultural experimentation engendered youth delinquency, but it placed its front-page *Howl* trial report adjacent to what the *Chronicle* regarded as a nauseating example of southern youth behavior: a photograph of a white high school student in Little Rock, Arkansas, merrily beating a hanging black effigy.[32]

Ultimately, support in court and in the media for the expansion of cultural pluralism depended on both parties erasing untraditional racial and sexual perspectives from the *Howl* debate. The *Chronicle*'s descriptions of the trial audience, for instance, never acknowledged the presence of black people at the proceedings.[33] The newspaper further focused the story on the rights of white men by almost totally ignoring the role Murao, a Japanese American, played in the affair. Similarly, by defending *Howl and Other Poems* as an indictment of homosexuality and a collection of professional poems, Ferlinghetti's attorneys framed the case around the rights of university scholars and professional artists who were assumed to be heterosexual, not the rights of culturally and sexually non-conforming bohemians. Thus, even the culturally and sexually conservative *Examiner* found itself endorsing Horn's decision. The *Examiner* emphasized that Horn rejected the obscenity charge precisely because the poetry was "disgusting" and "revolting"; the work thus produced "the antithesis of pleasurable sexual desires." Like the *Chronicle*, moreover, the *Examiner* comforted itself in the thought that the poem was the product of an "author" experimenting with "coarse and vulgar language." Neither the *Chronicle* nor the *Examiner* pondered whether Ginsberg's work revealed the presence of untraditional sexual perspectives within the population at large.[34]

Thus, the *Howl* verdict did not open the floodgates for culturally transgressive and sexually explicit speech. But from Hanrahan's and District Attorney Thomas Lynch's perspective, the *Howl* case did broaden the rights of male artists to use homosexually themed language. Previously artists had courted trouble if they presented gay people in any way other than according to a desexualized, effeminate stereotype. The *Howl* defense forced Hanrahan and Lynch to accept the prerogative of San Francisco's male, professional, and heterosexual or closeted poets and writers to describe homosexual people, albeit in a negative context, as sexually motivated and sexually active individuals.[35] It was not clear, however, that judges like Horn were prepared to extend sexual speech rights to other San Franciscans. Judge Horn, for one, continued denying bohemian and gay men basic civil liberties during the late 1950s. In one case over a young man's purportedly gay behavior in North Beach's bohemia, Horn opined that the defendant was guilty before the accused had presented his case. The judge then refused to let the defendant take the stand. An appeals court later vacated Horn's judgment in the case.[36]

PROFESSIONALIZED OBSCENITY POLICING: THE LENNY BRUCE AND THE VORPAL GALLERY CASES

The *Howl* trial convinced the SFPD's Juvenile Bureau to moderate its already limited pursuit of obscenity. Between 1958 and 1963, the bureau never issued more than ten obscene literature charges in a single year. In the aftermath of the *Howl* defeat, the SFPD could see how failed formal prosecutions complicated the Juvenile Bureau's preferred informal tactics. In 1955, for instance, the SFPD had frightened the publisher of *American Sunbather* and *Nudist Leader* into pulling his magazines from San Francisco through threats of legal action. When the publisher learned of the *Howl* verdict, he excitedly asked the ACLU whether Judge Horn's ruling provided him with enough legal cover return his magazines to San Francisco's newsstands. By the end of the decade, the periodicals were back in the city.[37]

The Juvenile Bureau also understood that courtroom defeats were now more likely because the *Howl* episode had created a durable and motivated anticensorship coalition of journalists, lawyers, professors, writers, and artists. In 1961 San Francisco's Democratic Assembly member Jack O'Connell strengthened the courtroom arm of this network by slipping the clause "utterly without redeeming social importance" into California's obscenity statute—a surreptitious maneuver he managed during the bill's reconciliation process. After Horn's verdict and O'Connell's legislative machinations, San Francisco's law enforcers recognized that any obscenity charges against an artistic work would need to overcome the technical defenses of field-leading scholars. Cosmopolitan liberal journalists, meanwhile, stood poised to publicize each prosecution and thus push sexually explicit works further into the mainstream.

The anticensorship network thus made courtroom victories harder to achieve and more costly to lose. District Attorney Lynch responded to these political perils by tightening his office's control over obscenity charges. The only instances during the early 1960s in which Lynch publicly upbraided police officers was when Juvenile Bureau inspectors issued obscenity arrests without his office's prior approval.[38]

Although the SFPD leadership and the district attorney used their authority to dial down obscenity prosecutions, police captains and prosecutors remained willing to bring charges over performances or materials they believed to be too explicit or too popular to enjoy the scholarly protections of art. In 1961 the SFPD and the district attorney's office agreed to prosecute Lenny Bruce when a performance by the so-called "sick comic" appeared to be both. On October 3 and 4, Bruce performed a two-night run at the Jazz Workshop, a North Beach nightclub. Police disregarded Bruce's opening-night shows, but a *Chronicle* journalist was present, and the following morning's newspaper reported on the act. Alongside a photograph of a howling audience and a mugging Bruce, the *Chronicle* related that much of the comic's monologue had pilloried Philadelphia police for his arrest a week earlier on drug charges. This antipolice riffing caught the attention of Central Station.[39] The SFPD understood that courts did not recognize antipolice rhetoric as obscene, so Central Station sent Patrolman James Ryan to Bruce's second night of performances to listen for material of a sexual nature.

When Bruce opened for his second evening, he did not mention the Philadelphia police department's overenforcement of drug laws but instead highlighted the SFPD's failed policing of gays. The comic first recounted that during his previous visit to the Bay Area in 1958, the owners of Ann's 440, a Broadway Street nightclub, had hired him because they believed he could attract a heterosexual audience and help them replace their "cocksucker" clientele. From Bruce's perspective, the story's humor rested on the crude gay word and the absurdity of the neighborhood relying on entertainers—rather than the police—to repel gay men from the area. Later in the performance, Bruce pressed the sexual boundaries further by parsing the erotic meaning of the term *to come* and then again by relating a nonsensical tale of a man who hung a "kiss it" sign from his penis. Officer Ryan had heard enough. He fetched his supervising sergeant, and after the performance the two officers booked Bruce for obscene speech.[40]

Two other Broadway Street establishments—a strip club called the Moulin Rouge and Finocchio's, a nightclub with a drag cabaret—offered popular sexual entertainment, but Ryan had no trouble distinguishing Bruce's language from this more acceptable fare. The Moulin Rouge staged an all-female, heterosexual show for an all-male audience and thus did not, in Ryan's view, threaten normative gender roles and hierarchies. Similarly, the patrolman doubted that the effeminate and inexplicit drag queens at Finocchio's would stimulate gay desires in its audience of heterosexual male and female tourists. Finocchio's cabaret, Ryan explained, was "a pretty average show, except that all the entertainers are female impersonators."[41]

Bruce's use of the word *cocksucker,* on the other hand, produced a more sexualized, active gay image that located gay identity in sexual acts rather than stereotypical effeminate behavior. During Bruce's trial, Assistant District Attorney Albert Wollenberg Jr., a liberal Republican, pointed out the difference between inexplicit gay caricatures and explicit gay descriptions when he asked one defense witness, "Why did he have to use the word 'cocksucker?' Wouldn't 'faggot' or 'fairy' have done as well?"[42] In the aftermath of the North Beach beat scene, moderate officials expressed little concern over untraditional gender behavior, but they continued to fret over the corruptive power of gay sexual perspectives.

Three years later, similar fears over the corruption of mixed-gender audiences prompted the SFPD and the district attorney to charge Muldoon Elder with obscenity for displaying a series of Ron Boise statuettes in his art space, the Vorpal Gallery. Eighteen-inch figures crafted from the metal of old car fenders, Boise's statuettes depicted explicit heterosexual sex scenes from the *Kama Sutra.* Central Station officers happened upon the works accidentally after a gallery staff person complained to police about a parked car that was illegally blocking the gallery's front door. The gaunt, twisted figurines offered depictions of sexuality that were both confusing and explicit in their three-dimensional renderings. Thus, on April 7, 1964, the SFPD Juvenile Bureau arrested Elder for distributing obscene matter and deployed fourteen police officers and three hulking police wagons to carry away the eleven diminutive works of art.[43]

San Francisco's prosecutions of both Bruce and Elder mobilized the city's free speech networks. In the Bruce case, Ferlinghetti introduced the comic to Bendich, the lawyer whose briefs had paved the way for the *Howl* victory. Later the ACLU offered Elder free legal representation.[44]

In both cases the courtroom defense capitalized on the prosecution's unwillingness or inability to address the sexual desire of the audience. California law dictated that speech had to raise prurient interests to be considered obscene, and in a 1959 exoneration of a Los Angeles–based homophile magazine, the U.S. Supreme Court had suggested that the state could not hold homo-

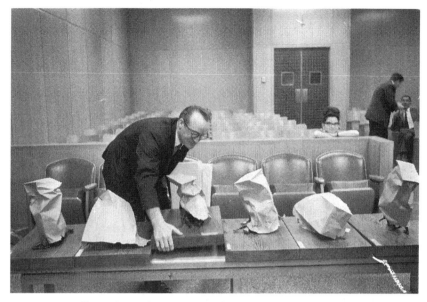

FIGURE 9. Officer Ed Castiglioni arranges Ron Boise's sexually explicit *Kama Sutra* statuettes for the Vorpal Gallery obscenity trial. The police and prosecution covered the statuettes in lunch bags to highlight the moral danger underneath. June 24, 1964. (Reprinted with permission, Bancroft Library, BANC PIC 2006.029: 138946.02.08.)

sexual works to a different standard than heterosexual publications. The prosecutor in the Bruce trial, however, wished to closet gay desire and thus made no attempt to identify any homosexual reactions within Bruce's putatively heterosexual audience. Bendich exploited the prosecutor's reticence and asked heterosexual audience members whether they had been aroused by Bruce's monologue. Bendich further disconnected Bruce's speech from titillation by forcing Ryan to admit that the officer had heard the word *cocksucker* used at the police station, a quintessential site of traditional male heterosexuality.[45]

Prosecutors in the Vorpal Gallery case attempted to inflame the jurors by covering the statuettes with brown paper bags, but then had a difficult time convincing people in the courtroom that emaciated, metallic forms excited prurient passion. When defense lawyers asked a scholar whether he found the statuettes titillating, the academic quipped, "The thought never occurred to me. But I'd rather make love to a bicycle."[46]

The defense lawyers in the two trials further defended the sexually explicit pieces by characterizing the two works as products of professional artists. In the Bruce case, a string of critics and scholars testifying for the defense wove the comic's monologue into a millennia-old, high-culture tradition of social satire. Similarly, the ACLU argued for Boise's works by asking professors and curators to place the statuettes in a long-standing artistic tradition exploring love. In the latter case, the *Chronicle* and the *Examiner* appreciatively likened the defense's testimony to a "college art seminar" and to "a sort of swifty summer course in Loving Art Through the Ages."[47]

Both defenses were significantly aided by the fact that their cases eventually landed in the court of Judge Horn. The respective defense teams requested jury trials, and at the conclusion of each hearing, Judge Horn delivered to the juries narrow deliberation rules that emphasized the centrality of a work's "social importance" and made convictions impossible. "Under the letter of the law," the jury foreman for the Bruce case lamented, "we had no choice" but to acquit. The Bruce and Vorpal Gallery victories incrementally expanded local boundaries of artistic protection for white San Franciscans. Bruce's not-guilty verdict established the prerogative of male heterosexuals to voice explicit gay descriptors in commercial settings. The Vorpal Gallery case solidified the freedom of male gallery owners to display explicit, plastic-art representations of heterosexual sex with confused moral messages.[48]

CENSORSHIP AND MASCULINE POSTURING

As civil liberties attorneys broadened speech rights in court, the lawyers teamed up with scholars and cosmopolitan liberal journalists to wage concurrent campaigns in the media. Male cosmopolitan liberals often attempted to legitimize sexually explicit works in public by impugning the masculinity of the censors. In 1957, for instance, the *Chronicle*'s editors associated MacPhee's Customs Office with feminine behavior by illustrating Harris's feature story on the office with a large photograph of Gayle Bennett—possibly the only woman working as a San Francisco translator. Later the *Chronicle* scorned Captain Hanrahan for "Making a Clown of San Francisco" and suggested that the Juvenile Bureau leader was a motherly prude bent on reducing the city's reading level to "Mother Goose [and] The Sleeping Beauty."[49]

Although these jabs at the would-be censors' masculinity were subtle, the intimations clearly struck a chord. *The Monitor,* the San Francisco Archdiocese's organ, responded to Harris's article with a long feature that made no mention of Bennett and instead profiled each of the male Customs Office staff members, with detailed descriptions of their working-class backgrounds and physical prowess. For instance, the newspaper described Joe Dillon, a translator, as a former fly-weight champion who "would be happy to square off with anyone who called him a censor for sidetracking a batch of printed filth." The newspaper even portrayed the balding and bespectacled MacPhee as a muscular protector of the city's families. "He's a product of the Mission [District]," the Catholic newspaper flexed, "and was initiated early in the tough neighborhood." Through his professional application of the law, *The Monitor* concluded, MacPhee had proved he was "a man" who believed "in enforcing law 'as she is written.'"[50]

Similarly, local police and male clean-culture activists reacted to harm-principle critiques by emphasizing that their censorship activities protected the physical well-being of the city's families. Following the *Howl* verdict, Captain Hanrahan insisted that he was far too "broadminded" to judge the content of sexually explicit material and yet also warned that these works served as a "dangerous stimulant to perverts." Similarly, Val King, a lay Catholic columnist and an aide to Assessor Russell Wolden, insisted that men must eliminate pornography because it could "arouse" "the nuts" "to do anything they want to our children, our wives or our mothers."[51]

These defenses of censorship leaned on traditional conceptions of masculine responsibilities and power. After World War II, cultural conservatives argued that men proved their strength by entering the business world, purchasing suburban homes, raising families, and embracing a culture that was uniform in its cultural, sexual, and racial standards. Conservatives claimed that when male liberals embraced cosmopolitanism, they did so because they lacked the fortitude to maintain traditional boundaries.[52] The association conservatives crafted between themselves and traditional forms of manliness proved electoral gold in the nation's suburbs.

Cosmopolitan liberals, however, capitalized on alternate visions of proper male behavior emerging among those male white-collar whites who found suburbanization unsatisfying. During the 1950s mass-culture publications like Hugh Hefner's stunningly successful *Playboy* magazine promoted a "lifestyle masculinity" that encouraged men to adopt hip urban identities by tolerating cultural and sexual pluralism, amassing modern art, and acquiring a surface knowledge of intellectual trends. Cosmopolitan liberals used this lifestyle masculinity rhetoric to defend the male prerogative to consume sexually explicit art.[53]

During the Vorpal Gallery case, the defense lawyers and the liberal journalists covering the proceedings suggested that sexually explicit speech had utility not only for scholars but also for white-collar men who wished to convey their modern manliness. In defense of the Boise statuettes, the ACLU lawyers called Michael Phillips to the stand. A member of the San Francisco Republican Central Committee, a past president of San Francisco's Young Republicans, and an employee of Bank of America, Phillips owned three Boise love statuettes. With his "button-down collar and rep tie," the *Chronicle* related to readers, Phillips was the "model of the young executive." In the witness box, he related how he displayed his Boise statuettes prominently inside the entrance of his home. Since the Vorpal Galley bust, he said, seventy people had come to his Cole Valley home to view these "beautiful" works. The press and ACLU attorneys made clear that embracing lifestyle manliness allowed male professionals like Phillips to earn the respect of their peers.[54]

Through their opposition to artistic censorship, San Francisco's male cosmopolitan liberals coupled their lifestyle masculinity with the manly, "vital liberal" posture being promoted by the nation's male liberal intellectuals. In the November 1958 *Esquire,* Arthur Schlesinger's "The Crisis of American Masculinity" proclaimed that America needed self-assured "vital liberal" leaders committed to seizing and wielding power. Confident independence, Schlesinger continued, allowed vital liberals to engage with opposing perspectives and pragmatically develop and implement effective policies. From this perspective, a man's cosmopolitanism reflected his rugged individuality. In San Francisco cosmopolitan liberals adopted this association of cosmopolitanism with manly policy making to ridicule male art censors as failed men. Wallace Stegner, an author, Stanford University professor, and founder of the Friends for the San Francisco Public Library, ridiculed timorous clean-culture advocates: "It would be absurd to expect writers to ignore the most powerful force in man. . . . The objections don't come from the radical left or the radical right. They always come from the terrified middle."[55]

The San Francisco anticensorship campaigns' fixation on male prerogatives ultimately ensured that the free speech victories of the early 1960s would benefit white men far more than white women. Indeed, Judge Horn initially used the professionalization of obscenity trials to constrict the legitimacy of female sexual expression. During Bruce's trial, Horn ruled that Mary Brown, a Jazz Workshop audience member, lacked the "expertise" to testify for the defense on whether Bruce's language had raised her prurient interest. (Horn forced Patrolman Ryan to answer this same question.) However, white women slowly forced their way into San Francisco's male-dominated obscenity debates by speaking as academics. In 1959 Phyllis Kronhausen, a psychologist and author, received local attention when she faced Molly Minrudi, a prominent clean-culture activist, in a television debate over censorship. The *Chronicle* accepted Kronhausen's professional expertise on "erotic realism" and reinforced her talking point that Minrudi lacked the academic background necessary to ban reading materials.[56]

Nevertheless, female scholars like Kronhausen often found male anti-censorship advocates more interested in their femininity than their intellectual expertise. During the Vorpal Gallery trial, for instance, the ACLU called Katherine Caldwell, a Mills College lecturer on Asian art, as a witness. Caldwell was the first female scholar to ascribe professional status to a censored artistic work in a San Francisco courtroom. The ACLU valued Caldwell for her ability to place the artwork in an intellectual context, but the *Chronicle* emphasized her femininity—describing her as a "sprightly little sparrow of a woman"—in order to highlight the absurdity of the male prosecutor's scandalized response.[57]

CENSORSHIP AND THE SHELLEY ADMINISTRATION

Through the early 1960s, progrowth mayors like Christopher often championed the traditional bounds of citizenship, but their overriding interest in redevelopment often steered them clear of centralized areas of law enforcement—such as artistic obscenity prosecutions—where they ran the risk of irritating their white-collar workforce. In Chicago, for instance, Mayor Richard J. Daley did not protest when *Playboy* hung its name on its downtown skyscraper, and he avoided condemning artistic works that crossed traditional sexual boundaries (including James Baldwin's 1962 novel, *Another Country*) out of fear for how such censuring might create a reputation unfavorable to downtown development. Mayors like Daley and Christopher instead looked to police to enforce cultural and sexual boundaries in less professionalized fields where officers could take discretionary actions that did not implicate police officials or city leaders.[58]

San Francisco's 1963 election of Democrat Jack Shelley—a traditional liberal who prioritized increased wages and salaries for breadwinning men, not downtown redevelopment, as the key to economic growth—raised the stakes of San Francisco's censorship debates. Unlike Christopher, Shelley was willing to defend the heterosexual, family-oriented standards of citizenship by directly involving himself in the clean-culture movement. For male activists on both sides of the censorship divide, Shelley's participation underlined the importance of electing a chief executive with an appropriate understanding of masculine prerogatives and responsibilities.

Jack Shelley stepped into the mayor's office hoping his tenure would serve as a victory lap to what had been a sparkling political career. A Roman Catholic and native son of the city's Mission District, Shelley had entered politics through the labor movement. During the early 1930s, he had joined the Brotherhood of Teamsters while supporting himself through law school as a bread truck driver, and by 1937 he had become the youngest man ever elected president of the American Federation of Labor's San Francisco Labor Council. One year later San Francisco voters selected Shelley as their sole state senator, and in 1949 the electorate chose him as the city's lone representative in the U.S. House of Representatives. He went on to score seven lopsided reelections to that office.[59]

A veteran of the Catholic Action movement, Shelley campaigned for mayor as a defender of the "general public welfare." He shared Mayor Christopher's belief that City Hall served the common good when it maintained traditional family values, but he regarded the managerial growth agenda as an elite power grab that threatened those mores. Shelley charged that his conservative opponent, Harold Dobbs of the San Francisco Board of Supervisors, "destroyed neighborhood values" when he coddled "fast buck real estate speculators and the wealthy downtown interests" and pursued "high-rise apartments" and waterfront freeways.[60]

In early 1964 the newly elected Mayor Shelley excited local clean-culture advocates with the assurance that he shared their concerns and would "do everything possible to curtail and eliminate obscenity in every form."[61] Shelley began making good on that vow later that year when he appointed John J. Ferdon, president of the Board of Supervisors, to the city's open district attorney position. (Governor Edmund "Pat" Brown had tapped District Attorney Lynch to fill the state's vacant attorney general post.) A devout Catholic, traditional liberal, and faculty member at the University of San Francisco Law School, Ferdon had crafted an urbane intellectual persona. He advertised his membership in the Bohemian Club, a local elite, all-male organization with artistic pretensions, and in 1964 one liberal reporter approvingly noted that Ferdon was reading a book on nineteenth-century French bohemians and had worked for "liberal candidates and causes." However, Ferdon's support for labor rights and civil rights stemmed from his desire to reinforce the power of male breadwinners, and Shelley was thus confident that the prosecutor would "keep San Francisco as it is" on matters of gender and sexuality.[62]

Clean-culture activists first forced Mayor Shelley and District Attorney Ferdon to prove their commitment to a single citywide clean-culture standard when they commandeered a North Beach neighborhood campaign charging inadequate policing. During the early 1960s, North Beach boosters grew increasingly angry over the temporary absence of a police station in their neighborhood. In 1961 the SFPD had closed the shared Hall of Justice and Central Station building in North Beach, transferring the Hall of Justice into new quarters in the South of Market neighborhood and establishing a short-term Central Station in the Marina District. City leaders promised North Beach residents that they would quickly construct a new, permanent North Beach home for Central Station, but over the next three years, the city failed to raise the funds, develop the plans, or even choose a location for the new building. As the city dawdled, North Beach boosters complained that their neighborhood was being overrun by panhandling, burglaries, street fights, obscene language, and some unmentionable activity in Washington Square Park (presumably gay male encounters).[63]

This neighborhood street-cleanup campaign emerged during a period of economic transition for North Beach. The neighborhood's upper Grant Avenue commercial beat scene had fallen into decline, and neon-lit nightclubs were appearing along Broadway Street. The Broadway commercial strip contained slightly fewer bars than in the past, but the establishments in earlier years had been, in the words of one state liquor agent, "little places run by Italians. . . . nothing quite like the scale we have now." Continued expansion of the city's downtown business sector spurred this commercial transformation. On weekdays male professionals from financial and advertising firms walked the short distance to Broadway for their lunch breaks and after-work drinks. In their competition for these patrons, Broadway Street club owners turned to sexually explicit entertainment. On June 16, 1964, the Condor Club set off a new craze when its featured dancer, Carol Doda, climbed atop a white baby grand piano and performed the swim in a topless bathing suit. Doda later used silicone injections to expand both her breasts and her popularity, and other Broadway clubs began offering their own panoply of semi-nude and fully nude entertainment. The sexually explicit entertainment quickly lured crowds of tourists on the weekends.[64]

Initially the North Beach boosters did not draw a link between the Broadway nightclubs and the street crime they feared. Central Station captain Charles Barca similarly expressed little concern over the new direction in Broadway Street entertainment. The chastening defeat of Central Station in the Vorpal Gallery trial and reports that Barca both patronized topless clubs and collected payoffs from them may help explain the captain's muted reaction. Police professionalization politics, however, brought Broadway Street to the mainstream's attention.[65]

In November 1964 club owners began organizing against what the *Examiner* obliquely described as police "oversight." Barca responded by issuing a public "suggestion": by Christmas Eve the North Beach clubs were to cover their performers with pasties, net, or mesh. The captain attached to this order a public reassurance that he intended to tame, not eliminate, the Broadway Street establishments. After all, he reasoned, in addition to drawing "undesirable elements" to the neighborhood, the clubs brought in a "wealthy set" with presumably healthy attitudes toward sex. "They attract anybody who likes a little action now and then," Barca rationalized, "and who doesn't?"[66]

Barca's threatening "suggestion" boomeranged horribly. Chief Cahill and Mayor Shelley mildly rebuked the captain for committing the cardinal sin in police professionalization—exerting district station authority over a so-called vice activity. The fact that club owners felt a need to organize against the police in the first place raised questions about whether the captain was already meddling in territory belonging to others. In addition to riling Cahill and Shelley, Barca's pasties command caught the attention of clean-government advocates in the press. In the early spring, Dick Hyer, a longtime clean-government proponent and reporter for the *Examiner,* penned a scathing exposé on the rise of narcotics sales and commercial sex in North Beach. The article presented the large topless clubs as "reputable" because they employed unionized workers, but inveighed against the "dubious" smaller, down-market bars that employed nonunionized servers and acted as dens of prostitution. Hyer left it to the reader to determine why the police department would allow this arrangement to persist, understanding that most politically savvy San Franciscans would recognize these telltale signs of corruption. The hints of police payola roused an immediate response from Shelley. "If the Police Department can't clear up this situation," he announced, "then I'll get a new chief and a new commission."[67]

The growing North Beach controversy spun around issues of sexuality and possible graft, but the episode did not play out as another gayola scandal. The Christopher administration's fealty to downtown interests had spurred the 1960 crackdown on police payoffs, but Shelley followed his traditional liberal commitment to the male breadwinner into an alliance with clean-culture activists. Father Lawrence Byrne, a Catholic priest and director of the Salesian Boys' Club at Saints Peter and Paul Church in North Beach, recognized that Mayor Shelley's involvement in the North Beach cleanup afforded an opportunity to extend Catholic principles, and he suddenly advanced himself as a leader of the North Beach neighborhood movement. A North Beach resident, Byrne had not been a prominent figure in the neighborhood's campaign against street crime, but in March 1965 he arranged meetings between local boosters and the mayor, insisted that the alleged surge in street crime stemmed from topless dancing, and urged Shelley to ban topless entertainment.[68]

The existing North Beach street-cleanup campaign gave Father Byrne access to rhetoric unavailable in earlier debates over censorship. By pointing to the danger of North Beach street violence, Byrne hoped to downplay his religious motivations, parry harm-principle critiques, and position himself as a defender of male breadwinners. Byrne insisted that he represented "working men, fathers of families, those who are known as 'regular guys' and popular in the district." The Broadway Street hoodlums, Byrne continued, humiliated these men by accosting their families and insulting their wives. "Men come to me," Byrne lamented, "and say they are afraid to go home at night."[69]

Censorship proponents' secular, masculine rhetoric soon attracted the culturally conservative *San Francisco Examiner* to the campaign against topless dancing, and on April 22, 1965, mounting political pressure motivated Mayor Shelley to take action. With District Attorney Ferdon prepared to prosecute any topless cases, Shelley ordered the SFPD to raid the Broadway clubs. The department timed the busts so Shelley could announce them during a speech to privileged Catholics at the University of San Francisco alumni banquet.[70]

The following morning cosmopolitan liberals responded with their own masculine posturing. The *Chronicle*'s editorial page ridiculed the *Examiner*'s pro-crackdown staff as "infuriated, frustrated, out-of-State migratory journalists" prone to "outbursts of journalistic puberty." The *Chronicle* then needled Mayor Shelley for submitting to the *Examiner*'s "ungentlemanly . . . pressure" and serving as the paper's "whipping boy." *Chronicle* reporters, meanwhile, attempted to elicit public sympathy by describing the arrested female dancers as passive, weeping, and fearful victims.[71]

Men dominated the initial cosmopolitan liberal critique, but female dancers began working their perspectives into the opposition. Dancers defied the ban and confronted the police, and cosmopolitan liberal reporters began recognizing that they could further impugn the masculinity of the censors by conveying these female perspectives. Five days after the initial bust, for instance, Doda ambushed Mayor Shelley at a North Beach luncheon to request an audience. Shelley hoped to avoid a confrontation in front of the media cameras, and he therefore rushed out onto the sidewalk and toward his car as Doda "trotted" along behind him. The next day local newspapers ran the headline "Mayor Eludes a 'Topless' Pursuer" and treated San Franciscans to an image of the leader of the eleventh largest city in America narrowly escaping "a girl with a complaint."[72]

As the women went to court, the topless clubs' lawyers turned the controversy toward questions of women's rights. Male liberals had long advocated for the male right to view female sexuality, but now the defense lawyers argued that women had a "civil right" to express their sexuality to men. Two brief trials in cases against topless clubs resulted in two directed not-guilty verdicts. Judge Leland Lazarus determined that topless dancing did not violate local

FIGURE 10. Police arrest an unidentified topless dancer from the Off Broadway nightclub. April 23, 1965. (Reprinted with permission, Bancroft Library, BANC PIC 1959.010—NEG PT III 04-23-65.7: 5.)

community standards, and Judge Lawrence Friedman argued that the bust violated the city's pluralist arrangement. Either "a public relations man whose contacts are city wide" or "social service workers who know what people think and feel throughout San Francisco," the judge ruled, could speak to community standards. But the raiding police officers, the judge intimated, were too isolated to grasp the social value the dancing held for all of the city's residents. A broader understanding of the city's interests, Friedman concluded, revealed that the women were presenting their topless performances as "theatrical" productions. Friedman's ruling established a local precedent granting women the right to artistically express their sexuality for the benefit of men.[73]

THE *LOVE BOOK* AND THE ART CENSORS' LAST GASP

Following the not-guilty verdicts in the topless club trials, many of the North Beach neighborhood boosters who had accepted anti-obscenity politicking as a strategy to increase police presence in the neighborhood disowned the topless issue. "We asked for more protection and not a crusade against nudity or anything else," the editor of the *Little City News* complained. The city's Catholic censorship proponents, on the other hand, emerged from the North Beach topless controversy more committed than ever to their fight against sexually explicit speech. A group of conservative Sunset District residents formed the Citizens for Law and Order, and as representatives of "the real San Francisco," they called on Mayor Shelley to sustain the city's anti-obscenity policing. These activists recognized that Shelley had proved himself a loyal partner in their clean-culture campaign.[74]

Shelley's administration, Cahill's command staff, and the Catholic Church's leadership responded to these community calls with a synchronized drive against sexually explicit speech. Early in 1966 Chief Cahill reorganized his Juvenile Bureau for a more aggressive assault by replacing retiring Captain Hanrahan with Lieutenant Daniel Quinlan. A devout Catholic, the forty-four-year-old Quinlan promised not to take a "tough cop" approach toward the city's youth, but the lieutenant vowed to defend traditional family values with vigorous prosecutions of pornography purveyors. He immediately created a full-time obscenity position within the bureau and assigned the post to Inspector Maloney, who was a graduate of the University of San Francisco and had a long history of busting smut dealers.[75] Bishop Joseph T. McGucken, meanwhile, urged a conference of area Catholic men to "put every judge on notice that people are against pornography." Four days after McGucken's pronouncement, and presumably in coordination with his call to arms, San Francisco's grand jury published an alarmist report warning of a "diabolical" local smut racket. The grand jury prescribed an SFPD crackdown on the homosexual and sadomasochistic literature circulating in the city, along with an education campaign designed to "thrust upon the conscience" of San Franciscans the dangers posed by pornography.[76]

On November 15, one week after a statewide procensorship proposition went down to defeat, Maloney and several other officers turned their campaign toward the city's avant-garde when they purchased a copy of Kandel's *The Love Book* from the Psychedelic Shop. The 825-word book of poetry's fusion of sexual and religious rhetoric appalled the clean-culture Catholics. Police arrested the Psychedelic Shop's co-owners, Cohen and Ron Thelin, for distribution of obscenity, and forty-eight hours later, Maloney and Weiner jailed Ron Muszalski for defiantly selling the poem at City Lights Bookstore.[77]

Although the city's professionalization of obscenity policing placed responsibility for *The Love Book* crackdown in the hands of the Juvenile Bureau and the district attorney, Mayor Shelley dove headlong into the controversy. Shelley had offered a tentative defense of topless-club arrests the year before (referring to the initial arrests as "test" cases), but this time around the mayor confidently condemned Kandel's poem as "hard core pornography." Insisting that the city maintain a single commercial cultural standard for the sake of families, the mayor pronounced, "I don't think this thing should be on sale where young kids can get hold of it."[78] The Supreme Court had long since dismissed the child protection rationale as a legal justification for censorship, but Shelley hoped that invocations of family values remained good politics.

As *The Love Book* trial got underway, Assistant District Attorney Frank Shaw, a talented attorney and devout Catholic, prosecuted the case by reasserting a traditional and homogenous vision of the city's cultural and sexual values. The prosecutor defined these standards around Catholic norms. Rather than condemning *The Love Book* for its coarse language, Shaw charged Kandel's work with attempting "to condition [San Francisco] into a new type of morality." He rejected a pluralist understanding of the city's interests as he questioned his first witness, columnist Val King. Together, Shaw and King attempted to resuscitate the roles of the "average person" and "community standards" in determining the city's cultural and sexual boundaries. The duo defined community standards around the locality of San Francisco (a narrow definition of community standards that the Supreme Court had rejected three years earlier in *Jacobellis v. Ohio*) and posited Catholicism as the primary prerequisite for expertise on the city's average persons. Shaw established King's knowledge of community standards by introducing him to the court not only as a former City Hall official, but also as a columnist for a Catholic newspaper, the host of a weekly Catholic television show, and a onetime teacher at a Catholic High School. King then testified that *The Love Book*'s blend of religion and sex violated community standards through its blasphemy.[79]

Marshall Krause, the ACLU staff attorney, and Vasilious Choulos, a private lawyer who hailed from the Mission District and frequently assisted Krause in free speech trials, defended Cohen, Thelin, and Muszalski by arguing that because the "average person" did not read poetry, average people should not be allowed to judge the social importance of *The Love Book*. But the magistrate hearing the case, Judge Lawrence Mana, was a moderate, cautious jurist who ultimately supported Shaw's efforts to reassert a homogenous understanding of the city's cultural and sexual interests. A former president of the Salesian Boys' Club, Mana also accepted the prosecutor's attempt to define those uniform values around traditional Catholic mores. Shaw thus called to the stand a string of Catholic figures who agreed that only medical professionals—"doctors . . . psychiatrists, nurses"—should publicly speak on female sexual perspectives.[80]

Mana's decision to drift so far from the judicial mainstream ensured that the jury's eventual guilty verdict would fail to withstand appeal. But because Mana allowed Shaw to transform the case into a local referendum on cultural and sexual pluralism, the three-week-long trial—the longest criminal hearing in San Francisco municipal court history—provided cultural conservatives and cosmopolitan liberals with one more opportunity to publicly debate over the cultural and sexual makeup of the citizenry.[81]

Shaw's prosecution of *The Love Book* warned that sexually explicit poetry threatened the rights of family men. "We are presently witnessing," Shaw inveighed, "a massive assault on human privacy." This "assault," the prosecutor continued, undermined the authority of husbands and fathers. Just as Father Byrne had charged that topless clubs overwhelmed North Beach fathers' ability to protect their wives and children on the street, Shaw argued that because *The Love Book* was a book of verse by a woman for women it subverted the husband's control over the sexual boundaries of his family. Dirty words in the mouths and ears of women were particularly scurrilous because the language could encourage wives to introduce sinful sexual acts and perspectives, including a homosexual viewpoint, into their husbands' bedrooms.[82]

The defense introduced one scholar to counter that the poem had social importance for academics, but Judge Mana's acceptance of the "average person" standard enabled Shaw to discredit this witness as lacking enough "contact with the average man" to issue an opinion on community standards. Krause and Choulos were thus forced to show how the new female power seemingly represented by *The Love Book* served the broader community. The lawyers took a birdshot approach, pointing to a whole range of San Franciscans who might benefit from Kandel's poetry. For instance, James M. Stubblebine, the chief of San Francisco's Mental Health Services, provided some of the trial's most attention-grabbing testimony when he insisted that high school students should read *The Love Book* in order to reduce "repression" and develop healthier attitudes toward sex. This argument reversed earlier defense strategies by admitting that the poetry produced sexual desire. Krause now insisted that *The Love Book*'s stimulating elements were a good in themselves. Shaw, in return, argued against *The Love Book*'s sexual potential, asking why, after a recent protest reading on a college campus, hundreds of students did not rush into bed together.[83]

Most of the defense's case, however, revolved around the "special value" *The Love Book* had for female readers as an "expression about sex from a woman's point of view." As the defense team well understood, Kandel believed that in both her professional and private lives she served society by exploring "What's a man, what's a woman?" Her investigation into these issues had sent Kandel crashing through barriers traditionally imposed against women in their professional and private lives. In 1960 she had arrived in San Francisco searching for the city's poetry scene, and Eric Nord, the North Beach impresario, had pointed her to the East-West House, a commune of beat poets inspired by Zen and Buddhist theologies, as well as an institution with sharp gender role divisions. Describing her relationship with Lew Welch, a central figure in the commune, Kandel recalled:

> In the beginning he had a vision that all the women folks would go off here and discuss all these feminine magicals, and all the men folks sit over here. And there were times when he'd get disturbed that I was talking with his poet friends instead of over with the women folk. He said, 'Why don't you want to be off talking about makeup and stuff rather than be in here talking about poetry?' I told him that poetry was what was interesting me.[84]

Kandel's self-confidence, unflappable demeanor, and formidable intelligence ultimately enabled her to fight through this sort of prejudice and to develop a professional reputation as a leading Bay Area poet.[85]

As Kandel sought to redefine women's opportunities in the professional arts, she also attempted to step outside women's traditional roles in private relations. Kandel married William Fritsch, a hippie, and the two gained notoriety within the local counterculture for their sexually impassioned relationship. Peter Coyote, an actor and member of their creative circle, remembered, "Their bed filled almost a whole room and was an epicurean marvel. Both sides were lined with boxes of cookies: Oreos, pecan sandies, and various whipped-cream and chocolate confections. There were dirty books, scented oils, and things to drink. It was a bed you could live in for days, and they often did." Kandel believed that her eroticized marriage enabled her to "worship" the holiness of herself and her husband.[86]

Kandel saw the gender-role boundary crossings in her professional and personal lives as a single project, but outsiders had little trouble divorcing her real-world challenges to male professional privilege from her poetic hymns to female sexual desire. Doing so transformed Kandel's work into a fulfillment of heterosexual male fantasies. *The Love Book* defense team defended Kandel's perspective by emphasizing its benefits to male interests. Its "expression about sex from a woman's point of view," the defense claimed, taught wives how to express their erotic love for their husbands. A marriage counselor testifying for the defense stated that women were often reticent to talk about sex and that they communicated their desires "indirectly by burning the food." (When Shaw incredulously asked why wives couldn't simply tell their husbands, "I want to make love," the counselor responded, "I think this lacks clarity.") The defense lawyers endeavored to show that *The Love Book* could create more exciting heterosexual marriages for the city's modern, self-assured husbands by providing women with the speech rights traditionally reserved for men.[87]

Krause and Choulos not only addressed the heterosexual population at large with their emphasis on erotic marriages, but also sought to hamstring the city's clean-culture movement through a redefinition of Catholic mores. The two attorneys called on a Catholic wife and a local priest to testify that cultural and sexual pluralism were consistent with Catholic morality. Margaret Krebs, the twenty-nine-year-old program chair of the Catholic Professional Women's Guild, a member of the Catholic Art Forum, and a lecturer on sex and art for priests in training, comfortably rooted her reading of *The Love Book* in her heterosexual marriage. Her husband had given her *The Love Book,* she explained, and she had found it to be "a beautiful statement of a woman's point of view" on heterosexual sex. The defense then brought to the stand Father Joseph Brophy. A new professor at the University of San Francisco, Brophy had caught the attention of Krause when he criticized the SFPD's Psychedelic Shop bust as an act of police repression in his university's newspaper. In court Brophy insisted that he testified as an "academician" and not a religious figure. But for Krause and cosmopolitan liberals in the press, Brophy's testimony was important as evidence of dissension within the Catholic establishment's ranks.[88]

On May 26 the jurors found *The Love Book* obscene and convicted the three *Love Book* sellers. Reporting that they had been split on whether Kandel's poems were "substantially beyond the customary limits of candor," the twelve jurors (ten women and two men) were "unanimous from the start" in rejecting the notion that a woman's point of view on sex held "social importance." On a quick appeal, however, Krause and Choulos used Judge Mana's decision to permit discussions of sacrilege to win a reversal.[89]

The defense also scored successes outside the courtroom. On the one hand, the episode enabled male poets and cosmopolitan liberal journalists to mock the censoring police as "children." More important, the trial reinforced the

institutional backing that academics, bookstore owners, and lawyers were prepared to provide for censored art. Shortly after the busts, local professors and
booksellers organized protest readings of *The Love Book,* and after the trial the
city's Barristers Group, a young lawyers organization within the San Francisco
Bar Association, invited Kandel to speak at a meeting. Krause remembered,
"We had never had such a huge crowd before. I mean . . . every square inch of
the place was completely filled with lawyers who wanted to come and see and
hear Lenore Kandel." This interest translated into legal aid: following the *Love
Book* case, a much wider body of San Francisco attorneys stood poised to serve
those accused of creating or selling obscene materials.[90] White female artists
therefore emerged from *The Love Book* trial with the power to communicate
erotically to the city's men and women.

MAYOR JOSEPH ALIOTO AND CULTURAL AND SEXUAL PLURALISM IN CITY HALL

Through the mid-1960s, censorship opponents asserted that young white-
collar men appreciated having access to sexually explicit art, and they attacked
Shelley's manliness when he used the SFPD's centralized obscenity policing
to threaten this growth-associated cultural expression. By the end of Shelley's
first term, downtown elites were impugning the mayor's manliness over his
failure to promote the growth economy itself.

Shelley repeatedly vacillated on questions of development. The mayor
blocked the construction of a controversial North Beach garage and initially
opposed removal of black residents from the Fillmore District. Later in his
term, however, Shelley reversed himself and threw his support behind Fillmore redevelopment while also advocating for a cross-city freeway. Neighborhood activists defeated the freeway project, and redevelopment stalled when
Shelley failed to win public support for two growth-oriented bonds on the
1966 ballot.[91]

Downtown growth advocates watching this political mess began pining
for the days of Mayor Christopher and business-led planning groups like the
Blyth-Zellerbach Committee. "What is actually missing in San Francisco today," one downtown growth proponent grumbled, "are those wonderful, awesome, elusive qualities of leaders of men—vitality, perceptiveness and guts."
The mainstream press, meanwhile, began to portray Shelley as "tired" and
"old." "No Mayor since the City Charter was enacted in 1932," one cosmopolitan liberal reporter charged, "has been delivered so much raw political control
of City Hall through his appointive powers. But Shelley, unaccustomed to

the executive attitude, has used it very little, and at times, ineptly, to help him achieve administrative goals."[92]

Heading into the November 1967 election, Shelley's reputation was in tatters. Shelley again faced San Francisco Supervisor Harold Dobbs, a law-and-order Republican and supporter of downtown growth, and in one July poll, the Republican had stretched out a twenty-point lead. Among Democrats, Dobbs trailed Shelley by only two points over all, and in predominantly white, middle-class neighborhoods like the Sunset District, Dobbs actually led Shelley among Democrats. Three months before the election, Shelley cemented his wizened image by being hospitalized for exhaustion. The incumbent decided to withdraw from the race, and attorney Joseph Alioto and Supervisor Jack Morrison jumped in to fill the Democratic void.[93] In the three-month, three-candidate race, Morrison forwarded himself as an opponent of downtown interests, Dobbs continued campaigning for law and order, and Alioto seized the cosmopolitan liberal banner.[94]

The son of a North Beach immigrant who made his living by fishing, Alioto had made a small fortune as an antitrust lawyer during the 1930s and 1940s. The 1967 mayoral race was Alioto's first campaign for public office, but the candidate entered the contest well known among political insiders. Since the early 1950s, Alioto had served as a member of the school board, as director of the San Francisco Redevelopment Agency, and as a campaign advisor to George Christopher. Alioto was also a friend of major redevelopment advocates like hotelier Ben Swig, and from the start of the shortened campaign, the press understood the "millionaire lawyer" to be a stronger "downtown candidate" than Shelley.[95]

Alioto ultimately cruised to a 16,332-vote victory by sweeping the city's middle- and working-class districts. Early in his campaign, he had picked up the endorsements of both the San Francisco Labor Council and the International Warehouse and Longshoreman's Union, having promised unions a role in and benefits from future redevelopment projects. This labor support had neutralized Morrison's advantage among liberal constituencies and had allowed Alioto to ignore Morrison and treat the race as a two-candidate contest with Dobbs. Both Alioto and Dobbs were wealthy attorneys, both spoke of themselves in the third person even in private conversation, both promised voters tax relief, and both vowed to pursue downtown growth policies. Alioto, however, sharply differentiated himself from Dobbs by adopting a cosmopolitan liberal approach to the citizenry.[96]

Dobbs, in addition to being a colorless candidate, stressed the importance of enforcing traditional family values and racial boundaries.[97] Alioto, by contrast, conceived of a citizenry in which the individual, rather than the family, served as the primary unit. Later, as mayor, Alioto spoke in a language evocative to young single professionals when he characterized the city as a place of "abrasive anonymity," where "the individual stands exposed to so many crosswinds of uncertainty, unshielded by the compactness and closeness of the big family or the small town." Alioto celebrated the fact that this environment fostered pluralist debate and thus made cities "the frontier of this greater democracy." During his campaign, Alioto cultivated his cosmopolitan liberal posture by hiring some of the young journalists who had been crafting the liberal ideology for the previous decade. Hadley Roff and Wes Willoughby, two former *San Francisco News* reporters who had written on the discretionary policing of the North Beach beats, worked the communications division of Alioto's campaign, and Roff then took over as the mayor's confidential secretary at the start of Alioto's first term.[98]

San Francisco's cosmopolitan liberals had effected a political realignment around new notions of citizenship, and when Alioto took the mayor's office, he needed to create a system of governance that would serve that citizenry. He proposed restructuring democracy around a deliberative democratic arrangement that promoted pluralist debate so long as it took place within formal political channels leading to the mayor's office. Rejecting Mayor Christopher's conception of government as an instrument that must "never degrade the spirit of unity," Alioto argued that with City Hall–mediated dialogues between pluralist groups government could become "an ordinance of reason for the '*common good.*'" In an inclusive government, Alioto elaborated, the citizenry's "disquiet" was "not impotent foot-stamping over a lost past," but became "purposeful" and would "bind the city into bold unity." Alioto fashioned his deliberative democratic message with the assumption that San Franciscans would discover a common interest in eradicating blight and reducing crime.[99] Through his mayor-oriented and redevelopment-directed governing strategies, Alioto introduced cosmopolitan growth liberalism into City Hall.

This cosmopolitan growth politics, Alioto insisted, required a leader with the mettle to draw together the city's competing perspectives into government-brokered dialogues. Alioto's emphasis on diving into fraught conflicts to reach consensus allowed the mayor to integrate the Catholic Action and vital liberal traditions. As William Issel has documented, Alioto established himself as a "leading light" of the local Catholic Action movement during the 1930s. Like earlier Catholic Action policy makers, Alioto personally maintained conservative attitudes on issues of sexuality. "I'm no more in favor of homosexuality," he assured the public, "than of opium smoking." But Alioto's primary goal was gathering broad-based support for downtown growth, not imposing cultural conformity, and he therefore saw in Catholic Action a model for consensus-building negotiations.[100]

The new mayor insisted that these dialogues required an energized chief executive. Warning about a loss of "vitality" from City Hall, Alioto channeled John F. Kennedy's vital liberal posture by promising to overcome San Francisco's supposed malaise with "a unique band of bright, young trouble-shooters and special assistants."[101] By accepting multiple viewpoints, Alioto vowed, these staff members would develop the "freshest," "boldest, most imaginative" solutions to "electrify all of the city government" and "get San Francisco moving again." Cosmopolitan liberals from the *Chronicle* responded to this rhetoric by extolling the shiny-headed, fifty-two-year-old candidate as a "fresh and vigorous," "dynamic," "energetic," "flamboyant," "new man" with "a new style of leadership." Indeed, supportive reporters championed Alioto as the most vital of all City Hall officials. In a feature titled, "The Busy Day of A Go-Go Mayor," a *Chronicle* writer swooned: Alioto "is a man in a hurry and very much accustomed to a frenetic pace which often leaves his staff people—and an occasional reporter—gasping for breath."[102]

Alioto first formulated his cosmopolitan growth liberalism and sold it to the public through discussions of policing and the harm principle. In an interview with Charles McCabe, a journalist who a decade earlier had patronized bohemian bars and romanticized beat gender transgressions, Alioto reported that he had traveled to the avant-garde city of Paris shortly after winning the mayoral election. "We in San Francisco have quite a reputation there," Alioto delighted. "We are known for narcotics, and hippies, and demonstrations against almost everything. We are still thought of, in many places, as the outlaw West." The mayor explained that rather than undermining this international repute with law-and-order prescriptions, he planned to craft a cosmopolitan liberal approach to crime. McCabe printed Alioto's proposal in bold type: "I think we have an opportunity to deal creatively with this reputation, by being at least as avant-[garde] on the question of what crime really is, as we are reputed to be in the area of personal behavior."[103]

Alioto promised an avant-garde approach, but his first proposal followed a strategy already in effect at the federal level. In 1967 President Lyndon B. Johnson assembled the Presidential Commission on Obscenity and Pornography, which investigated the laws surrounding the distribution of and—most controversially—the effects of pornography through a social-scientific rather than a moral lens. A year later Mayor Alioto began his first term by appointing community members, including liberal reporters like McCabe, to a City Hall–sponsored crime commission whose mandate was to define "what crime really should be in a modern society." Through negotiations within this commission, Alioto believed, citizens would find their common interest in reducing crimes against person and property. "I would like to see this new Crime Commission . . . do for the United States what the Wolfenden Report did in England," he signaled. "What criminals do to decent people is the relevant consideration." Alioto believed that acceptance of the harm principle would free police to combat "real crime . . . in the streets and elsewhere."[104]

At the federal level, liberals confronting harm-principle issues tied themselves in knots trying to reconcile their governing principles with their understandings of citizenship. The Presidential Commission on Obscenity and Pornography, for instance, took for granted that America's "basic institutions" remained "marriage and family." However, the commission also argued that commitments to empirical evidence and civil liberties necessitated a complete decriminalization of heterosexually explicit materials. Fearing that the commission's absolutist recommendations would allow material harmful to traditional family values, most Senate Democrats turned on their avowed commitments to individual rights and social-scientific study and rejected the commission's report.[105]

At the municipal level, however, cosmopolitan growth advocates like Mayor Alioto were able to use the promise of economic development to rationalize a middle way between traditional family values and an absolutist tolerance for cultural and sexual pluralism. Alioto repeatedly associated downtown growth with the arts. In his presidential nominating speech at the 1968 Democratic Convention, Alioto declaimed:

> From New York to San Francisco, our challenging cities—teaming, noisy, building—provide the surging pulse beat for our society. They are fountainheads of the creative genius of this nation. They set the new directions in art, music, education, architecture, business and all the other aspirations that give dimension and vitality to civilization.[106]

Alioto's first state-of-the-city address clung to the same themes: "San Francisco is rebuilding her skyline, revitalizing her waterfront, transforming her slums, giving energy to new creativity in music and the arts. In short, she is in the midst of a great renaissance."[107]

In the field of obscenity, opponents of censorship had succeeded in consolidating policing authority over sexually explicit art, and under Alioto the SFPD ceased its pursuit of sexually explicit expressions that young white professionals associated with a safe but exciting culture. Pornographers with connections to the art world were now able to legitimize their works by screening them in film festivals.[108] Purveyors of low-culture smut, on the other hand, received little protection from Alioto, white-collar professionals, and local academics; the ACLU was the only reliable defender of down-market pornography. Indeed, charges for "bringing and distributing obscene matter" skyrocketed under the Alioto administration, with arrests rising from eighteen in 1967 to eighty-nine in 1969.[109] Police also continued using their discretion to censor publications they found culturally or politically offensive by employing charges not related to obscenity. In the fall of 1969, police used a variety of charges, such as "soliciting for funds in public places without the chief of police's approval," to arrest at least forty-seven vendors selling the underground newspapers *Good Times, The Black Panther,* and *The Berkeley Tribe.*[110]

Alioto's avowed enthusiasm for the Wolfenden Report in 1968 placed the mayor and San Francisco at the forefront of a liberal transformation. In other cities with expanding white-collar populations, liberal politicians soon began finding electoral success with similar approaches toward sexually explicit material. In New York City, for instance, the professionalized obscenity policing under Mayor John Lindsay began turning a blind eye toward pornographic films screened in the art scene.[111]

Urban liberals elsewhere also began associating tolerance for limited sexual pluralism with economic growth and tougher law enforcement for violent crime. In Los Angeles liberal candidates for city council and the city attorney's office won elections by offering harm-principle defenses to gay bars that buttressed land values while withholding their support from low-end pornography vendors that depressed real estate prices. Councilor Robert Stevenson emphasized that while Los Angeles police officers were "trying to enforce unenforceable laws," the city had "a great crime problem that is not receiving a sufficient share of attention." Similarly, Mayor Wes Uhlman in Seattle, a Democrat who rose to power with support from a coalition of union members, academics, and feminists, vowed in 1974 that his administration would be "a lot more interested in seeing police officers out on the streets enforcing felony crimes that do have victims" than in watching police "wandering around Volunteer Park looking for gays looking for friends."[112] Like Mayor Alioto, these cosmopolitan liberals argued that a professionalized and tolerant approach toward cultural and sexual pluralism created a safer and more economically vital city.

CONCLUSION

During the 1950s and 1960s, the SFPD applied professionalized policing to sexually explicit speech. This centralized law enforcement ensured that the

SFPD's censorship attempts often implicated city and police leaders. Facing these raised stakes, traditional liberals found themselves in a quandary: their commitment to civil liberties permitted sexually explicit expressions that seemed to undermine their dedication to traditional family values. Republicans pounded Democrats over these contradictions in the suburbs, but in cities liberal politicians had access to the politics of downtown growth. Cosmopolitan liberals invoked the prospect of an expanding economy to rationalize a qualified defense for expanded speech rights. Between the late 1950s and late 1960s, cosmopolitan liberals in the press, local academics, and civil liberties attorneys repeatedly challenged the SFPD's traditional authority over morals and incrementally reduced police authority over sexually explicit expression. In 1968 Mayor Alioto took office with a cosmopolitan-growth liberalism explicitly associating expanded artistic boundaries with downtown development.

Through the debates over the North Beach beats, gay and lesbian bars, and sexually explicit entertainment, cosmopolitan liberals employed the harm principle in defense of cultural and sexual pluralism. In making these cases, cosmopolitan liberals repeatedly associated harmless acts with whites and placed a new emphasis on the citizenry's common interest in reducing violence. The debates over cultural and sexual pluralism thus left unanswered the question of what positive approaches cosmopolitan liberals would take toward harmful crimes and the perspectives of San Francisco's residents of color.

CHAPTER 5

Leader of the Pack: Gangs, Police Neglect, and Racial Pluralism

"Alright then baby, help me!" Orville Luster cried to the young men of Hunters Point. Standing alongside a still-smoldering car, Luster looked out on Third Street, a commercial thoroughfare now glittering with bullet shells and broken glass. Scores of young black men and women raced up and down the street, in and out of stores, hauling armloads of stolen clothes, food, and alcohol. The rioters targeted businesses whose owners lived outside the area or were associated with the San Francisco Police Department. In particular, young people vented their rage against Spotlight Liquors. Its Maltese-American owners, locals charged, often treated patrol officers to drinks, and when officers then exited the store, they were frequently drunk and chippy. Sparing the Vons liquor store directly across the street, the young people stripped Spotlight Liquors bare.[1]

The crowd paused from its looting and arson when Luster rose to speak. Over the clanging of alarm bells, the young black organizer issued a call to action:

> Here's what we'd like to do. We would like to get some fifty people who are serious about protecting the Hunters Point community and also helping this situation. We need fifty people who are willing people to get . . . excuse me mister, excuse me mister, thank you. We need to get fifty people who are willing to get on Third Street to move our children, our young people, and some of your kids on up out of our incident where they may be ki—I've got a wife and two kids who I've got to live for, and I do not want to see some idiot who wants a bottle of wine and some other things to kill me or my kid because they cannot chill![2]

During the Hunters Point uprising of September 28 and 29, 1966, peace-keepers like Luster and the young rioters to whom he appealed were reacting to two styles of unjust discretionary policing typical in low-income neighborhoods of color like Hunters Point. Across the country, one study noted, black city residents regularly protested the petty arrests, "humiliation," and "excessive force" they experienced at the hands of neighborhood police. In San Francisco, a patrol officer had ignited the anger leading to the Hunters Point conflagration when he fatally shot in the back an unarmed black teenager suspected of auto theft. After neighborhood tensions erupted over the incident, police had reverted to the second dominant pattern of Hunters Point law enforcement by removing themselves from the neighborhood and establishing a perimeter designed to contain but not extinguish the violence. This tactical stance mirrored the disproportionate neglect that urban police had long practiced in predominantly black neighborhoods. The 1968 National Advisory Commission on Civil Disorders found that in the nation's impoverished urban black enclaves, the "strength of . . . feelings about hostile police conduct" was "exceeded by the conviction" that residents of color were "not given adequate police protection."[3]

Regardless of what form of policing black residents critiqued, downtown growth advocates and traditional liberals dismissed their protests as illegitimate, race-conscious expressions. Charges of racially discriminatory law enforcement, the city leaders argued, violated the color-blind boundaries of discourse. Following the September 1966 police shooting of the young black suspect, Mayor Jack Shelley rejected the suggestion that the killing was part of a broader pattern of police discrimination, and he refused to meet with a group of young black men from the neighborhood who wished to negotiate policy reforms. Only after the mayor's rebuff did the neighborhood's young rioters take to the streets.

From the corner on Third Street, Luster repeated his stubborn refrain, calling for "fifty people." An audience member identified as "Ray" countered with a more confrontational plan, bellowing back, "We have to go beyond Third Street." "Right on, right on," Luster agreed. "We have to go downtown!" Ray persisted. Some audience members began muttering the epithet "coon" at Luster, but the street worker's prodding yielded results. He ultimately led a small band of young men off Third Street, up "the Hill," and into the district's housing projects. Armed only with megaphones, the men shepherded children indoors and urged the community's young people to cease their rampage.[4]

The back-and-forth between Luster and Ray illustrated the internal struggle among black San Franciscans as they attempted to balance their interest in compensating for police neglect with their desire to battle disproportionate

Conflict within black leaders re: violence

police violence. Ray was not alone in prioritizing the latter issue. Indeed, Mark Comfort, the activist whose audio recording captured this scene, had just returned from Lowndes County, Alabama, where he had picked up the name for a new, aggressive black organization, the Black Panther Party. By forming groups such as the Black Panther Party for Self Defense and the Brown Berets, young urban blacks and Chicanos were soon attempting to check unprofessional policing with armed self-defense.[5]

Luster believed that he too was communicating with downtown through his calls for peacekeeping. In a city where black residents never constituted more than 13 percent of the population, black activists often saw coalition building as a necessity. Luster now hoped to prove to the city's white cosmopolitan liberals that an acceptance of black perspectives could be used to abate violence. He did not, however, attach this call for racial pluralism to an emphasis on police professionalism. Instead, his peacekeeping illustrated how decentralized, community-driven governance could reduce harm. Through his peacekeeping, Luster urged cosmopolitan liberals to recognize the utility of inclusiveness, rather than top-down regulations, as a key to democracy and peace.

BLACK YOUTH AND THE POLICE IN HUNTERS POINT

Extending from the southeastern corner of the city, Hunters Point exhibited a landscape of segregation that often surprised East Coast liberals. The neighborhood was dominated by a large, irregular ridge that residents called the Hill, an elevated area that offered sweeping vistas of the bay and frequently the sunniest weather in San Francisco. Herb Cutchins remembered his reaction when he first arrived in the neighborhood in 1962 to begin his assignment as a neighborhood social worker:

> I had originally worked . . . in the '50s in Chicago on Skid Row. . . . And so when I was first assigned to Hunters Point, and you know, you drove out there for the first time, I was stunned because, you know . . . there were these breathtaking views and the apartments themselves. . . . I mean, I knew the South Side . . . and this bore no resemblance to any kind of poverty that I understood. And it doesn't take long to get convinced that this is poverty and deprivation of the first order. But the first blush is, "Oh, you know, this is really great stuff."[6]

In truth, Hunters Point residents faced the same structural obstacles in housing, employment, and politics confronting people of color throughout postwar urban America. Residents of the Hill, moreover, experienced a physical, social, and political isolation unmatched by any of San Francisco's other major neighborhoods. While downtown growth advocates obsessed over the Fillmore District, a centrally located neighborhood that served as the cultural, political, and professional heart of black San Francisco, City Hall and the mainstream media initially disregarded the outlying Hunters Point.

A residential neighborhood first appeared on the Hill during World War II, when the military built flimsy dormitories for war workers employed at the Hunters Point naval yard and dry docks. At the conclusion of the Korean War, the Navy simultaneously relinquished control over the Hill to the city and reduced its operations at the shipyard. Federal officials thus encumbered San Francisco with an area of declining employment and a fast-deteriorating housing stock.[7]

Like other West Coast governments inheriting deindustrializing shipyard communities, San Francisco's City Hall converted Hunters Point's wartime housing into a public housing ghetto. The city subdivided the shoddy barracks into apartments and then, in 1951, added permanent public housing complexes. By 1961 the San Francisco Housing Authority (SFHA) had concentrated 42 percent of the city's public housing into Hunters Point. In 1952 an NAACP lawsuit eliminated the SFHA's formal program of racial segregation, but the city continued to informally segregate public housing without judicial consequence. This policy, coupled with the discriminatory practices of San Francisco lenders and property owners, created an increasingly black population on the Hill. An integrated, 43 percent black neighborhood in 1950, the Hill was 75 percent black in 1960 and 97 percent black by 1967.[8]

A dearth of manufacturing jobs and the bigotry of local employers and unions produced high unemployment rates and low median incomes on the Hill. In 1960, a recession year, black male unemployment in Hunters Point hit 12.2 percent, as compared to a city average of 6.7 percent. While this rate compared favorably to Detroit's unemployment figures, it matched the black male jobless rate of West Coast cities like Los Angeles. San Francisco's high cost of living, moreover, placed special burdens even on residents who were employed. During the mid-1960s, 60 percent of Hunters Point families lived below the poverty line, compared with a citywide average for white families of 18 percent. Continuing deindustrialization, meanwhile, confronted young people with dimmer job prospects than those of their parents. By the early 1970s, male job seekers under age twenty faced a demoralizing 53 percent unemployment rate in Hunters Point.[9]

The mounting problems in Hunters Point provoked little attention from City Hall. Federal mandates required the World War II–era temporary housing structures to come down in 1970, but city officials failed to develop a plan for what it would do with the residents after the buildings were razed. Conservative supervisors advocated flattening the newer projects as well. Housing project inhabitants thus lived with a stressful uncertainty over whether Hunters Point, or even San Francisco, would remain their home. At the same time, the George Christopher and Jack Shelley administrations rarely applied their clean-government vision to governance in Hunters Point. In 1963 the SFHA's ledgers revealed that the housing agency had failed to account for $9,750,000 in Hunters Point rent. "An avowedly paternalistic Authority," the *Sun-Reporter* charged, "simply does not care—except to line its pockets." The fact that the *New York Times,* rather than a San Francisco newspaper, was the first to report on the glaring discrepancy only highlighted local elites' neglect.[10]

Under these conditions it was not surprising that many residents left Hunters Point at the first opportunity. Every year during the late 1950s and early 1960s, half of the families in the Hill's projects moved out of the temporary sites and a quarter departed from the permanent structures. Often residents left as soon as they secured a steady income and moved to the Bayview or Oceanview District. The common perception among black San Franciscans that Hunters Point was a jumping-off point helped produce a particularly young population. The average age in Bayview–Hunters Point was reported in 1960 as under twenty-six years old, roughly eleven years younger than the rest of the city.[11]

In an economically wanting and residentially fluid neighborhood with few connections to stable sources of power, community leadership proved a difficult undertaking. The handful of middle-class professionals and ministers who presented themselves as community representatives within mainstream politics rarely exhibited any influence over the neighborhood's population. The residents who exerted the greatest pull were often those who could provide their impoverished neighbors with basic necessities. Hazel Rutherford, for instance, enjoyed steady income from her work as a nurse and owned two homes from a previous marriage. Rutherford used these resources to take in youth experiencing trouble with their families or in need of a safe haven from police. Rutherford's house, one young man explained, represented "the bus station of the community." He continued, "The house is open to everybody, just like a church. So she can lay out five [dollars] when you need it, and many times if you come in and stay long enough, you're going to leave to drop five. . . . Momma never had to leave the pad. People would bring her stuff all the time just to be a part of that scene." Through the 1960s the Hill was checkered with adult powerbrokers like Rutherford, exerting their influence as far and as long as their limited resources extended.[12]

The lines of influence between Hunters Point's black male adolescents hung even more tenuously. Following patterns among black adolescents in other deindustrializing cities, some of the Hill's black male teenagers reacted to barriers in employment and residential markets by organizing gangs. The young people called their organizations "jacket clubs," after the jackets they wore bearing their club names and insignias. Each of the city's jacket clubs included an average of fifteen to twenty core male members, and by 1961 social workers estimated that San Francisco was home to more than a thousand gang members. The adolescents in these clubs rarely maintained fixed hierarchies. Gang leaders, in particular, often had to reestablish their authority by distributing goods they acquired through petty theft and by engaging in acts of physical heroism, mainly in fights with other gangs.[13]

Although young men organized their gangs as all-male groups, women played integral roles. The stature of employed mothers could redound to or reinforce the power of their sons. In the late 1950s, for instance, two of Hazel Rutherford's children—Robert and Vernard Rutherford—established themselves as the presidents of Hunters Point's two most powerful gangs, the red-and-yellow-jacketed Sheiks and the green-jacketed Savoys, which were separated by age but allied with each other. Female adolescents, meanwhile, could help protect gang members from the police. Police officers understood youth violence as a male problem and were unlikely to frisk young women. Thus female teenagers often transported male gang members' weapons.[14]

Gang members and police officers maintained predictably contentious relations. In the spring of 1956, an SFPD sergeant got a taste of gang members' antipolice antipathy when he attempted to break up a brawl between a Hunters Point jacket club and an invading Fillmore District gang. The officer threatened to call a police wagon if the youth did not disperse. "That was when the rocks started flying," he later recounted. The two jacket clubs joined together to pelt the police rushing onto the scene, and the SFPD required fifty officers to gain control of the area.[15]

Much of the gang members' hostility toward law enforcement stemmed from unprofessional policing practices. With little oversight and with access to sweeping legal codes such as the nightly curfew, Juvenile Bureau officers working out of the Hall of Justice and patrol officers based in Potrero Station wielded considerable discretion in their dealings with the Hill's residents. The SFPD's command ranks helped ensure that this discretion yielded poor policing by filling Potrero Station with inexperienced rookies and officers who had been punished for transgressions elsewhere in the city. For instance, SFPD leaders gave Sergeant Alfred Cecchi and Patrolman Michael Sugrue disciplinary postings in Potrero Station following their acquittals in the gayola scandal. One patrol-man explained why Potrero officers never feared punishments: "When you're at Potrero, you're at the very bottom of the list. You can't go down any further." Police of all ranks, Chief Richard Hongisto later agreed, regarded the remote, dilapidated Potrero Station as "the anal sphincter of the police department."[16]

The new strategy of aggressive preventive patrol, reflected in programs like Operation S, encouraged police to use their discretion to stop and interrogate residents of predominantly black neighborhoods. In a mid-1960s survey of the Watts neighborhood of Los Angeles, 44 percent of young males reported they had been subjected to "a roust, frisk, or search without good reason." Another study found that when SFPD officers detained Hunters Point youth in these field interrogations, the officers, like urban police elsewhere, frequently disre-garded the "nature and intent of crime" and instead policed youth on the basis of the young people's "attitude . . . towards the idea of the law itself." Local youth recognized these rules of engagement. "If you kiss their ass," one gang member explained, "and say, 'Yes Sir, No Sir,' and all that jazz, then they'll let you go. If you don't say that, then they gonna take you in. And if you say it funny they gonna take you in."[17]

Police in Hunters Point perceived clear patterns in the "attitudes" of the neighborhood's black male adolescents. One officer groused:

They have no regard for the law or for the police. They just don't seem to give a damn. Few of them are interested in school or getting ahead. . . . Furthermore, many of these kids try to run you down. They say the damnedest things to you and they seem to have absolutely no respect for you as an adult. I think I am prejudiced now, but frankly I don't think I was when I began police work.

The tendency for youth in Hunters Point to run from the police especially peeved the area's officers. "Resisting arrest is normal recreation," the newspa-per for the San Francisco Police Officers' Association (POA) complained.[18]

Some police associated the disrespect Hunters Point youth displayed for the law with a more generalized criminal culture. Police occasionally harassed Hunters Point parents over the behavior of their children, and rank-and-file officers expressed fear toward the local population. In 1959, a year with his-torically low murder rates, the POA newspaper's description of Third Street limned horror: the thoroughfare's "brassy bars and cafes" were "constant sources of violence," where "hot heads, steeped with alcohol, explode; knives flash; blood is spilled." Among some officers the sensations of frustration and fear mixed with attitudes of racial hatred. Describing his 1960 assignment to a patrol car on the Hill, Richard Hongisto related his shock over his supervising officer's easy use of the word *nigger*. Indeed, Hongisto remembered that during his first three days in Potrero Station, "I heard, 'Rughead, burrhead, jigaboo, nightfighter, jungle bunny, ape, spear-chucker, mau-mau, cannibal,' and I thought, 'Damn, I joined the Ku Klux Klan by accident.'"[19]

Across urban America, similar brews of police irritation, dread, and bigotry fed a schizophrenic style of law enforcement. In Hunters Point officers spent much of their time using their discretion to abdicate their responsibilities to Housing Authority police, who performed few services beyond helping locked-out residents get back into their apartments—for a five-dollar fee.[20] But on those occasions when Potrero Station police felt compelled to respond to disorder on the Hill, they unleashed disproportionate levels of force. "The Police Department in this neighborhood is lousy," one resident explained in 1965. "A policeman is never seen until he's been called and then it seems like the whole force comes out, with paddy wagons and police dogs." Two years later a black community group in New Haven, Connecticut, expressed parallel concerns. New Haven police, the activists charged, generally responded "too slowly or not at all," but then if they did arrive, they brought "many more men and cars than necessary," "brandishing guns and adding to the confusion."[21]

In Hunters Point the location of the disturbance often influenced police response. Officers expressed fear that residents of the Hill would "turn our city into a jungle," and they proved committed to protecting the upwardly mobile, white working-class residents of Bayview from their black neighbors in Hunters Point. "The animals on the Hill," one sergeant explained, "prey on the property owners" down below. Hunters Point gang members wearing their telltale jackets drew particular attention when crossing neighborhood lines. One Hunters Point gang member explained that the police "don't want us to come out of Hunters Point to tell the truth. Because every time we come out, man, they think we going to fight. But that ain't always true, and it ain't us that always starts the stuff. We on our way home. And they gonna pick us up for fighting."[22]

Rank-and-file police were notorious, by contrast, for their dawdling responses to calls for help from within Hunters Point. Police often showed little concern about acts of violence on the Hill. One youth described the SFPD reaction to brawls outside a community dance in the summer of 1964:

Fights going on, girls screaming, everything. And then this cat pulls out a gun and starts firing. Man, he was five feet away from them cops and they stood there! Just stood looking! Somebody coulda got killed or something. Or maybe they just didn't care. Maybe they was saying, "Why not let them niggers go kill each other anyway. They ain't got no sense."[23]

This reading of police attitudes hit close to the mark. One sergeant explained that police did not apply a "gung-ho type" of law enforcement to police districts like Potrero, because they "accepted the lifestyle of the people."[24]

As residents of poor urban neighborhoods searched for levers with which to reduce the brutality and neglect arising from discretionary policing, they faced politicians who rejected out of hand the notion that the police used discretion in a racially discriminatory manner. Machine politicians and managerial growth advocates alike assumed that SFPD officers, like the rest of the city's citizenry, had evolved beyond race consciousness.[25] In 1949 Mayor Elmer Robinson's police chief explained that the department did "not recognize minority groups as such." Rather than seeing skin color, the SFPD leader continued, police "recognize only two groups of persons in the process of its functions—those who are lawless and those who are law abiding." A decade later, Chief Thomas Cahill was still recycling these claims. When state legislators in 1960 questioned the chief about a black male car owner who had been pulled over on three separate occasions while driving along Market Street, downtown's main arterial road, Cahill replied, "I think if it happened to me, I would say, 'Well, I am out late and at unusual hours of the night and I'm certainly glad to know that the police are around to protect me.'"[26]

City and police officials claimed that charges of police racism introduced new racial divides into the city's otherwise color-blind arrangement. Chief Cahill, for instance, defended the use of "boy" with black adults by referring to his relationship with his own children. Apparently oblivious to the paternalism in his remarks, Cahill related, "I have three sons of my own and there are many times that I will say, 'Listen boy, go to bed. Listen boy, shut off that television.' And I don't feel that I am hurting him in any way or reducing him to any lower standard of citizen." "Don't carry the things that bother you in another area into San Francisco with you," Cahill admonished black migrants to the city, "but accept the life that we have here in San Francisco, which I think is very good." Managerial growth advocates' avowed commitment to color-blind liberalism thus facilitated the continued discretionary policing of Hunters Point.[27]

THE WHITE PRESS AND BLACK CRIME

Through the 1950s the mainstream media paid little attention to Hunters Point, and much of the neighborhood's gang activity took place outside the blinders of the civic sphere. Black—and, to a lesser extent, Latino—youth violence that occurred in more racially integrated and centrally located neighborhoods, by contrast, drew increasing notice from downtown newspapers toward the end of the 1950s. Crime statistics did not drive the white press's expanded coverage of black youth fighting. During the 1950s black men were overrepresented in the city's murder and robbery rates, but those levels of disproportion did not change at the end of the decade. Rather, the city's rates for both murder and robbery remained relatively low and stable. The downtown press's new focus on black youth crime coincided instead with a sharp increase in the city's young black male population. During the latter half of the 1950s, the front end of the city's postwar baby boom generation entered adolescence, and by 1960 young black men constituted 18 percent of the city's males ages fifteen to thirty.[28]

In 1958 the national media began taking notice of disparities in arrest rates for urban blacks. In the article "The Negro Crime Rate," *Time* magazine highlighted San Francisco as one of several cities outside the South struggling with disproportionate levels of black crime. The SFPD's published arrest statistics buttressed this characterization. Occasional reporting discrepancies in San Francisco's homicide rate and low clearance figures for reported robberies make it difficult to assess crime rates for black San Franciscans with accuracy. But from 1951 to 1959, the department's annual reports showed that black people accounted for approximately 44 percent of the city's murder arrests. Over the same period, one-third of all robbery arrests were of black people.[29] The *Time* report attributed "Negro crime" to the frustration black people felt as white discrimination prevented black assimilation into mainstream society. The article turned to San Francisco to make this final damning point. Quoting a black San Francisco deputy city attorney, the article concluded, "Slam enough doors in a man's face and he may break one of them down."[30]

Time's embarrassing national indictment of San Francisco as a city suffering from black crime and white discrimination spurred San Francisco's downtown newspapers to begin their own investigations into "Negro crime." Like the national coverage, local ruminations on race and crime ignored the crime rates of other groups of color and remained fixated on black San Franciscans. In 1959 police officers were openly discussing the language difficulties they faced with Latino residents and charging that the "large Spanish-speaking community" in the Mission District "keep police in that district on the go twentyfour [*sic*] hours a day." University researchers in Berkeley, meanwhile, were beginning to recognize rising tensions between police and Latinos in other cities. Nevertheless, San Francisco's mainstream press did not characterize clashes between white police and Latino residents as evidence of racial conflict until the early 1970s.[31]

Drawing on the pattern set by the *Time* piece and the arguments being made by San Francisco's black middle-class spokespersons, San Francisco's white journalists concurred that mainstream society incited black criminality by failing to "digest" black migrants. Local middle-class black spokespersons noted that while they themselves embraced color-blind liberalism, many of San Francisco's new black migrants had grown up in the Jim Crow South and had come of age viewing the law as an unjust tool of white supremacy. The southern police officer, the local head of the Urban League summarized, "was a white man carrying a club."[32]

Black professionals and white journalists and policy makers all assumed that black migrants from the South were carrying this race-consciousness into San Francisco. "Cheating is no crime among many of these people," one black social worker noted regarding San Francisco's black migrants. "That's a hangover from the South, where in the white man's home you took whatever you could get away with." Traditional liberals and managerial growth proponents expressed concern that the city's migrants would confer their color-conscious hostility to their children. When the average black migrant arrived in San Francisco, one white liberal professed, he "got a tenement room and a common-law wife and a bottle and settled down to pass his defeat on to his children." Juvenile delinquency, Chief Cahill agreed, was rooted in "parental neglect, personal defiance or community inadequacies." Most of the male critiques of black families blamed black mothers for hindering the development of black male breadwinners. Characterizing black mothers as both overbearing and unloving, one black male professional complained that black women's "dominance . . . emasculates" black males, while another black male spokesperson hypothesized that youth turned to gangs because those groups provided the only "affection many . . . know."[33]

White liberals and black professionals concurred that San Francisco's black migrants had developed a disrespect for the law in the South, but the two groups diverged over the role mainstream San Francisco played in sustaining the supposed culture of crime. Black professionals who arrived in San Francisco during World War II followed a political trajectory similar to the black intellectuals who rose to prominence in East Coast cities at the start of the century. Black middle-class activists in both locations and time periods initially highlighted what they considered the cultural deficiencies of black migrants but also asserted that local discrimination—particularly in the employment and housing markets—prevented black migrants from shedding their

4

supposed backward southern ways. Then, continuing along the path set by East Coast black intellectuals after the first Great Migration, San Francisco's postwar black spokespersons responded to the white mainstream's persistent double standard for black and white criminality by dropping the emphasis on cultural deficiency and focusing instead on white bigotry as the prime motivator for black lawbreaking.[34]

San Francisco's postwar white cosmopolitan liberals, by contrast, remained committed to the southern-black-culture argument. White liberals explained away the black population's difficulties in San Francisco's housing and labor markets as further evidence of the migrants' "heritage of prejudice and second class [sic] citizenship." "To many recent arrivals from the agricultural South," one liberal journalist averred, "the city is strange and frightening. It's impersonal, anonymous." This focus on southern culture allowed white locals to transform their laments over the problem of black crime into paeans to San Francisco's growth economy. Unlike "the South's slow-moving agrarian society," one cosmopolitan liberal reporter asserted, San Francisco maintained a "brisk-paced, highly technological economy" that offered "few jobs for the unskilled, and almost none for the back grown strong behind a plow." White journalists insisted that while San Francisco challenged blacks arriving with a damaged southern culture, the city had "given opportunities unequaled in many other parts of the U.S. to the schooled and sophisticated Negro."[35]

In addition to limiting the city's culpability for black crime rates, the white press's emphasis on southern culture allowed downtown newspapers to assume a color-blind posture when discussing black crime. Stereotyped depictions of obedient Asian Americans were also useful for this task. In an article on the "atmosphere of defeat that so often marks the young in the Fillmore," one liberal journalist highlighted a contrast:

It must be noted that the Chinese and Japanese immigrants to San Francisco faced a racial discrimination in the past more formal and rigid than that ever practiced here against the Negro. Why is the crime rate among those groups even lower than the white's [sic]? One reason is that the Oriental came from a far different culture than the Negro. . . . When subjected to discrimination by the white community, [the Chinese-American] had a refuge—pride in his racial heritage. After all, he could tell himself when the whites strove to make him feel inferior, his ancestors were blowing each other up with gunpowder in a civilized fashion while these Caucasians were still running around barbarically sticking each other with spears.

Chinese-Americans could draw pride from their early ability to move beyond a "spear" culture, but "the Negro had no defense." "His ancestors," the article concluded, "were the white man's slaves and his cultural heritage was centuries of oppression."[36]

Despite the white press's repeated gestures toward color-blind liberalism, the newspapers' discussions of community deficiencies often made their environmental and cultural explanations for crime scarcely distinguishable from biologically deterministic explanations of lawbreaking. Unsurprisingly, white reporters occasionally slipped into biological metaphors. In August 1961 the mainstream press issued its very first series on Hunters Point. The opening article speculated, "Perhaps the problem can best be described through the children and the grass. The children grow everywhere, but the grass does not at Hunters Point." Conjuring a narrative of racial invasion, the reporter warned that Hunters Point contained more "weedy and wild" children "per acre" than any other neighborhood in San Francisco.[37]

Local white liberals regarded the black birth rate as "the major ammunition" leading in the direction of an "explosion" because they assumed that black San Franciscans harbored predatory racial perspectives toward whites. Black youth, white officials and reporters stressed, were adopting the hostile racial perspectives of their parents. Hunters Point children "as young as eight, or nine," the *Examiner* warned, had already learned from their elders to "face the white stranger with eyes of suspicion, distrust, or hate."[38]

Because white liberals often identified the black population's supposedly backward, race-conscious culture as the source of antiwhite violence, liberal commentators regarded all untraditional black behaviors suspect. Thus, at the same time that cosmopolitan liberals were using the harm principle to expand the cultural and sexual boundaries of white San Franciscans, both traditional and cosmopolitan liberals continued to point to a "culture of easy violence and easy virtue" in the black community. By rooting black violence in black culture, white cosmopolitan liberals omitted untraditional cultural and sexual activities of African Americans from their harm-principle defenses.[39]

The link white officials and journalists drew between black culture and antiwhite violence made race-conscious politicking and all-black organizations like gangs particularly frightening. In 1961 Hadley Roff, a cosmopolitan liberal reporter, prognosticated that the city's gangs represented "battle lines of future racial warfare." That same year Roff also warned, in two separate series, that Black Muslims were capitalizing on the mainstream's failure to integrate black migrants. Roff stated that the religious group hoped inculcate the black population with a "racist and separatist" ideology bent on rejecting San Francisco's color-blind unity for "an all-Negro nation."[40]

The concern over organized and violent black youth spiked in the summer of 1961 when a gang fight on the Hill introduced many white San Franciscans to Hunters Point. On August 24, 1961, six members of the Magnificent Seven, a newly established Hunters Point jacket club, challenged the Rutherford boys' Sheiks and Savoys. The Magnificent Seven discharged two rifle shots into the air at the neighborhood's hilltop gymnasium and fired two more rounds through the front window of the Rutherfords' home, including one bullet that nearly struck Hazel Rutherford's daughter. Hazel Rutherford called the police, but they were slow to respond, and Robert and Vernard Rutherford's gangs used that lag time to intercept the Magnificents on top of the Hill. After the two sides pummeled and slashed each other with tire irons, bricks, and razors, police finally appeared. Over the next twenty-four hours, authorities arrested thirteen gang members involved in the melee.[41]

The use of the rifle and the targeting of a city-owned gym riveted downtown attention on Hunters Point for the first time. The "unruly youngsters," one columnist noted, "received more coverage in the local press than did the flight of Commander Shepard to outer space." For a week after the fight, policy makers and reporters lit up the front pages with a debate over the appropriate response to the Hill's gang members. The director of the SFHA declared his intention to evict from public housing the families of the arrested youths. Liberal commentators and Mayor Christopher, however, rejected this hard-line approach and reasserted their faith in the mainstream's ability to integrate the youth by technocratically addressing the "root of the problem."[42]

Managerial growth advocates and traditional liberals concurred that color-blind elites should determine the solutions to the Hill's problems. The *Examiner* suggested that gang violence had arisen from the city's naive encouragement of black participation in policy making. On the one hand, the newspaper celebrated the Hunters Point Boys' Club, a private agency that disaggregated black youth through the individualistic sport of boxing. In contrast, the newspaper noted, the Hunters Point Community Recreation Center—the site where the Magnificent Seven issued their challenge—had allowed Hunters Point residents to congregate on their own terms. "Doors open to all is truly democratic and a much exalted goal in our society," the *Examiner* offered. "But at the Hunters Point recreation center it has not worked." The article admonished the city to relinquish this "beautiful dream"; Hunters Point residents, the analysis made clear, could not be trusted to govern themselves.[43]

YOUTH FOR SERVICE

In Chicago and San Francisco, where managerial growth advocates' buoyant promises of technocratic assimilation were belied by the persistence of unjust discretionary policing, small clusters of social workers began experimenting with community-driven responses to youth "delinquency." Postwar social workers drew particular inspiration from the prewar Chicago Area Project (CAP). Devised during the 1920s by sociologists at the University of Chicago, CAP theorized that when migrants arrived in cities they struggled to assimilate into mainstream culture and underwent a period of disorganization that bred delinquency among youths. CAP leaders insisted that they could simultaneously inculcate migrants with mainstream values and rebuild community organization by democratically involving migrants in the design and implementation of their own uplift activities. CAP planners organized their programs around individual migrant neighborhoods, and they attempted to involve as many of the neighborhood's residents as possible by deploying "street workers" who identified and worked through "natural" neighborhood leaders. Among youth, CAP workers pointed to gang leaders as the adolescents with natural authority.[44]

During the late 1950s, Chicago and San Francisco social workers began initiating new CAP-style organizing programs. In San Francisco Carl May, a thirty-six-year-old former amateur boxer and a recent Quaker convert, formed Youth for Service (YFS) in November 1957 with financial backing from the American Friends Service Committee. YFS followed CAP's precedent by reaching out to San Francisco's low-income adolescents and young adults through gang leaders on the street. But May's program introduced two novel wrinkles. First, YFS involved low-income residents in volunteer service projects such as painting houses or tending gardens for poor and elderly people. Second, YFS operated as a citywide agency and used its service projects to mix together young people from different neighborhoods.[45]

By accepting gang structures and encouraging young men to cross neighborhood lines, YFS ran afoul of the SFPD's avowed interests and actual policies. In 1961 Chief Cahill pronounced that he had "always been opposed to the Friends' Youth for Service operation" because the agency's tolerance of racially homogenous gang structures flew in the face of color-blind liberalism. "They organize different groups with different names and this makes for trouble," Cahill warned. "We should not have separate clubs or club rivalries. We should have togetherness." Juvenile Bureau captain William Hanra-

FIGURE 11. Youth for Service leaders and participants pose at a meeting that brought together forty San Francisco jacket club presidents. At this confab, gang leaders tentatively agreed to bring future "beefs" to Youth for Service's Peace Council. The journalist covering this meeting reported that because Youth for Service founder Carl May "talks the language of the juveniles," "even the toughest of them treat him as an equal." Standing in the rear are (left to right) William Randle, 26, of the San Francisco Gents; Orville Luster, the soon-to-be Youth for Service secretary; Roy Wilson, 16, of the Warlords; and Emile Conner, a Youth for Service street worker. Seated are (left to right) Carl May, the Youth for Service secretary; Al "Moose" Heicke, 20, of the Geneva–Mission District gang; and Percy Pinkney, 21, leader of the Fillmore-based Aces. September 4, 1959. (Reprinted with permission, Bancroft Library, BANC PIC 1959.010—NEG PT III 09–04–59.12.)

han, meanwhile, noted that YFS frustrated the SFPD's practice of ghettoizing low-income youth. "Interclub rivalry," Hanrahan insisted, "can only be stopped if these gangs of hoodlums are confined to their own neighborhoods."[46]

Despite police predictions that YFS's gang-tolerant, cross-neighborhood approach would devolve into bloodshed, May and local gang leaders quickly realized that they could employ this arrangement in the service of peace. In the fall of 1958, the YFS founder began interceding in jacket club confrontations and working to convince the leaders of these gangs to negotiate truces. This cross-neighborhood brokering captured the imagination of gang leaders, and YFS's new peacekeeping work sparked a surge in youth participation.[47]

May's peacekeeping also enthralled young liberal journalists. In YFS's negotiation efforts, reporters saw both an effective violence-prevention project and great news copy.[48] When one journalist joined May out on the streets for an evening of peacekeeping, his subsequent report combined the narrative styles of a pulp thriller and a Western. "Darkness overpowered the feeble street lamps," the article opened, ". . . as if to hide what was about to happen." The Warlords and Los Bandidos, gangs with thirty to forty members each, were gathering in the Bernal Heights Playground for "a slugfest that would shatter the evening quiet of the neighborhood." But then a "lone man"—Carl May—"got out of [an] auto and walked onto the playground." The YFS leader, "a wiry package of nerve and nerves," bravely strode between the two clubs and asked, "What do you men want to fight for?" "Precisely in the right tone of voice," May then talked the two groups down and brokered a peaceful settlement.[49]

Cosmopolitan liberals endorsed YFS's involvement of young adults in violence prevention because the liberals were beginning to recognize the hypocrisy of the SFPD's discretionary policing regime. For instance, in the same 1961 series in which Roff warned of the Black Muslims' recruiting drives among black residents, the young liberal journalist also reported that putatively colorblind police were detaining black youth with petty vagrancy charges and assaulting jacket club members "in station-house backrooms." Roff suggested the consequences of this race-conscious law enforcement when he included a nineteen-year-old black man's roguish threat: "Too much harassment and a guy could feel: 'If you are going to get busted, why not make it big?'"[50]

Roff contrasted the racial politicking of the Black Muslims and the bigoted law enforcement of local police with the "bold" approach taken by YFS. He believed that although Black Muslims and the police prodded black consciousness toward violence, YFS used the youth's race-conscious gang structure productively. By accepting gang members on their own terms, Roff predicted, YFS would ultimately be able to break down the subculture and "guide individual club members" into the color-blind mainstream.[51]

GRASSROOTS PEACEKEEPING
AND BLACK CIVIC LEGITIMACY

During the early 1960s, a change in leadership and a massive infusion of outside money moved YFS to the forefront of Hunters Point politics. Carl May left the organization in the early fall of 1959, and on October 1 the American Friends Service Committee replaced him with Orville Luster, a young black social worker. Luster had previously made a name for himself in local delinquency prevention circles as the first black supervisor at San Francisco's detention center for male delinquent youth. There Luster had won the respect and trust of many of the detention center's young people with his strictness and physical stature. Indeed, Luster's six-foot, 230-pound frame and his ever-present cigar created a striking image. "Orville was a great big guy," a former YFS staff member remembered. "His presence, you know, you don't want to mess with him, just on the basis of his size. And [he had] a high-pitched voice, which sort of belied this imposing presence. But he was not a man you ever wanted to cross or to get mad or angry at you, which he did with regularity with anyone who worked for him."[52]

Shortly after Luster took over, YFS finished negotiating a three-year Ford Foundation grant enabling the agency to expand its street-worker program. The foundation had spent the late 1950s conducting a national search for innovative programs dedicated to the assimilation of low-income youth. Ford funders combined CAP's older understanding of delinquency as a period of assimilation with newer theories hypothesizing that youth entered this stage because they felt frustrated with the impediments standing between them and integration.[53] Luster hoped his street workers could help youth overcome these obstacles, but he disabused his staff members of the notion that they might achieve lasting leadership over the city's young men. Instead, he insisted that peace could be achieved only through daily acts of negotiation.[54] YFS, like postwar street-work programs in Chicago, found peacekeepers who were endowed with the self-assuredness to engage in these sorts of talks by recruiting young men from local pool halls and other areas associated with working-class culture. Luster ultimately hoped to create a path from San Francisco's gangs to YFS staff work by molding promising gang leaders into street workers.[55]

Hezekiah "Zeke" Singleton, YFS's Hunters Point street worker, possessed the qualities necessary for effective peacekeeping. A black working-class migrant from Louisiana, Singleton was hired by Luster in 1961 and immediately impressed the Hill's youth with his empathy and courage. Describing young street workers' responses to rumbles in Hunters Point, Walter Turner, a member of the Savoys, remembered:

We would sit back and we would look at them coming in and we would be saying, "They are *so* out of place. What are they doing?" But you know, it was like . . . they wasn't from the projects like we were. But, you know, they would still be there, and they wasn't afraid, and . . . that's what we had to respect them for. Because you couldn't find a lot of people that would come into a situation like that, but when somebody would you'd have to respect it. . . . Because it would be like why are they here when they don't have to be? They could be somewhere else, far away from here. But they were there trying to help.

Singleton further awed Hunters Point young men with his physical prowess and quick-thinking intellect. "Zeke had a marvelous way of making everything seem simple," a YFS staff person remembered, "and yet he was such an imposing presence. . . . You know, he was bigger than any of the guys in Hunters Point. And he sometimes would kind of stammer around like he wasn't sure what he was going to do, and yet he always knew exactly what to do. . . . and he never got taken on." YFS street workers like Singleton exhibited remarkable violence-prevention abilities. Between November 1960 and the summer of 1964, San Francisco experienced only one major rumble.[56]

YFS scored these peacekeeping successes at a time when city elites were growing ever more concerned with what they perceived as escalating racial disorder. In 1963 and 1964, a new group of so-called militant and radical San Francisco black activists dropped the liberal black activists' commitment to reform through formal political channels and instead began mobilizing large-scale direct-action civil rights protests. The radicals marched on the Hall of Justice to protest a vicious police beating of a black family inside their own home and conducted a series of sit-ins targeting the racially discriminatory hiring practices of a downtown hotel and downtown auto dealers. Like their peers in other cities, San Francisco's managerial growth proponents worried that television footage of central city demonstrations would scare away tourists and shoppers.[57]

Equally frightening to local elites was the upswing in criminal bloodshed and the race riots occurring in other American cities. In his 1964 run for the presidency, Senator Barry Goldwater introduced a law-and-order conservatism encouraging white Americans to view downtown civil rights demonstrations, street crime, and race rioting as symptoms of a single moral breakdown. San Francisco's downtown dailies had little difficulty connecting race riots elsewhere with violent crimes in San Francisco. Following New York City's 1964 Harlem race riot, for instance, San Francisco's mainstream press gave three days of front-page coverage to a Hunters Point assault in which a group of black youths beat and robbed a Chinese immigrant restaurant owner. The press's coverage did not consider how this attack might reflect social tensions between blacks and Chinese-Americans, and instead presented the incident as a clear-cut example of the black community's violent and race-conscious predilections.[58] Later that summer San Francisco newspapers followed a Philadelphia race riot with a string of local stories recounting black youths' assaults on white youth. Under headlines such as "Attacks on Whites" and "Racial Grudge," the newspapers put race-conscious motivations behind all of these beatings.[59]

The civil rights protests, crime rates, and rioting confronted San Francisco's managerial growth advocates and traditional liberals with a potential crisis of legitimacy. Growth proponents and liberals had long insisted on their ability to assimilate black residents, but the accumulating instances of disorder appeared to reveal the elites' failure. Now, in the mid-1960s, the mainstream white media, Police Chief Cahill, and various white policy makers all began deflecting responsibility for black crime and black peacekeeping.

Proponents of law-and-order conservatism explained crime as a problem of individual responsibility, and managerial growth advocates and traditional liberals joined conservatives to declare that black leaders bore responsibility for reducing the black crime rate. One white columnist insisted that San Francisco would never find a "solution" to the "high incidence of Negroes involved in crimes . . . unless the leaders of Negro pressure groups make the enforcement of old laws rather than the passage of new ones their No. 1 project." Another white San Francisco journalist responded to the 1965 Watts uprising in Los Angeles by demanding that local black leaders summon "the courage" to remind black youth of whites who fought for black rights—people like Abraham Lincoln and the modern-day white college student protesters. Similarly, during a 1964 sit-in seeking to integrate employment at a downtown hotel, the *Examiner* related that Mayor Jack Shelley blamed the "responsible Negro leadership" for abdicating its power and allowing "young militants" to lead "youth" in a "challenge of law and order."[60]

As white politicians and commentators leaned on the "Negro leadership" for solutions to black crime, some considered the terrifying possibility that recognized black spokespersons lacked influence over the black populace. San Francisco's liberal black spokespersons had never exhibited real clout over the poorer black population. The so-called radical activists championed increased political participation by the poor, but their mobilizing efforts rarely captured the involvement of Fillmore or Hunters Point residents. The radicals' large-scale downtown sit-ins had relied instead on the participation of white college students. The concern over potentially leaderless black youth grew even more pitched after the 1965 Watts riot. During that uprising young black people chilled outside observers by destroying large swaths of their neighborhood and dismissing the civil rights spokespersons, including Martin Luther King Jr., who attempted to quell their anger. Following the Watts riot, the *San Francisco Examiner* sent a journalist into Hunters Point to investigate whom the neighborhood's three thousand sixteen-to-twenty-one-year-olds considered their leaders. One male youth gave the reporter his headline with the unnerving reply, "Man, nobody speaks for me, I speak for myself."[61]

Established black spokespersons—liberal and radical alike—bristled that they were "about fed up" with white reporters and officials saddling them with a new crime-prevention mandate. White leaders, after all, were not forced to correct and "apologize" for the actions of white criminals. "I know of no person who carries a greater burden in current society than the so-called Negro leader," grumbled Cecil Poole, a liberal black United States Attorney in San Francisco. "People set the leader aside as something special. They think of a tribal hierarchy. In other words, all you have to do to deal with 'them' is 'find the chief medicine man.'"

By contrast, Luster recognized that the city elites' growing association of black leadership with black peacekeeping opened a political opportunity for the young black members of YFS. Through peacekeeping, young black men might achieve recognition as leaders in the civic sphere. Luster first began linking violence prevention and the civic legitimacy of young black males during the fallout over Hunters Point's 1961 hilltop brawl. The political elites' aloof debate over the future of the Hill's housing project occupants infuriated local residents, and Luster worked with a handful of other professionals to channel this grassroots anger into lasting political organization. These efforts helped housing project residents—in particular, a small cadre of energized housing project mothers—to establish committees dedicated to lobbying for the Hill's interests.[62]

Luster also exploited the media attention engendered by the brawl to demand that city officials begin recognizing the lines of "leadership" among the Hill's "children." Pointing to gangs as civic building blocks within the youth population, Luster admonished, "Whether the Mayor and Chief of Police like it or not, kids will organize into clubs or gangs or whatever the groups are called. They are as much a part of our national pattern as groups like the Lions or the Kiwanis." The YFS director rejected the notion that government leaders could technocratically serve the interests of the Hill's young people. "Who's going to lobby for them?" Luster asked. "Who speaks for them? The cops? No. The Recreation Park Dept.? No. The schools? No." Instead, he proposed that local officials create a lasting peace by accepting the legitimacy of the youth's perspectives and negotiating with the young people through YFS "ambassadors."

Failing to engage in these dialogues, he concluded, would provoke further bloodshed. "Unless we involve these people in the planning, we're going to have problems," Luster cautioned. "Everybody will come down to look at the beautiful new building and then some day somebody will try to tear it down."[63]

The YFS leader's strategy for black political integration forced him to affirm white mainstream perceptions that black male youth were potentially dangerous. Luster repeatedly corrected the press when they misidentified personal clashes as acts of race-conscious violence, but when he wanted to bring his youth attention or funding, he toyed with white fears. In 1964 Luster strode into a grant application interview with the United Community Fund, overturned a burlap bag on the boardroom table, and emptied out a clattering pile of knives, brass knuckles, meat cleavers, and blackjacks. Luster intoned he had taken these weapons from local youth the night before and that if YFS was to continue this work it would need funding for its street workers. The foundation quickly inked a check for $48,000. City Hall officials encouraged this sort of threat-based politicking from black spokespersons by refusing to offer concessions unless faced with a sense of imminent danger. "The only time anything is done for Negroes in San Francisco," one black liberal complained, "is when there is a crisis." In an article on San Francisco politics, Tom Wolfe famously labeled this intimidating style of poverty-agency fundraising "mau-mauing." When Wolfe identified the "genius in the art of confrontation who had mau-mauing down to what you could term a laboratory science," he pointed to Luster.[64]

Luster's desire to integrate the perspectives of young and impoverished males into civic debate paralleled the agenda of the city's black radical activists. However, Luster identified more with black liberals by presenting YFS as an agency willing to work through or alongside local business owners and existing government institutions. When merchants in Potrero Hill complained of a lack of police officers on the street, for instance, YFS offered to fill that void with its own street workers. Meanwhile, YFS's self-defined mission—responding to negligent policing rather than overpolicing—enabled Luster to limit his direct confrontations with City Hall and the SFPD. Finally, the YFS director's interest in increasing political participation in Hunters Point fit with the electoral agenda of Democratic powerbrokers. During the early 1960s, Republican operatives had begun working to suppress Democratic voting by intimidating voters away from polling stations in Latino and black neighborhoods, including Hunters Point. The young men of YFS were well equipped to neutralize this thuggery. The vote-marshaling efforts of YFS workers and a concurrent organizing movement among the Hill's housing project mothers vaulted Hunters Point from the bottom to the top San Francisco's voter turnout list. The heavily Democratic lean of that vote, in turn, won Luster new allies in traditional Democrats like Mayor Jack Shelley and younger cosmopolitan liberals like member of Congress Phillip Burton.[65]

VIOLENCE PREVENTION, JOBS,
AND THE WAR ON POVERTY

As Luster forged a path leading black male youth toward peacekeeping and civic legitimacy, he needed to convince the young black members of YFS to follow his lead. As the first generation of members aged, Luster encountered new complications. First, the youth were experiencing increasingly hostile interactions with the police. Luster attempted to address this problem by seeking top-down professionalization reforms through the SFPD's high brass. YFS street workers served as in-service training consultants for the SFPD, and Luster provided officers with direct youth contact by organizing Always Be Cool meetings between himself, YFS youth, and the SFPD's leadership. During these gatherings Luster didn't mince words. "You are hated and mistrusted" by the youth, Luster informed one group of police officials. "You are not seen as unique human beings, but as a representative of a mistrusted class. You are a faceless individual. You are the man who carries the gun, who carries the stick, the protector of the power structure."[66]

These interactions between the youth and police department leadership produced mixed results. Occasionally, there were revelations, such as when a police captain admitted that he had put a gun to a YFS member's head, and sometimes youth received restitution: in one case the leader of the police-community relations unit bought new shoes for a youth whose sneakers had been stolen by a police officer. But although the meetings provided youth with a safe atmosphere in which to vent their frustrations, police leaders refused to respond with reforms. During a 1963 conference between YFS members and the police, the youth expressed particular concern over the use of dogs, and one attendee claimed, "One night a cop sic'd one of them dogs and he come and sat on my leg. . . . The police called him back, he wouldn't come. You said they trained. How come he wouldn't come when he called him?" Police Chief Cahill responded with characteristic indifference: the department's use of dogs was nonnegotiable and the teenagers would be wise to shape up.[67]

Through the 1960s YFS felt it could better protect young people from violence by working around the SFPD than by working through it. Agency street workers, however, found it increasingly difficult to maintain their influence over the first generation of YFS members as these young people aged and assumed new financial responsibilities. Luster believed that in order to continue negotiating with the young men and grooming the more promising gang leaders for positions as street workers, he would need to begin offering them jobs. Luster argued that in neighborhoods as economically strained as Hunters Point, residents followed the command of whoever provided them with basic services and "fresh money."[68]

In 1965 the federal government opened new opportunities for "fresh money" when it initiated the War on Poverty. Following the philosophical and programmatic tradition set by the Ford Foundation's antidelinquency efforts, many of the War on Poverty's architects believed that frustrated assimilation created a culture of poverty. As federal planners looked to fund efforts that eliminated the obstacles separating poor people from mainstream culture, Luster saw the possibility for a new organizing model. By capitalizing on the connections he had made with Representative Burton and other local liberals, Luster won control over an early War on Poverty initiative, the Neighborhood Youth Corps, which distributed short-term jobs to adolescents to provide them with the experience of employment. YFS was the only private organization in the country to oversee a citywide Youth Corps program, and soon the agency was employing 231 low-income youth. The Youth Corps funding propelled YFS's political stature forward and ultimately increased the agency's leverage in its peacekeeping efforts out on the streets. But the program failed to produce much change in attitude among city elites. When a Shelley spokesperson addressed Neighborhood Youth Corps workers at the end of a summer job stint, he ignored the fact that no employers had offered the young people permanent positions. Instead, he moralized, "You have got to get in the stream . . . [and] flow with the rest of us."[69]

The federal antipoverty agenda not only provided a boon for Luster, it created new streams of funding for a second generation of street-work programs. Locally, the War on Poverty organized itself around "target area" neighborhoods suffering from concentrated levels of poverty, and neighborhood residents staffed the target areas' offices. In Hunters Point the housing project mothers who first organized in the aftermath of the 1961 hilltop brawl guided many of the target area decisions. Having watched YFS use peacekeeping to earn grants and employment programs, the Hunters Point poverty workers established their own neighborhood-based, street-work agency. The target area street-work program provided the Hill's young men with a new avenue to political legitimacy.[70]

In contrast to the citywide and integrative YFS, the target area's street-work program offered politically motivated young men a neighborhood-based approach more consistent with their old jacket club identities. The Hill's target area office also sponsored the *Spokesman*, a newspaper through which young residents could publicly protest against the SFPD and other government institutions. Under these conditions, a YFS staff member recalled, the target area street-work program "scooped up" many of the "sharp" men who had been among YFS's first generation of jacket club members. Their shift represented a modification of tactics, not goals. Like Luster and YFS, the target area's street workers ultimately hoped to reduce community violence, garner job grants, and achieve civic legitimacy.[71]

HUNTERS POINT'S "SO-CALLED RIOT"

An outburst of police and community violence in the fall of 1966 allowed the Hunters Point peacekeepers to begin integrating themselves into the city's cosmopolitan liberal coalition. Early in the afternoon of September 27, Matthew "Peanuts" Johnson and two friends ditched school to joyride through the streets of Hunters Point. As they motored down Griffith Street, they happened upon a parked squad car. Suspecting that the officer inside knew that the car was stolen (the officer did not), the boys panicked. Johnson and his friends slammed their vehicle to a halt, jumped out in the middle of street, and scattered in three directions. Witnessing this scene through the window of his cruiser, Patrolman Alvin Johnson recognized that something was amiss, so he took to foot and huffed after Matthew Johnson, shouting for the boy to stop. Officer Johnson fired four shots that he later claimed were pointed into the air and intended as warnings. The fourth blast, however, struck Matthew Johnson square in the back and killed him instantly. Patrolman Johnson was later acquitted of any wrongdoing. The penal code made homicide justifiable "to apprehend any person for any felony committed."[72]

As residents ringed the slain youth and talk of rioting entered the air, thirty young black male War on Poverty workers rushed to the target area office to plan a response. The organizers recognized that by rescuing their community from harm they might achieve civic legitimacy among white cosmopolitan liberals and finally garner the resources necessary for neighborhood uplift. Thus the assembled activists focused on peacekeeping. The young men informed human rights commissioners sent to pacify the neighborhood that a riot could be prevented only if Mayor Shelley met with them and negotiated reforms addressing City Hall's racially discriminatory governance over Hunters Point.[73]

Shelley, however, remained committed to color-blind, City Hall–dictated leadership in Hunters Point, and the traditional liberal mayor rebuffed the young men's negotiation request. He took to the steps of a Hunters Point community center and, with liberal black spokespersons to his side and riot-geared police to his back, the mayor delivered a speech. Shelley implored the neighborhood's residents to view the shooting in color-blind terms. Bruce Kennedy, a Catholic priest and the only white staff member in the Hunters Point target area office, later described Shelley's oration:

> When the mayor first got up to speak the first thing he said was, "I can't tell you how sorry I am about the death of that boy. It could have been my own son." From then on, nobody was listening. Because everybody in the place knew that it could not have been his own son. That was the very issue on which the whole thing was based, that this was a Hunters Point Negro, stealing a car, a boy with no influence.[74]

Shelley announced that Officer Johnson had been suspended from the force, but many listeners wondered whether the politician grasped that their grievances encompassed a much wider range of issues. Eggs, rotten vegetables, and cries of "motherfucker" rained down on the city's chief executive. Shelley and his entourage beat a hasty retreat, leaving one city representative behind to try to work with the residents. Within minutes that official's Mercedes Benz was ablaze, and the uprising began in earnest.[75]

Downtown journalists and politicians took away three lessons from the subsequent Hunters Point riot. First, white reporters and officials regarded the uprising as exclusivist and political. White media members arrived in the neighborhood expecting to find the former theme, and young black residents made sure that they left the neighborhood understanding the latter message. On the third day after the shooting and after most of the neighborhood violence had subsided, a white television crew ventured onto Third Street and asked a young black man if he wanted to "kill some white people." Startled by the complex of fears and prejudices underlying the question, the resident sputtered, "Do I want to kill some white people? Do I want to kill some white people?! Not as of yet, no. Not yet—unless something's done about this and today. Right today. I might change my viewpoint about wanting to kill some white people." Pointing out that he had a clean police record, the young man continued:

> I'm not out trying to make a name for myself. I'm out trying to help my people. . . . I'm proud to be black, and I think everybody else who's black

should be just as proud as I am. I don't think they should have any Uncle Toms on the police force or in the white man's army. I don't think they should send a nigger over there to Vietnam to kill a Vietnamese when they're over here getting killed in their own home. . . . I think they oughta let them brothers come back over here and shoot—and start fighting for their own homes, their own people, their own property, for their own family, for their own pride, for their own cause.

San Francisco's mainstream media slowly grasped the political fury fueling the Hunters Point violence.[76]

The second observation downtown observers made after the Hunters Point uprising was that although the Hill's residents were angry and harbored racial and politicized perspectives, they had wreaked relatively little destruction. The final tallies for the riot were lower than those for many other urban conflagrations of the period. In the 128 hours after Matthew Johnson's killing, police arrested 359 people (most for curfew violations), and 51 people suffered injuries, including six police officers, two firefighters, and one municipal bus driver. The city estimated that property damage was less than $100,000, and the neighborhood avoided any additional fatalities. With little bloodshed and few lasting physical scars, Hunters Point residents soon referred to the incident as the "so-called riot." In the Fillmore District, where people had also looted stores, many residents asked, "What riot?"[77]

Pointing to the uprising's small scale, the media argued that the third lesson to be taken from the riot was that liberal responses—including restrained law enforcement and nonviolent peacekeeping—mitigated the damage to human life and property. Following a pattern set by liberals in postriot Philadelphia, San Francisco's liberals focused on the successes of peacekeepers and thereby drew attention away from the liberal failures that precipitated the violence in the first place. Throughout the uprising YFS and target area street workers had roamed the streets attempting to calm both the rioters and the police. "The difference . . . between San Francisco and Watts," a liberal *Chronicle* reporter opined, was that "there were fingers in the ghetto, Negro leaders people trusted, who cautioned against lawlessness, against rioting." As usual, reporters celebrated Luster's role. "Again and again," one *Chronicle* reporter proclaimed, "the name of Orville Luster was mentioned and the significant part he and some 100 youths from his organization had played in keeping violence at a minimum."[78]

White cosmopolitan liberal journalists had been praising Luster for years, but they now also began specifically identifying young target area street work-

FIGURE 12. Street workers from Youth for Service and the neighborhood War on Poverty office carry a wounded man across Third Street during the Hunters Point riot. September 28, 1966. (Reprinted with permission, Bancroft Library, BANC PIC 2006.029: 140126B.03.16.)

ers. Liberal policy makers in Chicago during this period were postulating that gang leaders might have the capacity to not only "mobilize but also. . . . demobilize" riots. Now, San Francisco's cosmopolitan liberals pointed to the efforts of the former gang members in YFS and the target area office as evidence proving that theory. One Hunters Point minister urged the white reporters to view the young men's peacekeeping abilities as signs of power. "This is a new leadership," the pastor affirmed. "These young men are really doing things."[79] Thus, at the same time that cosmopolitan liberals were reorienting their understanding of citizenship around a shared interest in reducing violence, the young men of Hunters Point stepped forward as potential partners in the city's pursuit of a common good.

YFS and target area peacekeepers emerged from the riot hoping to translate this new downtown recognition into concrete assistance. The street workers formed Young Men for Action (YMA) as a political advocacy group dedicated to the interests of Hunters Point's young black men.[80] YFS street workers played a prominent role in the organization while YFS itself continued serving the neighborhood's youth, but Adam Rogers, a young target area staff worker, eventually established himself as the new group's leader.[81]

Born in San Francisco in 1944, Rogers grew up on the Hill and earned his street credibility through a successful run in amateur boxing. As a teenager he participated in YFS projects, and agency leaders quickly recognized the young man's extraordinary leadership potential. "He was clearly a community leader," a female YFS staff member attested. "He was a very sharp kid and he was really respected." She continued: "He was the kind of leader Orville wanted." But the soft-spoken Rogers was also self-assured and independent. He did not flinch in the face of authority figures (one City Hall official later recalled that when police "sassed him . . . he sassed them back"), and he kept Luster at arm's length. "He was always sizing up what the situation was," a YFS staff member explained. "He didn't do something just because he related well to someone." In 1966 he joined the Hill's target area office and quickly climbed the ranks. All the while, Rogers was developing the kind of physical presence the cosmopolitan liberal coalition valued. With a trimmed goatee and a six-foot-two-inch, 220-pound frame, Rogers was, in the words of one black city official, "a magnificent goddam physical specimen."[82]

During the Hunters Point uprising, Adam Rogers, Percy Pinkney of YFS, and a handful of other street workers attempted to mediate between the police and the rioters. Standing between the two groups, Rogers urged a police captain, "For God's sake, don't send any more cops down here. We'll clear it up for you." Police answered Rogers's entreaties with rifle fire. "The word came," Kennedy later reported, "that Adam Rogers was among those who had been hit."[83]

Kennedy commended Rogers's work during the previous day and a half:

Adam had been one of the key men in the whole attempt to keep tempers down, to keep people calm and cool. He had been for two days wandering through the crowd with a bullhorn, warning them to be careful about this and careful about that and not to lose their heads about this and that, trying to calm them down. He's a natural leader. . . . Out of the whole thing, he was the one man who stood out as the hero of this riot, so-called riot.

The police shooting wounded Rogers's leg, and this injury magnified his legend. When Rogers then established himself as a YMA leader, he followed the YFS model by attempting to parlay his peacekeeping ability into employment grants and a civic voice.[84]

As Rogers pivoted to fill the peacekeeping gaps left by city negligence, other groups appeared on the Hill prepared to focus on police abuse. In February 1967 the Black Panther Party made its presence felt by providing security for a

Hunters Point event honoring Malcolm X. The Black Panther Party and YMA initially coexisted peacefully as each sought to address different manifestations of discriminatory law enforcement. However, the two groups adopted markedly different postures toward City Hall. While the Black Panthers spoke of "revolution," Rogers called on youth to bring about change "legally" and expressed his hope that the Hill could work through City Hall to make "the Mayor get on his job." Like YFS, Rogers and the rest of YMA looked to the government to provide the resources and political validation they felt they needed to reduce bloodshed among the Hill's young people.[85]

MAYOR ALIOTO AND RACIAL PLURALISM IN CITY HALL

YMA entered the 1967 mayoral election a political free agent, searching for a patron who could provide it with a voice in City Hall and jobs to distribute. In September, during the final month of the city's mayoral race, YMA sponsored a large hilltop festival designed to celebrate black culture and remind downtown of the Hill's unmet needs. A disappointingly small number of whites joined the thousands of blacks attending the sunny festival, but early in the afternoon, Joseph Alioto and his campaign entourage puttered onto the grounds in a bus adorned to look like a cable car.[86]

Alioto was one of a growing number of urban liberal candidates during the late 1960s who responded to a lack of machine support by enlisting the campaign assistance of young black men. New York City's mayor John Lindsay, for instance, built alliances with "local troublemakers" in preparation for his 1969 reelection campaign. In San Francisco Alioto understood that his liberal opponent, Supervisor Jack Morrison, had used an alliance with Representative Burton to secure the endorsements of the city's black liberal spokespersons, including Luster. However, Alioto believed that the mass of black voters could be peeled away from the black professionals, and he was cognizant of the electioneering power the Hill's gang members had exhibited in previous campaigns. Alioto later recounted his introduction to the YMA leaders: "I told them that after I was elected I wanted them to be leaders—I wanted them to be involved in the community. So I told them what my programs were and they went out with them house to house."[87] This agenda, Alioto told Hunters Point residents, would increase access to jobs and better protect black residents from crime.[88]

This campaigning earned Alioto an upset over Morrison in Hunters Point. The new mayor quickly repaid his YMA supporters with job grants. Alioto's signal achievement for Hunters Point was his success in securing for the neighborhood a spot in the Model Cities program, a federal initiative that allocated five-year grants to selected neighborhoods in the hopes of producing visible physical improvements to the community. Shelley's administration had put forward an application for Hunters Point, but opposition from a group of middle-class homeowners, who were rightly concerned that their property would become vulnerable to redevelopment, had scuttled the submission. When the application deadline then passed, it appeared that Hunters Point had missed its chance. Alioto, however, used his close ties with Vice President Hubert Humphrey to submit a new Hunters Point application that did not include the middle-class homes, and thus secured a last-moment grant for the neighborhood. Alioto's achievement, the first director of San Francisco's Model Cities later explained, made the new mayor a "god" on the Hill.[89]

With widespread support in the community, Alioto moved forward on a series of Hunters Point redevelopment projects, including construction of a post office and replacement of the Hill's original housing projects. In contrast to Mayor Christopher, who had placed redevelopment decisions in the hands of technocrats, and Mayor Shelley, who had attempted to limit his dealings to black professionals, Alioto promoted grassroots support for his growth agenda by appointing Hill residents, including members of YMA, to key positions in the San Francisco Redevelopment Agency (SFRA). The mayor also formalized Rogers's role as a peacekeeper for the government by giving him a contract to establish security forces at the neighborhood's various redevelopment sites. Through this arrangement, City Hall relied on Rogers to escort nervous white developers and investors through the community. Within the first two years of Alioto's administration, Rogers transformed himself into what one female activist approvingly described as "Alioto's guard" in Hunters Point.[90]

During these same two years, however, San Francisco suffered stomach-wrenching spikes in its murder and robbery rates. Recorded statistics in these two categories had been climbing unevenly for the previous eight years. Between 1959 and 1967, San Francisco's annual murder rate rose from 39 homicides to 70 homicides, and the reported annual robbery rate increased from 1,287 to 3,964. San Francisco's homicide figure then jumped to 97 in 1968 and 140 in 1969. Meanwhile, the robbery rate raced upward by a dizzying 67 percent between 1968 and 1970, with the city experiencing more than 6,400 robberies over each of those years.[91]

The end-of-decade eruption in street violence reflected a qualitative change in criminal behavior. Traditionally, the black population's disproportionate murder and robbery arrest rates had been driven by black men in their late twenties and early thirties from across the city. In both 1968 and 1969 black men were half of those arrested for these two crime categories, but the surge in murders was primarily propelled by new violence among younger black men living in Hunters Point. In 1969, the city's peak murder year, Potrero District led the city in murder. Meanwhile the murder arrests for young men aged eighteen to twenty-two jumped from one in 1960 to thirty-eight in 1969.[92]

Alioto's patronage politics was born out of the mayor's desire to promote redevelopment, but in the face of the exploding crime rates, Alioto used his alliance with young men like Rogers to convince white San Franciscans that his cosmopolitan growth liberalism could protect them. Administration members like Roff were mindful of how YFS leaders like May and Luster had spent the previous decade using negotiations to adopt a violence-prevention posture appealing to white liberals. Alioto thus responded to the horrifying criminal bloodshed by highlighting street-work negotiations as a centerpiece of his governing approach.

The new mayor found it easy to promote his peacekeeping-through-negotiation model as an extension of the city's existing vital liberal and Catholic Action traditions. All three postures emphasized his eagerness to march into fraught conflicts and broker pragmatic resolutions serving the common good. In advertising his alliance with Rogers, Alioto stressed that he had "personally . . . made direct contact with the young men. It was deliberate and certain." Through these parleys, Alioto claimed, he had been able to "corral the younger tough element" and "channel their energies" toward a violence-reduction policy that benefited all.[93]

Alioto's negotiation strategy drew national attention from commentators across the political spectrum. The liberal *New York Times* covered Alioto's alliance with YMA in an approving feature, but New Left activists criticized Alioto's policies as a hypocritical co-option of the black community, and white conservatives scorned the mayor's negotiations as acts of spineless capitulation. In 1970 Wolfe's celebrated *New York* magazine essay "Mau-Mauing the Flak Catchers" skewered the Alioto administration from both of these latter directions. Wolfe argued that San Francisco's poverty program was based on choreographed confrontations between "mau-mauing" activists of color and the low-level white functionaries Alioto sent to serve as his "flak catchers." In these exchanges a white bureaucrat offered poor people few concrete concessions but provided the activist—"some bad dude"—the opportunity to trample his white "dignity" and "manhood" with threats of community violence. Ultimately, Wolfe concluded, the bureaucrats pacified black activists with a "shit-eating grin," and black spokespersons left with nothing more than the psychological validation that they were "right" and that the pencil pusher was "chickenshit."[94]

Mostly concerned with the state of white manhood, Wolfe's article did not pay much attention to the storms of violence raging in the black community. However, the swelling murder rate was rocking street workers back on their heels. In Hunters Point a newly expanding heroin market fueled much of this late-1960s carnage. The underground economy offered youth the potential for high-income work in a viable neighborhood industry and thus eroded what meager negotiating power the Hunters Point street workers wielded with their low-wage, government-funded jobs. Heroin's financial value, meanwhile, both raised the stakes of youth conflicts and enabled young people to purchase firearms. The increasingly agitated and armed environment made YFS's traditional negotiation strategy far more perilous.[95]

Across the country, liberal city leaders struggled against the confluence of escalating street violence and intensifying New Left and conservative critiques. New York's Mayor Lindsay and San Francisco's Mayor Alioto weathered this storm with a message similar to the pitch Luster delivered to white funders earlier in the decade. By tolerating race-conscious perspectives and negotiating with young black leaders, these liberals insisted, cities could offer blacks democracy and whites security. Alioto's cosmopolitan liberal conception of citizenship diverged sharply from Mayor Christopher's managerial growth politics and Mayor Shelley's traditional liberalism. Like Luster, Alioto insisted that racially pluralist politics could detach "militant"—that is, race-conscious—perspectives from "violent" activities. "Be militant, but never violent . . . Come to us before you go to the street with your problems," Alioto directed the young men of Hunters Point.[96]

As liberals began accepting a racially pluralist understanding of the citizenry, they needed to illustrate how they intended to organize government to incorporate that pluralism in the service of peace. Growth liberals like Mayors Alioto and Lindsay emphasized the special role of the mayor in promoting inclusiveness. Both leaders earned national attention for their approaches when their two cities avoided the rioting that hit a hundred other urban centers in the wake of the April 1968 assassination of Martin Luther King Jr. Lindsay, a liberal Republican, won accolades by rolling up his shirt sleeves and taking to the streets to personally implore residents to keep their cool. In San Francisco YFS and YMA helped avert violence, and on the day after the assassination Alioto invited Rogers and other members of YFS and YMA to stand alongside him during a memorial rally on the steps of City Hall.[97]

As Alioto's cosmopolitan growth liberalism privileged the role of the mayor in facilitating pluralism, the mayor diverged from two core elements of the YFS approach. First, Alioto rejected YFS's participatory democratic understanding

FIGURE 13. Flanked by Adam Rogers (left) and Sylvester Brown (right), and with other members of Youth for Service and Young Men for Action standing behind him, Mayor Joseph Alioto addresses a packed Civic Center on the day after Martin Luther King Jr.'s assassination. The previous day, Young Men for Action and Youth for Service helped avert rioting in Hunters Point. Mayor Alioto insisted that his alliance with these young activists was what spurred the young black men to keep the city "cool." April 5, 1968. (Reprinted with permission, *San Francisco Chronicle.*)

of the roots of power and location of democracy. YFS leaders insisted that by negotiating through gang leaders, they were simply working through the organic hierarchies that already existed on the street. At the same time, the youth agency regarded power in neighborhoods like Hunters Point as fluid and thus emphasized that the streets were sites of democracy. Under this philosophy YFS street workers engaged in constant negotiation to locate the proper powerbrokers and maintain their own influence. Alioto, by contrast, asserted that he personally created black leaders. YMA members had calmed rioters during the Hunters Point uprising, but Alioto dissembled that those who stood at his side during his memorial rally "had participated in San Francisco's riot in 1966 and are still aggressively militant." After King's assassination, Alioto continued, the young people "have been among the most forceful leaders in averting violence and keeping the City cool" only because he had opened "lines of communication." Explaining that when he found Rogers and the members of YMA, the young men were only "tough kids" with "qualities of leadership," Alioto stressed his decision to "consciously make an effort to develop leadership."[98]

Second, Alioto diverged from the YFS philosophy by arguing that he had the ability to create permanent leaders within Hunters Point. Through this conception of stable leadership, Alioto reassured white voters that his negotiations would reliably produce peace and that he could conduct these deliberations from his chair in the mayor's office. After identifying the area's leaders, Alioto explained, he had given them his telephone number and invited them to "talk to City Hall any time of day or night."[99]

By showing how a pluralist government centered on City Hall could reduce violence, mayors like Alioto and Lindsay hoped to sustain and legitimize their authority over their respective cities' prodevelopment agendas.[100] That overriding commitment to growth circumscribed Alioto's approaches to peacekeeping, however. The mayor said little of the quotidian tumult within Hunters Point and instead emphasized how his negotiations with Rogers spared the city from race riots and black power violence—spectacular forms of bloodshed with seemingly great potential to harm whites and derail the growth agenda in other parts of the city. At the same time, he withheld his support from peacekeeping groups whose messages threatened the growth agenda. In Chinatown, for instance, Alioto turned a blind eye to a crackdown by local police and Chinatown's business community against Leway, Incorporated, a new peacekeeping group attempting to draw attention to immigrant deprivation and intraneighborhood gang violence. The Leway's message, to the consternation of growth advocates, endangered Chinatown's reputation as a "safe and clean" tourist site for white families.[101]

Stressing that his deliberative democratic approach prevented violence, Alioto also insisted that when residents removed themselves from City Hall's development-oriented deliberations they sowed the seeds of disorder. The Black Panther Party drew these sorts of charges from the mayor after they engaged in violent confrontations with San Francisco police, attempted to block the SFRA's planned razing of the Fillmore District, and issued personal threats against him (for example, they published a cartoon depicting a bullet hurtling toward Alioto's temple). Alioto refused to entertain the notion that Black Panthers could serve as peacekeepers. In April 1969 reporters saw Panthers responding to a small, police-instigated uprising in the Fillmore District by calming rioters and rescuing white motorists and journalists from assaults by black residents. Alioto, however, credited "Youth for Service, Western Addition Youth and Young Men for Action" for containing "what might have been an ugly situation." He suspected that reporters had "probably mistaken" young men from those organizations for Black Panthers. The Black Panthers' strategy of shouting down public meetings, Alioto further claimed, facilitated race-conscious bloodshed. Following the earlier cosmopolitan liberal narrative warning of the violent potential underlying the Black Muslims' racial exclusivism, Alioto associated what he considered unchanneled racial perspectives with antiwhite, criminal mayhem. "The hate 'whitey' racism of Panther militancy," Alioto intoned, was possibly already "finding outlet in brutal crime." Alioto saw the results of Panther agitation in the recorded upswing of local "robbery murders committed by young Negro males against white owners of small business establishments."[102]

For Alioto, Rogers and YMA thus served not only as peacekeepers, but also as political antidotes to the Black Panther Party. The mayor related that he would "pick out young militants," then explain to the young men that they could be "quite assertive in their claims" as long as they worked "within constitutional consent" and "the system." Then he had granted these young men "credentials" to indicate his office's intent "to work closely with them on housing, on jobs, on education." This arrangement, Alioto concluded, had been instrumental "to blocking the progress of the Black Panthers." Alioto relished reciting an Eldridge Cleaver quote in which the Black Panther Party leader complained that Alioto's alliances with men like Rogers had "virtually destroyed the revolutionary morale of the people in Hunters Point."[103]

Alioto claimed credit for the Panthers' failure to consolidate power in Hunters Point, but the fact was that no black activists during the late 1960s—including Rogers and the young men of the YMA—succeeded in organizing the impoverished neighborhood. YMA members had initially hoped that by allying themselves with Alioto, they could acquire access to jobs with which to galvanize and uplift the entire community. But the necessary funding for a feat of that magnitude never materialized. Instead, Alioto diluted power, helping Rogers secure a spot on the Model Cities commission but then divvying up positions in other policy areas to other Hunters Point power players. "Alioto," Luster later observed, "was very cognizant of the leadership on all levels" of Hunters Point. Alioto eventually broadened his Hunters Point alliances to include the female housing project activists and Luster himself.[104]

YMA leaders initially expressed a willingness to work with other Hunters Point groups, including the Black Panther Party. In April 1969 a YMA organizer announced that his organization regarded the Black Panthers as "a member of this community" after a patrol officer shot and killed a nineteen-year-old Hunters Point youth who crashed a car in which he had been joyriding. Residents on the Hill, meanwhile, embraced both groups. At a 1969 fall festival celebrating a summer without rioting, an event organizer praised YMA's peacekeeping while selling copies of Cleaver's *Soul on Ice*.[105] YMA's inability to parlay their government and Model Cities positions into a stable, widespread base of community support, however, pushed the organization to grow dependent on Alioto for continued resources and political legitimacy. That tightening relationship with the mayor placed Rogers in a strained position with the Black Panther Party as police violence continued.

In the early spring of 1970, community anger toward the police swelled when two off-duty members of the SFPD's tactical squad gunned down Miles Beavers, a YFS Hunters Point street worker.[106] Beavers's killing, which the district attorney's office later determined to be justifiable homicide, and the community outrage it elicited produced contradictory responses from Hunters Point's various community organizations. The Black Panther Party attempted to use the killing to rally the community against Alioto. YFS and Rogers, however, worried that the Panthers' militarized bravado would tip the neighborhood toward self-destructive rioting. Moreover, their government-dependent solutions to the SFPD's underpolicing made it difficult to pivot toward an attack on Alioto for the SFPD's disproportionate use of force. YFS thus posted street workers at the house of Beavers's widow in order to turn away Panther recruiters, and they organized a press conference at which Pinkney linked Beavers's killing to the long list of earlier violent police actions. Pinkney angrily demanded a City Hall–directed investigation, but Alioto was content to let the issue pass. Rogers meanwhile issued no public protests against the government. Instead, the young activist broke up a Black Panther Party meeting where activists were planning a memorial demonstration.[107]

On the day of Beavers's funeral service, the slain street worker's brother and brother-in-law shot Rogers twice with a pellet gun. Rogers blamed the Panthers for the attack, but he had a contentious history with the Beavers family. While Rogers recuperated in the hospital, the Black Panther Party organized a free food rally and mounted a public relations campaign in which they pilloried Rogers as a "moron," a "stupid nigger," and a "parrot" for Alioto, who "should not be trusted." "Here is a fool that lives in the community and talks like Alioto," the Black Panthers' newspaper charged. Local residents continued to support the Panthers in the wake of this incident, and some expressed hope that the Panthers and YMA could make peace. In May 1970 a young black man told a television reporter that he valued both the YMA and the Panthers for encouraging him "to get off my behind and do something." "To get out and help," he continued. "To help my people better ourselves."[108]

part Rogers became "part of the" (handwritten margin note)

Following the shooting, Rogers committed himself to Alioto's delibera-tive democratic arrangement, and by 1972 Alioto's administration had made Rogers the assistant director of Hunters Point's poverty program. However, Rogers still lacked the resources to secure widespread community influence, and allegations began mounting that he was compelling obedience through force. One rival accused Rogers of urinating on disobedient youth and beating former jacket club presidents who during his youth had denied him member-ship in their gangs. Eventually, Rogers began intimidating and manhandling fellow organizers. Luster and other Hunters Point activists claimed that they had been physically assaulted by Rogers.[109]

As Rogers followed his alliance with Alioto into increasingly contentious relations on the Hill, Alioto used the partnership to win reelection. In Alioto's 1971 mayoral bid, the incumbent faced liberal and conservative opponents who, in the words of one observer, all "tried to outdo each other as advo-cates for law and order." Alioto downplayed the intraracial violence emanat-ing from the city's drug economy and instead centered his campaign around the "toughness" he displayed when forging the "coalition" that kept the city "cool" and free of antiwhite riots. This message allowed Alioto to build on his first election's coalition of working-class union members and downtown professionals as he now made inroads into white, middle-class, family-oriented enclaves like the Inner Sunset. Meanwhile, voters in Hunters Point rewarded Alioto for providing jobs and services by delivering the cosmopolitan liberal candidate a romping eight-to-one victory. On election day, Alioto cruised to a 27,000-vote win.[110]

Rogers's reputation on the Hill, by contrast, disintegrated. The controversy over his leadership style peaked in January 1972 when several Model Cities commissioners resigned from the board out of fear that Rogers might hurt or murder them. The following month Hill residents rebuked Rogers from the safety of anonymous polling booths and voted him off the Model Cities com-mission. Alioto's ability to dole out postings allowed the mayor to weather Rogers's defeat. The mayor retained the loyalty of the housing project mothers serving in the SFRA, and he transferred the coveted security job positions to other young, physically imposing neighborhood men.[111]

During the early 1970s, YFS buckled in the face of the militarized drug trade and the ever more aggressive SFPD.[112] Between mid-1968 and mid-1971, a chilling six YFS street workers and former street workers were killed while they were off the job. Experiencing a crisis of conscience, Luster pulled his staff away from on-the-street peacekeeping and instead bolstered business and labor alliances in an attempt to transform YFS into a job-training organization.

Regarding the street-work strategy, Luster later lamented, "We put so much pressure on some of these young people sometimes by saying that they're leaders, when they've just negotiated this for a short term. And a lot of times what they've negotiated doesn't even help them. *Especially* if they end up dead." In 1972 Luster's employment strategy ran aground when he tried to create jobs for low-income youth with a nonunion McDonald's restaurant and lost his support from organized labor. Dumped by this critical ally, Luster left YFS, and the program fell into decline.[113]

Bloody confrontations between police and black male activists on the streets were leading civil rights activists across urban America to reevaluate their violence-abatement strategies. During this period women moved to the vanguard of law enforcement politics. In Hunters Point, housing project mothers concentrated their efforts on overaggressive policing rather than police neglect, and like female activists in Philadelphia, they decreased the number of direct showdowns with police by shifting their activities off the streets and into City Hall. Through the Black Women's Committee for Concern, the Hunters Point women demanded top-down professionalism reforms. This sort of politicking fit easily into Alioto's new style of governance. The mayor quickly integrated these Hill activists into City Hall's police policy-making discussions by providing the group's leader a seat on a City Hall–sponsored committee dedicated to devising a fresh "criminal justice plan."[114]

CONCLUSION

During the 1950s and 1960s, the poor black residents of Hunters Point faced a knot of policing and political problems common to the nation's urban black residents. On the one hand, the SFPD's traditional, discretion-based policing regime subjected Hunters Point to both police violence and police neglect. On the other hand, the city leadership used its avowed commitment to color-blind perspectives to dismiss as illegitimate protests against racially discriminatory law enforcement. Unable to find allies committed to solving underpolicing with professionalized, rule-of-law reforms and desperate to save the city's low-income young people from harm, social workers and low-income residents turned to decentralized strategies emphasizing inclusiveness.

Community peacekeepers argued that a tolerance for expanded racial pluralism, similar to a tolerance for expanded cultural and sexual pluralism, could enable the city to reduce violence. White cosmopolitan liberals eventually accepted this argument, but only with a caveat: unchanneled black racial perspectives, many white liberals continued to assume, would result in antiwhite bloodshed. On these compromised terms, the cosmopolitan liberal coalition acknowledged the legitimacy of a race-conscious citizenship.

As cosmopolitan liberals achieved political power, they confronted the new problem of crafting a governing style that reflected their expanded tolerance for pluralism. In cities like San Francisco and New York, liberal mayors supportive of redevelopment emphasized City Hall–oriented inclusiveness. That approach, Mayor Alioto found, allowed liberals to provide white voters a sense of security amid skyrocketing bloodshed. The cosmopolitan growth arrangements offered much less to Hunters Point residents. Rogers's generation of young black men were instrumental in introducing principles of racial pluralism into San Francisco's City Hall, but they achieved their civic voice on the presumption that they would bear responsibility for reducing violence in their communities. Facing deindustrialization, drugs, and police brutality, Hunters Point peacekeepers were ultimately overwhelmed by an upsurge in bloodshed in the late 1960s and early 1970s.

CHAPTER 6

"If You Are Very Liberal toward Dissent, You Can Be a Little Bit Tougher": Cosmopolitan Liberalism and the Use of Force

"There is no code with me," Bob Jeffrey later declared. "One cop protecting another? If he was wrong, his ass was out with me." A black patrolman, Jeffrey had joined the SFPD during the early 1960s in order to "get into" and "serve" "the black community." In that capacity Jeffrey soon found San Francisco's black residents calling on him to police the police.[1]

City leaders, civil rights activists, police, and black residents all acknowledged that SFPD officers and black residents maintained a violent relationship, but they explained this bloodshed through competing conceptions of the citizenry. Civil rights activists assumed that San Franciscans maintained pluralist racial perspectives and saw police violence as race-conscious, antiblack brutality. Across the nation, black spokespersons called on managerial growth advocates and traditional liberals to make good on their promises of top-down, rule-of-law governance by punishing acts of racially discriminatory law enforcement. For instance, civil rights activists repeatedly proposed civilian review boards that could simultaneously draw together pluralist perspectives and adjudicate police misbehavior from above. Managerial growth proponents and traditional liberals, however, assumed that police maintained an apolitical stance vis-à-vis black residents and served the public good through their use of force. In most cities, including San Francisco, officials thus dismissed civilian review boards as a threat to color-blind discourse and a violation of expert-driven police professionalism.[2]

From the perspective of city leaders in San Francisco and elsewhere, the violence arising between police and black residents was a product of the black community members' race-conscious contempt for the law. As a solution to this supposed problem, police professionalizers during the late 1950s and early 1960s introduced police-community relations (PCR) units, proposing that these units would train officers to communicate with communities of color and then deploy these officers to inculcate marginalized residents with a color-blind respect for law enforcement.

However, the SFPD's PCR unit unexpectedly opened opportunities for local civil rights activists. Unable to achieve top-down oversight, black community spokespersons instead pushed police officials to fill the unit with Jeffrey and other officers who were, in the words of one criminologist, willing to work "together with minority group leaders" in "an established and ongoing, mutually cooperative arrangement." San Francisco's black activists recognized that although city officials stymied their efforts to restrict discriminatory and autonomous police discretion from above, PCR members like Jeffrey might allow them to secure rights through cooperative police discretion.[3]

Patrolman Jeffrey agreed to partner with black activists and thereby challenged both the physical prerogatives and apolitical posture of the rank and file. Initially Jeffrey represented black community interests by personally intervening against acts of police violence. Jeffrey later related that he had "saved a lot of people 'cause I was there. I questioned it. They [other police] knew how I felt. . . . So people weren't going to be treated certain ways in front of me." In early 1968 Jeffrey took this campaign into the civic sphere when he announced to a meeting of neighborhood activists that he had witnessed acts of police brutality. That declaration made it into the press, and Jeffrey later rhetorically asked, "Can you imagine what other police thought of me when I said, 'I have seen it'?" Jeffrey's public, political stance against autonomous discretion fueled an ongoing interdepartmental firestorm over PCR reforms. By the end of the year, the Hall of Justice had pulled Jeffrey off the PCR unit, and the rank and file had hounded the young officer out of the SFPD.[4]

Cosmopolitan liberals achieved formal political power in the midst of this civil war in the SFPD. As a political faction promising peace through inclusiveness, the cosmopolitan liberals needed to address the fray and explain their own position on a police officer's physical and political rights and responsibilities. Through the resulting interactions between cosmopolitan liberals and rank-and-file police, the two groups began persuading one another to consider the positive roles police officers could play in an inclusive democracy.

USE OF FORCE IN THE FILLMORE DISTRICT

During the 1950s, black activists living in San Francisco's centrally located Fillmore District regarded the SFPD rank and file's discretionary use of force as their neighborhood's most urgent policing problem. White patrol officers acknowledged that police-community interactions in the Fillmore often became physical. "Violent encounters were part and parcel of your work," recalled John Mindermann, a Fillmore Street patrolman in 1960 and 1961. "Very, very violent encounters," Mindermann continued. "And the encounters would continue into the patrol wagon and they would sometimes—depending on the intensity and the duration—they would carry over into the station at 841 Ellis."[5]

Police attributed their use of force to the Fillmore residents' propensity for committing criminal violence and resisting arrest. Officers could point to the city's arrest rates to substantiate the contention that black residents represented a particularly violent segment of the population. Each year from 1957 to 1961, black San Franciscans accounted for 33 to 67 percent of the annual homicide arrest rate and 23 to 39 percent of the annual robbery arrest rate. (These figures should be evaluated cautiously, however. The SFPD published inconsistent murder statistics for 1960 and 1961, and the soundness of the department's arrests remains unclear because the SFPD did not track the disposition of cases that were not resolved during the year of arrest.) Cognizant of these disproportionate arrest rates, police approached what officers termed the Fillmore "Jungle Beat" warily. "There was always a fear amongst police officers with respect to dealing with blacks," Mindermann recalled. "So there was a perception that when you dealt in a black neighborhood there was a higher degree of danger."[6]

The Fillmore District's black spokespersons countered that black San Franciscans encountered wild displays of police force even when the residents were acting peaceably. The San Francisco NAACP served as the primary clearinghouse for grievances about local discrimination against blacks during the late 1950s, and shortly before being elected president of the San Francisco NAACP in 1959, Terry Francois broadcast that police beatings were "the most common complaint" the NAACP received. These complaints often recounted nightmarish story lines in which an unexpected encounter with a patrol officer suddenly transformed a banal, everyday activity—ringing the doorbell of a friend's house, driving in a car, waiting for a taxi, or entertaining evening company in an apartment—into a horror show of batons and blood.[7]

The SFPD's structure and culture prevented the department from establishing internal checks against inappropriately violent arrests. In theory, a district patrol officer's arrests were supposed to be reviewed by both the officer's station sergeant and the station lieutenant. However, patrol officers usually bypassed station sergeants and sent detained prisoners directly to the Hall of Justice or the Youth Guidance Center. Meanwhile, the station lieutenants' shifts started and finished two hours earlier than their patrol officers' stints. As a result, station lieutenants usually exerted little oversight over their own patrol shift and instead rubber-stamped reports for an earlier shift over which they had little responsibility.[8]

Even when supervising officers became aware of a line officer's violent behavior, department norms prevented commanders from taking action. Supervising officers assumed that their commanders would interpret any disobedience among patrol officers as evidence of the supervisor's failed leadership. Furthermore, supervising officers did not punish or even seek to monitor police violence because they often valued officers who employed force. Lieutenant Dante Andreotti commented on this culture when describing how he had once earned a Class B citation for successfully capturing an armed-robbery suspect. Andreotti had effected this arrest without firing his weapon, and after his award ceremony, his captain commended his "good work," adding, "If you had used your gun you would have gotten A class."[9]

During the early 1950s, police violence emerged as the Fillmore District's most animating political issue. The NAACP, black church ministers, the local office of the American Civil Liberties Union, and the Fillmore District press all networked to identify, investigate, and contest the violent policing of black residents.[10] Initially, this loose coalition addressed the pattern of discretionary violence by working through the city's established political channels. The government offered victims of police abuse formal avenues of redress through the civil courts and the SFPD.

In civil court injured parties could sue the offending police. During the mid-1950s, however, the California legislature complicated this process by denying victims of abuse the right to sue if they were convicted of any charge. It was not hard for violent officers to concoct minor cover charges of resisting arrest or drunkenness; this not only protected officers from conviction but often meant that recipients of police beatings then faced additional fines or jail time.[11] When black victims of police brutality successfully managed to get their cases into court, juries sometimes ruled in their favor. But patrolmen often lacked the assets to make civil lawsuits worthwhile. Civil rights proponents attempted to increase the payout in these cases and raise the city's financial interest in preventing acts of police violence by lobbying the city to bond police officers for brutality. Oakland and New York City, a Fillmore-based newspaper pointed out, both maintained remuneration policies for victims of abuse. Mayor Christopher's administration rejected this proposal, and instead San Francisco's city attorney regularly provided free legal defense for police accused of brutality in cases in which the city was not liable.[12]

In addition to allowing victims of police abuse to seek judgments in civil court, the city charter permitted injured residents to seek punishment for the offending officers through the police department itself. It is unclear how many citizen grievances were filed or what the SFPD did with these complaints because the SFPD did not keep a central index of citizen protests, in spite of a city mandate that it do so. Regardless, victims of abuse faced a variety of challenges when submitting charges. First, a complainant had to file a grievance at a police station, but there was no guarantee that a police station would have a complaint form on hand, and citizens lodging grievances tempted a fresh round of harassment and abuse. In 1947 Alvin G. Sweetwyne, a black metalsmith and father of four, entered the SFPD's Hall of Justice to report that a special police officer had beaten him.[13] The station's desk officers ignored Sweetwyne's accusation and instead booked him for disturbing the peace, resisting an officer, and "$1000 vagrancy." Widespread reports of police intimidation against alleged victims of brutality continued though the early 1970s.[14]

Once a complaint was lodged, the chief of police maintained discretion over who, if anyone, would investigate the case before the Police Commission issued a disciplinary determination. Through the mid-1960s, the Police Commissions of Mayors Robinson, Christopher, and Shelley never expressed public concern with police violence against black residents and instead joined police commanders in whitewashing investigations of antiblack violence. In these so-called rinky dos, commissioners accepted the accused police officers' often unoriginal, stock explanations for the victims' injuries and dismissed charges of brutality. Francois claimed that he was "not aware of one complaint by a negro where the Department found any merit" from 1950 to 1958. He considered the commission's acquittals in NAACP cases particularly galling because the civil rights organization only pursued cases "where we thought the victim was innocent of any violation and was a person whose record was such that they would not show in a bad light in the public press."[15]

As black San Franciscans ran up against dead ends in both the civil courts and the SFPD's internal investigations, black spokespersons tried appealing directly to local elites, and they achieved top-down policing reforms when they framed their grievances in terms of clean-government professionalization. At the start of the 1950s, for instance, the *Sun-Reporter,* a Fillmore-based newspaper and black San Francisco's leading organ, forced police to allow black entrepreneurs to participate in the Fillmore's police-tolerated gambling industry by printing—under the guise of a cleanup campaign—embarrassing features exposing the underground economy.[16]

The issue of police brutality failed to fit into discussions of political corruption, so black activists' protests over police violence fell on deaf ears. The *Sun-Reporter*'s increasingly graphic descriptions of police violence illustrated the black activists' growing exasperation over the hypocrisy of managerial growth officials who claimed to govern by color-blind principles but refused to apply professionalization reforms to police violence against black people. In 1956 the newspaper began illustrating its articles with grisly photographs of the victims' cut and swollen faces, and two years later the newspaper started publishing periodic recaps of SFPD carnage. All the while, San Francisco's leaders refused to take even the small step of introducing a race relations course into the Police Academy curriculum, a concession granted by white officials in Oakland, Chicago, and New York City. Reporting on yet another police beating in February 1960, a *Sun-Reporter* writer fumed, "The details are so familiar as to be unimportant here."[17]

RANK-AND-FILE PREROGATIVES UNDER PROFESSIONAL POLICING

The formidable discretionary prerogatives rank-and-file officers enjoyed on the street masked the ways in which the city's centralized, elite-driven political arrangement demanded the patrolmen's near-total subservience inside the department. The Catholic, white, Irish, and Italian identities that most police officers shared sometimes created a unified approach to the citizenry, but this common culture failed to create solidarity between patrol officers and the SFPD's politically connected inspectors and commanders.

Police brutality hearings illustrated both the extent and limits of the patrol corps's various forms of power. Through the mid-1960s, the SFPD's high brass and the Police Commission never used police brutality accusations to punish an officer for violence against black residents. Police officials, however, often exploited the investigations as opportunities to flex their own authority over the lower ranks. They ignored the question of whether officers improperly used their discretion to inflict pain on black people and instead focused the hearings on transgressions of workplace rules. In 1947, for instance, black patrons of a Fillmore District bar accused three police officers of drunkenly beating them. Police commissioners acquitted the charged officers on the assault indictments, but then suspended the three for being inebriated on duty. In a 1955 case, at least five neighborhood witnesses accused two police officers of battering and then arresting two young black men. Rather than punishing the accused officers for these assaults, the Police Commission reprimanded the pair for failing to carry their service revolvers and thus needing to use their fists.[18]

High-ranking opponents of professionalism, on the other hand, exploited brutality hearings to scold patrol officers for taking their professional stature too far. Officer Gale Wright, who was on the scene of a rough, high-profile arrest while serving at Ingleside Station, later recalled his debriefing at the hands of the district command: "They just—three or four guys in the office—it was really a piss, because they just toyed with me for about an hour, an hour and a half, two hours, whatever it was. You know, and there was really no support at all, just taking their shot." One aggressive captain showed little concern over the arrest in question and instead suggested that Wright had violated the standards of a good patrolman by pursuing an education. Wright remembered the captain remarking, "'I see by your record . . . you have two years [in] city college.' And I said, 'Yes, sir.' And he said, 'Do you plan on going back to college?'" Wright answered affirmatively, and the captain responded, "Well we frown on that in the department." "In other words," Wright concluded, "he wanted to be the only educated bastard around."[19] The dispositions of these brutality hearings reflected the rank and file's workplace vulnerability. Patrol officers had no opportunity for recourse against the persistent bullying of the high brass. "Your sergeant, your lieutenant, your captain," Sergeant Jerry Crowley bluntly summarized, "could shit on you 'til the cows came home."[20]

During the 1940s and 1950s, machine politicians and managerial growth advocates across the country permitted rank-and-file officers to establish their own organizations, but only if they adopted apolitical postures. In 1941 the SFPD leadership allowed the rank and file to found the Police Officers' Association (POA) on the shared assumption that the group would never seriously confront the department's leadership. The POA was open to all officers, although it drew primarily from the patrolman and sergeant ranks, and primarily dedicated itself to organizing entertainment activities and social welfare services. The POA boasted impressive membership rolls—claiming 1,600 of the SFPD's 1,734 officers in 1961—but its feeble political posture limited enthusiasm from the rank and file. The POA operated as a paper organization with a small circle of active members playing musical chairs among its leadership posts, and it remained so politically marginal that on one occasion the police commissioners did not recognize the association's president.[21]

The POA maintained close relations with the white law-and-order truck drivers in the Teamsters Union's Local 85, and in the late 1950s, the Teamsters began offering to help organize the association's membership into a formal union. (Such overtures would carry more weight after 1961, when the state's governor and legislature affirmed the right of public employees to collectively bargain.) The POA advertised the Teamsters' gestures to capture attention from city officials and newspapers, but its leaders' conception of their own civic responsibilities prevented them from seriously considering unionizing. "I don't believe in police unions," Sol Weiner, the POA's president in 1959, later explained, " . . . because the power of a union is [the] strike and stuff like that. . . . I believe police have a responsibility to the public they serve."[22] POA leaders accepted the professionalization precept that police departments represent shared, apolitical civic interests and should thus remove themselves from open politicking.

This understanding of common interests grew strained, however, in the face of continued downtown-driven police professionalization. In January 1961, five months after the gayola trials, the Blyth-Zellerbach Committee, an institutional voice of San Francisco's managerial growth interests, published a study proposing that the city apply "business principles" to the SFPD. In particular, the downtown representatives recommended that the department funnel more power to the chief by consolidating the department's nine police districts into four. Downtown police professionalizers had long desired station consolidation; in both 1937 and 1957, Chamber of Commerce–approved police studies had recommended reducing the SFPD to seven district stations.[23]

The consolidation proposal aimed to curb the autonomy of station captains and lieutenants, but it also threatened to eliminate scores of lower-ranking desk positions. This potential reduction in the number of desk jobs represented a new incursion into the already limited labor opportunities available to the rank and file. San Francisco patrol officers emphasized their manly, independent, physical street image, but few officers dreamed of walking the beat forever. For officers who had missed out on a promotion to lieutenant or lacked the political juice to land an inspectorship or Traffic Bureau transfer, the SFPD's station house appointments offered an opportunity to move away from the physical demands and dangers of the street. Chief Cahill ultimately rejected the station consolidation plan, arguing that district stations gave residents a greater sense of security. Nevertheless, the proposal's frightening potential and the support it received from San Francisco's real estate interests motivated POA leaders to create "a stronger, more militant Association."[24]

The POA leadership pursued this more vigorous political stance without violating the managerial growth advocates' desire for elite-led governance. Rather than speaking publicly for themselves, POA officials hired Jacob "Jake"

Ehrlich to serve as both the association's lawyer (for a negligible $300 per month) and its proxy in policy debates. A flamboyant figure in San Francisco's well-heeled social circles, Ehrlich approached clean-government reforms ambivalently. During the Atherton scandal in the 1930s, he had defended police from charges of corruption, and in 1961 he told a private POA meeting that he recognized that the Blyth-Zellerbach Report infringed on the "opportunity" of patrol officers. The consolidation plan, he vowed, would "become the law of the land when I have a long, grey beard." "And gentlemen," he concluded, "I shave every day."[25]

Ehrlich expressed equal commitment to the notion that San Franciscans shared interests that could be identified and met through elite-dominated governance. The POA reported that Ehrlich promised not to "launder" POA grievances "in public" and vowed to instead serve the association's interests through conciliatory "private" meetings with Chief Cahill. The association elaborated that the lawyer's overriding goal was to "build with the front office because we are all in the same family."[26]

A law-and-order reaction to a violent attempted murder first tested Ehrlich's ability to simultaneously serve the rank and file's labor interests and honor the city's elite-brokered policy-making arrangement. Late in the evening on April 18, 1962, April Aaron, an attractive, blonde twenty-two-year-old woman, was walking to church through the Panhandle, a Haight-Ashbury park, when an unknown assailant, reported to be black, tackled her and then repeatedly hacked at her with a butcher knife.[27] She survived, but the attack cost Aaron her eye and partial use of her arm and leg. In the days that followed, downtown newspapers breathlessly recorded other attacks against white San Franciscans. The *Chronicle* began a front-page report on an SFPD-sponsored crime study with a discussion of purse snatchings and the department's finding that there appeared to be "a greater tendency for white persons to become victims of attack by other racial groups than for the contrary to occur." The newspaper buried the relevant additional point—in the story's final, page-twelve paragraph—that reported assaults during that year against males outnumbered assaults against women 152 to 6.[28]

Following the attack on Aaron, Police Chief Cahill whipped up white fears of black male violence against white women and introduced two programs designed to buttress the street-level power of his patrol corps. He won support from managerial growth advocates by characterizing both strategies as advances in professionalism. First, he requested funds from the Board of Supervisors to establish a K-9 unit. The plan was to expertly transform dogs donated by the citizenry into obedient tools of law enforcement. San Francisco's

Board of Supervisors had rejected a similar proposal after the 1960 anti-HUAC demonstration and police riot, but in the wake of the Aaron slashing the supervisors readily offered their approval.[29]

The reactions to the K-9 proposal illustrated the citizenry's competing understandings of democratic governance. Black civil rights activists associated dogs with the antebellum period, noting that white slaveholders used the animals to "brutalize Negro slaves." However, the K-9 program's emphasis on centrally directed, expert preparation captured the imagination of managerial growth proponents, liberals and conservatives alike. The K-9 unit, these professionalization supporters emphasized, would reduce dialogue between police and residents. "You can argue with a cop but you can't argue with a dog," one officer quipped. In the place of dialogue, the K-9 unit promised consolidated decision making. Even cosmopolitan liberal reporters like the *News-Call Bulletin*'s Hadley Roff underscored that police dogs were "meticulously trained" to attack only on command.[30] Alongside descriptions or pictures of K-9 hounds interacting docilely with white children, white cosmopolitan liberals assured their readers that the department would only utilize this power in a color-blind manner, targeting burglars, muggers, and violent criminals. The *Chronicle*'s blithe assumption that professional arrangements would produce color-blind ends allowed the newspaper to report without irony that the SFPD's dog trainer had once worked for the Nazi army and that one donated dog arrived with the name Rommel.[31]

Rank-and-file officers expressed no reservations over the K-9 program, but they bristled at the second reform in Cahill's self-described "War on Crime." In order to release more patrolmen for "front-line" street duty, Cahill announced, he would introduce female "civilian" clerks in the district stations. The 1961 Blyth-Zellerbach Report and managerial growth advocates throughout the country had identified this so-called civilianizing of non-law enforcement tasks as a core professionalism goal. In San Francisco the mainstream press cheered Cahill's plan because it would be cost effective (incoming female clerks would be paid less than the male officers who had previously occupied the positions) and would increase the SFPD's physical presence on the street.[32]

The SFPD's civilianizing program illustrated the limits of the POA's politics by proxy. POA officials feared that female clerks would spoil the district stations' all-male work cultures and eliminate and feminize one of the few rewards available to patrolmen after a career of service on the beat. Nevertheless, POA officers and Ehrlich bit their tongues and offered only a muted protest to the hiring of female clerks.[33] Two years later, when the department announced its conversion to female meter maids, POA leaders declared that it was "Time for a Stand" and, through Ehrlich, submitted to the Police Commission a ten-point list of demands covering both bread-and-butter issues and workplace treatment. The SFPD leadership and the city's mainstream newspapers dismissed the POA's protests as illegitimate, and Ehrlich showed little interest in engaging in a public fight over workplace rights. This POA stand thus came to a quick and anticlimactic end, and the civilianizing trend continued. Between 1950 and 1970, the number of civilians working in the SFPD tripled, and civilian labor grew to 15 percent of the department's workforce.[34] POA leaders groused over the conversion but stopped well short of going to war over these labor interests.

THE EMERGENCE OF COOPERATIVE DISCRETION

Across the country, civil rights spokespersons faced city leaderships willing to infringe on rank-and-file interests in nearly every area except the patrol officers' prerogative to use discretionary force against people of color. In city after city, civil rights proponents began abandoning traditional, color-blind, elite-oriented approaches to police reform and instead sought to secure reform beachheads within their police departments. For instance, they emphasized the importance of introducing officers of color. In San Francisco the *Sun-Reporter* had already started suggesting race-conscious solutions during the early 1950s when it urged the SFPD leadership to increase the number of the department's black hires. The black newspaper asserted not only that black applicants had earned the right through color-blind merit, but that black residents preferred to be policed by black officers. The newspaper further intimated that both race consciousness and discretion could be used productively when it complained of the "lassitude" exhibited by white officers and insisted that black officers would provide the Fillmore District with more "persistent" policing.[35]

Through the 1960s and early 1970s, the SFPD distinguished itself among the nation's metropolitan police forces by resisting demands for racial integration. Elsewhere in urban America, civil rights activists convinced Democratic administrations to hire more black officers on the argument that officers of color possessed more understanding of and credibility within communities of color. In San Francisco, however, the SFPD's color line proved resistant to pressure from Shelley's and Alioto's Democratic administrations. In 1965 the department had 55 black officers on its 1,726-person roster, along with 3 Asian-Americans and 54 officers with Spanish surnames. Six years later black officers constituted only 5 percent of the police corps at a time when black people made up 13.4 percent of the city's population.[36]

Whether serving in the SFPD or another urban police force, African-American police faced daily reminders that many of their white peers considered them second-class. Patrolman Jeffrey, who worked in plain clothes both on the narcotics squad and as a PCR officer, noted that he spent much of his time contending with patrol officers who "refused to believe my identification and badge was real." The high brass reinforced this sense of illegitimacy by denying black officers promotions—no black officer made sergeant grade until the Alioto administration—and segregating black officers in low-value "Siberia" positions. One black patrolman recalled that when he and a group of other black police officers protested their postings, the high brass spitefully punished them by moving "us all to Traffic where we were all assigned to a single intersection—one man on each corner."[37]

By the early 1960s, Fillmore spokespersons recognized that rank-and-file integration was not a realistic near-term solution for curbing police violence.[38] Black activists therefore began casting about for new models of governance through which they could leverage their perspectives into the SFPD. On occasion, black activists demanded that the city join Philadelphia and New York City in instituting independent review boards. Downtown newspapers like the *Chronicle,* however, considered these propositions nonstarters because they plainly violated the city leadership's avowed principles of professionalism and color-blindness. During the early 1960s, the *Chronicle* supported infringements on police autonomy in artistic obscenity cases, arguing that in a culturally and sexually pluralist society, artists and scholars deserved oversight over SFPD censorship decisions. But Scott Newhall's cosmopolitan liberal newspaper continued to oppose the notion that the city maintained racially pluralist interests and thus questioned the grounds on which black residents would enjoy authority over professional police.[39]

Black activists received a more sympathetic hearing when they promoted the PCR unit, a new policing model arising out of the School of Criminology at the University of California, Berkeley. The school had generated the nation's dominant professionalization model during the mid-1950s, and at the start of the 1960s it promoted the PCR unit as the next major advance in professionalism. The school's dean invoked the supposed cultural deficiencies of black migrants when explaining why San Francisco needed a PCR unit. "The Negro hasn't found San Francisco yet," he averred. "This is still like a frontier to him." The PCR unit, Berkeley scholars proposed, would train officers to communicate with black residents, and unit officers would then use their expertise to teach black migrants "essential human values" and to "absorb" them into the city's modern, color-blind culture.[40]

While Berkeley scholars conceived of the PCR unit as a clear effort at professionalization, San Francisco's black activists recognized that the model's emphasis on communication made the unit a potential Trojan horse for black perspectives. A PCR unit would provide activists with a permanent link to the SFPD and potentially a police department representative. Thus in 1960 Berkeley criminologists, local professionalization proponents, long-established black activists in the NAACP, and the newly organized housing project mothers from Hunters Point began assembling annual conferences dedicated to advertising the community relations concept to the city's press and politicians.[41]

Chief Cahill initially condemned the PCR plan as a violation of color-blind principles. "Special race units," Cahill scoffed, "would be perpetuating the bias, a cure worse than the disease." Youth for Service, however, was already illustrating to mainstream journalists that citywide groups could use race-conscious language to guide black people into the city's purportedly color-blind culture. Meanwhile, reported incidents of violence from community members against police—including one episode in which community members allegedly tackled a police officer and threatened to execute him with his own sidearm—pushed the *Chronicle* and the *Examiner* into endorsing the PCR concept. The *Examiner* cautioned that "violence and tragedy" would follow if the department did not find ways to deal with the "influx of minority groups . . . with inbred hostilities towards the police."[42]

In the spring of 1962, Cahill finally relented and formed a PCR unit. Cahill assigned the unit to Lieutenant Andreotti, who had a reputation for defending the street-level prerogatives of the patrol officers and who had once fatally shot a fleeing suspect. Cahill provided Andreotti with a sergeant and a patrolman, making PCR the smallest unit in the police department, and Andreotti deployed his two officers to work in the districts with the largest black populations. During Shelley's term in City Hall, the chief added PCR officers to work with Latino, Chinese-American, and gay residents as well. Designing the PCR unit along professionalization principles, Cahill placed Andreotti under his direct command, dressed the PCR officers in plainclothes, and vowed that the detail would "teach minorities respect for law and order."[43] The chief understood police-community communications as a one-way conversation.

Following professionalism principles, the SFPD established a PCR executive committee based in the Hall of Justice and made up of citizens from across the city. This group held monthly meetings to advise Andreotti on PCR policies. The *Chronicle* applauded the decision not to provide the executive committee with any formal power within the SFPD, concurring with Mayor Christopher's contention that Cahill "should not be handicapped by a citizens' debating society."[44] Indeed, Cahill was not "handicapped" in the slightest as he proceeded to ignore the PCR unit altogether.

Chief Cahill had organized the PCR around a professional, centralized model, but then refused to interact with the PCR because he believed that community participants would introduce illegitimate perspectives into SFPD policy making. This contradiction resulted in a total lack of oversight over the PCR unit. PCR officers were assigned to specific districts but worked in those areas outside the district's regular command structure. Local residents immediately capitalized on this lack of supervision by pushing the unit toward greater decentralization. Mary Jane Scharff, the director of the PCR executive committee, began organizing volunteer PCR committees at the neighborhood level.[45]

These neighborhood committees urged their assigned PCR officers to use their discretion to negotiate with them in devising policing priorities. The committees, in other words, asked their PCR officers to accept a relationship based on cooperative discretion. On some occasions, PCR officers used the district meetings to serve as mouthpieces for downtown interests. Patrolman Elliot Blackstone, for instance, screened *To Build a Dream,* a film depicting the "phases and accomplishments" of the regional Bay Area Rapid Transit train line construction. Far more often, however, district committees spent their time considering how to direct PCR officers toward neighborhood-generated policies. These efforts produced a range of activities. Various PCR officers helped community members acquire job training, educated community members on their rights vis-à-vis the police, and worked with groups like Youth for Service to negotiate truces among battling youth. PCR officers Julio Fernandez and Inocente Cisneros served the outer Mission District by providing a weekly Spanish-language radio program answering Latino San Franciscans' law enforcement questions. Andreotti, meanwhile, startled the command ranks by disavowing top-down models and declaring, "Community relations is not selling the police product. You can communicate or fat-mouth to your heart's content, but if people don't see tangible results happening in other areas of their lives, you have lost them."[46]

The city leadership's efforts to deflect African-American demands for the right to be spared state brutality had ironically produced an institution that extended black residents—and then other marginalized groups—a host of new state services. Black activists understood that when confronting discretion-oriented institutions, achieving the negative right to be left alone by the government was harder than winning the positive right to government assistance. The former objective required civil rights activists to take away old prerogatives through rules enforcement, while the latter objective could be accomplished by granting police new powers through partnership. In creating a democratic police force, civil rights activists now began pairing their demands for top-down regulations with new emphases on inclusiveness and cooperation.

By the mid-1960s some PCR committees were pressing PCR officers to serve as their spokespersons in the civic sphere. The PCR unit represented one of the only points of access marginalized citizens enjoyed with any branch of government, and they thus looked to PCR officers as "all-purpose om-budsmen" who could help them with other city institutions. In 1965, when San Francisco initiated its War on Poverty program, the target area offices in Hunters Point, Chinatown, the Mission District, and Central City all made the political role of PCR officers even more explicit by providing them with desks, column space in the target area newspapers, and a voice in target area policy-making discussions.[47]

By engaging in decentralized, collaborative, discretion-based policing and open politicking, the PCR unit breached nearly every professionalization boundary. Chief Cahill attempted to keep the unit's experimentation in check by denying it a budget and refusing to promote PCR officers for their service in the unit.[48] These policies not only constricted the officers' ability to gain independence from Cahill but also limited the unit's muscle among the rank and file. Without funds or rank, PCR officers had little ability to compel other officers to follow their lead.

Cahill stopped short, however, of fully reining in the PCR unit's unconventional work. Andreotti recalled that the chief initially "went along with all the maverick ideas." In 1963 Cahill offered positive lip service to the unit's cooperative, root-cause approach to crime fighting. PCR officers, he concurred, needed "to go far beyond the concepts of law *enforcement, per se*" and reach "away out into the social service sphere." Cahill's equanimity regarding the PCR unit stemmed from his ignorance of the goings-on within the dispersed district committees; his failure to appreciate the gathering strength of the civil rights leaders with whom Andreotti and the other PCR officers were associating; and most important, the enormous political capital the PCR unit was earning him among liberals in San Francisco and the nation at large. Locally, Cahill found that he could mollify critics after acts of police repression with token expansions of the PCR unit's ranks. Following the New Year's Day Ball fiasco, for instance, Cahill added a PCR officer to work with gay and lesbian residents. Later that year, when a resident won a civil lawsuit against a violent officer, Cahill defused pressure for top-down controls over the rank and file by expanding the PCR unit's personnel from seven to eleven.[49]

The PCR unit's cooperative discretion fascinated police reformers and the national media.[50] As the unit's novel approach to policing expanded its reputation, Cahill earned national standing as "one of the brightest stars in the police firmament." It was widely assumed that President Lyndon Johnson's administration selected Cahill in 1965 as the only police chief to serve on the President's Commission on Law Enforcement on the basis of his department's PCR unit. That commission found the SFPD's PCR unit to be "unique to American police departments" for its "action"-oriented work with the "grass roots." The irony of Cahill's growing prominence was not lost on local black activists. "Cahill fought the idea of a Community Relations Unit for three years," Carlton Goodlett noted wryly. "Since its inception, he has become a national police figure. . . . We pushed him into greatness."[51]

THE WAR WITHIN THE SFPD

Unable to convince city leaders to address race-conscious perspectives, civil rights activists had used the PCR unit to exact reform from within the SFPD. The PCR officers had no real influence over patrol work, but both the department's district station captains and much of the rank and file quickly regarded the unit as a menace to the compromises they had accepted within police professionalism. Some concerns of the rank and file revolved around petty resentments, such as the PCR officers' ability to wear plainclothes like the detectives. Others grumbled over the PCR unit's ability to win the affections of residents of color. "We are out in the street dealing with the garbage. We see the real slum," one officer sniped. "Those guys wear their suits and make out like good guys."[52]

Patrol officers were most vexed, however, that PCR officers used their cooperative discretion to second-guess the autonomous discretion of the rank and file. During the mid-1960s, PCR officers began helping job applicants with rap sheets to explain away their past petty criminal charges to potential employers. For many of San Francisco's male low-income youth, the record of a misdemeanor or false arrest served as a major impediment to employment. Often these arrests involved a "suspicion of felony" charge. In their attempts to regulate black youth, police officers often used their discretion to detain youth with such charges, and they frequently made them as specific and serious as possible. Thus, black male youth could develop long records peppered with "suspicion of robbery" and "suspicion of rape" accusations. PCR officers became expert at explaining away these sorts of arrests with prospective employers or erasing the past bookings altogether. During one two-month period in the PCR unit, Patrolman Jeffrey "explained" an astounding two hundred San Franciscans into jobs.[53]

PCR officers further challenged the autonomous discretion of the rank and file by collecting police brutality accusations from community members. This practice, the SFPD's uniformed patrol officers objected, increased the number of brutality allegations and heightened the severity of the charges. Community members often felt more comfortable with PCR officers than with the desk clerks at the district stations, and they therefore provided the unit's members with less inhibited (or, in the view of the rank and file, more fantastic) descriptions of police bloodshed. Some PCR officers went even further in violating the district stations' code of silence by reporting the acts of brutality they witnessed themselves. "No one was about to beat a black man while I was around," one PCR officer commented. "I once saw a cop punch a black kid at Park Station. I spoke up and that sort of stuff ended, though all the cops stopped speaking to me."[54]

Rank-and-file officers seethed over the PCR-generated brutality probes despite the fact that the PCR unit's work did little to increase the likelihood that patrol officers would be punished for their use of force. Many rank-and-file officers erroneously believed that the PCR officers investigated the brutality complaints they collected. On the contrary, PCR officers forwarded the citizen grievances to the department's normal chain of command. The PCR unit thus confronted violent patrol officers with few new legal consequences. Local civil rights attorneys and activists actually reported upswings in antiblack police assaults in late 1963 and again in late 1964 and early 1965.[55]

Even though the PCR unit lacked the power to affect the day-to-day decisions of police officers, the rank and file, Mindermann recalled, viewed the PCR programs as "a direct repudiation of their vigilant, honest, forthright efforts to contain crime—a disproportionate amount of which [was] being generated by black people." Rank-and-file officers were particularly incensed that "direct repudiation" from within the SFPD originally arose from black residents outside the department. The perspectives of black activists were now being represented in SFPD policy. Sergeant Crowley of the Potrero District later vented this anger:

It's like the French Revolution, right? They send out the priests into the ghetto . . . to allay the people. . . . Well, when the mob came, the guys in the front were the priests, screaming and yelling. So, they [the PCR] identified with the community, not with a balance between the police department and the community. They thought they were speaking for the community rather than the police department.[56]

Michael Hebel, a Park Station patrolman, also described resentment over the authority marginalized residents enjoyed through the PCR unit: the "general perception was that community relations was not police, it was community. And there was no balance. So that community relations was [a] police voice, inside the police for the people we have been talking about"—bohemians, gays and lesbians, and African Americans.[57] The prerogatives police maintained under professionalism were arranged around the assumption that all citizens possessed preexisting shared interests. Black activists, however, resisted autonomous police discretion by refusing to play by the rules of professionalism. As Crowley's and Hebel's later references to balance illustrated, the PCR challenge led some rank-and-file officers to begin conceiving of San Francisco's police politics in pluralistic terms.

Rank-and-file police lashed out against PCR officers for what was perceived as a betrayal of rank-and-file interests. On a daily basis, rank-and-file officers subjected PCR members to the silent treatment, office pranks (like permanently stealing desks), and a range of invectives. Richard Hongisto, a white PCR officer, recalled being told that an officer had pointed to him and said, "You see that guy? You know what he is? There goes a pot-smoking, Communist, homosexual, nigger lover." By the late 1960s, there were reports of white and black officers drawing their service weapons on each other, and PCR officers began avoiding some district stations out of fear for their physical safety. One black veteran PCR officer abandoned any pretense of intradepartmental comity when he remarked:

> Some of the policemen in the San Francisco police department are clear and distinct racists, the type who would be prime Nazi material. . . . Changing racial attitudes of a bigot is fairly impossible. We're not concerned with how the average policeman thinks, but how he acts. If a cop does something wrong we want him punished so neither he nor his buddies will do it again. That's the most we can do. . . . There are a number of men in the department that I would immediately fire. There are others that I would put in jail because I know what they have done and that is where they belong. That's not politically realistic, however.

Andreotti ceased viewing the city's lawbreakers as his unit's primary concern. "Our war," he later explained, "was with the police department."[58]

The 1966 Hunters Point riot expanded the battle lines of this war beyond the SFPD. Racial conservatives worried that inclusive institutions like the PCR unit had facilitated this explosion of neighborhood destruction by encouraging race-conscious perspectives and hamstringing police efforts to enforce color-blind laws. Ehrlich, in particular, jumped headlong into the intradepartmental fray. Earlier in the decade, Ehrlich had warned that civil rights activists threatened to "usher in a new era of National Socialism" with their race-conscious demonstrations against lily-white hiring practices. At the same time, he had illustrated his own brand of color-blind politics by festooning his office walls with intertwining American and Confederate flags. Following the Hunters Point riot, Ehrlich battled the race-conscious approach of the PCR unit by working with the Oakland Police Department and the *San Francisco Examiner* to manufacture a public scandal involving a black Hunters Point PCR officer and an Oakland prostitute. Meanwhile, a POA ally on the grand jury police committee and the SFPD's nine district captains issued closely timed calls for Cahill to dissolve the PCR unit.[59]

The Hunters Point riot had left Chief Cahill receptive to these requests. Prior to the Hunters Point uprising, the chief had frequently bragged that because of his benevolent professional leadership, "We don't have race riots in San Francisco." The violence in Hunters Point, Cahill growled, had "spoiled" that "record," and he, like Ehrlich, assumed that the rioting could only be the result of the work of race-conscious instigators. Under these circumstances, Cahill no longer viewed Andreotti's association with black activists as benign. Indeed, Cahill concluded that one black PCR officer already served as a plant for the city's Black Muslims.[60]

Mayor Shelley believed that the PCR unit's employment efforts helped assimilate young black men as breadwinners, and he prevented Cahill from eliminating the unit outright. Shelley did nothing, however, to stop Cahill from creating a competing PCR infrastructure. The chief detailed new uniformed PCR officers to district stations, where they answered to their district station captains, not Andreotti. Cahill's power grab dashed Andreotti's hopes of reforming the SFPD from within, and in August 1967 the disillusioned PCR leader left the SFPD for a position in the Community Relations Service of the U.S. Department of Justice. With Andreotti out of the way, Cahill forbade PCR officers from collecting citizens' brutality complaints, and he replaced Andreotti with Lieutenant Gus Bruneman. The paternalistic chief justified Bruneman's selection by noting the lieutenant's role in founding the SFPD's Police Athletic League, a police-youth sports organization. But black activists saw equal significance in Bruneman's previous assignment as the head of the despised K-9 division. Four of the PCR unit's six black members resigned from the department within months of Bruneman's appointment. Chief Cahill, meanwhile, continued using the hollowed-out PCR, as well as his widely advertised human relations conferences, to burnish his national reputation as a police reformer.[61]

MAYOR ALIOTO'S COSMOPOLITAN LIBERAL POLICING

In 1968 Mayor Alioto took office amid fierce fights—inside and outside the SFPD—over the relationship between inclusiveness, police use of force, and community violence. Alioto responded to these debates with a cosmopolitan liberal growth message that, like Mayor John Lindsay's governing style in New York City, promised both to increase democratic participation and to retain the traditional privileged position of City Hall.[62] As Alioto sought a middle ground, however, he kept his focus on the tensions between marginalized residents (especially African Americans) and the city's anxious middle-class whites. The new mayor never addressed how the new citizen-state relationship would affect the institutional interests of San Francisco police.

As soon as Alioto took office, the mayor encouraged civil rights activists by increasing the access residents of color enjoyed in City Hall's police policy discussions. Most dramatically, the mayor appointed Washington Garner, a doctor, as the city's first black police commissioner. Garner, in turn, revivified the PCR unit. The unit's work channeling marginalized perspectives into government-oriented dialogues paralleled Alioto's deliberative democratic vision. The mayor therefore accepted the decentralized, cooperative discretion of the PCR officers on the assumption that they would strengthen the connection between his office and the citizenry. PCR officers had proved their ability to fulfill this role during his mayoral campaign. Facing a compressed electoral timeline, Alioto's campaign advisors had learned that PCR officers and the PCR neighborhood committees could rapidly introduce them to the spokespersons, needs, and desires of the city's low-income voters. Alioto continued using the PCR neighborhood committees for outreach after his election. In March 1968, for instance, he attended the Bayview PCR committee meeting to discuss policing with two hundred neighborhood residents.[63]

Mayor Alioto and Commissioner Garner strengthened the PCR unit by forcing Chief Cahill to replace Lieutenant Bruneman as its head with Lieutenant William Osterloh. The new PCR leader echoed Alioto's emphasis on the importance of embracing pluralism at the upper levels of government: "If you have a captain out in a district station who cares, who has sergeants who care, who have lieutenants who care, then you will have patrolmen who care."[64] After Osterloh's appointment, Alioto's administration pressed Cahill into adding more officers to the PCR detail, increasing the size of the unit back to fourteen officers by 1970, and Commissioner Garner then ensured that the department filled the unit's five new posts with officers supported by, and sometimes handpicked by, local black and Latino powerbrokers.[65]

As Alioto accepted the PCR unit's cooperative discretion as a means of expanding City Hall's inclusiveness, he championed the Hall of Justice's deployment of professionalized force as protection for City Hall pluralism. Earlier in the decade, cosmopolitan liberal reporters had thrown their support behind the K-9 unit on the contention that disciplined, expert uses of force could serve the city's common values. Alioto now took another step toward professionalized force by unveiling the tactical ("tac") squad. Arranged in four separate groups of eight, the tac squad dressed its officers in masked helmets and all-black coveralls and schooled the men in judo, wrestling, karate, baton use, antisniper control, and house-to-house combat. Neither City Hall nor the Hall of Justice made any attempt to downplay the tac squad's physical capabilities. Department leaders described its members as "outstanding physical specimens," and one squad sergeant summarized, "We don't want little guys."[66]

Alioto and the SFPD leadership stressed that the department leadership would firmly control the tac squad so that its awesome power would be directed only against "civil disturbances" that threatened the civic good with "violence." Police discretion supposedly had no place in the squad. In contrast to beat officers who were expected to act autonomously, tac squad officers were, in the words of one sergeant, "trained to operate as a unit." The police leadership, Alioto explained, would deploy the tac squad in a "scientific," nonlethal manner. "The precision tactics," Alioto later asserted, "avoided the use of buckshot, bayonets, or tear gas." (Some squad members allegedly compensated for their lack of weaponry by cutting their riot sticks diagonally across the end so they could administer sharper kidney blows.) The unit's very name suggested its emphasis on planning and forethought, in contrast to the physical, onomatopoeic connotations of the Los Angeles Police Department's SWAT team.[67]

The tac squad made its debut in January 1968 when it broke up an anti–Vietnam War demonstration in which protesters attempted to disrupt a speech by Secretary of State Dean Rusk. The squad's national reputation spread quickly; during the squad's first year in operation, the FBI invited its leaders to coauthor the federal agency's report on riot control. Tac squad members complicated Mayor Alioto's attempts to portray their squad as a defender of democracy, however, when they involved themselves in extracurricular violence. In July 1968, for instance, two to four drunken tac squad officers rampaged through the Mission District, assaulting seven to nine mostly black and Latino young men. The details on this assault spree were sketchy because the district police and district attorney both obstructed and bungled the investigation, but even with the resulting evidentiary challenges, a jury found one of the two charged tac squad officers guilty of two counts of battery.[68]

Community activists claimed that on-duty tac squad officers also engaged in discretionary violence. In one incident Hunters Point residents charged the tac squad with using Mace against a middle-class black mother and her two adult daughters while the three were detained in a police wagon. In another episode, schoolteachers and administrators accused the tac squad of attacking students and instructors indiscriminately during a fight following a high school basketball game. The same month school desegregation activists alleged that the tac squad intentionally failed to help civil rights supporters who were attacked by white thugs (reported to be Teamsters) at a school board meeting. Black spokespersons, meanwhile, charged that tac squad members spent the long periods between high-profile demonstrations roaming "high criminal incidence" areas and abusing black San Franciscans. Alioto attempted to deflect these allegations of tac squad unprofessionalism with minor reforms aimed at tightening the department's top-down control over the squad, and by issuing homilies like: "Even the Lord in selecting 12 disciples, only got 11 good ones." However, the mayor was unequivocal about his intention to maintain the tac squad "until the acts of violence end."[69]

Alioto had more political latitude when regular patrol officers engaged in unprofessional use of force. During his first year in office, the accusations of rank-and-file brutality kept pace with the charges of tac squad violence. One student claimed six officers "creamed" him during an antiwar party; witnesses accused another officer of subduing a fourteen-year-old girl and her mother by breaking the girl's arm and banging her mother's head; and police confirmed that yet another officer drunkenly fired his service weapon at a noisy cat, missed the animal, and instead creased the forehead of his neighbor. These "three incidents," Alioto was willing to admit, had "justifiably . . . disturbed" "a large group of legitimate and reasonable people."[70]

Nine months into Alioto's administration, civil rights activists confronted the mayor with a citizen slaying that forced him to take a clear stand on the issue of rank-and-file discretionary violence. On September 29, 1968, a minor traffic mishap set off a chain of events ending in Michael O'Brien, an off-duty SFPD patrol officer, killing George Baskett, a black twenty-eight-year-old father of two and husband to a pregnant wife. O'Brien had already been arrested twice for theft when the SFPD accepted him into its ranks in 1966. The department initially assigned the twenty-six-year-old officer to the interracial Potrero Hill, but public protests over his outlandish racial provocations soon forced his supervisors to transfer him to another neighborhood. During this same period, O'Brien was allegedly exhibiting a worrisome habit of drawing his weapon in off-duty situations. A seventeen-year-old black Bank of America employee charged that O'Brien had pulled a gun on her in late July 1968, and the following month, a witness claimed, O'Brien fired a gun at a door lock during a nightclub argument.[71]

Late in the afternoon of September 29, O'Brien, a second off-duty officer, and two female companions were lounging outside a garage where O'Brien kept his boat trailer. The garage opened onto Brush Place, a narrow residential alley in San Francisco's impoverished and interracial South Park neighborhood. O'Brien had left his boat trailer jutting out of the garage and was in the process of drinking a "great portion" of a gallon jug of wine when a black Brush Place resident turned his car into the cramped alley. The driver attempted to maneuver his car around the boat, driving partially on the opposite sidewalk, but his car made contact with the boat's trailer and left a small scratch in its fender.[72]

Stories diverged wildly over what occurred next. According to O'Brien, he and the driver got into an argument, and the driver's wife fetched a pistol and began shooting at the off-duty officer. Brush Place residents, O'Brien continued, began pouring out onto the street and joined in the attack. Amid this assault, O'Brien charged, Baskett began thrashing O'Brien with the rung of a chair, and on the third blow, O'Brien accidentally discharged his gun into Baskett's body. The tac squad arrived in the nick of time, O'Brien concluded, and arrested four residents, including the original driver of the car, who now held the gun that O'Brien insisted had been fired at him. Tac squad officers corroborated O'Brien's version of events, failed to mark the spot where Baskett fell, and neglected to preserve the scene. Chief Cahill accepted their report, announced that O'Brien's shooting had been "accidental and in self-defense," and attempted to put the issue to rest.[73]

Incensed civil rights activists and social service agency workers, however, began flooding Alioto's office with messages, and liberal *Chronicle* and *Examiner* journalists uncovered what they interpreted as a police whitewash.[74] These newspaper reports compelled the SFPD to reopen the case, and the department's captain of inspectors, a civil rights moderate, assigned two officers from the reenergized PCR unit to conduct the new investigation.[75]

The PCR officers assembled a narrative sharply at odds with O'Brien's. Residents told the community relations police that O'Brien, a six-foot, five-inch, 235-pound man, had flown into a rage after seeing his fender nicked. Locals claimed that O'Brien had immediately tossed the apologizing driver against a telephone pole and called the driver's wife a "nigger bitch." At no point, witnesses asserted, did the off-duty O'Brien identify himself as a police officer. Thus everyone was startled when O'Brien suddenly unholstered a side-arm. Residents reported that Baskett, a 160-pound man, then stepped forward to challenge O'Brien to put down his weapon so they could settle the conflict with their fists. Instead, O'Brien allegedly pulled the gun's trigger three times without any shots firing (he was running through empty chambers or had for-gotten to remove the safety), before looking at the weapon, counting aloud to three, and unloading the fatal round into Baskett's chest. Following the killing, residents related, O'Brien turned to rest of the neighbors and screamed, "I want to kill a nigger so bad I can taste it. Just make one move and I'll kill you."[76]

Witnesses were unanimous in exculpating the four arrested residents. In-deed, the driver charged with handgun possession claimed that tac squad of-ficers had forced the pistol into his hand while he was lined up against a wall at gunpoint. This testimony and the appearance of physical evidence directly contradicting O'Brien's version of events compelled the district attorney to release the four arrested witnesses without charge. With the case now receiv-ing statewide coverage, Alioto's Police Commission suspended O'Brien, and under mayoral pressure, the district attorney took O'Brien to trial for man-slaughter.[77]

The POA immediately turned to Ehrlich, their elite proxy, for help.[78] Eh-rlich followed a straightforward courtroom strategy: the defense attorney used the jury-selection process to impanel an all-white jury, then, with the judge providing him tremendous leeway, Ehrlich race-baited the jurors. Referring to Brush Place as a "hellhole" and to its mostly black residents as "some 200 hyenas," Ehrlich warned the jury: "You must realize we're dealing here with people of little or no moral honesty or integrity." Playing on base fears, Ehrlich further intoned, "Those people would have killed . . . O'Brien, and they would have killed you, too. If you'd been there."[79]

During the trial Ehrlich dramatized his contempt for Alioto's new style of pluralist discourse by manufacturing a confrontation with a Black Panther in the courtroom audience. Pointing to the young black radical, Ehrlich de-manded, "What's your name boy? Stand up!" The young man retorted that his name was not Boy, and Ehrlich postured, "Well, I'm put out. I don't like this childish infantile feeling that someone's trying to offend these people.

I've fought for them, defended them without fee, . . . and I won't take any backtalk out of them." Ehrlich followed this grandstanding with an attack on the mayor for pandering to black interests. Alioto had forced the prosecution to press charges, Ehrlich insisted, so he could lock up the "minority vote" for his anticipated gubernatorial run.[80]

As Alioto worked to curb unprofessional police violence through the O'Brien prosecution, the mayor used a concurrent student and faculty strike at San Francisco State College to illustrate how the professionalized use of force could stimulate City Hall–oriented democracy. Student unrest at the college had been building for years, and in November 1968 a multiracial coalition of San Francisco State students initiated a strike over fifteen "non-negotiable" demands. By January 1969, 350 professors and an unknown number of black activists from the Fillmore District and Hunters Point had joined the student picket lines at the campus entrances.[81]

A year prior to the strike, black student activists had assaulted a white student newspaper editor, and just weeks before the walkout, a Black Panther leader had exhorted student activists to "bring guns to school." The mainstream media had made front-page news of both of these incidents, but during the four-month strike, the mass of participants proved committed to nonviolence. Demonstrators attempted to close the school with picket lines, marches, and acts of disruptive vandalism (such as the emptying of bookshelves at the library), and Alioto responded to these nonviolent tactics with force. The tac squad took up permanent duty at the college and swept up gatherings of protesters with drawn batons and lockstep maneuvers. Between December 2, 1968, and January 30, 1969, doctors reported, police injured eighty of the strikers whom they arrested.[82]

Alioto defended the tac squad's bloody toll by emphasizing how the students threatened his administration's democratic arrangement with their non-negotiable demands and their school-closing tactics. Like government institutions, the mayor argued, colleges were sites where inclusive discourse could manufacture common values. "The clash of ideas on the anvil of debate," he proclaimed, "has been this Nation's surest means of hammering out the truth, and our institutions of higher learning provide the spirited arena where this can be done." When students conducted a sit-in inside the school's administration building, Alioto rationalized his decision to clear out the protesters by terming the demonstration an act of "force or violence" because it stifled democracy and "effectively excludes anybody else." This was a form of "violence," an Alioto spokesperson elaborated, that could spread into other parts of the city. By exhibiting eagerness to deploy police on college campuses, Alioto differentiated himself from other liberals, like New York's Mayor Lindsay. When in early March 1969 Alioto was himself assaulted by student protesters at Georgetown University, he promptly criticized the school's leadership for failing to initiate "professional police action."[83]

At the same time, the San Francisco mayor distanced himself from conservatives like California governor Ronald Reagan by stressing that his use of force encouraged democratic negotiation. During the spring of 1969, Governor Reagan unleashed the National Guard against student demonstrators at the University of California, Berkeley, with the simple aim of crushing the protests. At San Francisco State, Reagan's appointed college trustees resisted negotiations, and the governor advocated humbling the strikers "at the point of a bayonet, if necessary." Alioto ridiculed conservatives like Reagan for exposing themselves as "gutless and soft" for their unwillingness to negotiate. Brushing off his confrontation with Georgetown University students, the mayor swaggered, "Frankly, I have no fear of our younger generation and its heady, impetuous idealism." Conservatives' fearfulness, Alioto continued, endangered the citizenry. He argued that the haphazard use of "bayonets" and "aerial gas attacks" that sought only "repression"—a reference to National Guard tactics at Berkeley—would "inflame" students further.[84]

Through self-assured negotiations, Alioto insisted, students could be controlled. From the start of the strike, he offered City Hall as a venue and agent for negotiations between the strikers and the college regents. He also established the Citizens Committee on San Francisco State to broker a resolution and rooted the committee's work in the Catholic Action tradition by assigning Roman Catholic auxiliary bishop Mark J. Hurley as the group's chair. Alioto also claimed that he was willing to provide students with a microphone and platform at a "campus Hyde Park"—a reference to the Speakers' Corner protest space in London's Hyde Park—so the students could "advocate" as much as they wanted. "After debate," he suggested, San Franciscans could hold a "plebiscite" to determine popular will. His system accounted for pluralist values on policy matters, but the mayor pointed to the governing system itself as a civic interest. On these grounds Alioto denied students the right to interfere with government-approved venues for democratic participation. "We have to tell them," he explained to Congress, "that we are going to let you participate in decision [*sic*] without abdicating leadership."[85] For Alioto, democracy was located not out "in the streets," but under the dome of City Hall.

Over a seventy-two-hour period in March 1969, both the O'Brien trial and the San Francisco State strike came to an end. At San Francisco State, drained and battered protesters finally agreed to talk, and through negotiations sponsored by Alioto's Citizens Committee, the strikers and trustees reached a settlement. Alioto declared that his policing strategy had sustained democracy. His tac squad's arrests had enabled him to reach "a negotiated settlement between the trustees, who at one time said they would not negotiate, and the students, who at one time said they would not negotiate either, and the teachers, too, who at one time said they would not negotiate."[86]

Meanwhile, Ehrlich proved a good judge of his jury, and on March 20, O'Brien received a not-guilty verdict. But the officer's victory was short-lived. Ehrlich's histrionic defense had placed the liberal administration's commitment to racial pluralism on trial, and the *Chronicle*'s headline "'Stand Up, Boy': Angry Ehrlich's Court Outbursts" illustrated that his strategy had caught liberal attention. On March 31, Alioto's Police Commission found O'Brien guilty of "unofficer-like conduct" (a charge mostly stemming from the patrolman's admitted use of "profanities and . . . threats"). The possible punishments for this violation ranged from simple reprimand to outright dismissal, and the Police Commission unanimously voted for the latter.[87] Patrolman O'Brien was the first officer in SFPD history to lose his position over an act of belligerence against a black person.

In just a year and a half in office, Alioto had shored up the PCR unit, introduced the tac squad, and used the two policing groups to help score simultaneous victories over the student strikers at San Francisco State and Patrolman O'Brien and his POA defense. Alioto celebrated his successes with state and national victory laps. On these tours, Alioto met with U.S. Attorney General John Mitchell, presented an address at Yale University, gave the keynote speech at Philadelphia's National Law Day ceremonies (where Philadelphia mayor James Tate, a Democrat, was also attempting to square liberalism with tough policing), and delivered the presidential nominating speech at the Democratic Convention in Chicago.[88]

The mayor explained to his various out-of-city audiences that his efforts to expand access to government and crack down on the discretionary use of force justified his use of professionalized force against demonstrators. "It seems to me," Alioto told Congress, "that, if you are very liberal toward dissent, you can be a little bit tougher, even, in terms of law enforcement, because you have removed one of the frustrations." Similarly, Alioto insisted that "when you have been very very liberal" in the disciplining of wayward officers, you can "afford to be a little tougher about law enforcement." As both of these formulations revealed, Alioto predicated his understanding of democracy and the use of force on the assumption that the mayor could maintain his authority over the rank and file.[89]

CONCLUSION

During the 1950s and 1960s, the nation's urban civil rights activists and city officials debated over the rank and file's use of force over residents of color. This fight implicated both the rank and file's street-level interests and their workplace and political prerogatives. Initially rank-and-file police officers in San Francisco and elsewhere accepted an arrangement with police professionalizers that excluded them from the political sphere and gradually diminished their workplace rights. In exchange, city elites defended the rank and file's autonomous discretion over black residents by dismissing out of hand charges of race-conscious police brutality.

Unable to achieve recourse through City Hall, some civil rights activists looked for new avenues for reform within the SFPD. Spokespersons for the black community—and later, advocates for gays and lesbians, bohemians, Chinese Americans, and Latinos—found liberal officers in the PCR unit willing to partner with residents and challenge the rank and file's autonomous discretion with their own cooperative discretion. Inside and outside the police force, the PCR unit's work fueled arguments over whether the city should respond to rising crime rates with greater inclusiveness or tougher law enforcement.

Mayor Alioto took office insisting to voters they did not have to choose between these two approaches. Instead, he promised San Franciscans both participation and order through a City Hall–oriented democracy. Alioto embraced the PCR unit as an entity that drew community voices into government policy-making discussions, but he then used that inclusiveness to rationalize centralized policing by the tac squad. Forwarding his City Hall as an identifier and defender of the common good, Alioto claimed the prerogative to act against San Franciscans—police officers and community members alike—whose behavior challenged his democratic arrangement.

"City Hall Can Be Beaten": Haight-Ashbury Activists, Rank-and-File Police, and a Cosmopolitan Localism

A motley congregation of men, women, and children lazed on the grounds of the Golden Gate Park amphitheater. As the "sweet pungent aroma" of marijuana "wafted up at times," one reporter reminisced, the fall 1972 gathering looked like "another impromptu love-in, the kind that made headlines in the days of flower children and cosmic happenings." Counterculture singers, dancers, and acrobats entertained the onlookers, with the performances occasionally pausing for short political speeches. Hippies from the Church of the Good Earth, young white professionals and middle-class blacks representing the Haight-Ashbury Neighborhood Council (HANC), and a new generation of white officers speaking for the Police Officers' Association all took the stage to protest Mayor Joseph Alioto's decision to close Park Station, the small district police station serving the Haight-Ashbury neighborhood. Paraphrasing the orators, one journalist conveyed that Haight-Ashbury residents and Park Station officers felt that although their relationship was "not always cordial" it was nevertheless "close." On those terms, the activists urged the small crowd of 150 to reverse Alioto's action by heading to the polls on November 7 and voting to reopen Park Station.[1]

Earlier that year Alioto and his new police chief, Donald Scott, had announced Park Station's closing as the first step in a long-term plan to consolidate San Francisco's nine district police stations to four major headquarters. This centralization effort extended from Alioto's broader agenda to make City Hall both the locus of the city's democratic debate and the executor of the citizenry's decisions. Following the lead of Mayor John Lindsay in New York City, Alioto hoped to make the police more effective and democratic by initiating rapid-response police strategies dedicated to arresting criminals who caused harm.[2]

At the Golden Gate Park protest, opposition arose from blacks, hippies, police, and perhaps most startlingly, the young white professionals whom Alioto had intended to court with his policing agenda. Across the country white-collar workers living in unredeveloped neighborhoods like the Haight-Ashbury were demonstrating against cosmopolitan growth liberalism with a cosmopolitan localist liberalism. Although this marriage of cosmopolitanism and localism struck growth liberals like Alioto as contradictory, cosmopolitan localists insisted that pluralist democracy necessitated decentralized neighborhood-based decision making. The diverse set of organizers behind this first annual Haight-Ashbury Police-Community Picnic resisted further police professionalism and instead championed the "close and not always cordial relationship" patrol officers and residents developed on the sidewalks as a model for their localist democratic vision.

LOCALIST POLITICS IN THE HAIGHT-ASHBURY

During the 1950s and 1960s, San Francisco's cosmopolitan liberal coalition arose around the notion that expanded bounds of citizenship could attract the young, college-educated white-collar workers needed to grow the city's service, banking, information, and government sectors. To the delight of cosmopolitan growth advocates, the downtown jobs produced through redevelopment and the expanded culture facilitated through police professionalism brought young white-collar workers streaming into the city.[3]

Yet, although young professionals had benefited from City Hall's reform policies, some chose to keep the downtown's centralization agenda at arm's length from their home lives. Across the nation, segments of the young urban professional workforce spurned the modernist apartment towers jutting up across their cities' skylines and instead gravitated to those pockets still untouched by redevelopment wrecking balls. These "postindustrial" workers, historian Suleiman Osman has shown, rushed into historic neighborhoods, such as Atlanta's Inman Park, Boston's South End, Toronto's Yorkville, and Washington, DC's Capitol Hill. Many of these white migrants, Osman found, arrived hoping that the small scale of these unmodernized "urban villages" would enable them to develop more personal and "authentic," or humanizing, relationships.[4]

In San Francisco many young white migrants landed in the Haight-Ashbury, a neighborhood near the geographic center of the city. The Haight-Ashbury offered newcomers stately Victorian homes; the vibrant, long, rectangular Panhandle park; and an intimate two-lane, five-block commercial strip along Haight Street. Between 1960 and 1970, the neighborhood's population dropped by 5.8 percent, but the number of single people climbed 30 percent and the number of male professionals jumped by 180 percent. By 1970 a city planning report found "an increasing number of residents who are under 35, well educated, single, and white."[5]

Young white professionals poured into the Haight-Ashbury's northwestern flatlands and southwestern hills. Property owners in the flatlands had subdivided their colorful Victorian homes into rental units, and during the 1950s and early 1960s, these apartments attracted not only white-collar professionals and government clerks but retirees, Eastern European immigrants, San Francisco State College students, a brief influx of gay men, and bohemians priced out of the gentrifying North Beach. To the south and across Haight Street, wealthier young professionals moved onto the neighborhood's southwestern slopes. Here migrants found an older and more privileged population of white homeowning professionals, including doctors and professors from nearby medical and university campuses.[6]

By the end of the 1950s, property owners in the northeastern quadrant of the neighborhood had begun renting their units to working-class black residents displaced by redevelopment in the adjacent Fillmore District. As black San Franciscans achieved a foothold in the neighborhood, property owners also accepted Latino, Chinese-American, and Filipino-American tenants. This inflow of people of color into the neighborhood's northern end remade the neighborhood's social makeup. In 1950 the Haight-Ashbury's population was roughly 97 percent white, including a very small number of Latinos, and by 1970 the neighborhood was roughly 33 percent black, 14 percent Latino, and 10 percent Asian-American.[7]

The Haight-Ashbury's sectors were divided by wealth and racial composition, but a variety of factors tied residents together around a common neighborhood identity. As part of their day-to-day lives, residents of all the Haight-Ashbury's pockets shopped along the Haight Street commercial corridor. This experience contributed to a village environment appreciated by longtime residents and newcomers alike.[8] Explaining that many of the homeowners living in the southwestern portion of the neighborhood had consciously chosen to forgo "better addresses" for the Haight-Ashbury's unmodernized setting, a San Francisco–based journalist noted that the area's older residents

had firm views clustering about the conviction that three-story Tudor and Victorian dwellings are preferable to skyscrapers, that streets should serve people before automobiles, that a neighborhood was meant for living as well as sleeping, that habitation implies some human dirt, that small shops foster human acquaintance as department stores don't, and that schools which are integrated are more educational than schools which are segregated.[9]

In the Haight-Ashbury and "urban villages" elsewhere, young white professionals and working-class blacks also bonded around a common antipathy toward centralized governance. These residents associated City Hall decision making with material, psychological, and emotional dangers. In the Haight-Ashbury, residents had personally witnessed the centrally planned and executed demolition of the neighboring Fillmore District. As San Francisco's growth advocates looked for other redevelopment opportunities, Haight-Ashbury residents were rightly concerned that city planners and downtown executives might next seek to demolish their neighborhood. Haight-Ashbury locals also protested that when they had no input in the government policies affecting them they felt less vital (what the New Left later described as "alienated"). Area residents insisted that they would become more human by taking a personal role in neighborhood policy making. On these twin motivations, historians Osman and Guian McKee have shown, urban village whites and urban African Americans both turned to do-it-yourself neighborhood uplift strategies. Haight-Ashbury residents—local women in particular—initiated myriad self-consciously small-scale and neighborhood-oriented institutions and services.[10]

Fears of street violence motivated the first sustained neighborhood organizing effort in the Haight-Ashbury. In June 1958 the interracial murder of Connie Sublette (the North Beach beat strangled in a Haight-Ashbury alley) rattled locals, and within months residents had established the Haight-Ashbury Neighborhood Council. HANC leaders announced that the Haight-Ashbury was "a state of mind as well as a geographical area," and spokespersons defined that mind-set around local self-improvement. With this philosophy HANC initiated an advertising campaign designed to attract outside shoppers into Haight Street businesses, a successful lobbying effort to persuade the city to install litter cans on neighborhood street corners, and a volunteer street-sweeping program.[11] HANC members believed that these collaborative efforts affected more than the neighborhood's physical well-being. "The impact of citizens lifting themselves by their own bootstraps," a HANC consultant rhapsodized, "instills a new vitality in the neighborhood—a vitality that cannot immediately be evaluated in terms of material achievement."[12]

HANC leaders characterized black-and-white interracial cooperation as particularly invigorating. The organization originated as a predominantly white group, and Latinos and Asians never acquired a prominent role during the 1960s, but HANC drew in a growing number of black participants over this period. In 1969 HANC's membership elected Ray Waller as the organization's first black president.[13] HANC acknowledged the racial imbalances between the neighborhood's residential southwestern and northeastern sectors, but HANC activists, black and white alike, celebrated the racial diversity experienced in neighborhood-wide groups such as HANC and in common spaces like Haight Street. In 1963 HANC may have been the only neighborhood association in the nation to send its own delegation—a white man and black woman—to the March on Washington. A year later Haight-Ashbury residents overwhelmingly rejected a California proposition defending the rights of home sellers to discriminate on the basis of race. (The rest of San Francisco, excluding the Haight-Ashbury vote, approved the measure by nine points.) Following the 1965 riot in Watts, Los Angeles, Richard Boyle, publisher of a Haight-Ashbury newspaper, lionized his neighborhood as "a model for the nation of good race relations."[14]

Most HANC members identified with the developing cosmopolitan liberal understanding of the citizenry, but whereas many of the city's mainstream journalists promoted the cosmopolitan liberal definitions of crime and citizenship as a path to downtown growth, HANC's membership believed that the city could best foster and capitalize upon pluralism through localist decision making. This neighborhood-oriented approach eventually placed HANC at loggerheads with both the methods and goals of downtown growth advocates. In 1964 HANC entered citywide politics when Mayor Jack Shelley, in a concession to downtown business leaders, approved state plans to build a raised Golden Gate Freeway through the Panhandle. In exchange for the homes of the mostly black residents living along the proposed freeway line, the thoroughfare promised to save mostly white suburban commuters and shoppers an estimated six minutes of travel time between the Golden Gate Bridge and the downtown. However, the freeway proposal required the Board of Supervisors' approval, and HANC packed the board's freeway hearings with residents decrying the government's "imperial" plans to wipe out "one of the few . . . well integrated neighborhoods in our city." In 1964 HANC's lobbying secured a shocking single-vote victory from the Board of Supervisors, blocking the freeway's construction.[15]

The localists' faith in the ability of area residents to solve neighborhood problems extended to issues of crime. In 1961 a seminal localist treatise by Jane Jacobs, *The Death and Life of Great American Cities,* contended that the public peace was "not kept primarily by the police" but by "an intricate . . .

network of voluntary controls and standards . . . enforced by the people themselves." HANC members first asserted their role in neighborhood peacekeeping following the April 1962 slashing of April Aaron in the Panhandle. Proposing what the *Chronicle* labeled a "Neighborhood's Do-It-Yourself War
on Crime," HANC averred that individual small-scale physical rehabilitation
efforts could reduce violence. Pointing out that City Hall had disregarded its
earlier requests for an increased number of street lamps, HANC now urged
area residents to illuminate the nighttime sidewalks by leaving on their porch
lights. HANC further suggested that its existing network of volunteer sidewalk
sweepers could serve as a model for a resident-driven neighborhood watch
program. Volunteer block captains, HANC recommended, would patrol the
streets with police whistles and harness the surveillance power of residents.[16]

In explaining the rationale for the block captains, however, HANC emphasized that the state had a positive role to play in neighborhood peacekeeping. HANC president Anna Guth explained that the primary function
of resident block captains would be to "get neighbors better acquainted with
each other" so local residents might "more easily recognize something suspicious and . . . report it to the police." HANC regarded police officers as critical partners in the maintenance of law and order. The organization promoted
police-community cooperation by urging the SFPD to allow male resident
volunteers to ride along in the police patrol cars cruising their community.[17]

While HANC's early battles against freeway construction sought to purge
state influence from the neighborhood, the organization's discussions of crime
and law enforcement illustrated the activists' desire to shape state services
rather than to abolish government intervention altogether. The "*only duty*" of
"*public officials,*" HANC underscored, is "*to serve the public—and not domi-
nate it.*" HANC officials focused on cooperation within patrol cars because
cruisers removed police from the sort of face-to-face contact HANC members
thought critical to democratic policy making. To the consternation of local
residents, the SFPD's leadership (following the recommendations of the 1961
downtown-staffed and -funded Blyth-Zellerbach Committee survey) had recently initiated a shift from walking beats to patrol car beats. HANC officials
witnessing the expansion of Park Station's patrol car fleet from four to seven
now hoped that through their ride-along program they would be able to bring
local patrol officers back in touch with the community.[18]

Through the mid-1960s, white Haight-Ashbury spokespersons located a
template for their ideal government-resident relationship in the interactions
between Haight-Ashbury residents and SFPD foot patrol officers walking
their neighborhood. In particular, localists venerated Haight Street's daytime

foot patrol veteran Patrolman Leo Maguire. A "muscular, six foot plus heavy-weight," Maguire possessed what Michael Hebel, a younger Park Station patrol officer, recalled as "a certain presence [and] command." Maguire, Hebel continued, also possessed "a great a gift of communication. . . . He was certainly an excellent talker." Maguire represented precisely the sort of cooperative government official the Haight-Ashbury localists desired. In 1965 Boyle, the white editor of the weekly *Haight-Ashbury Independent,* lauded Maguire and other Haight Street patrol officers in a series of newspaper profiles. Boyle's newspaper reported on accusations of police violence and racism in other parts of the city, but its coverage of Haight Street foot patrol officers characterized them as peaceful, color-blind community servants. Boyle praised Patrolman Maguire for handing out candy to children, giving "directions to Haight-Ashbury neighborhood housewives looking for a particular market or pharmacy," "suggest[ing] to over-time parkers that they move on," and protecting residents from black con artists performing the elaborate "Jamaican switch."[19]

When contrasted with the campaign by black activists for police-community relations (PCR) officers who could combat rank-and-file violence, Boyle's grandfatherly image of Patrolman Maguire, coupled with the editor's conviction that the neighborhood's only criminal danger emanated from black people, could all appear unthreatening to the downtown agenda setters. Following Aaron's slashing, however, Police Chief Thomas Cahill bitingly mischaracterized the group's police reform proposals as a "vigilante idea." Cahill supported autonomous police discretion so long as officers used their independence to serve the values of the managerial growth advocates. He clearly felt threatened when localists proposed to steer police independence in a collaborative direction. Similar to the black activists promoting the PCR unit, HANC members hoped to use the rank and file's discretion to promote local inclusion rather than top-down control.[20]

THE HIPPIES AND LOCALIST FEARS OF CENTRALIZED POLICING

The expansion of the hippie scene during the mid-1960s moved the sharp contrasts dividing the Haight-Ashbury and Hall of Justice visions of law enforcement to the forefront of San Francisco politics. An unpublicized counterculture community first took root in the Haight-Ashbury flatlands during the early 1960s. The middle period of the decade then provided the bohemians room to expand as the prospect of the Golden Gate Freeway project frightened a number of longtime store owners and residents out of the area. The press labeled participants in the subculture "hippies" in early 1966, and by the end of that year, roughly thirty hippie-catering commercial establishments operated in the neighborhood. Police leaders regarded this new bohemian world criminal because the community rejected traditional gender roles, romanticized drug use, and eventually harbored a sizeable population of teenage runaways.[21]

The SFPD's initial response to this hippie scene followed the pattern the department had set with the North Beach beats. SFPD leaders relied on uniformed Park Station patrol officers to maintain order, and the officers did so with broad "public nuisance" charges.[22] Hippies, in return, charged that the "subjectivity" wielded by "policemen on the beat" (including Patrolman Maguire, who participated in the *Love Book* bust) led to harassment and brutality.[23]

When the hippie population continued to swell, SFPD leaders began seeing the need for a new, more centrally directed approach. In early 1967 a hippie festival in Golden Gate Park drew ten thousand to twenty thousand participants. Two months later the Diggers, an anarchist hippie collective committed to providing free meals and beds to indigent bohemians, publicly predicted that in months a hundred thousand young people would arrive in the Haight-Ashbury for a "Summer of Love." The Diggers called on city officials to prepare for this self-fulfilling forecast with food, shelter, and medical services. Instead, the Inspectors Bureau deployed the narcotics squad for neighborhood sweeps; Park Station commanders directed raids on Digger communes and "Victorian tenements"; and the Hall of Justice flooded the Haight-Ashbury with Operation S, the professional policing program that saturated so-called crime hot spots with plainclothes officers.[24]

The San Francisco Department of Public Health used these crackdowns as an opportunity to exploit the mainstream media's caricature of barefoot, panhandling, "dirty" hippies. *Look* magazine, for example, conjured this image when it described the typical hippie flat as "a filthy litter-strewn, swarming dope fortress that was a great deal less savory and sanitary than a sewer."[25] In March 1967 the health department deployed teams of health inspectors to visit 691 buildings in the Haight-Ashbury flatlands. Unfortunately for city officials, the investigators found only 39 residences in need of sanitary repair, and of those, a paltry six were occupied by hippies. Most of the offending units were rented by black tenants whose building managers refused to engage in upkeep. Undeterred, health department officials began working hand in hand with raiding police, temporarily condemning apartments after police sweeps for drugs and runaways.[26]

The fast-expanding hippie scene stirred a range of emotions among longtime residents of the Haight-Ashbury. Traditional merchants expressed the most hostility as they worried that the bohemians would drive away their middle-class customers. The Haight-Ashbury Merchants and Improvement Association illustrated its support for one Haight Street patrolman's work in controlling the hippies by presenting him with a flower-bedecked night stick. The Haight-Ashbury's hippies and localist liberals, however, slowly found that they shared common values, and by the middle of 1966, HANC as an organization ceased expressing any opposition to the hippies.[27]

The localist liberals and the hippies bonded over their mutual appreciation for the Haight-Ashbury's social diversity and their common belief that neighborhood residents could propel their own neighborhood's uplift. Michael McClure, a hippie poet and playwright, explained to a television reporter that the neighborhood's racial and ethnic "integration" and "tolerance" attracted the first wave of hippie settlers. He then expressed his interest in and pride over bringing "a new vitality . . . into the neighborhood." McClure asserted:

> When I first moved into the neighborhood there was a certain amount of narcotics in the neighborhood, there was a certain amount of prostitution in the neighborhood, and I don't see any of that now. The young people have come in, they've taken over the neighborhood, and they've really cleaned it up.[28]

Haight-Ashbury liberals saw the revitalization potential of the hippie community in the hippie businesses lining Haight Street. According to the *San Francisco Bay Guardian,* one of the city's growing number of underground newspapers, the hippie merchants' most reliable customers were not bohemians or tourists, but neighborhood-dwelling "academic types" and "civil servants in all categories." The hippie merchants and liberal consumers, the newspaper continued, both believed that hippie shops fostered a more authentic commercial relationship in which hippie businesspersons "reversed the current mass-economics trend toward bigness and automated specialization." By "returning to a bastardized form of Medieval craft shops and guilds," hippie store owners, in the eyes of localist liberals, reinforced the urban village environment.[29]

Localist liberals and hippies also organized meetings around their shared opposition to the Hall of Justice's centralized policing campaign. In 1967 neighborhood liberals said little about the Haight Street patrol officers' discretionary policing of the hippies, but tore into Chief Cahill, Mayor Shelley, and leaders of the Department of Public Health when these city officials involved themselves in anti-hippie law enforcement. "HANC asks that Chief Cahill accept the fact," one missive began, "that the Police Department is . . . not the guardian of the public's morals." The organization insisted that any tensions existing between the Haight-Ashbury's established population and the new hippies could be resolved within the bounds of the neighborhood and "that the primary function of the police" was "to help people to live peaceably together." HANC bristled that the current efforts of outside officials to combat pluralism in the Haight-Ashbury would only "further divide a community that has made a great effort to integrate its diverse populations."[30]

Haight-Ashbury activists—localist liberals and hippies alike—were particularly vexed that City Hall and the Hall of Justice used the centrally orchestrated hippie crackdown to promote narratives about a "dirty" neighborhood. These story lines, Haight-Ashbury residents worried, cleared a path for downtown-operated bulldozers.[31] During the 1967 Summer of Love, Kenneth Rexroth, a poet and North Beach transplant, warned that downtown interests and local mass media outlets hoped to use crime in the Haight-Ashbury as a pretext for replacing the Victorians with high rises. Similarly, localists agonized that the "little busts" were leading to "the big bust, . . . redevelopment," and even some of the area's more conservative traditional business owners suspected "that there was a 'master plan' to 'get' the neighborhood." David Sacks, a vice president of the American Broadcasting Company and the local station manager of KGO-TV, encouraged this sort of paranoia when he editorialized that the city could solve the problems of the Haight-Ashbury with freeways and apartments towers.[32]

Neighborhood activists hoped to reestablish order through partnerships with the police, but Park Station officers showed little interest in cooperation. Localists complained, for instance, that Park Station police failed to attend the Haight-Ashbury's PCR committee meetings. Without assistance from the state, Haight-Ashbury liberals and a handful of hippies initiated their own local responses to the issues of drug use and runaway youth. Viewing speed and heroin users as "sick" people in need of affection and rehabilitation (Haight-Ashbury activists seldom expressed concern over marijuana smoking), the organization helped launch the Haight-Ashbury Free Medical Clinic and Huckleberry's for Runaways.[33]

The SFPD leadership took seriously the challenges the Haight-Ashbury community institutions presented to both the police department's traditional understanding of crime and its commitment to professional, top-down governance. The department thus subjected neighborhood service centers to threats, raids, and trumped-up charges. Meanwhile, the SFPD's continued campaign against hippies in the streets, parks, and flats succeeded in driving many of the original bohemians out of the neighborhood. A second wave of younger and poorer hippies took their place, and these bohemians proved less interested in expanding their consciousness through LSD than in popping speed (methamphetamines) and shooting heroin. The SFPD leadership exploited this change in the scene to justify an even greater emphasis on centralized law enforcement. Localist liberals, meanwhile, struggled to maintain their neighborhood-based services for the increasingly desperate hippie population.[34]

CENTRALLY ORCHESTRATED POLICING
IN THE HAIGHT-ASHBURY

Mayor Alioto took office in January 1968 insisting that the Haight-Ashbury activists' desire for policy-making input could coexist with the SFPD's centrally directed campaign against violence. Indeed, he believed that by promoting the former, he could justify the latter. Mayor Alioto ridiculed the "institutionalized indolence of the hippie movement," but defended "their right to dress and to speak as they please, no matter how unorthodox, so long as they don't interfere with the rights of others." When a local conservative exclaimed that hippies had transformed Golden Gate Park into a "jungle" unsafe for women and children, Alioto sanguinely responded that hippies had a right to the public grounds and then illustrated his confidence in the midst of the counterculture by organizing a made-for-media, tongue-in-cheek picnic in the park.[35]

Mayor Alioto also buttressed police-community dialogue through appointments. Alioto's Police Commission transferred Captain Mortimer McInerney from the SFPD's Bureau of Complaint, Inspection, and Welfare to the head of Park Station. A bright, fast-rising officer, McInerney willingly met with neighborhood activists to discuss area policing policy.[36] Alioto's commissioners then transferred Richard Hongisto, a young, ambitious patrolman, to the PCR unit. Initially assigned to the city's gay community, Hongisto eventually responded to rising tensions in the Haight-Ashbury by taking on the hippies as an additional concentration.

Hongisto excited Haight-Ashbury activists by helping area hippies and culturally mainstream residents "work together" to make "a truly fine model community."[37] Eventually Hongisto began broadcasting the Haight-Ashbury's desire for inclusive, neighborhood-based policy making at the city's local development planning sessions. At a gathering sponsored by the San Francisco Planning and Urban Renewal Association, Hongisto criticized the public-private planning agency for excluding both the neighborhood's white hippies and its black residents from the city's Haight-Ashbury planning process.[38]

Mayor Alioto believed that his tolerance for his sort of politicking in formal political channels justified deployments of the tac squad against those who defied the state. On a late Sunday afternoon in February 1968, a group of hippies snarled neighborhood traffic with an impromptu street dance. Captain McInerney's patrol officers successfully cleared the intersection, but the Hall of Justice nevertheless called the tac squad into service. Residents milling around on the sidewalk or peering out their windows watched in astonishment as phalanxes of tac squad officers marched onto Haight Street. Their faces concealed by Plexiglas helmets and gas masks, officers began attacking hippies. They employed Mace and, for the first time since the waterfront strikes of the 1930s, tear gas. Tac squad officers then turned their attention on liberal residents, firing blanks at people watching from their windows and launching tear gas canisters at the Haight Street Free Medical Clinic. The city's official tally for the police action listed eight injuries and over ninety arrests. The Haight-Ashbury Free Medical Clinic, however, claimed that it saw a hundred young people, most with scalp lacerations or chemical burning in their eyes.[39]

Alioto dismissed the notion that the squad's tactics hampered democratic dialogue. When questioned about why participating tac squad members had removed their identifying badges, Alioto gamely responded that the police stars had pointy edges that could stab an officer through his shirt. Explaining that a "commercial element" of—in the *Chronicle's* paraphrase—"outsiders" had introduced drugs into the neighborhood, the mayor portrayed the tac squad as neighborhood defenders. Drugs, Alioto asserted, were a medical problem because they made youth "mindless," but they became a criminal issue when "hoodlums" transformed unthinking drug users into "storm trooper[s]" dedicated to "violence." The *San Francisco Chronicle* elaborated that the supposed mindlessness of the "drug-taking hippie" necessitated the use of force. Unlike "black militants" and "draft card burners," the newspaper explained, the drug takers were "an ugly enigma" who lacked "motives" that could be understood and were thus incapable of reasoned negotiations.[40]

With the mayor's blessing, the Hall of Justice kept up its pressure. Indeed, the same day Alioto held his self-assured picnic in Golden Gate Park, the tac squad raided the park's so-called Hippie Hill. Later that evening the squad swept up twenty-eight people as suspected juvenile runaways along Haight Street. Police ultimately booked only ten as runaways and released twelve without charge. Through the rest of the spring, the narcotics squad followed a similar big-bust strategy with late-night raids on hippie communes.[41]

FIGURE 14. Tac squad officers with ammunition belts make arrests on Haight Street during a night of clashes with local hippies. July 18, 1968. (Reprinted with permission, Bancroft Library, BANC PIC 2006.029: 140285J.01.05.)

The swelling tensions between hippies and the police over these sorts of busts cracked open on a Tuesday evening in July 1968 when local residents began hurling sticks and rocks at two undercover narcotics agents attempting to detain a suspected drug dealer. Park Station police and the tac squad dashed to the scene, imposed a curfew, and began making arrests. For two consecutive evenings, police and residents battled, with the latter hurling rocks and bottles at the police and Molotov cocktails onto the street pavement. This violence, one reporter ruefully noted, made the neighborhood "probably the only truly integrated community in the country to riot." Alioto praised the efficiency of the centralized SFPD response and invoked the ominous rhetoric of neighborhood deterioration. Emphasizing "the litter, the debris, the broken glass," and "the derelicts," Alioto opined that the Haight-Ashbury was "taking the aspect of the old Third and Howard area (Skid Row)."[42]

The Haight-Ashbury's localist liberals—white and black alike—fumed over Alioto's centralized policing approach. The tac squad members not only brought violence upon longtime residents who "could not possibly be mistaken for hippies," they did little to protect residents from the very real rise in day-to-day drug-trade bloodshed. Beginning in late 1967 and continuing through 1968, neighborhood violence spiked as drug dealers competed over the new markets in speed and heroin. In the first two months of 1969 alone, the Haight-Ashbury experienced an unprecedented seventeen murders. The director of the Free Medical Clinic stated that this official tally did not include the homicides that he believed had been disguised as drug overdoses.[43] Merchants fled the neighborhood, and the commercial vacancy rate soared from 4 percent in 1965 to 35 percent in 1971. HANC officials charged that the SFPD's professional-ized response—raids and sweeps orchestrated by the Hall of Justice—netted narcotics-using "victims" while failing to address the "root of this evil," "the organized suppliers and dealers of illegal drugs."[44]

HANC continued to plead for police-resident cooperation. In doing so they diverged from those hippies who insisted that neighborhood residents could provide their own law enforcement. For instance, hippies connected with the Church of the Good Earth—a collective following in the tradition of the by-then-defunct Diggers—took it upon themselves to intimidate speed dealers out of the neighborhood. HANC's leadership, by contrast, saw police as necessary for neighborhood safety. In 1969 HANC members elected Waller as the organization's first black president after he campaigned on his record as a former SFPD officer who "specialized in Community Relations." (Waller had not served in the PCR unit.)[45] Meanwhile, HANC's Safety Committee, headed by David Johnson—a forty-three-year-old black photographer, civil rights proponent, and employment counselor at the nearby University of California Medical Center—paired his condemnations of Chief Cahill's attitude toward blacks with assurances that "patrolmen on foot in the area" could reduce harmful crimes.[46]

HANC leaders continued demanding a greater emphasis on foot patrol officers—and on black beat officers, in particular—through the end of the decade. The group's spokespersons claimed that neighborhood beat officers, including Maguire, understood how to effect arrests without resorting to a level of force that might spark a riot. They also believed that foot patrolmen possessed a familiarity with the neighborhood that enabled them "to distin-guish between residents and transients and . . . to identify the suppliers and dealers in drugs in the area." When HANC activists lodged their concerns over anonymous, centralized policing to Captain McInerney, the Park Station leader agreed to encourage greater familiarity between police and residents by assigning two foot patrol officers to fixed Haight Street shifts (younger patrol officers' shifts and beats often rotated). However, McInerney possessed little authority over the narcotics and tactical squads periodically whipping through his district's streets.[47]

RANK-AND-FILE POLITICIZATION

As Alioto and Haight-Ashbury localists both looked to police officers to represent their vision of proper governance in a pluralist city, officers recognized that the conflict between the mayor and the localists provided them an opportunity to step into the civic sphere and advance their own institutional interests. A small cluster of liberal PCR officers, including Hongisto, were the first to break toward explicit politicization. These officers had grown infuriated with the POA when it had defended Patrolman Michael O'Brien after he killed George Baskett but had then rejected the appeals of black officers ensnared in their own off-duty legal troubles. In the fall of 1968 Henry Williams, a black sergeant; Palmer Jackson, a twenty-six-year-old black PCR officer; and Patrolman Hongisto formed Officers for Justice (OFJ), a liberal-leaning alternative to the POA.[48]

The OFJ officers mounting their challenge followed local and national precedents. Since 1962 the SFPD's own PCR unit had been taking increasingly political stances in their work against discretionary police violence. In 1967 black police officers in Chicago had responded to their department's racially discriminatory stop-and-frisk policies by forming the Afro-American Patrolmen's League of Chicago. A year later Cleveland's black police officers turned their social organization, the Shield Club, in a confrontational direction when they sued Cleveland's Fraternal Order of Police for donating their membership dues to George Wallace's 1968 presidential campaign.[49]

The OFJ in San Francisco sought to adopt a similar political stance. Police Commission approval was required for all SFPD organizations, and OFJ founders appealed to Alioto's commissioners by emphasizing how their group would expand civic pluralism. When Alioto and his commissioners beseeched the OFJ to instead merge with the POA, local civil rights activists scoffed at this proposal, dismissing it as Pollyannaish. The Police Officers' Association, Reverend Cecil Williams said bluntly, "is one of the most racist organizations in the City. The John Birch Society is not that uptight." Elaborating on the POA's resistance to racially pluralist politics, OFJ organizers noted that "not a single Black member has ever been selected to represent the Association on its policy committees, in its meetings with other organizations, nor in any form that would indicate that they were necessary to the organization." With the outcome of the O'Brien trial still in question and tensions reaching a fever pitch amid the strike at San Francisco State College, Alioto's administration needed to mollify his coalition's liberal flank. Seeing an opportunity to display their continued commitment to pluralism, his Police Commission relented and provided the OFJ its official consent.[50]

After the OFJ exploited Alioto's avowed commitment to political pluralism in City Hall, it quickly pivoted toward a localist critique of the mayor's
centrally orchestrated law enforcement. During the San Francisco State College strike, for instance, OFJ organizers held a press conference at which they
advised students and faculty to provide the PCR unit with reports of questionable tac squad behavior. Unlike associations of black police officers mobilizing
elsewhere, the OFJ initially hoped to recruit liberal white police officers with
this localist orientation, but only liberal black officers joined the new association.[51] By June 1970 the group claimed to represent a majority of the SFPD's
eighty-two black policemen. Thus the OFJ followed the pattern of other black
police unions in the United States. Lacking numerical might inside the SFPD,
the OFJ drew its leverage from sources of power outside the police force. PCR
officer Jackson explained, "We knew that our strength was in the community,
not in the police department. So. . . . we went to the people."[52]

The OFJ hoped that its new relationship with the people in the civic
sphere would produce more democratic law enforcement on the street.
Pledging to remove itself from technocratic decision making and adopting
the mission statement of the Afro-American Patrolmen's League of Chicago,
the OFJ promised:

> We will no longer permit ourselves to be relegated to the role of brutal pawns
> in a chess game affecting the communities in which we serve. We are husbands,
> fathers, brothers, neighbors, and members of the black community. Donning
> the blue uniform has not changed this.[53]

The OFJ and civil rights activists first sought to enact their racially pluralist and localist principles by securing control over the PCR unit's leadership.
In early 1969 the department's command staff harassed PCR leader Lieutenant William Osterloh into retirement after he participated in the PCR unit's
investigation of Patrolman O'Brien. Cosmopolitan liberal growth advocates
initially proposed conducting the search for Osterloh's replacement according to traditional professional principles. If a lieutenant had not been able to
compel respect and obedience from other officers, the *Chronicle* suggested,
the department should now assign the unit to a captain. OFJ members, by
contrast, believed that the PCR unit would be better equipped for a fight with
the rank and file if it reinforced its power in black neighborhoods. Thus on
the same day the jury acquitted O'Brien of manslaughter, the OFJ publicly
petitioned the city to install Rodney Williams, a black PCR patrolman and
twelve-year veteran of the department, as the head of the PCR unit.[54]

Civil rights activists endorsed the OFJ's request, and San Francisco's liberal Democratic Central Committee tacked on additional recommendations aimed at increasing community influence over the police department. The committee pressed the Police Commission to appoint twenty-five additional officers to the PCR unit, provide the unit with formal authority over brutality and harassment investigations, and elevate the PCR leader's *position* to the rank of deputy chief—a move that would place the unit directly under the Police Commission rather than the chief of police. The Police Commission, however, desired palliative concessions that would promote pluralism without transferring power from the police chief to local residents. The commissioners thus appointed Williams to the head of the PCR unit and rejected the Democratic Central Committee's additional proposals.[55]

Alioto's compromise had taken care to protect the institutional authority of the police chief, but many white patrol officers saw Williams's appointment as an impingement upon their own workplace rights. The alliance between black community activists and OFJ officers, POA leader John Lehane later charged, gave the latter the "juice" they needed to "get ahead of everybody else." The PCR unit, Lehane continued, allowed liberal police to say, "'Hell with your examination. I can't pass it, but give me the job anyway.'"[56]

The POA had trouble persuading voters to view their opposition to Williams in color-blind terms. A decade earlier the group had not protested when Mayor Christopher's Police Commission elevated Frank Ahern and Cahill—two patrolmen—to the position of chief of police. Rodney Williams's leapfrogging only differed insofar as it placed a black patrolman in a position of authority over PCR sergeant Gene Simmons, a higher-ranking white officer. Most of the POA's leaders, moreover, belonged to the Inspectors Bureau but had not ever seriously addressed that bureau's long tradition of choosing members on the basis of outside sponsorship. Thus when the POA suddenly professed an interest in favoritism and crafted a charter amendment specifically worded to allow for Williams's removal, liberal spokespersons regarded the proposition as racially motivated, and San Franciscans rejected it at the polls.[57]

In addition to confronting the rank and file with the outside political influence of black civil rights groups, Rodney Williams's appointment threatened to constrict the rank and file's street-level powers by ensuring that the PCR unit would continue its practice of collecting police brutality complaints. Indeed, by 1970, one study concluded, a PCR officer's primary function was to take grievances about the police. This additional monitoring of police discretion came at a time when rank-and-file officers across the nation had reason to fear for their safety. The exploding rates of lethal urban violence represented more than abstract statistics to the officers mandated to keep the peace. In Chicago firearm attacks killed thirty police officers between 1966 and 1970. A sniper in San Francisco's Hunters Point neighborhood murdered a black patrol officer in November 1967, and half a year later Black Panthers wounded two white San Francisco police officers in a shootout.[58] In October 1968 dynamite detonated outside Richmond Station, and then, just weeks before Rodney Williams's appointment, a Noe Valley neighborhood SFPD patrolman was fatally shot. In this final incident, police falsely pinned the killing on seven Latino youth and young men. Soon dubbed "Los Siete" by Chicano activists, all seven received acquittals in court.[59]

Police encountered particularly heavy violence in Park District. In February 1970 a bomb explosion just outside Park Station unleashed a spray of upholstery staples that killed Sergeant Brian McDonnell, a member of the POA's board of directors, and injured eight other officers and station staffers. Later in June a Park District sergeant was shot in the back of the head while issuing a traffic citation. Park Station officers responded by heading out to duty with two or three guns. "We didn't have bullet proof vests, we didn't have the things for communication we have now," Hebel remembered. "It was a pretty isolating and isolated experience." Elsewhere in the city, a car bomb ripped apart a police cruiser. That blast did not injure any police, but by end of 1970, two more police officers had been killed in the line of duty.[60]

At the same time officers were seeing a dangerous gulf opening between police and city residents, many in the rank and file felt electrified by the exploits of the tac squad. For years, officers had griped over the department's disorganized responses to large-scale demonstrations.[61] "The way they used to do things," former Captain Kevin Mullen scoffed, "is . . . if something happened, they just sent a bunch of cops over there. There was no military structure to anything. They just send a bunch of cops, you know. 'Oh, we need help,' and then everybody comes charging in from all over." These anarchic reactions had sometimes placed officers in embarrassing positions. John Mindermann recalled the frustration he felt during a 1964 civil rights demonstration when he watched his lieutenant wade into a massive sit-in only to get his legs knotted amid the protesters' interlocked arms. Mindermann and his fellow officers had to help pull their superior out. It "really angered us," Mindermann continued, to see the demonstrators' greater tactical organization.[62]

The tac squad's clear mandate to use force and its visually impressive lockstep maneuvers thus came as a revelation to many rank-and-file officers. Young patrolmen in particular clamored for a turn in the tac squad rotation. When the constant on-call status at San Francisco State College stretched the tac squad's endurance, the department capitalized on rank-and-file enthusiasm by establishing a secret "second platoon" as an augmenting force. (The press learned of the second platoon a month after the strike had ended.) Under the command of Lieutenant Ray White, a former POA president, the second platoon included three hundred officers at the height of the San Francisco State strike and provided participating officers with the opportunity to engage in tac squad training and maneuvers. The second platoon, one supervising captain remarked, proved "good for morale."[63]

The phrase *second platoon* soon developed into a moniker for a culturally, sexually, and racially right-wing police subculture. Within this fraternity, Lieutenant "No Head Shots" White handed out "battle streamers" for the second platoon's various engagements (for example, the "Battle of Dolores Park"), members published an underground *Second Platoon News,* and officers began organizing annual second platoon celebrations. The "slap-stick comedy routines" performed at these gatherings included skits featuring male officers in drag, a black officer in African tribal costume (complete with a large bone scepter), and patrolmen acting out the misadventures of the "Fag One" patrol car.[64] The SFPD leadership likely believed, with Alioto, that the department was reinforcing its power over the rank and file with its militarily oriented tac squad and second platoon. Lieutenant White was loyal to the SFPD command and, as a former POA president, supportive of the association's politics-by-proxy approach. The tac squad and second platoon, however, were stoking a rank-and-file self-confidence and brotherhood that neither the top brass nor City Hall controlled.

While uniformed patrol officers developed an intensifying esprit de corps, some of the same officers also wished to build bridges with citizens on the street. Hebel, a Park District radio car driver and one of the few POA officials representing the patrol division, remembered that he and a handful of other officers were beginning to feel that professionalism's emphasis on "answering calls for service" "was not a very effective way to do policing." Instead, officers like Hebel saw "the necessity of having . . . community ties in order to do policing effectively." Following events like the bombing at Park Station, Hebel continued, "There was both a little bit more suspicion about the community groups, but also a greater awareness of them" and a realization of officers' "dependency on them, as well as their dependency on us."[65]

Across the nation the sometimes contradictory and sometimes overlapping feelings of embattlement, fraternalism, and dependence pushed officers toward grassroots activism. Usually, this organizing took a distinctly right-wing cast as police officers resisted the expanding boundaries of citizenship through political campaigns against civilian review boards and through organized and vigilante violence against New Left activists. In San Francisco, however, the rearguard fight by Jake Ehrlich and the traditional POA leadership was yielding disappointing results. First, the gratuitous charges Ehrlich lobbed at Alioto and black San Franciscans during the O'Brien case failed to protect O'Brien's job security. Then in November 1969 the POA again found itself on its heels when the OFJ sponsored two ballot propositions that elevated the PCR from a unit to a bureau, improved police officers' fringe benefits, and eliminated political influence from the promotion process. Ehrlich and the traditional POA leadership were loath to support any measure that might raise the OFJ's stature and thus sheepishly opposed the bread-and-butter proposals. OFJ officers reveled in how their propositions brought the POA's inaction on issues of favoritism into sharp relief and enabled them to generally "make fools" of the association's leadership.[66]

Ehrlich in particular appeared to be lost in the cosmopolitan liberal city. That did little, however, to temper his self-confidence. When the lawyer announced the POA's "unalterable opposition" to the OFJ ballot measures, he commented that he (rather than the POA membership) had not yet decided how the association would defeat it. "As a general," Ehrlich explained, "I can't commit my troops until all the facts are in. George Washington and Napoleon learned that."[67]

The OFJ's propositions fell to defeat at the polls, but some uniformed officers questioned why they were taking marching orders from this "Napoleon." In 1969 three officers—Lieutenant Jerry D'Arcy of the K-9 unit and Sergeant Jerry Crowley and Patrolman Lou Calabro of Potrero Station—mobilized an insurgent group named the Blue Coats. Blue Coat leaders advocated transforming the POA into an aggressive, openly political group for the rank and file. These officers took inspiration from both the OFJ in San Francisco and the right-wing grassroots police movements arising in other cities. More practically, they hoped to capitalize on recent judicial rulings and legislative reforms. A series of court decisions permitting public employees to engage in politics now led city officials to doubt that San Francisco's prohibitions against police politicking were constitutional. The state legislature, meanwhile, created a new bureaucracy in 1969 to handle collective bargaining between city councils and police associations.[68]

Social and political developments within the SFPD also facilitated the Blue Coat power play. During the late 1960s, department personnel was undergoing a transformation. Alioto's administration pressed the SFPD to pursue recruits with a college education, and by 1971 the average SFPD officer had two years of postsecondary schooling. Thus many of the department's young officers had experienced at least peripheral contact with the period's campus movements and were more apt to regard public confrontation as a normal means of pursuing interests.[69] Even those who had not been to college could look to the city's marginalized groups as an example for how patrol officers could begin forwarding their perspectives into the civic sphere. Patrolman Hebel, the only POA official to make the jump from the old guard to the Blue Coats, had served on Patrolman O'Brien's POA defense team, and he later recalled his distress over the rank and file's political marginalization:

> There were beginning to be huge imbalances in terms of the political process and the political structure, in which many groups in society that hadn't had a voice, mostly minorities, and in particular, African-Americans, women, gays, colleges, environmentalists, the war movement—were suddenly getting a huge voice. . . . The voices were loud, boisterous, heckling, and to a person who had just come into the department watching this, a small number of us began to say, "Well, where is our voice in all of this? Where is the response to this? Do we just take it?"[70]

The college-exposed recruits entered the SFPD during a period of tremendous personnel turnover, and this rapid replacement rate disrupted the department's established hierarchies. Traditionally, district station veterans transmitted a culture of deference to the relatively small number of recruits coming into the department each year. During the late 1960s, however, the bubble of officers hired in the immediate aftermath of World War II began reaching the mandated retirement age of sixty-five, and the department was compensating for the exodus with a hiring surge.[71] Captain Mullen, who joined the SFPD in 1959, later described how the outflow of veterans and influx of rookies unsettled power relations at the station level:

> When I came into the department, like, you'd go to the station [on your first permanent assignment], right? Like I did out of the academy. Maybe there'd be two of you on the watch, two new guys. And then everybody else had been around for five to twelve years—they were seasoned people. They dictated the culture of the watch. You *joined* them, right? . . . [But] by '68 they started doing a lot of hiring . . . plus a lot of retirement. So what would happen is, so maybe four or five guys would be going out onto a watch. Well, they could form their own little subculture within the larger culture, and I mean, they were not so overawed by the people that were there before them. And I think a lot of the

change came from below, from those people. I think they started demanding different things.[72]

The Blue Coats capitalized on the rush of new officers and new values. Following the PCR unit's and OFJ's model of searching for power outside downtown and the Hall of Justice, the Blue Coats built bases of support at Northern and Potrero Stations, both of which were responsible for the neighborhoods with the city's largest black populations. The Blue Coats refocused police officers away from downtown growth advocates' concerns over making police into professional representatives of the state and toward the issue of the rank and file's rights vis-à-vis the state. Hebel later explained that when he joined the department in the summer of 1966, the department was struggling with how to identify itself: "Are we a profession or are we a craft?" But the Blue Coats argued: "This shouldn't be the discussion. . . . We shouldn't be talking about those things. We should be talking about how do we get our own voice and how do we improve our wages, hours, and working conditions." These concerns, Hebel noted, were "what labor is all about."[73]

THE RANK-AND-FILE ALLIANCE WITH COSMOPOLITAN GROWTH PROPONENTS

Multiple movements envisioning politicized police officers marched into San Francisco's 1971 election. Cosmopolitan localists in the Haight-Ashbury, Fillmore, Hunters Point, and upper Market Street (Castro) neighborhoods backed Hongisto, now a former PCR officer, in his successful bid for the office of San Francisco sheriff. After Hongisto formed the OFJ, department leaders had denied him time off to earn a criminology doctorate at University of California, Berkeley. Hongisto quit the force in 1970, and the following year the self-described "one-man coalition" transformed his PCR connections into an electoral network.[74] Hongisto ran for sheriff on a cosmopolitan localist message, propounding the harm principle (he supported the decriminalization of both marijuana and homosexual sex) and railing against both centralized, expert-driven policing reforms and the city's emphasis on "superior weaponry." Hongisto's close associations with black civil rights activists, Haight-Ashbury liberals, and radical feminists (Hongisto briefly took the name Blair-Hongisto when his wife, Sandra Blair, became active in the women's liberation movement) all contributed to Hongisto's understanding of and opposition to centralized governance. Hongisto charged that consolidation of authority produced dehumanizing networks, higher taxes, a loss of civil liberties, and "social chaos."[75]

Despite Hongisto's message, it is unlikely that Mayor Alioto regarded Hongisto's victory as a repudiation of cosmopolitan growth politics. Hongisto secured only 36 percent of the vote; he won because his three opponents (including last-place finisher and former "scourge of the Beatniks," William Bigarani) split the city's more moderate and conservative voters. In fact, Hongisto received fewer votes than an anti-high rise proposition that was crushed by twenty-four points. Alioto, meanwhile, used the 1971 mayoral race to draw the Blue Coats into his electoral coalition and thus further illustrated how his City Hall-oriented democracy reinforced inclusiveness and law enforcement simultaneously.[76]

Alioto first began signaling his willingness to dialogue directly with police officers in the immediate wake of the O'Brien trial and San Francisco State College strike. He likely saw a political alliance with the POA as smart defense. Elsewhere in the urban United States, rank-and-file police organizations were using the white mainstream's law-and-order ferment to wreak havoc on municipal governments. Police officers in New York City, Detroit, and nearby Vallejo, California, all ground the mayoral agendas in their cities to a halt with walkouts and "Blue Flu" sick-outs.[77] At the same time, San Francisco's Blue Coats were signaling a declining fealty to the city's growth interests when they blasted the "near-sighted" Downtown Association, Apartment Owners Association, and Chamber of Commerce for their opposition to increased fringe benefits for police. By building bridges with a politicized POA, Alioto aimed to avoid a full-scale police revolt against his redevelopment agenda.[78]

Accepting the Blue Coats also enabled Alioto to appear pro-police while marginalizing elite racial conservatives like Ehrlich and Cahill.[79] In earlier years Chief Cahill would have quickly quashed the Blue Coats' and Alioto's political gestures to each other as clear violations of police professionalism. The veteran chief's power, however, was on the wane. During the late 1960s, the department's lengthening record of civil rights violations and the continuing escalation of crime rates eroded the Cahill's support among managerial growth advocates. He was finally pressured into retirement in January 1970, and Alioto tapped Deputy Chief Al Nelder to replace him.[80] Nelder lacked deep political reserves, and when the POA held its election only one month later, the new chief could do little to prevent a Blue Coat wave.

In February 1970 San Francisco's rank and file, particularly those serving in the tac squad or assigned to Potrero or Northern Station, elected two Blue Coats, including the group's first black member, to the POA's executive council.[81] The Blue Coats also captured control of the *Notebook,* the POA's monthly journal.[82] Through these positions the Blue Coats ousted Ehrlich

F I G U R E 1 5 . A police officer looks out a Hall of Justice window at a campaign banner promoting the Blue Coats in an upcoming Police Officers' Association election. The banner's bold lettering and clear visibility reflect the Blue Coats' assertive approach to rank-and-file politicking. January 26, 1970. (Reprinted with permission, © Bettman/Corbis.)

as the association's legal representative. Meanwhile, the remaining traditional POA leaders continued suffering embarrassing setbacks in the city's political sphere. In late 1970, for instance, the POA faced a civil rights challenge from Fred Lau, a recent San Francisco State College graduate. Lau had applied to the SFPD and had missed the department's minimum height requirement by three-quarters of an inch. Department officials mockingly suggested that he try stretching exercises, but Lau instead decided to take his case to the Civil Service Commission.[83]

The department's 5'8" height requirement had long prevented Asian-American and Latino applicants from disturbing the SFPD's overwhelmingly white, monolingual composition. (In 1970 the SFPD's 1,800-person force included only three Chinese-American officers.) The SFPD's standard put San Francisco behind New York City, where a reduced height requirement had already increased the number of Spanish-speaking officers. Over the previous half-decade, activists in Chinatown and the Mission District had mobilized their neighborhoods around the issues of poverty and education, and these constituencies now leaned on the Civil Service Commission. In December 1970, against the objections of Chief Nelder, the Police Commission, and the POA, the Civil Service Commission lowered the height requirement by a single inch. Lau entered the department; in 1996, he would be appointed SFPD chief of police. In 1970, however, POA president Lehane reacted incredulously to the commission's decision. "If you drop the limit to 5-7," he asked, "why not drop it more and let midgets in the department?" Alongside these political defeats for the POA, two more police officers were wounded in an assassination attempt in the Haight-Ashbury. In 1971 the Blue Coats rode the rank-and-file frustrations to win outright control of the POA's executive committee.[84]

Rank-and-file officers in other cities followed their conservative attitudes toward citizenship into alliances with law-and-order politicians. Republicans could be counted on to defend autonomous police discretion against top-down regulatory strategies like the civilian review board. However, conservatives in San Francisco and elsewhere often opposed allowing rank-and-file officers an organized voice in debates over police personnel policies.[85] Weighing rank-and-file antipathy toward expanded pluralism against their institutional interests, the Blue Coats diverged from other police unions. Blue Coats recognized that their street-level powers would be moot if they could not protect themselves against civil rights activists in the political sphere. The more astute members of the Blue Coats thus recognized—slowly—that they could begin currying Alioto's support and achieving that legitimacy by downplaying the POA's traditional public hostility toward racial pluralism.

During the 1970 POA campaign, Sergeant Crowley, the Blue Coats' candidate for POA president, disarmed City Hall officials and news reporters with color-blind rhetoric. Crowley reassured liberals that the Blue Coats' concerns with promotion and patronage reflected their support for meritocracy and not their hostility toward Rodney Williams and the PCR unit. "We're not interested in colors," Crowley told the media, "only equal opportunity within the department, no matter what a man's complexion, race or religion may be." Indeed, Crowley claimed that Blue Coats represented patrol officers of all racial perspectives. Explaining the genesis of the Blue Coats' name, Crowley related, "There was a question of whether or not blacks or whatever—you know, there weren't that many of them—should be in this, and 'Crazy' Joe Pierce says, 'Hey, we don't give a shit.' And he says, 'As long as he's a 'blue coat.' And I think, 'Hey, that's great.'"[86]

With their avowed commitment to inclusive democracy, the Blue Coats took bold public stances. In February 1971 they announced their intention to document and publicize the decision records of local judges. Black spokespersons immediately understood the plan as a "transparent effort to intimidate" liberal jurists, but Lieutenant D'Arcy defended the proposal in the cosmopolitan liberals' language of self-assured civic participation. "We should have the right to express ourselves," D'Arcy declared. "Policemen have been neglectful of this in the past for fear of press and media criticism. But we are emerging out of that era and we are starting to speak out and starting to be heard." The mainstream media and Alioto offered guarded approval. "If the police wish to comment as a body on judicial decisions," the mayor reasoned, "they obviously have a right to do so."[87]

Later that year Alioto and the Blue Coats formalized an alliance. The Blue Coats inserted a clause into the POA constitution permitting the association to endorse political candidates, and the Blue Coat leadership extended its support to Alioto in his reelection effort.[88] The incumbent then confirmed the Blue Coats' political legitimacy by delivering a campaign speech at a POA meeting. Hebel recalled how this event signaled a shift in power relations between the rank and file, the high brass, and the mayor:

> The second time Alioto was up for election, the POA was endorsing and I can recall being out at an endorsement meeting where suddenly—the first time I'd ever seen it before—the top police command and most of the brass, a lot of the captains, show up. And they show up specifically to make sure that Alioto gets the endorsement. First time I'd ever seen them there, last time I'd ever seen them there. But it was clear to me that that was the defining moment, that the shift in power, the shift in political power, was moving from the chief to the association. . . . Tom Cahill was there for sixteen years, he was the spokesperson. If you wanted the spokesperson for police officers in the department you got it from Tom Cahill. . . . That stopped. If you wanted the voice of police officers, that election defined when you no longer went to the police [chief], you went to the POA.[89]

Chief Nelder recognized the changing political currents and resigned in advance of Alioto's reelection. Alioto replaced Nelder with Scott, who was loyal to the mayor and amenable to the newly politicized POA. Immediately after his reelection, Alioto signed a "Memorandum of Understanding," a twenty-nine-page series of declarations concerning grievance procedures, promotion policies, and the right of police officers to engage in off-duty political activities. Blue Coats hailed the document as the "Magna Carta for San Francisco police."[90]

THE RANK-AND-FILE ALLIANCE WITH
COSMOPOLITAN LOCALISTS

With his resounding reelection, Alioto appeared firmly in control of both the city's redevelopment and its law enforcement agendas. By accepting the political legitimacy of the OFJ and the Blue Coat–led POA, he had built an electoral coalition around policing and pluralism that encompassed both residents of color and police officers. Through negotiations, Alioto assumed, his administration could neutralize any opposition to his centralized governing strategy. The mayor could draw further confidence from the fact that major crimes, although still perilously high, were on the decline and that successful business interests—including the world's largest bank, the nation's leading railroad, the biggest privately owned public utility, and nearly a hundred other national corporations—continued to draw white-collar workers into the city.[91]

Alioto, like the nation's other liberal growth-oriented mayors, continued to look for ways to apply his centralized governing approach to police practices. In New York City, Mayor Lindsay's administration trailblazed the "rapid-response," radio car–driven "911" strategy. Taking this same path, Alioto and Chief Scott followed the mayor's 1971 victory by immediately announcing their plans to close Park and Southeast (formerly Potrero) Stations. The SFPD would make up for the lost foot patrols, the city leaders explained, by expanding the number of motorized responders from the remaining stations. Police district consolidation had been a goal of downtown redevelopment advocates since the 1930s, and SFPD officials announced that the Park and Potrero closures were but the first step in a multistage process aimed at replacing the city's nine existing "neighborhood police stations" with "four headquarters." San Francisco's big-business organizations, such as the Municipal Conference, praised the plan for its promised cost savings and its centralized understanding of democracy. "Stations are not community centers," the municipal group scoffed, "but are merely for the reporting and assignment of personnel."[92]

Police commanders presenting the plan averred that the station consolidation would serve the rank and file's and public's shared interest in increasing physical security. City officials promised that it would allow the department to put desk-bound officers on the streets, and they invoked the recent Park Station bombing to insist that the city could better safeguard its officers by reducing the number of stations it needed to defend. Confident that Alioto's electoral coalition with police would act as a governing coalition and certain that policies for responding to violence served the common good, Alioto's administration developed the plan with little regard for the inclusive policy-making process the mayor had long touted. The POA's new Blue Coat leadership, for instance, learned of the consolidation plan from the media.[93]

The consolidation proposal quickly ran into a wide range of constituencies who both opposed the plan and possessed the political infrastructure necessary to fight it. New leaders of the POA, such as Crowley, immediately recognized the station closure plan as a threat to their promotional opportunities. Similar to the SFPD's earlier introduction of female clerks, the shuttering of the district stations promised to reduce the number of police desk jobs. The elimination of Southeast Station, moreover, would wipe out the first and subsequently most active Blue Coat organizing site.[94]

The Blue Coats worried over how Alioto's plan might infringe on their workplace rights, and they realized that they could defend those institutional interests by again exploiting intraliberal tensions over government arrangements. POA officials never suggested curbing the physical power of the tac squad, but gestured to localists by acknowledging the immense powers that style of policing afforded to City Hall and the Hall of Justice. The city leadership, POA president D'Arcy charged, thought "the police should be a para-military organization beholden to the Police Commission alone." D'Arcy assumed that city leaders would use that authority to serve downtown interests. Regarding the station closures, D'Arcy speculated that "downtown merchants may have muscled the idea through." After all, he continued, the plan promised to "bring many district police into the downtown area where merchants are concerned about the rising crime rate and the decrease in the number of shoppers." Rather than promoting the autonomous discretion that undergirded traditional policing or the top-down arrangements celebrated by advocates of professional policing, D'Arcy now embraced the cooperative discretion promoted by localists. Police, D'Arcy proposed, should serve as "representatives of their community and should act as liaison between the community and the government."[95]

Neighborhood organizers, meanwhile, began coordinating responses to the station closures through the PCR unit. The unit's citizen executive committee, led by Mary Jane Scharff, brought together activists from the Park and Southeast Districts, and neighborhood groups united under a newly created umbrella organization, People's Voice. Reporting on one station consolidation hearing before the Board of Supervisors, a cosmopolitan liberal journalist marveled at the diversity of People's Voice: "Citizens from Hunters Point to the Haight-Ashbury, from neighborhood merchant to bearded long-hair, from right-wing Republican to left-wing Democrat—some 250 who choked the supervisors' chamber yesterday—were distinctly united in the demand that stations stay open."[96]

Localist approaches to law enforcement attracted conservative small merchants who regarded foot patrol officers as their protectors. The citywide San Francisco Council of District Merchants Associations registered its opposition to the station closures, and the president of the South-East San Francisco Merchants Association warned that without foot patrols, "trouble" would ensue and people would "begin to arm themselves." Leland Guth, a member of the Haight-Ashbury Merchants and Property Owners Association (and husband to former HANC president Anna Guth), issued a similar warning. "There has been talk," he reported, "of vigilante groups being formed to supplement the police as a result of the closings of these stations."[97]

Cosmopolitan localists shared the merchants' concern over street safety, but they emphasized how district stations promoted order through inclusiveness. Rejecting Alioto's City Hall–oriented democracy as a mirage, Haight-Ashbury activists insisted that a "dehumanized" and *"militarized* force" would naturally "result from the centralization of police."[98] After all, neighborhood spokespersons declared, "You can't talk with a cruising police car." Reverend Lyle Grosjean, a HANC member who identified with and served the hippies, argued that decentralized governance would result in more authentic and just policy making. He characterized the fight against station consolidation as a struggle for "people over institutions, flesh and blood over blind bureaucracy, the needs and wishes of citizens over the schemes and programs of experts and politicians."[99]

The Haight-Ashbury hippie community approached patrol officers with far more suspicion than their liberal neighbors did, but hippie activists joined People's Voice on the assumption that reform could be achieved more easily within decentralized arrangements. *Haight Action* voiced this counterculture attitude: "The reason community people opposed the Park Station closing was that folks realized that the Haight would continue to be policed, but that effective contact and *to some degree* control over police patrols would be removed. Special squads—TAC Squad, helicopters, park & beach units, etc—controlled from downtown, unfamiliar with neighborhood patterns, styles and needs would greatly harm our community." Reverend Grosjean concurred: "All we are saying is keep the police as close as possible to the people. We want to visit them in their dens. No one should be deceived that we love the police, but . . . we prefer . . . having them in our neighborhoods." Some hippies even hoped that their cooperative campaign for Park Station would increase the neighborhood's influence over the rank and file. *Good Times,* a local underground newspaper, predicted that as the SFPD's chief inspector "and his downtown mob gain control over the PD, the cop on the beat may have to look for allies among the people." The POA, for its part, encouraged these dreams of more equanimous relationships by co-organizing the Haight-Ashbury Police-Community Picnic in Golden Gate Park.[100]

The People's Voice–POA coalition initially attempted to prevent the station closures through lawsuits. Those failed, and the SFPD shuttered Park and Southeast Stations in late April and early May 1972. The anticonsolidation campaign then turned its attention to the media and the electorate. When police leadership announced Southeast Station's closure, the district's POA representative and a member of the Southeast Station PCR board were both on hand at the station to provide journalists with a reaction. At Park Station's closing, members of the POA, HANC, and Church of the Good Earth held a press conference and offered reporters a tour of the building.[101]

Alioto's police leadership reinforced the connection neighborhood activists drew between centralized law enforcement and antidemocratic governance by harassing and arresting Good Earth commune members. The Church of the Good Earth had already developed a contentious relationship with the Alioto administration by protesting against the mayor's redevelopment agenda, but during the eleven-month fight over Park Station, centrally orchestrated police pressure against Good Earth noticeably rose.[102] Between January 1972 and February 1973, police jailed Good Earth commune members a total of 111 times for various marijuana charges. In mid-May 1972, police and federal agents teamed up to raid twelve Good Earth houses and flats. SFPD leaders claimed that concerns over heroin had motivated the raids, but the officers only found three pounds of marijuana and left the communes smashed and overturned. "It was," an underground journalist reported, "a search & destroy mission."[103]

The raids seemed to confirm all of HANC's worst nightmares of Hall of Justice–directed law enforcement. HANC president Ed Dunn explained, "We were fearful this would happen when they closed Park. We had good relations with the Park patrolmen." POA president D'Arcy concurred that these sorts of busts were stifling peace and democracy. "I know these men," D'Arcy said of Good Earth members. "If the Haight were my beat, we'd have no reason for beefs. By closing this station the Police Commission is attempting to destroy contacts and dialogue between cops and citizens in this community." According to members of HANC and the Good Earth commune, the raid was "political, a response" to the "efforts to keep the Park station open" and to Good Earth's anti–Vietnam War activism.[104]

The POA–People's Voice coalition responded to this politicized law enforcement by reaching out to liberal politicians. Democrats such as Sheriff Hongisto, Willie Brown and John Burton of the State Assembly, and State

Senator George Moscone used the station-closing debate as an opportunity to unite with cosmopolitan localist activists around the principles of neighborhood governance and to win over rank-and-file police officers on issues of labor rights.[105] Even the Democrats on the Board of Supervisors—especially Quentin Kopp, Robert Gonzales, and Dorothy Von Beroldingen—rallied behind the localist movement. Traditionally, the board had been a reliable defender of redevelopment-oriented proposals, and in the previous election supervisors had uniformly opposed an antigrowth measure setting building-height limits. However, Democratic supervisors were personally affronted by Alioto's aggrandizement of power and were ready to prioritize the board's institutional interests over the centralization agenda of downtown businesses. The Board of Supervisors went to the ballot and sponsored Proposition K, a charter amendment that mandated both the reopening of the two stations and the Board of Supervisors' approval for any future station closures. In November 1972 Proposition K passed by a slender 3.8 percent margin, and Park and Southeast Stations reopened the following year.[106]

For localist liberals, Proposition K's victory offered important political lessons. The measure's passage alerted neighborhood activists to the swath of San Franciscans they could capture with a message of inclusive, decentralized, cooperative governance. In 1973 HANC spearheaded a failed campaign for a charter amendment to make San Francisco's Board of Supervisors positions district-based rather than at-large. In this unsuccessful effort they associated their movement with top-down regulations on downtown development. In 1976 Haight-Ashbury activists resubmitted their district-election charter amendment, but this time returned to the message that had won them the station reopening fight. By linking district elections with self-determination, localists narrowly passed their district-election reform plan.[107]

The Proposition K campaign revealed to neighborhood activists strategies for reaching out to the broader electorate, but it did not lay the foundation for a long-term alliance with rank-and-file police. In 1973 the OFJ followed the pattern of other black police groups, such as Chicago's Afro-American Patrolmen's League, by filing a lawsuit challenging the police department's racially discriminatory hiring practices. The OFJ's briefs pointed out that between 1969 and 1973 the number of black SFPD officers had declined. According to one survey, only one other city in the nation—Bridgeport, Connecticut—had experienced a decrease in the number of black police officers over that period. This legal challenge quickly detonated the station reopening coalition as the Blue Coat–led POA defended the SFPD's traditional hiring policies in both the courts and the local media.[108]

244 Chapter Seven

The victory over the station consolidation plan also failed to eliminate the centralized policing practices Haight-Ashbury activists found so abhorrent. The neighborhood's liberal and hippie activists had hoped that a reopened Park Station would provide them with a beachhead from which to reform the rest of the department. "No one was fooled that Park Station was a good thing before the closing," a neighborhood newspaper insisted. "The job was to re-open and re-structure the new station." Local activists, however, never articulated how they intended to leverage the power of the district stations against officials within the Hall of Justice. After Park Station reopened, the tac squad remained, and locals griped as the narcotics squad continued raiding the Good Earth commune "every time the Good Earth joins in opposing something the police want."[109]

The POA, by contrast, cheered the policing arrangements left in Proposition K's wake. The Hall of Justice's centralized use of force operated under no new constrictions, and the POA understood that it could now draw on localists when downtown's agenda infringed on the rank and file's workplace rights. "One thing, it's gratifying to know," the POA newspaper crowed, "we have proven that City Hall can be beaten."[110]

CONCLUSION

San Francisco's cosmopolitan liberal coalition arose around new conceptions of citizenship, but by the mid-1960s, liberals were fracturing over how to best organize the government to serve that citizenry. Cosmopolitan growth advocates propounding City Hall–oriented democracy faced off against localists championing neighborhoods as the fount of democracy. As rates of criminal violence rose and cosmopolitan liberals emphasized the citizenry's shared interest in reducing bloodshed, their fight over democratic arrangements turned to questions of law enforcement. Cosmopolitan growth advocates and cosmopolitan localists dismissed the radical position—forwarded by the Black Panther Party in the Fillmore District, the Red Guard Party in Chinatown, and occasionally the Church of the Good Earth commune in the Haight-Ashbury—that advocated abolition of the police and the devolution of law enforcement responsibilities to the residents themselves.[111] Instead, both sides insisted that their interactions with police served as democratic models.

The competing attempts by cosmopolitan growth proponents and localists to build police alliances poured fuel on an ongoing conflagration within the SFPD. Similar to urban police departments elsewhere in the country, the SFPD spawned a liberal organizing effort by black officers and right-wing expressions from white officers. In San Francisco, however, a new generation of Blue Coat organizers came to recognize how the predominantly white rank and file could defend its institutional interests by placing conservative definitions of crime and citizenship on hold and instead exploiting the cosmopolitan liberal debates over democracy. Following the path blazed by the OFJ, the Blue Coats earned political legitimacy by offering to strengthen the mayor's message of City Hall pluralism and defended their workplace and street-level rights by joining localists in a fight to save district stations. Through both of these efforts, Blue Coats began convincing liberals to value inclusiveness and cooperation over regulation as the basis for democratic governance. San Francisco thus entered the mid-1970s with an increasingly pluralist politics and an ever more powerful police department.

CONCLUSION

Warming up for a jeremiad against Democratic foreign policy proposals, Jeane Kirkpatrick electrified the attendees of the 1984 Republican National Convention by scorning the recent "Democratic National Convention" and then adding, gratuitously, "in San Francisco." Kirkpatrick's speech went on to tag national Democratic leaders as "San Francisco Democrats" six more times. Invoking the epithet in her concluding rallying cry, Kirkpatrick declared, "The American people . . . will reject the San Francisco Democrats and send Ronald Reagan back to the White House!"[1]

With her San Francisco Democrats slur, Kirkpatrick suggested that liberals were too meek to stand up to Communist leaders abroad and antiwar demonstrators at home. The phrase resonated powerfully among Republicans because it evoked a much broader conservative fever dream of weak-kneed liberal permissiveness inducing moral decline. On those terms, conservatives have repeatedly returned to the "San Francisco Democrats" and "San Francisco values" smears. In the 2006 midterm congressional elections, for instance, Republican candidates nationalized their local campaigns by tying their district opponents to San Francisco representative and Democratic House Minority Leader Nancy Pelosi. Representative Sam Graves, a Republican from Missouri, flayed his female Democratic challenger for representing "San Francisco–style values" with a cheaply produced thirty-second spot featuring yuppies sipping champagne and an effeminate African-American man in club clothes gyrating between a black woman and a white woman and rubbing his back side against the latter. As conservative spokespersons made hay of San Francisco policies protecting undocumented workers and sexually explicit street fairs, some condemned San Francisco's liberal leadership for "straightjacket[ing]" the city's police.[2]

The conservatives' caricature placing San Francisco Democrats at odds with law enforcement reflects a deep misunderstanding of the relationship between San Francisco liberals and the SFPD. The cosmopolitan liberal coalition's growing tolerance for cultural, racial, and sexual pluralism did not lead it to reject hard-nosed law enforcement. Quite the opposite, new liberal leaders defended expanded pluralism on the basis of their insistence that inclusiveness enabled tougher policing against violent crime; San Francisco's modern understandings of citizenship and law enforcement developed in tandem. By the late 1970s, liberals in other American cities were using debates over policing to draw similar conclusions regarding pluralism, democracy, and policing.

San Franciscans during the post–World War II period placed their city at the forefront of successive interrelated and national transformations in urban liberalism. Through the 1950s and 1960s, cities across the North and West experienced influxes of migrants of color, growing tax-base competition from the suburbs, and rising rates of criminal violence. Managerial growth proponents and traditional liberals—in San Francisco and a range of other cities—promised their followers economic, social, and civic stability through a commitment to their cities' traditional definitions of citizenship. Proud of their tolerance for divergent class and religious identities in the civic sphere, San Francisco's local elites never questioned the notion that the citizenry maintained shared interests that were color-blind, heterosexual, and fixed to traditional gender roles. Mayors George Christopher and Jack Shelley both insisted that their economic agendas would reinforce the social and economic power of the city's white male breadwinners.

As managerial growth advocates and traditional liberals prepared to enforce traditional values on the street, however, they confronted police departments rooted in machine-era arrangements. Crucially, old urban machines had enhanced the ability of the police to serve the machine's electioneering interests by granting patrol officers tremendous autonomous discretion. When managerial growth advocates took power, they vowed to apply their technocratic governance to the police by professionalizing officers away from their old role as venal bagmen. Traditional liberals, meanwhile, pledged to defend civil liberties through top-down regulations designed to bring police officers under the rule of law. Following these doctrines, managerial growth advocates and traditional liberals both pushed police departments into a new professional era of law enforcement.

Under police professionalism, city officials promised to create apolitical police departments that consolidated personnel management and policy-making power into the hands of an all-powerful, expert police chief. These reforms were followed by a national decline in large-scale, organized police corruption.[3] As managerial growth advocates and traditional liberals cracked down on payola, however, they stopped well short of entirely eliminating autonomous discretion. Although their governing principles seemed to foreclose the possibility of an independent patrol officer, neither faction wished to fully relinquish the rank and file's power to enforce traditional behavioral standards with unwritten laws.

Marginalized residents and a new generation of white-collar professionals capitalized on the dissonance between police professionalism's stated commitment to top-down governance and the discretionary activities of patrolmen on the beat. In San Francisco, marginalized groups and liberal white journalists and politicians highlighted those moments when rank-and-file discretion over the city's racial, cultural, and sexual boundaries appeared to violate Mayor Christopher's and Mayor Shelley's avowed state-building principles and growth-oriented goals. Out of these critiques, a cosmopolitan liberal philosophy and coalition emerged.

Cosmopolitan liberals exploited police debates to redirect urban liberalism toward new understandings of citizenship and democratic governance. Taking advantage of the administrative debates over police professionalism, the cosmopolitan liberal coalition argued that by tolerating a culturally, sexually, and racially pluralist citizenry, city residents could discover and unite around their true common interests: economic growth and reduced criminal bloodshed. However, the young white journalists and politicians promoting that cosmopolitan liberal vision also used their understandings of shared interests to impose new boundaries and expectations. These advocates for cosmopolitan liberalism, for instance, frequently reserved their defenses of cultural and sexual pluralism for behaviors that appeared to facilitate economic growth. Many of the young white liberals continued to associate black race consciousness with antiwhite violence and thus accepted racial pluralism on the presumption that black residents would use their civic participation to reduce black criminality.

These various caveats meant that the cosmopolitan liberal realignment afforded different marginalized groups with different rights and responsibilities. White North Beach beats, white gay-bar owners, and white sexually explicit artists used the harm principle to persuade liberal city and state officials to enact top-down police reforms designed to free them of the rank and file's discretionary power. Groups whom liberal elites associated with violence or regarded as impediments to growth, by contrast, had difficulty obtaining these negative freedom-from rights. Instead, representatives for the city's young black men and the Haight-Ashbury localists looked to achieve rights to new state services by cooperating with—rather than establishing control over— members of the SFPD.

Cosmopolitan liberalism's understanding of democratic governance thus continued to value top-down regulations but also now elevated the principles of inclusiveness and partnership. The new liberal emphasis on cooperation accelerated when cosmopolitan growth advocates in Joseph Alioto's administration squared off against cosmopolitan localists in the Haight-Ashbury. The two liberal camps each turned to the SFPD—which was oriented around both a citywide Hall of Justice and neighborhood district stations—as an institution through which they could illustrate the efficacy of their doctrine. The OFJ and, eventually, the Blue Coats recognized that they could advance their departmental interests by taking sides in these intraliberal debates. Together, cosmopolitan liberals and rank-and-file police officers convinced each other that the city could reinforce pluralism by granting police officers new powers grounded on inclusive principles. San Francisco police officers thus played an important role in defining the new cosmopolitan liberal conception of democracy.

Following Alioto's second term, San Francisco elections continued to rotate around the issues of economic development and the struggle between centralized governance and neighborhood autonomy. Police officers were political free agents in these debates, alternately emphasizing their ability to serve City Hall and local communities and thereby expanding their own physical prerogatives, workplace powers, and political might. At the same time, cosmopolitan growth proponents and localists repeatedly exploited the differences of rank, race, station, and political ideology (and, by the 1980s and 1990s, gender and sexuality) dividing the police force. As various constituencies leveraged different SFPD factions, successive police reforms had the tendency to overlap with, rather than replace, earlier agendas. Thus, seemingly contradictory police policies—such as stop-and-frisk, police-community relations, and tactical law enforcement—all coexisted in the cosmopolitan liberal police department. Nevertheless, cosmopolitan liberal policing maintained new and distinct principles: the rank and file lost their unquestioned autonomous discretion over the city's morals and the use of force, but achieved a political voice and regained legitimacy for discretion through cooperation.

When San Francisco's electorate embraced cosmopolitan liberalism during the late 1960s, the city briefly fell out of step with much of the rest the urban United States. In cities including Chicago, Los Angeles, Minneapolis, and Philadelphia, law-and-order conservatives achieved power by promising anxious white voters that they intended to unleash autonomous police discretion in defense of traditional standards of behavior.[4] But by the early 1970s, liberal politicians in many of these same cities were injecting harm-principle arguments into discussions of discretionary law enforcement. Similar to San Francisco's cosmopolitan liberals, liberal candidates in Los Angeles, Chicago, New York City, and Seattle cobbled together coalitions of white-collar professionals and marginalized residents around the notion that cities could promote growth and reduce violence through an acceptance of expanded pluralism.

By the 1980s urban liberalism was on the rebound, and officials propounding cosmopolitan growth principles were governing Cleveland, Los Angeles, Atlanta, and Boston. These Democrats promoted redevelopment, political inclusiveness, and more open cultural and sexual environments for middle-class residents. Over the same period, liberals across the nation redefined the citizenry's common interests around a reduction in harmful crime. The legal scholar Jonathan Simon notes that this process was already underway in 1968, when President Lyndon Johnson's Safe Streets Act conceived of the model citizen as a crime victim. San Francisco's experience reveals that the expansion of cultural and sexual boundaries and the increased commitment to fighting violent crime were interrelated trends. In the hands of cosmopolitan liberals, the harm principle emphasized both harmless and harmful activities.[5]

When cosmopolitan liberal politicians began achieving power in the urban United States, they found that they lacked the institutional might to compel rank-and-file officers to embrace their vision of citizenship. Police officer associations had emerged from the 1960s as formidable political powers.[6] The independent muscle of these associations and of police departments more generally expanded through the 1980s. New forfeiture and asset-seizure rules enacted in the Comprehensive Crime Control Act of 1984 provided police with fresh federal revenue streams that severely curtailed the budget-making leverage City Halls had traditionally enjoyed over their police departments.[7]

In most cities police officials and rank-and-file associations initially threw their political weight behind law-and-order conservatism. Police officers recoiled at liberal tolerance for expanded pluralism and regarded civilian review boards as a threat to their political and physical security.[8] Liberals, in turn, reacted to revanchist police politics with a continued emphasis on top-down regulation, either through outside civilian review or an increased reliance on specialized, tactical-but-non-lethal policing squads.[9] These police-liberal rifts did not disappear from San Francisco politics. In 1978 San Francisco Police

Officers' Association (POA) officials backed the law-and-order campaign of Dan White, a former police officer running for San Francisco supervisor. Then a year later, when White assassinated Mayor George Moscone and Supervisor Harvey Milk, two cosmopolitan localists, a number of POA officials participated in White's defense.[10]

Urban historians have identified how police officers and police departments during the 1970s often made themselves banner holders for law-and-order conservatism.[11] In San Francisco, however, the POA's Blue Coat leadership exhibited political flexibility when they put aside their conservative definitions of citizenship and worked with liberals to defend their bread-and-butter interests and the legitimacy of discretion. The new POA leadership understood that cosmopolitan liberalism opened a host of new opportunities for police empowerment. By the late 1970s, big-city police union organizers in other cities were coming to the same conclusions.[12]

Thus, during the 1980s, urban police across the United States bolstered the legitimacy of their discretion through a new emphasis on inclusiveness. As legal scholar David Sklansky has illustrated, this national turn unfolded in two directions. First, in the 1980s cities began adopting modern civility laws, banishing tactics, and the widely hailed broken-windows law enforcement strategy. Early proponents of these order-maintenance approaches advocated granting police the power to arrest citizens for activities deemed disorderly (such as panhandling or congregating on street corners) even when those activities did not cause immediate physical or material harm to others. Police reformers in liberal-controlled cities rationalized these proscriptions by arguing that unruly behaviors created a culture of fear and disorder and inspired crimes against person and property. Liberal city officials further insisted that because these policies were generated within open and inclusive political arrangements, the police tactics represented an expression of the citizenry's common will.[13]

Cities adopting this perverted version of the harm principle—including San Francisco during the 1980s—generally applied order-maintenance law enforcement to people of color. Many of San Francisco's white liberals had been using this sort of slippery-slope harm-principle argument to police nonviolent activities by black people for decades. Indeed, cosmopolitan liberalism had never regarded the cultural and sexual behaviors of African Americans as innocuous. That deep tradition perhaps explains why repeated empirical studies debunking the efficacy of order-management tactics have failed to shake popular faith in broken-windows law enforcement.[14]

Along a second trajectory, in the 1980s and 1990s the nation's police forces reinforced their discretion by fostering inclusive community-policing programs in strategic partnerships with cosmopolitan localists. This new reform agenda emphasized continuous, face-to-face neighborhood-based collaboration between rank-and-file police and community members and encouraged police and residents to cooperatively identify local criminal dangers and strategize police responses. By the late 1980s and into the 1990s, community policing was the nation's dominant reform model.[15]

Scholars have often explained the origins of community policing by highlighting the role that academic criminologists and a handful of influential police chiefs played in conceiving of the program from above. In San Francisco, however, the governing principles behind community policing were already apparent among community members and police during the 1960s. Indeed, the criminologists in academia promoting community policing frequently referenced the SFPD's police-community relations unit's sustained collaborative engagement with residents as a template for the new reform agenda. The 1972 alliance between Haight-Ashbury localists and select Blue Coat leaders provided an even clearer precedent for community policing. At Park Station, rank-and-file officers had embraced participatory democratic rhetoric to defend their workplace interests. When Michael Hebel, the Blue Coat official who had begun to question the effectiveness of the rapid response strategy when he was a Park Station patrol car officer, returned to Park Station during the early 1990s as a captain, he joined with neighborhood activists to devise the SFPD's community policing program.[16]

As this book has shown, the post–World War II street-level meetings between urban residents and police officers were interactions where community, City Hall, and police department politics collided. In the resulting debates over law enforcement and democracy, a number of political factions wielded particular influence. Downtown business elites, for instance, made sure that police reforms rarely impinged on their own agenda. After all, city officials initiated most changes to police discretion on the basis of a promise of downtown economic growth. Scholars note that even the community policing strategies emerging out of localist politics frequently played into the hands of corporate leaders by legitimizing reduced central-state regulation.[17]

The downtown business community's sway over the police reform program, however, did not equate with day-to-day control over street-level law enforcement. Individual police officers enjoyed tremendous discretion during the post–World War II period, and police used that power to defend institutional values and prerogatives that occasionally failed to match the interests of downtown elites or law-and-order conservatives. Indeed, rank-and-file officers found that some of their values served as bridges to liberals. The nation's modern-day policing arrangements thus represent not only negotiated agreements between liberal and conservative politicians and activists, but also compromises between those same political actors and the police.

Finally, attention to street-level interactions between community residents and police reveals both the pivotal role liberals played in the development of postwar law enforcement and the central place of police politics in the transformation of liberalism itself. The cosmopolitan liberalism that arose during the second half of the twentieth century did not evolve amid a defensive posture toward issues of law and order. Instead, white-collar professionals and marginalized residents placed themselves at the forefront of the postwar debates over law enforcement and used those discussions to develop a cosmopolitan liberal ideology and coalition. By engaging with issues of street-level policing, the cosmopolitan liberal coalition ultimately reconceived definitions of crime, the boundaries of citizenship, and the proper shape of government in an urban democracy.

ACKNOWLEDGMENTS

In these closing pages, I offer heartfelt thanks to the dozens of peers, archivists, interviewees, and family members whose insights and helping hands are evident in these pages.

I first happened into the history of San Francisco policing while searching for a crime-themed paper topic that could be rapidly researched in a single semester. Kerwin Klein, my mentor, pointed me to an intriguing local police scandal he had come across named "gayola." At the time, both of us were new to the Bay Area archive scene, but we speculated that the trials for this case had produced abundant and readily accessible court and police documents. Within a couple of weeks, I learned that the courts had long since purged the trial transcripts and that the San Francisco Police Department maintained no collected records from the pre-1973 period. The success of my work would need to rely instead on the generosity of local San Franciscans.

As my early interest in the gayola scandal broadened into a larger study of postwar urban liberalism, San Franciscans from throughout the city extended to me their time and trust through interviews and personal papers. My first interviewees—a group including former gay bar workers, such as Bill Plath and Bob Ross, and former police officers, including Elliot Blackstone and Kevin Mullen—showed particular patience as they walked me through the basics of midcentury urban law enforcement.

Most important, these interviewees made clear to me that my initial questions were incomplete. I had entered the project expecting to write a power-politics history revolving around police raids and sweeps that were directed by City Hall and the Hall of Justice and reported in the local press. My interviewees, however, repeatedly drew my attention toward the less visible day-to-day interactions between residents and officers on the street. These residents forced me to consider how their dispersed and highly personalized encounters fit into our understanding of urban political history.

A handful of local people—including Orville Luster, Richard Hongisto, Thomas Fleming, Kevin Killian, and Susan Stryker—opened their contact books and provided me with introductions to a wide range of communities. Orville, John Mindermann, Michael Hebel, and Hadley Roff sat down for multiple conversations, and Orville, Ray Shine, Al Baccari Jr., and David Dodd granted me access to rafts of documents unavailable in local archives. When the project began leading me toward formal collections, I received assistance from the archivists and librarians at the California Historical Society; San Francisco Public Library; San Francisco African American Historical and Cultural Society; American Civil Liberties Union of Northern California; Archdiocese of San Francisco; and Gay, Lesbian, Bisexual, Transgender History Society. James Eason, Susan Snyder, and the rest of the Bancroft Library staff deserve special thanks for their help in pulling hundreds of photographic negatives out of cold storage and then processing the handful of images I selected.

I entered this project hoping to mix fields and methodological approaches, and my peers and mentors in the UC Berkeley History Department were instrumental in showing me the broad possibilities open to historians. No one expanded my scholarly horizons more than Kerwin Klein and Richard Cándida Smith. Kerwin and Richard have both remained involved in this project as it has developed, receiving new versions of the manuscript on a nearly annual basis for the last six years. This constant presence provided both of them with a tremendously helpful before-and-after perspective as I made dramatic revisions. I also deeply appreciate Bill Issel and Martin Meeker, two other friends and colleagues from the Bay Area, for helping me make sense of San Francisco's often complicated history. My good friend Kevin Adams read an early draft of the manuscript and offered a very diplomatic critique. Since then, Kevin has been my most important professional mentor, showing me the ropes of academia beyond the archives and classroom.

All of my contacts at the University of Chicago Press have had an intuitive sense of when to step back and when to check in. Robert Devens shepherded my book into the press, and here at the end, Russ Damian, Meg Murphy-Sweeney, and Tim Mennel have taken my book into production. My anonymous readers helped me—repeatedly—to reconceptualize my argument through their questioning. From reading the acknowledgment pages of other books in this series, I know that authors have already commented on the herculean efforts Tim Gilfoyle, the series editor, puts into his manuscript edits. These stories are all true! I extend my deep appreciation to Tim for his line-by-line edits and detailed reviews. His comments were invaluable.

A number of scholars showed extraordinary generosity by looking over large sections or an entire draft of the manuscript as a professional courtesy. I have a lot to pay forward following the assistance I have received from Matthew Lassiter, Eric Schneider, Mark Rose, David Sklansky, and those who served as anonymous readers. My friend Heather Ammermuller also assisted with a late-stage proofread.

In terms of ensuring that I would complete the book, there is perhaps no one more important than Myra Rich, my former chair in the University of Colorado, Denver, history department. In 2007 a series of unsuccessful tours through the academic job market had me sending out resumes to Bay Area nonprofits. My job search, however, had introduced me to Myra, and she had faith in both my research and my ability to teach. Singlehandedly, she secured me a visiting assistant professorship at UC Denver, and she then made a variety of sacrifices to get me a tenure track line. The support I have since received from my department colleagues at UC Denver has left me feeling exceptionally lucky. Marjorie Levine-Clark, Bill Wagner, Thomas Andrews, and Myra have all read full drafts of my book. Pam Laird has guided me through every mechanical and contractual step of the publishing process.

I am fortunate that my best friend is also an extraordinary historian. Khal Schneider read a decade's worth of rough drafts, provided me a futon for my Bay Area research trips, and served as a constant sounding board. His instincts and his insights into my project have always been dead on, and, perhaps most important, he is a major reason I can look back on my early years in academia and describe them as "a whole lot of fun."

My parents, Bob and Jan; my sisters, Megan and Brooke; my uncles, Claude and Tom; and my in-laws, Peter and Barbara, always made it clear that they were proud of what I was trying to accomplish with this book. They also had a very real role helping me learn how to articulate my story and its significance. None were ever satisfied with a two-sentence response to the question, "How's the book going?" Their indefatigable interest kept my nose pointed forward. Barbara passed away this last year, but one of my last and most treasured memories with her and Peter and Becky, my wife, occurred at a dinner in Ithaca. Barbara and Peter were, as usual, peppering me with questions about the manuscript and making me feel important. It meant a lot to me—and I think to Barbara, as well—that after years of these sorts of conversations, I was able to describe to her the finish line.

My father was the most unequivocal cheerleader. He encouraged me to take a chance on the visiting professor position in Denver, and he then took it upon himself to help Becky and me set up our new life here, with multiple drives across the Nevada deserts and Rocky Mountains. My mother's influence, meanwhile, appears on every page of this book. Her childhood stories of growing up in "the City" were what first brought me to consider San Francisco's past. She also, through a lifetime of devotedly reading my work, was the person who taught me how to write. For the rest of my career, whenever I teach writing—to either my students or my own children—I'll be passing along lessons from my mother.

Finally, there's Becky. I knew I'd lucked into something pretty special when she showed up to hear me give my very first public talk on this project. Over the next year, Becky was a constant source of encouragement as I closed in on what I declared the original product's "final draft." What I'm sure she didn't anticipate, however, was that for six more years, I would go through redraft after redraft after redraft, repeatedly resurrecting the word *final* only to then remark, "Well, maybe I need another new chapter or two." Becky made those years of rewrites not simply bearable, but exhilarating. As thanks, I dedicate to her the notebook redrafts of another—slightly more talented—writer. She and I later heard these Springsteen lyrics during a special moment in time:

> ~~By~~ In the day we sweat it out on the streets of a runaway American Dream/
> At night we ~~stalk the jungle in heat with murder in our gears~~ ride through
> ~~Spanish thunder rebel powers mansions of pain mansions of pride~~
> mansions of glory in suicide machines/
> (marginalia: ~~only suicide~~)
> Sprung ~~honed~~ from ~~steel chrome~~ cages out on Highway 9/
> chrome-wheeled, fuel-injected/
> And steppin' out over the line/
> (marginalia: ~~surf city~~)
> ~~here in~~ Baby this town ~~trys to~~ rips the ~~flesh~~ bones from your back/
> It's a death trap[,]
> [It's] a suicide rap/
> We gotta get out while we're young/
> 'Cause. . .

Becky, thank you.

ABBREVIATIONS

ACLUN: ACLU News (newspaper of the American Civil Liberties Union of Northern California)

ACLUP: American Civil Liberties Union of Northern California Papers, California Historical Society Archives

BL: The Bancroft Library at the University of California, Berkeley

CHSA: California Historical Society Archives

CW: Chinese World

GLBTHS: Northern California Gay, Lesbian, Bisexual, and Transgender Historical Society Archive

HA: Haight Action

HAI: Haight-Ashbury Independent

HAIL: Haight-Ashbury-Ink-Link

HAMR: Haight-Ashbury Midtown Record

HAR: Haight-Ashbury Record

JLAP: Joseph L. Alioto Papers, San Francisco Public Library

LCN: Little City News

N&V: News and Views

SBP: Scott Bishop Papers, San Francisco Public Library

SFAP: San Francisco's Arguello Park: Community Builds a Neighborhood Park Papers, Bancroft Library at the University of California, Berkeley

SFBG: San Francisco Bay Guardian

SFC: San Francisco Chronicle

SFE: San Francisco Examiner

SFEC: San Francisco Sunday Examiner and Chronicle

SFN: *San Francisco News*

SFNCB: *San Francisco News-Call Bulletin*

SFPD: San Francisco Police Department

SFPL: San Francisco Public Library

SR: *The Sun-Reporter*

SSJ: Shedding a Straight Jacket Oral History Collection, Northern California Gay, Lesbian, Bisexual, and Transgender Historical Society Archive

TGSFR: Tavern Guild of San Francisco Records, Northern California Gay, Lesbian, Bisexual, and Transgender Historical Society Archive

TS: *The Spokesman*

NOTES

INTRODUCTION

1. *SFC,* May 14, 1960, 1; Ralph Tyler, "Why It Happened in San Francisco," *Frontier,* June 1960, 6; *SFNCB,* January 24, 1961, 5.

2. *SFE,* April 17, 1965, 19; April 26, 1961, 12. *SFC,* February 19, 1961, 1; May 14, 1960, 1. Tyler, "Why It Happened," 8.

3. "Letter from Communitywide Committee to Secure ACLU's Legal Defense for May 13 Arrestees to Rabbi Alvin Fine, Chairman of the Board of Directors of ACLU of Northern California," June 8, 1960, ACLUP, Folder 642; *SFE,* April 26, 1961, 12; *SFNCB,* April 21, 1961, 7; *SFC,* May 14, 1960, 3, B.

4. Capital Film Labs, *Operation Abolition* (Washington, DC: Capital Film Labs, 1960), accessed at http://archive.org/details/6239_Operation_Abolition_01_00_52_09.

5. Lisa McGirr, *Suburban Warriors: The Origins of the New American Right* (Princeton, NJ: Princeton University Press, 2001), 62; Todd Gitlin, *The Sixties: Years of Hope, Days of Rage* (New York: Bantam, 1987), 83; James Miller, *"Democracy Is in the Streets": From Port Huron to the Siege of Chicago* (New York: Simon and Schuster, 1987), 46.

6. Robert Self, *American Babylon: Race and the Struggle for Postwar Oakland* (Princeton, NJ: Princeton University Press, 2003), 224; Michael Flamm, *Law and Order: Street Crime, Civil Unrest, and the Crisis of Liberalism in the 1960s* (New York: Columbia University Press, 2005).

7. *SFNCB,* January 23, 1961, 6.

8. *SFC,* February 12, 1961, 20; February 9, 1961, 12. *SFNCB,* May 3, 1961, 7; April 20, 1961, 6.

9. Peter Dreier, John Mollenkopf, and Todd Swanstrom, *Place Matters: Metropolitics for the Twenty-First Century,* 2nd ed. (Lawrence: University Press of Kansas, 2005), 171, 177. Also see Terry Nichols Clark, "Race and Class versus the New Political Culture," in *Urban Innovation: Creative Strategies for Turbulent Times,* ed. Terry Nichols Clark (Thousand Oaks, CA: Sage Publications, 1994), 23.

10. United States Bureau of Census, *Census of Population: 1940,* Volume 2, Part 1, Section 6, Table 25, 567, and Table 21, 54; *Census of Population: 1950,* Volume 2, Table 4, 5–11. Albert

Broussard, *Black San Francisco: The Struggle for Racial Equality in the West* (Lawrence: University Press of Kansas, 1993), 138. William Issel, "Faith-Based Activism in American Cities: The Case of the San Francisco Catholic Action Cadre," *Journal of Church and State* 50, no. 3 (2008): 520. The 1940 Census counted Latinos as white, but foreign-born Mexicans and Central and South Americans only accounted for 1 percent of the total population.

11. United States Bureau of Census, *Census of Population: 1940,* Volume 2, Part 1, Section 6, Table 21, 542; *Census of Population: 1950,* Volume 2, Table 47, 5–179; *Census of Population: 1960,* Volume 1, Table 21, 6–141; *Census of Population: 1970,* Table 23, 6–105. The Immigration and Nationality Act of 1965 renewed large-scale Chinese immigration, but in 1970 residents of Chinese descent still only made up 8 percent of San Francisco's population.

12. Thomas Sugrue, *Origins of the Urban Crisis: Race and Inequality in Postwar Detroit* (Princeton, NJ: Princeton University Press, 1996); Self, *American Babylon,* 25–26, 42; United States Bureau of Census, *Census of Population: 1960,* Volume 1, Table 5, 6–21.

13. Robert Self, *All in the Family: The Realignment of American Democracy since the 1960s* (New York: Hill and Wang, 2012), 4. Also see Whitney Strub, *Perversion for Profit: The Politics of Pornography and the Rise of the New Right* (New York: Columbia University Press, 2011), 44.

14. William Issel, "'Land Values, Human Values, and the Preservation of the City's Treasured Appearance': Environmentalism, Politics, and the San Francisco Freeway Revolt," *Pacific Historical Review* 68, no. 4 (1999): 619–20; Dreier, Mollenkopf, and Swanstrom, *Place Matters,* 167.

15. Ira Katznelson, *City Trenches: Urban Politics and the Patterning of Class in the United States* (New York: Pantheon, 1981), 16; Robert Self, "Sex in the City: The Politics of Sexual Liberalism in Los Angeles, 1963–79," *Gender and History* 20, no. 2 (2008): 290; Guian McKee, *The Problem of Jobs: Liberalism, Race, and Deindustrialization in Philadelphia* (Chicago: University of Chicago Press, 2008), 6; Self, *American Babylon,* 13–14.

16. *Crime in the United States: Uniform Crime Reports—1960,* issued by J. Edgar Hoover, Director, Federal Bureau of Investigation (Washington, DC: U.S. Government Printing Office, 1961), 33; *Crime in the United States: Uniform Crime Reports—1971,* issued by L. Patrick Gray III, Acting Director, Federal Bureau of Investigation (Washington, DC: U.S. Government Printing Office, 1972), 60; Flamm, *Law and Order,* 127.

17. Robert Fogelson, *Big-City Police* (Cambridge, MA: Harvard University Press, 1977), chapters 1–3.

18. A. C. Germann, "Community Policing: An Assessment," *Journal of Criminal Law, Criminology, and Police Science* 60, no. 1 (1969): 94; San Francisco Committee on Crime, *A Report on the Police Department, Part II, The Ninth Report of the Committee* (San Francisco: Committee on Crime, June 17, 1971), 126; The President's Commission on Law Enforcement and Administration of Justice, *The Challenge of Crime in a Free Society* (Washington, DC: U.S. Government Printing Office, February 1967), 103.

19. San Francisco Committee on Crime, *Report on the Police Department, Part II,* 130, 125.

20. "Summary of Police Department Personnel" and "Schedule of Uniformed Members," in SFPD, *Annual Reports* (San Francisco: City of San Francisco, 1952–1970). San Francisco's official rank and civil-service title for the lowest-level uniformed police officer was *patrolman. Police woman* referred to a separate civil-service title and status. The SFPD did not begin transitioning away from these gender-specific ranks and civil-servant statuses until 1976.

21. John Mindermann interview with author, March 29, 2004.

22. Mindermann interview.

23. Frank Donner, *Protectors of Privilege: Red Squads and Police Repression in Urban America* (Berkeley: University of California Press, 1990), 1; Ernesto Chávez, *"¡Mi Raza Primero!" (My People First!): Nationalism, Identity, and Insurgency in the Chicano Movement in Los Angeles, 1966–1978* (Berkeley: University of California Press, 2002), 45, 6; Marylinn Johnson, *Street Justice: A History of Police Violence in New York City* (Boston, MA: Beacon, 2003), 203, 253, 288–89; Ian Haney López, *Racism on Trial: The Chicano Fight for Justice* (Cambridge, MA: Belknap, 2003), chapter 6; Edward Escobar, *Race, Police and the Making of a Political Identity: Mexican Americans and the Los Angeles Police Department, 1900–1945* (Berkeley: University of California Press, 1999), 11; Mike Davis, *City of Quartz* (New York: Vintage, 1992), 267, 252.

24. Michael Willrich, *City of Courts: Socializing Justice in Progressive Era Chicago* (New York: Cambridge University Press, 2003), 60; Mae Ngai, *Impossible Subjects: Illegal Aliens and the Making of Modern America* (Princeton, NJ: Princeton University Press, 2005), 90; Margot Canaday, *The Straight State: Sexuality and Citizenship in Twentieth-Century America* (Princeton, NJ: Princeton University Press, 2011), 5–6, 152; Kelly Lytle Hernández, *Migra!: A History of the U.S. Border Patrol* (Berkeley: University of California Press, 2010), 2–4.

25. Don Kates Jr., "Police Malpractice," Folder 744, "Reporter's Transcription for the Appeal of *People v. Charles C. Pierce*," Folder 1606, and "Letter from Elizabeth Lenhart to Ernest Besig" (no date, but shortly before June 19, 1959), Folder 781, ACLUP.

26. David Alan Sklansky, *Democracy and the Police* (Stanford, CA: Stanford University Press, 2007), 33. Liberal definitions of *rule of law* varied, but liberals generally employed the term to suggest that the government should follow stable rules and that those rules should be determined by democratic processes.

27. Flamm, *Law and Order*, chapter 3.

28. Alison Isenberg, *Downtown America: A History of the Place and the People Who Made It* (Chicago: University of Chicago Press, 2004), 205; John D'Emilio, *Sexual Politics, Sexual Communities: The Making of a Homosexual Minority in the United States, 1940–1970*, 2nd ed. (Chicago: University of Chicago Press, 1998), 23–31; Allan Bérubé, *Coming Out Under Fire: The History of Gay Men and Women in World War Two* (New York: Free Press, 1990), 113, 216; Richard Cándida Smith, *Utopia and Dissent: Art, Poetry, and Politics in California* (Berkeley: University of California Press, 1995), 80–82; Elizabeth Schrank, *Art and the City: Civic Imagination and Cultural Authority in Los Angeles* (Philadelphia: University of Pennsylvania Press, 2009), 66; Josh Sides, "Excavating the Postwar Sex District in San Francisco," *Journal of Urban History* 32, no. 3 (2006): 356.

29. Flamm, *Law and Order*, 2, 68.

30. Eric Schneider, *Smack: Heroin and the American City* (Philadelphia: University of Pennsylvania Press, 2011), 132.

31. Christian Parenti, *Lockdown America: Police and Prisons in the Age of Crisis* (New York: Verso, 2000), 63; James Patterson, *Restless Giant: The United States from Watergate to Bush v. Gore* (New York: Oxford University Press, 2005), 3, 81, 223, 341–42; Dreier, Mollenkopf, and Swanstrom, *Place Matters*, 214.

32. United States Bureau of Census, *Census of Population: 1950,* Volume 2, Table 35, 5-122, and *Census of Population: 1960,* Volume 1, Table 74, 6-321.

33. Bernard Harcourt, *Illusion of Order: The False Promise of Broken Windows Policing* (Cambridge, MA: Harvard University Press, 2001), chapter 7.

CHAPTER 1

1. *SFC,* January 14, 1956, 10.

2. Jon Teaford, *The Rough Road to Renaissance: Urban Revitalization in America, 1940-1985* (Baltimore, MD: Johns Hopkins University Press, 1990), 55, 57-60; *SFC,* March 2, 1955, 4.

3. *Police and Peace Officers' Journal of the State of California* (January-February 1954), accessed at http://archive.org/stream/policepeaceoffic19561957sanf/policepeaceoffic19561957 sanf_djvu.txt. *SFC,* January 14, 1956, 10; August 2, 1955, 4.

4. *SFC,* January 14, 1956, 10.

5. "Thomas Cahill Interview," SBP, 90-11, Box 1; Sol Weiner interview with author, March 2, 2003; Elliot Blackstone interview with author, October 16, 1999.

6. Robert Fogelson, *Big-City Police* (Cambridge, MA: Harvard University Press, 1977), 263; Samuel Hays, "The Politics of Reform in Municipal Government in the Progressive Era," *Pacific Northwest Quarterly* 55, no. 4 (1964): 157, 159; Frederick Wirt, *Power in the City: Decision Making in San Francisco* (Berkeley: University of California Press, 1974), 117; John Mollenkopf, *The Contested City* (Princeton, NJ: Princeton University Press, 1983), 151.

7. Wirt, *Power in the City,* 114, 118-120; Chester Hartman, *City for Sale: The Transformation of San Francisco,* rev. and updated ed. (Berkeley: University of California Press, 2002), 48. On other business-led charter reform efforts, see Guian McKee, *The Problem of Jobs: Liberalism, Race, and Deindustrialization in Philadelphia* (Chicago: University of Chicago Press, 2008), 19-20.

8. William Issel, "'Land Values, Human Values, and the Preservation of the City's Treasured Appearance': Environmentalism, Politics, and the San Francisco Freeway Revolt," *Pacific Historical Review* 68, no. 4 (1999): 619-20; Hartman, *City for Sale,* 7.

9. Clarence Stone, *Regime Politics: Governing Atlanta, 1946-1988* (Lawrence: University Press of Kansas, 1989), 38; Robert Fogelson, *Downtown: Its Rise and Fall, 1880-1950* (New Haven, NH: Yale University Press, 2003), 376.

10. Hartman, *City for Sale,* 16; Allan Temko, "San Francisco Rebuilds Again," *Harper's Magazine,* April 1960, 53.

11. Fogelson, *Big-City Police,* chapter 1; *SFE,* March 17, 1937, 14; Charles Raudebaugh, "San Francisco: The Beldam Dozes," in *Our Fair City,* ed. Robert Allen (New York: Vanguard, 1947), 352.

12. *SFNCB,* October 12, 1959, 6.

13. Samuel Walker, "Origins of the Contemporary Criminal Justice Paradigm: The American Bar Foundation Survey, 1953-1969," *Justice Quarterly* 9, no. 1 (1992): 54; David Alan Sklansky, "The Persistent Pull of Police Professionalism" (unpublished paper, courtesy of the author, 2010), 2. On earlier and similar efforts at school reform, see David Tyack, *The One Best System: A History of Urban Education* (Cambridge, MA: Harvard University Press, 1974), part IV.

14. Fogelson, *Big-City Police,* 176–77; SFPD, *Annual Report* (San Francisco: City of San Francisco, 1937), 43–44.

15. Raudebaugh, "San Francisco: The Beldam Dozes," 352, 363; San Francisco Committee on Crime, *A Report on the Police Department, Part I, The Ninth Report of the Committee* (San Francisco: Committee on Crime, June 17, 1971), 37. The city charter placed marginal checks over the Police Commission's (and, by extension, the mayor's) authority by freezing the size of the SFPD's workforce. The addition of a single sergeant, under this system, required a citywide referendum. Wirt, *Power in the City,* 12.

16. *SFNCB,* October 13, 1959, 4; October 14, 1959, 4; October 15, 1959, 11. *SFN,* February 4, 1948, 1, 7. *SFE,* February 9, 1948, 1. Mollenkopf, *The Contested City,* 151. San Francisco Committee on Crime, *A Report on the Police Department, Part II, The Ninth Report of the Committee* (San Francisco: Committee on Crime, June 17, 1971), 2–3. *SFC,* December 17, 1957, 9; February 1, 1955, 2. An SFPD study in the early 1970s reported that detail commanders within the Inspectors Bureau estimated that no less than 15 percent of their officers were "completely ineffective and unproductive." San Francisco Committee on Crime, *A Report on the Police Department, Part II,* 2–3.

17. *SFC,* February 5, 1948, 16.

18. George Dorsey, *Christopher of San Francisco* (New York: Macmillan, 1962), 92. On the musical-chairs quality of high-brass appointments, see *SFNCB,* October 12, 1959, 6.

19. Kevin Mullen, *Chinatown Squad: Policing the Dragon from the Gold Rush to the 21st Century* (Novato, CA: Noir, 2008), 13; *SFE,* March 22, 1950, 7.

20. *SFC,* September 23, 1949, 17; March 22, 1950, 1, 10.

21. *SFC,* September 14, 1970, 10; August 26, 1949, 17.

22. *SFE,* October 21, 1970, 9; August 26, 1949, 7. *SFC,* September 23, 1949, 17; October 3, 1964, 5. Mullen, *Chinatown Squad,* 157–58.

23. *SFNCB,* October 14, 1959, 4.

24. *SFE,* November 7, 1947, 2; *SFEC,* February 15, 1948, TW2; *SFN,* February 4, 1948, 1, 7.

25. *SFC,* March 10, 1950, 2; December 26, 1950, 2.

26. Nayan Shah, *Contagious Divides: Epidemics and Race in San Francisco's Chinatown* (Berkeley: University of California Press, 2001), 225.

27. *SFN,* February 4, 1948, 1, 7. *SFC,* March 9, 1950, 1; February 11, 1956, 4. Chiou-ling Yeh, *Making an American Festival: Chinese New Year in San Francisco's Chinatown* (Berkeley: University of California Press, 2008), 31.

28. *SFC,* March 10, 1950, 2; April 6, 1950, 2.

29. *CW,* June 21, 1954, 2.

30. *SFC,* August 26, 1949, 17. *CW,* June 21, 1954, 2; February 15, 1956, 2.

31. *SFE,* June 21, 1954, 3.

32. William Rivers and David Rubin, *A Region's Press: Anatomy of Newspapers in the San Francisco Bay Area* (Berkeley: Institute of Governmental Studies, University of California, 1971), 35; Frederick Wirt, "Alioto and the Politics of Hyperpluralism," in *Politics/America: The Cutting Edge of Change,* ed. Walter Dean Burnham (New York: D. Van Nostrand, 1973), 357, 359; Wirt, *Power in the City,* 120. By the late 1960s and continuing into the 1970s and 1980s, mayors reinforced their connection to the media by hiring reporters directly into their administrations. Hartman, *City for Sale,* 39.

33. Scott Newhall, *A Newspaper Editor's Voyage across San Francisco: SFC, 1934–1971, and Other Adventures: Oral History Transcript* (Berkeley: University of California, Berkeley, 1990), 217–18. The Catholic archbishop wielded veto power over the *Examiner*'s police chief nominations. Malcolm Glover interview with author, July 7, 2004. For a story of Wren dictating a police policy position to Mayor Robinson, see Dorsey, *Christopher of San Francisco,* 89.

34. *SFC,* January 19, 1971, 2; "Letter from Jim Benet to Abe Mellinkoff," December 2, 1960, Scott Newhall Papers, BL, Carton 8, Folder: City Desk. The *Chronicle*'s most vocal police professionalization advocates were Charles Raudebaugh and Dick Hyer. In 1949 the *Chronicle*'s owners broadened their newspaper's influence by founding the KRON television station. Through the 1950s local television and radio stations relied on newspaper journalists for their local crime and police reports. Glover interview.

35. Rivers and Rubin, *A Region's Press,* 29–30. Both newspapers fawned over the city's well-to-do in their society pages. The *Examiner,* however, focused on the traditional Catholic elite, while the *Chronicle* concentrated on Jewish and Protestant social happenings. Warren Hinckle, *If You Have a Lemon, Make Lemonade* (New York: G. P. Putnam's Sons, 1974), 20.

36. *SFC,* January 31, 1955, 1; April 23, 1953, 1. Newhall, *A Newspaper Editor's Voyage,* 217–19.

37. *SFC,* October 23, 1953, 18; William Keller, "The Cocky Milkman," *Frontier,* February 1958, 15; Dorsey, *Christopher of San Francisco,* 72.

38. Dorsey, *Christopher of San Francisco,* 88; *SFC,* January 26, 1956, 11; *SFNCB,* October 12, 1959, 6.

39. Dorsey, *Christopher of San Francisco,* 67, 91, 99. Under Christopher's board presidency, the supervisors ordered the internal SFPD efficiency survey. *SFC,* April 1, 1950, 8.

40. Dorsey, *Christopher of San Francisco,* 99.

41. Ibid., 100. *SFC,* August 2, 1955, 4; March 2, 1955, 1; December 29, 1955, 1. Newhall, *A Newspaper Editor's Voyage,* 219. *CW,* November 11, 1955, 1.

42. *SFC,* January 7, 1956, 1, 2; January 17, 1956, 1. The Treasury agents had handpicked SFPD Inspector Frank Ahern to assist them with their raid. *SFC,* January 26, 1956, 11.

43. Matthew Countryman, *Up South: Civil Rights and Black Power in Philadelphia* (Philadelphia: University of Pennsylvania Press, 2006), 164; Marc Stein, *City of Sisterly and Brotherly Loves: Lesbian and Gay Philadelphia, 1945–1972* (Chicago: University of Chicago Press, 2000), 158.

44. Ethan Rarick, *California Rising: The Life and Times of Pat Brown* (Berkeley: University of California Press, 2005), 44–45; *SFC,* January 22, 1956, 4.

45. *SFC,* September 5, 1958, 5; January 22, 1956, 4.

46. *SFE,* February 24, 1954, 1. *SFC,* March 23, 1954, 1; April 16, 1954, 1, 4; January 26, 1956, 1. *SFNCB,* October 15, 1959, 11.

47. *SFNCB,* October 12, 1959, 6; October 13, 1959, 4. *SFC,* January 17, 1956, 1, 5.

48. David Johnson, *American Law Enforcement: A History* (Saint Louis, MO: Forum Press, 1981), 121; Samuel Walker, *Popular Justice: A History of American Criminal Justice,* 2nd ed. (New York: Oxford University Press, 1998), 173.

49. Yeh, *Making an American Festival,* 54. *CW,* February 11, 1956, 2; January 9, 1956, 1; January 27, 1956, 1.

50. *CW,* July 30, 1955, 2; February 15, 1956, 2.

51. *SFC,* February 10, 1956, 1; February 9, 1956, 4; February 18, 1956, 1; February 20, 1956, 1, 17.

52. *SFC*, February 26, 1956, 1; February 27, 1956, 2. *SFE*, December 14, 1959, III:8. Also see *SFNCB*, October 20, 1959, 12. *CW*, February 27, 1956, 2; February 28, 1956, 2.

53. *SFC*, September 2, 1958, 1; September 5, 1958, 1.

54. *SFC*, September 7, 1958, 11; September 3, 1958, 6. *SFE*, June 24, 1967, found in Thomas Cahill Papers, SFPL, Folder 17. SFPD, "Chief Cahill: A Life in Review" (no date), accessed at http://sf-police.org/index.aspx?page=1630.

55. Fogelson, *Big-City Police*, 187; *SFE*, December 16, 1959, II:3.

56. *SFC*, December 8, 1958, 1, 5.

57. Karl Beitel, "Transforming San Francisco: Community, Capital, and the Local State in the Era of Globalization, 1956–2001" (Ph.D. dissertation, University of California, Davis, 2003), 32.

58. *SFE*, December 16, 1959, II:3. The similar rationales behind police professionalism and redevelopment encouraged growth proponents to mix the rhetoric of the two campaigns. In 1959, for instance, a celebration of Police Chief Frank Ahern proclaimed, "Ahern Bull-Dozed S.F. Police into Top Force." *SFNCB*, October 19, 1959, 11.

59. *SFC*, December 8, 1958, 5.

60. Fogelson, *Big-City Police*, 187; William Turner, *The Police Establishment* (New York: Putnam, 1968), 145; National Advisory Commission on Civil Disorders, *Report of the National Advisory Commission on Civil Disorders, March 1, 1968* (Washington, DC: U.S. Government Printing Office, 1968), 159.

61. Samuel Walker, *Taming the System: The Control of Discretion in Criminal Justice, 1950–1990* (New York: Oxford University Press, 1993), 7; Walker, "Origins," 57.

62. Walker, *Taming the System*, 7; Walker, "Origins," 58; Walker, *Popular Justice*, 173; O. W. Wilson, *Police Administration* (New York: McGraw-Hill, 1950).

63. Walker, *Taming the System*, 6, 8.

64. Walker, "Origins," 62, 64, 66, 68. University of California, Berkeley, criminologist Arthur Sherry devised the survey's pilot project. Walker, *Taming the System*, 7.

65. Yeh, *Making an American Festival*, 98–99.

66. John Mindermann interview with author, March 29, 2004.

67. *SFE*, December 16, 1959, II:3.

CHAPTER 2

1. *SFE*, December 2, 1958, 5.

2. *SFC*, December 2, 1958, 3.

3. *SFE*, December 2, 1958, 5; "Notes" (no date), ACLUP, Folder 1545.

4. John Maynard, *Venice West: The Beat Generation in Southern California* (New Brunswick, NJ: Rutgers University Press, 1991); Lisa Phillips, ed., *Beat Culture and the New America, 1950–1965* (New York: Whitney Museum of American Art, in association with Flammarion, 1995); Steven Watson, *The Birth of the Beat Generation: Visionaries, Rebels, Hipsters, 1944–1960* (New York: Pantheon, 1995); Clinton Robert Starr, "Bohemian Resonance: The Beat Generation and Urban Countercultures in the United States during the Late 1950s and Early 1960s" (Ph.D. dissertation: University of Texas, 2005). Through their creative work, beats challenged traditional bounds of citizenship. As historian Richard Cándida Smith has noted, beats

condemned white-collar husbands and family-oriented wives as slaves to consumer culture. Male beats advocated for broadened understandings of legitimate male behavior, while female beats often sought to annihilate the conception of gender distinctions altogether. Richard Cándida Smith, *Utopia and Dissent: Art, Poetry, and Politics in California* (Berkeley: University of California Press, 1995), chapters 6–7. Also see Jack Foley, "'And They Began to Call *That* Beat': Transmutations of a Word" (no date, courtesy of the author), 1.

5. *SFEC*, August 15, 1958, TW4. *SFC*, June 14, 1958, 2; August 30, 1960, 6. "The Bored, the Bearded and the Beat," *Look,* August 19, 1958, 65.

6. Arthur Sherry, "Vagrants, Rogues and Vagabonds—Old Concepts in Need of Revision," *California Law Review* 48, no. 4 (1960): 562; California State Assembly Interim Committee on Judiciary, Subcommittee on Constitutional Rights, *A Public Hearing of the Assembly Interim Committee on Judiciary, Subcommittee on Constitutional Rights,* held in San Francisco, California, July 28–29, 1958 (Sacramento: Interim Committee on Judiciary, 1958), 139 (hereafter, Constitutional Rights hearings of 1958); Caleb Foote, "Vagrancy-Type Law and Its Administration," *University of Pennsylvania Law Review* 104, no. 5 (1956): 614.

7. *SFE*, December 2, 1958, 5.

8. Real Estate Research Corporation, *San Francisco Housing Fact Book* (San Francisco: Real Estate Research Corporation, 1962), 59; Francis Joseph Rigney and L. Douglas Smith, *The Real Bohemia* (New York: Basic Books, 1961), 3; Frants Albert, "Urban Renewal Study for San Francisco's Telegraph Hill" (master's thesis, University of California, Berkeley, June 1960), 27; "Arthur Hanna Oral History," March 23, 1999, 34, in The Telegraph Hill Dwellers Oral History Collection, BL.

9. *Henri Lenoir Scrapbooks, 1941–1965, volume 1*, BL; Rebecca Solnit, *Secret Exhibition: Six California Artists of the Cold War Era* (San Francisco: City Lights Books, 1990), 27; Bill Morgan, *The Beat Generation in San Francisco: A Literary Tour* (San Francisco: City Lights Books, 2003), 24, 68; Lewis Ellingham and Kevin Killian, *Poet Be Like God: Jack Spicer and the San Francisco Renaissance* (Hanover, NH: Wesleyan University Press, 1998), 40.

10. David Meltzer interview with author, June 12, 2003.

11. Morgan, *Beat Generation*, 76; Barry Silesky, *Ferlinghetti: The Artist in His Time* (New York: Warner, 1990), 56–58; Ellingham and Killian, *Poet Be Like God*, 55; Margot Patterson Doss, *San Francisco at Your Feet: The Great Walks in a Walker's Town* (New York: Grove, 1964), 23; Rigney and Smith, *Real Bohemia*, 3.

12. Rose Doris Scherini, *The Italian American Community of San Francisco: A Descriptive Study* (New York: Arno, 1976), 26.

13. Leo Krikorian, "The Beatniks and 'The Place': The Golden Age of North Beach in San Francisco" (rough draft, no date, courtesy of Mary Kerr), 48. For an example of North Beach's traditional Italian-American artists and bohemians patronizing the new beat bars, see *LCN*, August 13, 1958, 3.

14. United States Bureau of Census, *Census of Population: 1950*, Volume 3, Part 4, Table 3, 6–7; *Census of Population and Housing: 1960*, Volume 10, Table P-3, 218–19, Table H-2, 365.

15. *LCN*, July 11, 1957, 1, 8.

16. *SFC*, September 4, 1959, 2; *LCN*, December 9, 1959, 3. Ruth Weiss, a white beat, recalled that an Italian-American restaurant owner once vouched for her when she was being questioned by a patrol officer. Ruth Weiss interview with author, July 3, 2003.

17. "The Bored, the Bearded and the Beat," 65; Dan Wakefield, "Night Clubs," *The Nation*, January 4, 1958, 19; Kenneth Rexroth, "San Francisco's Mature Bohemians," *The Nation*, February 23, 1957, 159–62; Bruce Bliven, "San Francisco: New Serpents in Eden," *Harper's Magazine*, January 1958, 38; "Personal and Otherwise: Among Our Contributors," *Harper's Magazine*, January 1958, 21; "The Cool, Cool Bards," *Time*, December 2, 1957, 71; "Beat Mystics," *Time*, February 3, 1958, 56; Noel Clad, "A Frigid Frolic in Frisco," *Playboy*, February 1958, 21–22, 74–75.

18. *SFE*, February 26, 1958, II:1; April 22, 1958, II:1. *SFC*, April 2, 1958, 15.

19. Ron Fimrite interview with author, June 21, 2004. *SFE*, May 4, 1958, 1. *SFEC*, June 15, 1958, TW4–6; June 22, 1958, TW4–6.

20. *SFE*, May 4, 1958, 3.

21. Timothy Stewart-Winter, "Raids, Rights, and Rainbow Coalitions: Sexuality and Race in Chicago Politics, 1950–2000" (Ph.D. dissertation: University of Chicago, 2009), 39. United States Bureau of Census, *Census of Population: 1960*, Volume 1, Table 74, 6–321, Table 13, 6–55, Table 105, 6–552; *Census of Population: 1950*, Volume 2, Table 10, 5–52, Table 57, 5–218. Suleiman Osman, *The Invention of Brownstone Brooklyn: Gentrification and the Search for Authenticity in Postwar New York* (New York: Oxford University Press, 2011), 65, 133.

22. *SFE*, May 4, 1958, 1. *SFEC*, June 15, 1958, TW4–6; August 31, 1960, 4. Norman Podhoretz, "The Know-Nothing Bohemians," *Partisan Review* 25, no. 2 (1958): 307–8, 317.

23. *SFEC*, June 15, 1958, TW6; *SFC*, June 19, 1958, 1; *SFN*, June 18, 1958, 1; *SFE*, June 19, 1958, 1.

24. *SFE*, June 20, 1956, 14; June 29, 1958, 14; June 19, 1958, 11. *SFC*, June 19, 1958, 1, 6; June 19, 1959, 7. *SFN*, June 18, 1959, 1, 4; June 19, 1958, 2.

25. *SFC*, June 19, 1958, 1, 6; *SFE*, June 19, 1958, 11.

26. *SFN*, June 18, 1959, 4. *SFC*, June 18, 1958, 1; June 19, 1958, 1. *SFE*, June 19, 1958, 11.

27. *SFE*, June 19, 1958, 11.

28. Rigney and Smith, *Real Bohemia*, 161; Watson, *Birth of the Beat Generation*, 260, 4. Similarly, some members of the judiciary failed to express alarm over beat defendants. On July 22, for instance, a municipal judge issued an injunction against the police department's harassment of Eric Nord's Party Pad. *SFC*, July 23, 1958, 30. *Playboy* meanwhile traded its earlier depiction of beat women as frigid with an alluring "Beat Playmate." "Playboy's Beat Playmate," *Playboy*, July 1959, 47. Also see Paul O'Neil, "The Only Rebellion Around," *Life*, November 30, 1959, 116.

29. *LCN*, June 11, 1958, 3; *SFNCB*, June 24, 1960, 21.

30. Danny Kathiner, "The Rise and Fall of Gaslight Square," *Gateway Heritage: The Magazine of the Missouri Historical Society* 22, no. 2 (2001): 42.

31. *SFN*, August 9, 1958, 1; Morgan, *Beat Generation,* 36; Meltzer interview.

32. Constitutional Rights hearings of 1958, 158. *SFC*, August 19, 1958, 3; August 12, 1958, 5; December 27, 1958, 2; July 23, 1958, 30. *SFE*, August 11, 1958, 1. *SFN*, August 9, 1958, 1.

33. *SFN*, July 29, 1958, 6. Brown approvingly explained that upper Grant Avenue provided gay men with a healthy place for them to become weekend beats and "find conformity for their non-conformity." *SFEC*, June 22, 1958, TW6.

34. Bernard Harcourt, *Illusion of Order: The False Promise of Broken Windows Policing* (Cambridge, MA: Harvard University Press, 2001), chapter 7.

35. *Evening Bulletin* (Philadelphia), February 18, 1959, 1; February 19, 1959, 14. Also see Marc Stein, *City of Sisterly and Brotherly Loves: Lesbian and Gay Philadelphia, 1945–1972* (Chicago: University of Chicago Press, 2000), 160.

36. *LCN*, April 16, 1958, 3; *SFC*, May 13, 1958, 17.

37. *LCN,* May 21, 1958, 3; *SFE*, June 20, 1958, 14; Rigney and Smith, *Real Bohemia*, 159; *SFC*, June 20, 1958, 4.

38. John Mindermann interview with author, March 29, 2004; *SFC*, September 25, 1971, 14. Also see "Letter from Rev. James A. McGee to Most Rev. John J. Mitty, Archbishop of San Francisco," March 10, 1955, San Francisco Archdiocese Archives, Folder: Police. Severe staffing shortages during World War II had forced the SFPD leadership to relax its traditional restrictions on white women and black men, but the postwar wave of white male recruits squelched any integrative momentum. In 1959 more than 1,000 of the SFPD's 1,300 patrolmen had joined after World War II. *SFNCB*, October 15, 1959, 11. The SFPD hired its first black officer in 1943, and the department hired five women for traffic duty in 1944. All these appointments were temporary and expired after the war's end. *SFE*, October 12, 1943, 3; *SFC*, August 28, 1947, 13.

39. "Summary of Personnel," in SFPD, *Annual Report* (San Francisco: City of San Francisco, 1947); Richard Hongisto interview with author, April 8, 2002; *SFE*, December 14, 1959, III:8; *SFNCB*, October 28, 1959, 7.

40. "Summary of Personnel," in SFPD, *Annual Reports* (San Francisco: City of San Francisco, 1945–1967); Mayor's Committee for Municipal Management, *A Report to the Blyth-Zellerbach Committee on Modern Management for San Francisco, Volume 1* (San Francisco: City of San Francisco, June 1961), 44; SFPD, *San Francisco Police Department Study* (San Francisco: City of San Francisco, 1957), 13; *SFNCB*, October 15, 1959, 11.

41. Mindermann interview.

42. *SFN*, June 19, 1958, 1.

43. Mindermann interview; *LCN*, May 20, 1959, 3.

44. Mindermann interview. *SFC*, June 18, 1971, 8; August 14, 1959, 4. Frederick Wirt, "Alioto and the Politics of Hyperpluralism," in *Politics/America: The Cutting Edge of Change*, ed. Walter Dean Burnham (New York: D. Van Nostrand, 1973), 356. Gale Wright interview with author, June 4, 2003.

45. "Letter from Ernest Besig to Thomas Cahill," April 7, 1959, ACLUP, Folder 781; Constitutional Rights hearings of 1958, 158. Also see "Letter from Ernest Besig to Thomas Cahill," June 20, 1959, ACLUP, Folder 781; *SFC*, August 1, 1959, 2.

46. *SFN*, April 14, 1959, 2; "Notes," October 13, 1959, ACLUP, Folder 780.

47. American Civil Liberties Union of Northern California, *Weekly Bulletin #2019*, November 23, 1959, ACLUP, Folder 780. In 1957 courts dismissed or ruled not guilty in 71 percent of San Francisco's vagrancy cases. *SFN*, July 29, 1958, 2.

48. American Civil Liberties Union of Northern California, *Weekly Bulletin #2019*, November 23, 1959, ACLUP, Folder 780.

49. Samuel Walker, "Origins of the Contemporary Criminal Justice Paradigm: The American Bar Foundation Survey, 1953–1969," *Justice Quarterly* 9, no. 1 (1992): 66.

50. Arthur Sherry, "Vagrants, Rogues and Vagabonds—Old Concepts in Need of Revision," *California Law Review* 48, no. 4 (1960): 562; Constitutional Rights hearings of 1958, 139; Foote, "Vagrancy-Type Law," 609; "Squaresville U.S.A. vs. Beatsville," *Life*, September 21, 1959, 31.

51. *New York Post*, March 15, 1959, M5. Also see O'Neil, "Only Rebellion," 130.

52. Constitutional Rights hearings of 1958; California State Assembly Interim Committee on Criminal Procedure, *A Public Hearing of the Assembly Interim Committee on Criminal Procedure: Laws of Arrest*, held in Sacramento, California, February 18–19, 1960 (Sacramento: State of California, 1960) (hereafter Laws of Arrest inquiries of 1960).

53. Constitutional Rights hearings of 1958, 108.

54. *SFN*, July 29, 1859, 2; April 14, 1959, 2.

55. Foote, "Vagrancy-Type Law," 627; *SFN*, July 29, 1958, 2. Elsewhere in the North and West, vagrancy law critics focused on police repression of docile indigents and hardworking laborers. Sherry, "Vagrants," 557–73; William Douglas, "Vagrancy and Arrest on Suspicion," *The Yale Law Journal* 70, no. 1 (1960): 1–14. Roff's coverage of the O'Connell hearing for the labor-friendly *News* directly associated the SFPD's unjust use of the vagrancy code against beats with earlier repression of labor radicals.

56. *SFC*, July 29, 1958, 26.

57. *SFE*, December 2, 1958, 5; "Notes" (no date), ACLUP, Folder 1545.

58. Ibid.; *SFC*, December 2, 1958, 3; *SFE*, December 19, 1958, II:1; *San Francisco Police*, September 1959, 7.

59. *SFC*, December 2, 1958, 3.

60. Sherry, "Vagrants," 563. *ACLUN*, July 1959, 1; July 1961, 3. Gene Marine, "O'Connell for Congress," *Frontier*, June 1962, 10.

61. Laws of Arrest inquiries of 1960, 90.

62. *SFE*, August 6, 1962, 18; August 5, 1962, IV:2. *SFC*, March 25, 1960, 1; May 11, 1958, 4; July 8, 1958, 3. Constitutional Rights hearings of 1958, 109. Also see "Letter From Ernest Besig to Thomas Cahill," October 3, 1958, and "Notes," April 16, 1959, ACLUP, Folder 780; "Letter from Ernest Besig to Thomas Cahill," March 13, 1959, ACLUP, Folder 781; Ellingham and Killian, *Poet Be Like God*, 108; Rigney and Smith, *Real Bohemia*, 161–62; *ACLUN*, May 1959, 3.

63. "Reporter's Transcription for the Appeal of *People v. Charles C. Pierce*," ACLUP, Folder 1606. In later years, when Bigarani served as an inspector, one *Chronicle* reporter claimed, the officer "loved to entrap homosexuals in public men's rooms" and other gay-associated spaces. Krikorian, "Beatniks," 66. Jerry Kamstra recalled that Bigarani once entered the Co-Existence Bagel Shop just as a gay poet was recounting a recent homosexual experience in a loud, "vibrating falsetto." Bigarani, according to Kamstra, paid the gay poet little heed and moved instead to the back of the bar, where he intimidated a racially integrated table of beats. Jerry Kamstra, *Stand Naked and Cool Them: North Beach and the Bohemian Dream, 1950–1980* (San Francisco: Peeramid, 1981), 41.

64. Krikorian, "Beatniks," 66; *ACLUN*, September 1959, 3; Kamstra, *Stand Naked*, 10, 49. Also see "Letter from Elizabeth Lenhart to Ernest Besig" (no date, but shortly before June 19, 1959), ACLUP, Folder 781. North Beach police officers were also on guard for white and Filipino inter-

racial co-mingling. "Notes," July 6, 1959, ACLUP, Folder 781. In contrast to these various North Beach habitués, Ruth Weiss, who is white, stated that she publicly associated with black men in North Beach and never experienced police harassment. Weiss interview. There are no public records or accounts of police harassing black female regulars within the beat scene.

65. United States Bureau of Census, *Census of Housing: 1950*, Volume 3, Part 4, Table 3, 52; *Census of Population and Housing: 1960*, Volume 10, H-1, 314. Chinatown was pushing outward into the western side of North Beach, but police officers expressed little concern for the expanding Chinese-American population. Scherini, *Italian American Community*, 27.

66. Laws of Arrest inquiries of 1960, 166; "Notes" (no date), ACLUP, Folder 781.

67. Laws of Arrest inquiries of 1960, 168; Rigney and Smith, *Real Bohemia*, 163.

68. Malcolm Glover interview with author, July 7, 2004.

69. Warren Hinckle, *If You Have a Lemon, Make Lemonade* (New York: G. P. Putnam's Sons, 1974), 31; Thomas Fleming, "The Black Press in the 1920s" (1998), Virtual Museum of the City of San Francisco, accessed at http://www.sfmuseum.org/sunreporter/fleming16.html; William Rivers and David Rubin, *A Region's Press: Anatomy of Newspapers in the San Francisco Bay Area* (Berkeley: Institute of Governmental Studies, University of California, 1971), 45–46.

70. Don Kates, Jr., "Police Malpractice," 20, ACLUP, Folder 744; *SFE*, May 21, 1958, 1, 17; *SFC*, May 21, 1958, 1, 4. Also see *SR*, May 24, 1958, 1.

71. *SR*, August 1, 1959, 1, 20; June 13, 1959, 1. *SFC*, June 15, 1959, 15; August 1, 1959, 2. *SFE*, July 31, 1959, CHSA, ACLU Clippings.

72. Brenda Knight, *Women of the Beat Generation: The Writers, Artists, and Muses at the Heart of a Revolution* (Berkeley, CA: Conari, 1996), 108, 113; Maria Damon, "Introduction," *Callaloo* 25, no. 1 (2002): 105.

73. *SFC*, February 21, 1978, 2; Weiss interview; A. D. Winans, "A Celebration of Bob Kaufman: A Hidden Teacher of the Beats" (no date or publisher, courtesy of Arthur Monroe); Kamstra, *Stand Naked*, 43. For examples of Kaufman's political consciousness, see *SFC*, August 12, 1958, 1; Damon, "Introduction," 106.

74. Ellingham and Killian, *Poet Be Like God*, 137–38; David Meltzer, *San Francisco Beat: Talking with the Poets* (San Francisco: City Lights Books, 2001), 201. Also see Pierre Delattre, *Episodes* (St. Paul, MN: Gray Wolf Press, 1993), 55. For a photograph of Bigarani seizing Kaufman in a bar, see Jerry Stoll, *I Am a Lover* (Sausalito, CA: Angel Island Publications, 1961).

75. *SFEC*, April 25, 1976, CLM:13. Kaufman references police censorship, vagrancy arrests, the death penalty, and jail in the *Abomunist Manifesto*. Robert Kaufman, *Abomunist Manifesto* (San Francisco: City Lights Books, 1959).

76. *SFC*, August 14, 1959, 1, 4. Rigney and Smith, *Real Bohemia*, 170. *ACLUN*, September 1959, 3. *SFE*, August 19, 1959, IV:2; August 9, 1959; August 15, 1959, 3.

77. *SFC*, August 14, 1959, 4.

78. *SFC*, August 17, 1959, 38.

79. *SFE*, August 15, 1959, 3. The San Francisco Police Officers' Association journal printed only one article on the Kaufman-Margolis episode and reported on subsequent police-beat confrontations in a comical tone. *San Francisco Police*, September 1959, 6–7; New Year's 1960, 9. The *Sun-Reporter* readily connected the censorship incident with the officer's history of "false arrests." *SR*, August 22, 1959, 10.

80. *SR*, August 1, 1959, 1, 14; August 8, 1959, 1; November 7, 1959, 1, 12. *SFE*, July 26, 1959, 14. *SFC*, August 6, 1959, 5.

81. *SFE*, January 23, 1960, 1, 5; January 24, 1960, 1, 3. *SFC*, January 23, 1960, 1, 4.

82. *SFE*, January 24, 1960, 3; Laws of Arrest inquiries of 1960, 168.

83. *SFC*, January 24, 1960, 1-3.

84. Ibid.

85. Rigney and Smith, *Real Bohemia*, 165; *SFE*, January 31, 1960, 10; *SFC*, February 7, 1960, 28.

86. *SFC*, January 31, 1960, 5; *SFNCB*, January 30, 1960, 1; *SFE*, January 31, 1960, 10.

87. *SFC*, January 31, 1960, 5; February 9, 1960, 26. *Underhound* 4 (1960): 4. *Underhound* was one of two beat journals edited by Anderson.

88. Laws of Arrest inquiries of 1960, 166, 168-69; Kates, "Police Malpractice," 15, ACLUP, Folder 744; *SFC*, March 25, 1960, 1, 9; Maynard, *Venice West*, 114; *New York Post*, March 17, 1959, 86; Maria Damon, "Triangulated Desire and Tactical Silences in the Beat Hipscape," *College Literature* 27, no. 1 (2000): 155. Also see *LCN*, March 9, 1960, 3.

89. *SFC*, August 30, 1960, 1, 6; September 16, 1963, 1.

90. *SFC*, August 9, 1960, 3; August 31, 1960, 4. *LCN*, September 28, 1960, 3. The liberal *Chronicle* reported covering the poetry raid explained that Bigarani busted the gathering because a poet was reading antipolice verse, but did not reveal that the poet reading the antipolice verse was gay. For discussion of the poet, see Kamstra, *Stand Naked*, 41.

91. Warren French, *The San Francisco Poetry Renaissance, 1955-1960* (Boston, MA: Twayne, 1991), 54; *SFC*, October 13, 1960, 3.

92. *Mapp v. Ohio* (1961) nationalized the Cahan rule, which forbade courts from accepting evidence without a warrant; *Miranda v. Arizona* (1966) forced police officers to affirmatively inform suspects of their rights; and *Papachristou v. Jacksonville* (1972) invalidated common vagrancy laws on grounds of "vagueness." In 1960 an American Bar Association survey into police discretion revealed that Wisconsin's exclusionary rule had no effect on policing in the state. Walker, "Origins," 58. For other studies illustrating the difficulties of curbing police discretion, see Thomas Johnson, Gordon Misner, and Lee Brown, *The Police and Society: An Environment for Collaboration and Confrontation* (Englewood Cliffs, NJ: Prentice-Hall, 1981), 178; David Simon, "Homicide: A Year on the Killing Streets," in *The Miranda Debate: Law, Justice, and Policing*, ed. Richard Leo and George Thomas III (Boston, MA: Northeastern University Press, 1998); Richard Leo, "From Coercion to Deception: The Changing Nature of Police Interrogation in America," in *The Miranda Debate: Law, Justice, and Policing*, ed. Richard Leo and George Thomas III (Boston, MA: Northeastern University Press, 1998).

CHAPTER 3

1. Bob Ross interview with author, October 5, 1999; "Bob Ross Interview," 45-46, SSJ, 97-026.

2. William Eskridge Jr., *Gaylaw: Challenging the Apartheid of the Closet* (Cambridge, MA: Harvard University Press, 1999), 7; Kyle Cuordileone, "'Politics in an Age of Anxiety': Cold War Political Culture and the Crisis in American Masculinity, 1949-1960," *The Journal of American History* 87, no. 2 (2000): 519.

3. John D'Emilio, *Sexual Politics, Sexual Communities: The Making of a Homosexual Minority in the United States, 1940-1970,* 2nd ed. (Chicago: University of Chicago Press, 1998), 177-82, 184-85; Martin Meeker, "Behind the Mask of Respectability: Reconsidering the Mattachine Society and Male Homophile Practice, 1950s and 1960s," *Journal of the History of Sexuality* 10, no. 1 (2001): 91.

4. Elizabeth Armstrong, *Forging Gay Identities: Organizing Sexuality in San Francisco, 1950-1994* (Chicago: University of Chicago Press, 2002), 1, 3, 34; Meeker, "Behind the Mask," 91; Nan Alamilla Boyd, *Wide-Open Town: A History of Queer San Francisco to 1965* (Berkeley: University of California Press, 2003), chapter 5; Marc Stein, *City of Sisterly and Brotherly Loves: Lesbian and Gay Philadelphia, 1945-1972* (Chicago: University of Chicago Press, 2000), chapter 6.

5. Robert Self, *All in the Family: The Realignment of American Democracy Since the 1960s* (New York: Hill and Wang, 2012), 81.

6. *SFE,* June 27, 1954, 18; June 28, 1954, 12; December 10, 1956, 1, 29. Eskridge, *Gaylaw,* 32, 61, 72.

Unlike the mainstream press, local tabloids occasionally raised the alarm of a homosexual invasion. Nan Alamilla Boyd, "San Francisco Was a Wide Open Town: Charting the Emergence of Gay and Lesbian Communities through the Mid-Twentieth Century" (Ph.D. dissertation, Brown University, 1995), 67.

7. SFPD, *Annual Report* (San Francisco: City of San Francisco, 1955), 8, and *Annual Report* (San Francisco: City of San Francisco, 1956), 12; Sol Stoumen and Russell Munro, *Appellant's Opening Brief in the District Court of Appeal: State of California, First Appellate District, Division Two, Sol M. Stoumen, Petitioner and Appellant, vs. Russell S. Munro, Director of the Department of Alcoholic Beverage Control of the State of California, et al.* (San Francisco: Pan-Graphic Press, 1963), 93. For an isolated example of Ahern cooperating with state liquor officials, see *SFC,* March 23, 1956, 3.

8. "Adults Arrested and Charged by Sex and Race," in SFPD, *Annual Report*s (San Francisco: City of San Francisco, 1955, 1956); The President's Commission on Law Enforcement and Administration of Justice, *Task Force Report: The Police* (Washington: U.S. Government Printing Office, 1967), 187; *SFE,* July 1, 1954, 12; Michael Rumaker, *Robert Duncan in San Francisco* (San Francisco: Grey Fox Press, 1978), 13. In later years the sex detail would be referred to as a sex crimes detail. The broader connotations of the sex-detail label reflected the squad's mandate to punish activities not specifically proscribed by law.

9. "George Mendenhall Interview," April 23, 1990, 5, and "Phyllis Lyon and Del Martin Interview," 3, SBP, 90-11, Box 1, Folder 7; Sherri Cavan, "Interaction in Home Territories," *Berkeley Journal of Sociology* 8 (1963): 26. Also see Sherri Cavan, "Social Interaction in Public Drinking Places" (Ph.D. dissertation, University of California, Berkeley, September 1965), 296; Minutes, Senior Armed Forces Disciplinary Control Board Western Area Board meetings, July 25, 1951, 15, and February 28, 1951, 10; Records of the Department of Alcoholic Beverage Control, California State Archives, F3718:342.

10. *San Francisco Police,* November 1959, 9; John Mindermann interview with author, March 29, 2004. For an example of Thomas Cahill chuckling over the policing of gay men in bathroom stalls, see "Thomas Cahill Interview," 110, SSJ, 97-026.

11. "Thomas Cahill Interview," SSJ, 97–026; "Don Lucas Interview," 325, SSJ, 97–032.

12. "Richard Hongisto Interview," 6, 7, SBP, 95–100, Box 1, Folder 11; Don Kates Jr., "Police Malpractice," ACLUP, Folder 744; *San Francisco Police,* September 1959, 9; Richard Hongisto interview with author, April 8, 2002.

13. Mindermann interview.

14. John Lehane interview with author, June 23, 2003; Cavan, "Social Interaction," 300.

15. Ross interview with author; "Charlotte Coleman Interview," 21, SSJ, 97–023; David Johnson, *The Lavender Scare: The Cold War Persecution of Gays and Lesbians in the Federal Government* (Chicago: University of Chicago Press, 2004), 149.

16. *Mattachine Review,* April 1960, 7.

17. Elliot Blackstone interview with author, October 16, 1999; Bill Plath interview with author, September 29, 1999; *SFC,* September 25, 1954, 1.

18. See, for example, Gary Atkins, *Gay Seattle: Stories of Exile and Belonging* (Seattle: University of Washington Press, 2003), 82.

19. Eskridge, *Gaylaw,* 94.

20. Mindermann interview. *SFNCB,* October 14, 1959, 4; October 15, 1959, 11.

21. Blackstone interview; Ross interview with author.

22. *SFC,* February 10, 1955, 1; Boyd, *Wide-Open Town,* chapter 2; Armstrong, *Forging Gay Identities,* 143; Martin Meeker, "Come Out West: Communication and the Gay and Lesbian Migration to San Francisco, 1940s–1960s" (Ph.D. dissertation, University of Southern California, December 2000), 28.

23. *SFE,* June 18, 1954, 1, 4; June 27, 1954, 1, 18; June 28, 1954, 1, 2; June 29, 1954, 1; July 1, 1954, 1, 12.

24. *SFE,* September 9, 1954, 1, 9; *SFC,* September 9, 1954, 1, 14.

25. *SFE,* September 9, 1954, 1, 9; September 11, 1954, 1, 10. *SFC,* September 9, 1954, 1, 14.

26. *SFC,* September 16, 1954, 1; September 22, 1954, 1, 13; September 23, 1954, 16. *SFE,* September 24, 1954, 10.

27. *SFC,* October 3, 1953, 2; Thomas Gill, "The State Board of Equalization and Liquor Control," *California Law Review* 38, no. 5 (December 1950): 892–93.

28. California State Assembly Interim Committee on Public Morals, *Report of the Assembly Interim Committee on Public Morals* (Sacramento: State of California, 1949), 29; "Bob Ross Interview," 62, SSJ, 98–12; Lewis Ellingham and Kevin Killian, *Poet Be Like God: Jack Spicer and the San Francisco Renaissance* (Hanover, NH: Wesleyan University Press, 1998), 41–42.

29. "Appellant's Petition for a Hearing by the Superior Court," *Stoumen v. Reilly,* Superior Court of the State of California, 14–15, 59, 60, GLBTHS, Box: 1, Legal Hearings, Folder: *Stoumen v. Reilly;* "Opening Brief for Appellant," *Stoumen v. Reilly,* 1 Civil No. 14,666, California District Court of Appeal (First District, Division 2), 59–60, 66.

30. Gill, "State Board of Equalization," 894.

31. Arthur Leonard, "The Gay Bar and the Right to Hang Out Together," *Sexuality and the Law: An Encyclopedia of Major Legal Cases* (New York: Garland Publishing, 1993), 192; *Stoumen v. Reilly* 37 Cal. 2d (1951), 713; Eskridge, *Gaylaw,* 94.

32. Caspar Weinberger with Gretchen Roberts, *In the Arena: A Memoir of the 20th Century* (Washington, DC: Regnery, 2001), 101; George Dorsey, *Christopher of San Francisco* (New York:

Macmillan, 1962), 94. Weinberger later served San Francisco's managerial growth agenda as a member of the San Francisco Planning and Urban Renewal Association's executive committee. Chester Hartman, *City for Sale: The Transformation of San Francisco,* rev. and updated ed. (Berkeley: University of California Press, 2002), 17.

33. Arthur Samish and Bob Thomas, *The Secret Boss of California: The Life and Times of Art Samish* (New York: Crown, 1971), 175; Weinberger, *In the Arena,* 106; *SFC,* November 4, 1954, 1.

34. "ABC Appeals Board Decision," *Marshall v. Stoumen,* No. 46892, AB-135, Alcoholic Beverage Control Appeals Board of the State of California, 2, 3, 7; Plath interview.

35. *One Institute Quarterly: Homophile Studies* 4, printed in Stoumen and Munro, *Appellant's Opening Brief,* appendix; Ira Deitrick, *Alcoholic Beverage Control in California: A Preliminary Study* (Stanford, CA: Stanford University Institute for the Study of Human Problems, 1962), 53.

36. *Koehn v. State Board of Equalization* 50 Cal. 2d (1958), 432. Also see Deitrick, *Alcoholic Beverage Control,* 93.

37. Stoumen and Munro, *Appellant's Opening Brief,* 50, 9–12.

38. Ibid., 283.

39. Ibid., 14, 41, 86–87, 155–56, 160; R. E. L. Masters, *The Homosexual Revolution* (New York: Julian Press, 1962), 184; Sol Stoumen and Russell Munro, *Appellant's Closing Brief in the District Court of Appeal: State of California, First Appellate District, Division Two: Sol M. Stoumen, Petitioner and Appellant, vs. Russell S. Munro, Director of the Department of Alcoholic Beverage Control of the State of California, et al.* (San Francisco: Pan-Graphic Press, 1963), xvii, xviii; Sol M. Stoumen and Russell S. Munro, *Petitioner's Petition for Hearing by the Supreme Court after Decision by the District Court of Appellate District, Division Two, and numbered therein 1 Civil No. 20,310: Sol M. Stoumen, petitioner and appellant, vs. Russell S. Munro, Director of the Department of Alcoholic Beverage Control of the State of California, et al.* (San Francisco: Pan-Graphic Press, 1963), 85. In one instance Judge Clayton Horn denied a gay man the right to cross-examine witnesses or present his own. "Reporter's Transcript on Appeal," *People v. Charles C. Pierce,* 9, ACLUP, Folder 1606.

40. "George Mendenhall Interview," 4, SBP, 90–11, Box 1, Folder 7; "Charlotte Coleman Interview," 21, SSJ, 97–023; Stoumen and Munro, *Appellant's Closing Brief,* xii; Stoumen and Munro, *Appellant's Opening Brief,* 73.

41. Meeker, "Come Out West," 28.

42. *The Ladder* 4, no. 3 (1959): 6–7; Stoumen and Munro, *Appellant's Opening Brief,* 98, 103, 193; Stoumen and Munro, *Appellant's Closing Brief,* 51. Published in San Francisco, *The Ladder* was the official organ of the Daughters of Bilitis.

43. Stoumen and Munro, *Appellant's Opening Brief,* 100.

44. *The Ladder* 4, no. 5 (1960): 6, 20.

45. "Charlotte Coleman Interview," 15, SSJ, 97–023.

46. Stoumen and Munro, *Appellant's Opening Brief,* 32. The ABC rewarded Sydney Feinberg for the *Vallerga* verdict by promoting him to area director.

47. *SFE,* February 1, 1956, 1.

48. John Mollenkopf, *The Contested City* (Princeton, NJ: Princeton University Press, 1983), 167; Dorsey, *Christopher of San Francisco,* 186; Jim Kepner, *Rough News—Daring Views: 1950s' Pioneer Gay Press Journalism* (New York: Haworth Press, 1998), 377, 379–380.

49. Kepner, *Rough News*, 386. *SFC*, April 8, 1959, 4; May 1, 1959, 35. *ACLUN*, June 1959, 1, 4.

50. Dorsey, *Christopher of San Francisco*, 187; *SFE*, October 9, 1959, 8.

51. *SFC*, October 9, 1959, 4; *SFNCB*, October 9, 1959, 1.

52. *SFNCB*, October 19, 1959, 11, 14.

53. *SFNCB*, October 9, 1959, 1; *SFC*, October 10, 1959, 1; *SFE*, October 12, 1959, 1; Dorsey, *Christopher of San Francisco*, 190.

54. "Bob Ross Interview," 45, SSJ, 98–012; Ross interview with author.

55. "Charlotte Coleman Interview," 62, SSJ, 97–023; Ross interview with author.

56. Stoumen and Munro, *Appellant's Opening Brief*, 75, 78.

57. William Thomas Allison, "The Militarization of American Policing: Enduring Metaphor for a Shifting Context," in *Uniform Behavior: Police Localism and National Politics*, ed. Stacy McGoldrick and Andrea McArdle (New York: Palgrave Macmillan, 2006), 15–19; Gerald Woods, "A Penchant for Probity: California Progressives and the Disreputable Pleasures," in *California Progressivism Revisited*, ed. William Deverell and Tom Sitton (Berkeley: University of California Press, 1994), 108–9; *SFNCB*, October 12, 1959, 1, 6; Mollenkopf, *Contested City*, 169.

58. Stoumen and Munro, *Appellant's Opening Brief*, 75. *SFE*, February 28, 1960, 1, 16; March 16, 1960, 5; May 14, 1960, 1, 6; May 13, 1960, III:1; August 4, 1960, III:2.

59. *SFE*, May 24, 1960, 14; July 26, 1960, 8. Ross interview with author. Unidentified newspaper, April 14, 1960, GLBTHS, Box: 1950s and 1960s Newsclippings, Folder: Gayola.

60. *SFE*, May 18, 1960, 4; July 12, 1960, 6; July 23, 1960, 3. *SFC*, May 13, 1960, 3. Walker, *A Critical History of Police Reform*, 170.

61. *SFC*, August 16, 1960, 3.

62. *SFE*, August 9, 1960, 7. *SFC*, August 10, 1960, 33; August 9, 1960, 12; July 28, 1960, 3; August 2, 1960, 3.

63. *SFC*, August 20, 1960, 1. The defense attorneys also exposed a number of errors and inconsistencies in Bauman's testimony. For instance, Bauman claimed that none of the accused had ever arrested a gay man at his establishment, but the defense showed that Sugrue had made two arrests in June 1959. *SFE*, July 27, 1960, 11. In addition, Sergeant Robert McFarland had been in the hospital when Bauman claimed to have made him a payment. Finally, a writing expert testified that the payoffs had been recorded in the Waterfront Hangout's ledger with a different pencil than all of the other entries, suggesting that the extortion numbers had been added after the fact. *SFC*, August 12, 1960, 3.

64. Stoumen and Munro, *Appellant's Opening Brief*, 80–81; *People of California v. Cardellini*, Criminal No. 57156, California Superior Court, San Francisco. ABC agents also took bribes from at least one North Beach beat bar. David Meltzer interview with author, June 12, 2003.

65. San Francisco Committee on Crime, *A Report on the Police Department, Part II, The Ninth Report of the Committee* (San Francisco: Committee on Crime, June 17, 1971), 3; *SFC*, August 3, 1960, 1; *SFNCB*, May 28, 1960, 4. The San Francisco Police Officers' Association tried to recoup the retroactive pay of four of the suspended officers, but the gayola prosecutions did not permanently strain interdepartmental relations. "You're always pissed off about something," Sergeant Jerry Crowley later recalled. "This was just a new thing for the police department to deal with." *The Notebook*, March 1961, 2; Gerald Crowley interview with author, May 20, 2003. From 1961 to 1970, the San Francisco Police Officers' Association printed its

journal under the name *The Notebook*. In 1970 the association renamed its organ *San Francisco Policeman*. Evidence of organized graft resurfaced toward the end of the 1960s. By that time Cahill was nearing retirement, and his desire to leave on a high note motivated him to turn a blind eye toward renewed corruption. Robert Jones, "Black vs. White in the Station House," *The Nation*, October 13, 1969, 370.

66. *SFC*, July 26, 1960, 4; August 2, 1960, 3; August 6, 1960, 1, 2. *SFE*, July 26, 1960, 8.

67. *SFC*, August 6, 1960, 15; August 14, 1960, 22; August 12, 1960, 26.

68. Timothy Stewart-Winter, "Raids, Rights, and Rainbow Coalitions: Sexuality and Race in Chicago Politics, 1950–2000" (Ph.D. dissertation: University of Chicago, 2009), 75; Atkins, *Gay Seattle*, 196.

69. *SFC*, June 29, 1960, 4; "Appellant's Opening Brief," *Stoumen v. Munro*, 176–77.

70. Stoumen and Munro, *Appellant's Opening Brief*, 176–77. *ACLUN*, July 1961, 3; July 1963, 2. "Adults Arrested and Charged by Sex and Race," in SFPD, *Annual Reports* (San Francisco: City of San Francisco, 1959, 1960, 1961). Arrests for "lewd and indecent acts" rose from 148 in 1959, to 330 in 1960, to 524 in 1961.

71. *SFE*, October 12, 1961, 3.

72. Ibid.; Eskridge, *Gaylaw*, 80. Also see *SFE*, May 21, 1960, 6; May 29, 1960, 8.

73. *SFC*, October 30, 1963, 41; November 4, 1963, 31.

74. *SFE*, August 14, 1961, 12.

75. *SFC*, May 29, 1960, 2; August 14, 1961, 3.

76. *SFNCB*, June 26, 1961, 15. The *Chronicle* had already printed the attorney's quote a week earlier in a report on the ABC's decision to revoke the liquor license of the Whoo Cares Bar, a gay drinking establishment on Haight Street. The newspaper covered the bar's closure neutrally, but felt unthreatened enough to jokingly headline its report: "Whoo Cares?—The Liquor Board." *SFC*, June 20, 1961, 11.

77. *SFE*, August 15, 1961, 1, 12; "Adults Arrested and Charged by Sex and Race," in SFPD, *Annual Reports* (San Francisco: City of San Francisco, 1961, 1962, 1963).

78. "Bob Ross Interview," 60, SSJ, 98–12; "Charlotte Coleman Interview," 72, SSJ, 97–023; Eskridge, *Gaylaw*, 80. For a discussion of San Francisco gay and lesbian bars serving as community service centers, see Cavan, "Social Interaction," 147–48, 276.

79. "Bob Ross Interview," 30, SSJ, 98–12; "Bill Plath Interview," 15, 16, SSJ, 97–024; Tavern Guild Foundation, "What We're All About" (no date), TGSFR, Box 1, Folder 1; Armstrong, *Forging Gay Identities*, 50; Minutes, San Francisco Tavern Guild (hereafter TGSF), July 14, 1964, TGSFR, Box 1, Folder 13; "Adults Arrested and Charged by Sex and Race," in SFPD, *Annual Reports* (San Francisco: City of San Francisco, 1963, 1964). Describing the minimal level of contact among gay and lesbian bar owners prior to formation of the Guild, Bill Plath, the gay owner of a homosexual bar in the Lower Haight neighborhood, stated that he would never have known of the post-gayola drive on the downtown and Embarcadero areas had it not been covered in the mainstream press. Plath interview. Because the rumor of a bust could be as financially crippling as a license revocation, bar owners used Tavern Guild meetings to reassure one another that they were still operating. Minutes, TGSF, February 19, 1963, TGSFR, Box 1, Folder 11; Minutes, TGSF, February 2, 1965, TGSFR, Box 1, Folder 14. When individual police officers tried to renew shakedown payments, Guild members notified the ACLU. A quick and

threatening phone call from the ACLU to Chief Cahill ensured a speedy end to the extortion attempts. Marshall Krause interview with author, May 26, 2003. D'Emilio and particularly Boyd have provided important examinations of the Tavern Guild. D'Emilio, *Sexual Politics,* 189; Boyd, *Wide-Open Town,* 223–26. As Boyd points out, bar owners possessed job security and a steady source of income that enabled open and vigorous challenges to the SFPD. They did not need to worry about losing their job or clientele over revelation of their sexuality.

80. *SFC,* October 30, 1963, 41; November 8, 1963, 41; July 22, 1964, 39.

81. Although the bar culture and the Tavern Guild included lesbians, most of the city's liberal politicians during this period spoke of a "gay" vote and defined homosexual political interests around the interests of white gay men. Armstrong, *Forging Gay Identities,* 125, 134.

82. Ibid., 50; Minutes, TGSF, May 19, 1964, and Minutes, TGSF, November 18, 1964, TGSFR, Box 1, Folder 13; Richard DeLeon, *Left Coast City; Progressive Politics in San Francisco, 1975–1991* (Lawrence: University Press of Kansas, 1992), 25; "Bob Ross Interview," 54, SSJ, 98–012.

83. Minutes, TGSF, November 24, 1964, TGSFR, Box 1, Folder 13.

84. "Charles Lewis Interview," Tape 1, SSJ, 02–169; Minutes, TGSF, July 14, 1964, and Minutes, TGSF, October 20, 1964, TGSFR, Box 1, Folder 13; "Phyllis Lyon and Del Martin Interview," May 1, 1990, 16–17, SBP, 90–11, Box 1, Folder 10.

85. "Herb Donaldson Interview," February 14, 1990, 2, SBP, 90–11, Box 1, Folder 5; Minutes, TGSF, December 22, 1964, TGSFR, Box 1, Folder 13; "Robert Cromey Interview," April 25, 1990, 11, 12, SBP, 90–11, Box 1, Folder 8.

86. *ACLUN,* February 1965, 4; "Phyllis Lyon and Del Martin Interview," 19, SBP, 90–11, Box 1, Folder 9; Boyd, *Wide-Open Town,* 234; *SFE,* January 2, 1965, 12.

87. *ACLUN,* February 1965, 4; "Herb Donaldson Interview," 50, SSJ, 97–025; "Charles Lewis Interview," Tape 1, SSJ, 02–169.

88. Boyd, *Wide-Open Town,* 234; *SFE,* January 2, 1965, 12. Also see "Here's What REALLY Happened . . ." TGSFR, Box 19, Folder 2.

89. *SFE,* February 11, 1965, 9; Krause interview; *SFC,* February 11, 1965, 2; "Phyllis Lyon and Del Martin Interview," 20, SBP, 90–11, Box 1, Folder 9.

90. Ross interview with author; *SFC,* February 12, 1965, 3. Also see Minutes, TGSF, February 16, 1965, TGSFR, Box 1, Folder 13.

91. *SFC,* February 12, 1965, 3; *ACLUN,* March 3, 1965, 3; Minutes, TGSF, February 16, 1965, TGSFR, Box 1, Folder 13; "Charles Lewis Interview," Tape 1, SSJ, 02–169; Krause interview.

92. "Herb Donaldson Interview," Tape 1, SSJ, 02–167; Krause interview.

93. "Bob Ross Interview," 57, SSJ, 98–12; Ross interview with author.

94. *SFNCB,* February 13, 1965, 1; Minutes, TGSF, November 5, 1965, TGSFR, Box 1, Folder 14.

95. Terry Eisenberg, Robert Fosen, and Albert Glickman, *Police-Community Action: A Program for Change in Police-Community Behavior Patterns* (New York: Praeger, 1973), 46; "Charlotte Coleman Interview," 72, SSJ, 97–023.

96. *N&V,* September 1966, 7; *SFC,* April 5, 1972, 3. In 1965 gay and black activists formed Citizens Alert, a police-harassment and brutality hotline service. TGSF, "What We're All About" (no date, circa 1967), TGSFR, Box 1, Folder 1; *SFE,* August 27, 1967, 20.

97. Stewart-Winter, "Raids," 168, 171–72; *Los Angeles Advocate,* June 1968, 9; Robert Self, "Sex in the City: The Politics of Sexual Liberalism in Los Angeles, 1963–79," *Gender and*

History 20, no. 2 (2008): 301–2, 305. During the late 1960s and early 1970s, California's lewd vagrancy code (Penal Code 647a) was also referred to as the *lewd conduct code* and the *public lewdness code*. *Los Angeles Advocate* was a gay liberation journal.

98. Robert Fogelson, *Big-City Police* (Cambridge, MA: Harvard University Press, 1977), 172.

CHAPTER 4

1. Lenore Kandel, *The Love Book* (seized edition) (San Francisco: Stolen Paper Review Editions, 1966). Reprinted by permission of the Estate of Lenore Kandel.

2. *SFC,* November 16, 1966, 1; November 23, 1966, 2; May 6, 1967, 3.

3. *SFC,* November 16, 1966, 15; November 18, 1966, 16.

4. *SFE,* May 9, 1967, 5; Leonard Wolf, *Voices from the Love Generation* (Boston, MA: Little, Brown, 1968), 34; *SFC,* November 17, 1966, 18.

5. Kyle Cuordileone, *Manhood and American Political Culture in the Cold War* (New York: Routledge, 2004), chapter 2; Robert Dean, *Imperial Brotherhood: Gender and the Making of Cold War Foreign Policy* (Amherst: University of Massachusetts Press, 2001); Michael Flamm, *Law and Order: Street Crime, Civil Unrest, and the Crisis of Liberalism in the 1960s* (New York: Columbia University Press, 2005), 6.

6. Whitney Strub, *Perversion for Profit: The Politics of Pornography and the Rise of the New Right* (New York: Columbia University Press, 2011), 78.

7. Marjorie Heins, *Not in Front of the Children: "Indecency," Censorship and the Innocence of Youth* (New York: Hill and Wang, 2001), 45–46.

8. *New York Post,* March 15, 1959, M5; *SFC,* March 26, 1965, 1; *ACLUN,* October 1958, 4; California State Assembly, Interim Committee on Judiciary, Subcommittee on Pornographic Literature, *Transcript of Proceedings* (Sacramento: State of California, 1958), 23, 24.

9. *ACLUN,* February 1954, 3; January 1949, 1. Between 1956 and 1963, the SFPD arrested fifty-six white men, five Chinese-American men, and five black men on obscene material charges. "Adults Arrested and Charged by Sex and Race," in SFPD, *Annual Reports* (San Francisco: City of San Francisco, 1956–1963).

10. William Issel, "'The Catholic Internationale': Joseph L. Alioto's Urban Liberalism and San Francisco Catholicism," *U.S. Catholic Historian* 22, no. 2 (2004): 110; William Issel, "Faith-Based Activism in American Cities: The Case of the San Francisco Catholic Action Cadre," *Journal of Church and State* 50, no. 3 (2008): 522.

11. *SFC,* May 11, 1951, 1; April 10, 1957, 24. Charles Raudebaugh, "San Francisco: The Beldam Dozes," in *Our Fair City,* ed. Robert Allen (New York: Vanguard, 1947), 354. John Mollenkopf, *The Contested City* (Princeton, NJ: Princeton University Press, 1983), 153.

12. "Besig Speech Notes, undated," ACLUP, Folder 739: Obscenity, 1960–1965; Michael Harris interview with author, July 13, 2004; Allan Temko, "San Francisco Rebuilds Again," *Harper's Magazine,* April 1960, 53.

13. *SFC,* December 16, 1956, 22; Jim Kepner, *Rough News—Daring Views: 1950s' Pioneer Gay Press Journalism* (New York: Haworth Press, 1998), 182–84. Prior to the various gay scares of late 1956 and early 1957, the Customs Office had allowed a shipment of *Howl* to enter the country.

14. Lawrence Ferlinghetti and Jacob Ehrlich, *Howl of the Censor* (San Carlos, CA: Nourse, 1961), 135.

15. *SFC,* March 26, 1957, 2.

16. Marshall Krause interview with author, May 26, 2003; Jonah Raskin, *American Scream: Allen Ginsberg's Howl and the Making of the Beat Generation* (Berkeley: University of California Press, 2004), 212.

17. Warren Hinckle, *If You Have a Lemon, Make Lemonade* (New York: G. P. Putnam's Sons, 1974), 32; Bill Morgan and Nancy Peters, eds., *Howl on Trial: The Battle for Free Expression* (San Francisco: City Lights Books, 2006), 103.

18. *SFC,* April 11, 1957, 5.

19. Harold McKinnon, *Catholic Action and the Lawyer: Outline of a Catholic Lawyer's Guild* (San Francisco: Catholic Men of the Archdiocese of San Francisco, 1939). *SFC,* May 30, 1957, 9; June 6, 1957, 4. When the SFPD impounded *Howl and Other Poems,* the *Little City News* noted with a hint of cosmopolitan pride that Henry Miller's banned *Tropic of Cancer* could also be purchased in North Beach for twenty dollars a copy. *LCN,* June 20, 1957, 3.

20. *SFC,* June 6, 1957, 1, 4; Morgan and Peters, *Howl on Trial,* 2–3.

21. *SFC,* August 16, 1957, 1, 4; June 7, 1957, 2.

22. *SFE,* November 1, 1967, 2; Barry Silesky, *Ferlinghetti: The Artist in His Time* (New York: Warner, 1990), 71; Ronald Collins and David Skover, *The Trials of Lenny Bruce: The Fall and Rise of an American Icon* (Naperville, IL: Sourcebooks MediaFusion, 2002), 44.

23. Jacob Ehrlich, *A Life in My Hands: An Autobiography* (New York: Putnam, 1965), 223. *SFC,* August 7, 1957, 2; June 8, 2003, D5.

24. Collins and Skover, *Trials of Lenny Bruce,* 45; Richard Cándida Smith, *Utopia and Dissent: Art, Poetry, and Politics in California* (Berkeley: University of California Press, 1995), 355; Victor Tulli, "Indecent Reading: Literature, Obscenity Law, and U.S. Culture, 1952–1966" (Ph.D. dissertation, University of Pennsylvania, 1999), chapter 3.

25. *ACLUN,* October 1949, 1; Strub, *Perversion,* 60; *Roth v. United States* 354 U.S. 476 (1957).

26. Tulli, "Indecent Reading," 147, 181.

27. *SFC,* August 23, 1957, 4; Ferlinghetti and Ehrlich, *Howl of the Censor,* 2, 94.

28. Albert Bendich interview with author, April 16, 2003; Tulli, "Indecent Reading," 199.

29. Ferlinghetti and Ehrlich, *Howl of the Censor,* 33; Tulli, "Indecent Reading," 194.

30. *SFE,* September 6, 1957, 3.

31. Tulli, "Indecent Reading," 187. In November 1957 the Supreme Court reversed a censorship ban on the film *Game of Love,* declaring that any redeeming social importance protected a work from censorship. Strub, *Perversion,* 63. Later, in the 1973 *Miller v. California* ruling, a more conservative High Court lowered the bar on prurient and offensive language, stating that the work must have "serious literary, artistic, political or scientific value" to receive First Amendment protections. Paul Boyer, *Purity in Print: Book Censorship in America from the Gilded Age to the Computer Age,* 2nd ed. (Madison: University of Wisconsin Press, 2002), 311.

32. *SFC,* October 4, 1957, 1.

33. See cover photo for Morgan and Peters, *Howl on Trial.*

34. *SFE,* October 4, 1957, 1, 4.

35. In 1961 Lynch dropped obscenity charges, which officers had issued without his consent, against a movie theater showing Kenneth Anger's gay-themed film *Fireworks*. *ACLUN*, July 1961, 3.

36. "Reporter's Transcript on Appeal—*People v. Charles C. Pierce*," 1, 6, 9, ACLUP, Folder 1606.

37. "Adults Arrested and Charged by Sex and Race," in SFPD, *Annual Reports* (San Francisco: City of San Francisco, 1958–1963); *ACLUN*, October 1958, 4; "Notes" (no date), ACLUP, Folder 503. The Juvenile Bureau responded to the declining power of its obscenity prosecution threats by employing a host of secondary charges. In 1962, for instance, San Francisco police issued a dubious "purchasing stolen books" charge against a purveyor of foreign "girlie" magazines. The charge was later dismissed. "Letter from Ernest Besig to Thomas Lynch," January 21, 1963, ACLUP, Folder 739. Similarly, in April 1963 Lenny Bruce returned to San Francisco after beating earlier SFPD obscenity charges, and the SFPD bullied the comic with an illegal search of his hotel room for narcotics. *ACLUN*, April 1963, 1.

38. Carole Hicke, "Oral History Interview with John A. O'Connell: Oral History Transcript" (Berkeley: Regional Oral History Office, University of California, Berkeley, 1988), 22. *ACLUN*, June 1961, 4; July 1961, 1. For the ACLU learning of a local censorship attempt from the *Chronicle*, see "Letter from Ernest Besig to Georgina Silva," February 9, 1961, ACLUP, Folder 739.

39. *SFC*, October 4, 1961, 9.

40. Collins and Skover, *Trials of Lenny Bruce*, 48–49, 53; *SFC*, October 5, 1961, 1, 8.

41. *SFC*, March 7, 1962, 2.

42. Maria Damon, "The Jewish Entertainer as Cultural Lightning Rod: The Case of Lenny Bruce," *Postmodern Culture* 7, no. 2 (January 1997): 23.

43. *ACLUN*, May 1964, 1; *SFC*, April 8, 1964, 8.

44. Damon, "Jewish Entertainer," 16.

45. Bendich interview; Strub, *Perversion,* 37; Damon, "Jewish Entertainer," 23.

46. *SFE*, June 24, 1964, 3; *SFC*, June 27, 1964, 2.

47. *SFC*, March 7, 1962, 2; June 27, 1964, 2; June 24, 1964, 5. *SFE*, June 24, 1964, 3.

48. *SFC*, March 9, 1962, 1, 12; July 3, 1964, 8.

49. *SFC*, April 11, 1957, 5; June 6, 1957, 22.

50. *The Monitor*, May 10, 1957, 3; May 3, 1957, 8.

51. *SFC*, June 6, 1957, 4; November 12, 1959, 8. California State Assembly, Interim Committee on Judiciary, Subcommittee on Pornographic Literature, *Transcript of Proceedings*, 21.

52. Cuordileone, *Manhood*, 40, 85–86.

53. Bill Osgerby, *Playboys in Paradise: Masculinity, Youth and Leisure-Style in Modern America* (Oxford, UK: Berg, 2001), 81; Barbara Ehrenreich, *Hearts of Men: American Dreams and the Flight from Commitment* (Garden City, NY: Anchor/Doubleday, 1983), chapter 4; Elizabeth Fraterrigo, *Playboy and the Making of the Good Life in Modern America* (New York: Oxford University Press, 2009), chapter 3.

54. *SFC*, June 30, 1964, 2.

55. Cuordileone, *Manhood*, 176, 173, 30; James Gilbert, *Men in the Middle: Searching for Masculinity in the 1950s* (Chicago: University of Chicago Press, 2005), 63, 68; *SFE*, February 9, 1962, 1.

56. Damon, "Jewish Entertainer," 19; Collins and Skover, *Trials of Lenny Bruce*, 65; *SFC*, December 2, 1959, 1.

57. *SFC*, June 26, 1964, 9.

58. Timothy Stewart-Winter, "Raids, Rights, and Rainbow Coalitions: Sexuality and Race in Chicago Politics, 1950–2000" (Ph.D. dissertation: University of Chicago, 2009), 105, 166.

59. *SFC*, September 8, 1967, 10; William Issel, "Faith-Based Activism," 532.

60. Issel, "Faith-Based Activism," 532; *HAI*, October 10, 1963, Political Section. Also see Josh Sides, *Erotic City: Sexual Revolutions and the Making of Modern San Francisco* (New York: Oxford University Press, 2009), 79.

61. "John Shelley Letter to Isabel Sheehy," January 24, 1964, John Shelley Papers, SFPL, Series 3, Box 5, Folder 5.

62. *SFC*, November 6, 1963, 9; August 18, 1964, 1, 18; August 19, 1964, 3.

63. *SFC*, August 13, 1965, 4. *LCN*, January 15, 1964, 1; April 29, 1964, 1; May 20, 1964, 1, 3; April 22, 1964, 8. Also see *SFE*, June 30, 1964, 13.

64. *SFC*, September 16, 1963, 1, 10.

65. Malcolm Glover interview with author, July 7, 2004.

66. *SFE*, December 18, 1964, 1, 15.

67. *SFE*, December 19, 1964, 1, 7; March 23, 1965, 1, 10; March 24, 1965, 1.

68. *SFE*, March 25, 1965, 4.

69. Ibid.; *The Monitor*, August 25, 1966, 9; *LCN*, May 5, 1965, 9.

70. *SFC*, April 23, 1965, 1, 10.

71. *SFC*, April 23, 1965, 38, 1.

72. *SFE*, April 28, 1965, 12; *SFC*, April 28, 1965, 18.

73. *SFC*, April 24, 1965, 6; May 8, 1965, 12. *SFE*, June 16, 1965, 1.

74. *SFE*, May 9, 1965, 1; *LCN*, May 19, 1965, 1, 8.

75. *SFE*, February 10, 1966, 8; *SFC*, November 18, 1966, 16. In 1965 and 1966, Inspector Maloney racked up eighteen convictions out of nineteen attempts. The local ACLU was too small to protect all of the targeted businesses. *SFC*, August 13, 1965, 4.

76. *SFE*, April 4, 1966, 1; *SFC*, April 8, 1966, 3. The *Examiner* helped Quinlan and Maloney fashion secular, professional images by reporting that fellow officers regarded Quinlan as an "intellectual" and noting that Maloney maintained a "well stocked" personal library that included books with "sex." *SFE*, February 10, 1966, 8; November 20, 1966, 24.

77. Smith, *Utopia and Dissent*, 342. *SFC*, November 16, 1966, 15; May 30, 1967, 3. *SFE*, November 17, 1966, 1, 3. Police and city officials had associated hippie art with obscenity prior to *The Love Book* bust. In 1965 the San Francisco Recreation Commission banned the Mime Troupe, a politically oriented counterculture theater group, from performing in Golden Gate Park on the rationale that the group was "obscene." No court proceeding arose from that accusation. Michael William Doyle, "Staging the Revolution: Guerrilla Theater as a Countercultural Practice, 1965–68," in *Imagine Nation: The American Counterculture of the 1960s and '70s,* ed. Peter Braunstein and Michael William Doyle (New York: Routledge, 2002), 71. In the late summer of 1966, SFPD inspectors arrested two actors performing Michael McClure's sexually explicit *The Beard*. The SFPD arrested the pair for obscenity, but prosecutors avoided prosecuting the actors for obscenity violations by charging them

with "lewd and dissolute conduct in a public place." *SFC*, August 9, 1966, 1, 11; August 10, 1966, 3.

78. *SFC*, April 24, 1965, 6; November 26, 1966, 1.

79. Jeffrey Burns, "The *Love Book*, the Counterculture, and the Catholic City" (no date, courtesy of the author), 3. *SFC*, May 9, 1967, 3; May 4, 1967, 2. Strub, *Perversion*, 105. *SFE*, May 3, 1967, 3; May 4, 1967, 5.

80. Krause interview; Alessandro Baccari Jr., Vincenza Scarpaci, and Rev. Father Gabriel Zavattaro, *Saints Peter and Paul Church: The Chronicles of "The Italian Cathedral" of the West, 1884–1984* (San Francisco: Alessandro Baccari Jr., 1985), 237, 246; *SFE*, May 24, 1967, 12.

81. *SFC*, May 27, 1967, 10.

82. *SFC*, May 26, 1967, 3.

83. *SFC*, May 20, 1967, 3; May 12, 1967, 4.

84. *SFEC*, October 21, 1979, CL:35–36.

85. *SFC*, April 29, 1967, 3; Wolf, *Voices*, 34; Brenda Knight, *Women of the Beat Generation: The Writers, Artists, and Muses at the Heart of a Revolution* (Berkeley, CA: Conari, 1996), 281; *SFEC*, October 21, 1979, CL:35–36; Peter Coyote, *Sleeping Where I Fall: A Chronicle* (Washington, DC: Counterpoint, 1998), 116.

86. Coyote, *Sleeping*, 116; *SFC*, May 6, 1967, 3.

87. Ronna Johnson, "Lenore Kandel's *The Love Book*: Psychedelic Poetics, Cosmic Erotica, and Sexual Politics in the Mid-Sixties Counterculture," in *Reconstructing the Beats,* ed. Jennie Skerl (New York: Palgrave Macmillan, 2004), 103. *SFC*, April 29, 1967, 3; May 18, 1967, 5. *SFE*, May 9, 1967, 5.

88. *SFC*, May 19, 1967, 3; Robert Brophy interview with author, June 24, 2003; *SFE*, May 17, 1967, 5. The 1963 Second Vatican Council inspired some priests during the mid-1960s to challenge old notions of Catholic morality. Burns, "The *Love Book*, the Counterculture, and the Catholic City," 5. A growing number of local Catholics were expressing tolerance for sexually explicit entertainment. Following the poetry trial, a coalition of lay Catholics, including San Francisco state senator George Moscone, mobilized to defend Brophy against conservative calls for his excommunication. *SFC*, July 17, 1967, 3; "Jeffrey Burns interview with Robert Brophy," July 1993, 3 (transcript courtesy of Jeffrey Burns). Also see *SFC*, April 14, 1967, 3; September 18, 1968, 6.

89. *SFE*, May 27, 1967, 3.

90. William Turner, *The Police Establishment* (New York: Putnam, 1968), 152–53. *SFC*, May 25, 1967, 3; November 22, 1966, 13; November 24, 1966, 24. Krause interview.

91. Frederick Wirt, *Power in the City: Decision Making in San Francisco* (Berkeley: University of California Press, 1974), 139; Karl Beitel, "Transforming San Francisco: Community, Capital, and the Local State in the Era of Globalization, 1956–2001" (Ph.D. dissertation, University of California, Davis, 2003), 38; William Issel, "'Land Values, Human Values, and the Preservation of the City's Treasured Appearance': Environmentalism, Politics, and the San Francisco Freeway Revolt," *Pacific Historical Review* 68, no. 4 (1999): 612; *People's World*, November 26, 1966, 33.

92. *SFEC*, August 22, 1965, TW28; September 10, 1967, A11. *SFE*, November 6, 1967, 41.

93. *SFC*, August 2, 1967, 1; September 8, 1967, 10; September 9, 1967, 8. *SFE*, July 2, 1967, 1.

94. *SFC*, September 12, 1967, 18; October 18, 1967, 6; October 27, 1967, 1; October 30, 1967, 4.

95. *SFC*, September 9, 1967, 8; September 8, 1967, 10.

96. *SFC*, November 8, 1967, 1; November 9, 1967, 1; September 9, 1967, 8. *SFE*, November 8, 1967, A; November 2, 1967, 38; September 19, 1967, 11; September 22, 1967, 7. Barbara Ferman, *Governing the Ungovernable City: Political Skill, Leadership, and the Modern Mayor* (Philadelphia, PA: Temple University Press, 1985), 58.

97. *SFE*, November 8, 1967, A. Earlier in the decade, Dobbs had achieved notoriety by resisting civil rights protesters demonstrating against the lily-white hiring policies of a local restaurant chain he owned. *SFC*, November 8, 1963, 4.

98. Joseph Alioto, "The Moral Basis of Violence," *Notre Dame Lawyer* 44, no. 6 (1969): 1045; *SFC*, December 5, 1967, 1. Willoughby became the director for public affairs in the San Francisco Redevelopment Agency. For additional examples of reporters making the jump to City Hall, see Hartman, *City for Sale*, 39.

99. Issel, "'The Catholic Internationale,'" 117; Joseph Alioto, "State of the City Message, October 14, 1969," 2, JLAP, Box 17, Folder 56.

100. Issel, "Faith-Based Activism," 525; *SFC*, December 20, 1967, 24. Alioto ultimately appointed more union representatives to government than his labor-serving predecessor, Mayor Shelley. Wirt, *Power in the City*, 175.

101. *SFE*, September 27, 1967, 5. Also see *SFC*, October 25, 1967, 4.

102. *SFC*, September 22, 1967, 6; November 6, 1967, 8; October 25, 1967, 4; September 9, 1967, 1; November 9, 1967, 34; April 1, 1968, 3. *SFE*, September 27, 1967, 5; November 8, 1967, 36; November 2, 1967, 38.

103. *SFC*, November 10, 1967, 2. In spring 1968 the Criminal Procedure Committee of California's Democratic-controlled State Assembly issued a widely reported 125-page study recommending parole for state prisoners who were neither habitual criminals nor perpetrators of bodily harm. *SFEC*, March 24, 1968, TW5.

104. Strub, *Perversion*, 151–53; *SFC*, November 10, 1967, 2. McCabe later sat on the crime commission's "Mass Disorders" and "Non-Victim Crime" subcommittees. "San Francisco Committee on Crime: Sub-Committees," JLAP, Box 2, Folder 28.

105. Robert Self, "Sex in the City: The Politics of Sexual Liberalism in Los Angeles, 1963–79," *Gender and History* 20, no. 2 (2008): 301; Strub, *Perversion*, 156–57, 134.

106. "Statement of Mayor Joseph L. Alioto, San Francisco, California, to the Platform Committee of the Democratic Party, Democratic National Convention, August 22, 1968, Chicago, Illinois," 1, JLAP, Box 17, Folder 24.

107. Joseph Alioto, "State of the City Message, October 14, 1968," 1, JLAP, Box 17, Folder 55. Also see "Inaugural Address By The Honorable Joseph L. Alioto, Mayor of San Francisco, January 8, 1968," 3, JLAP, Box 17, Folder 35.

108. Strub, *Perversion*, 164, 165.

109. The SFPD issued thirty-four charges of bringing and distributing obscene material in 1968. "Adults Arrested and Charged by Sex and Race," in SFPD, *Annual Reports* (San Francisco: City of San Francisco, 1967, 1968, 1969).

110. *The Black Panther*, August 25, 1973, 5; *SFC*, December 2, 1969, 4.

111. Strub, *Perversion*, 164.

112. Self, "Sex in the City," 302; Gary Atkins, *Gay Seattle: Stories of Exile and Belonging* (Seattle: University of Washington Press, 2003), 194, 206. Stevenson's rhetoric echoed the case made by San Francisco's Council on Religion and the Homosexual half a decade earlier. In 1965 the liberal ministers speaking for that organization charged that when police spent their time attempting to enforce "unenforceable laws" they failed to apprehend "murderers and robbers." *SFC*, September 25, 1965, 4.

CHAPTER 5

1. Bruce Kennedy audiotape, September 30, 1966; Mark Comfort audiotape, September 29, 1966. Thanks to Bruce Kennedy for providing me access to Mark Comfort's recording made during the Hunters Point uprising.

2. Comfort audiotape.

3. The President's Commission on Law Enforcement and Administration of Justice, *Task Force Report: The Police* (Washington, DC: U.S. Government Printing Office, 1967), 147, 148; The National Advisory Commission on Civil Disorders, *Report of the National Advisory Commission on Civil Disorders* (Washington, DC: U.S. Government Printing Office, 1968), 161.

4. Comfort audiotape.

5. Donna Murch, *Living for the City: Migration, Education, and the Rise of the Black Panther Party in Oakland, California* (Chapel Hill: University of North Carolina Press, 2010), 125, 145–47; Robert Self, *American Babylon: Race and the Struggle for Postwar Oakland* (Princeton, NJ: Princeton University Press, 2003), 226–27; Ernesto Chávez, *"¡Mi Raza Primero!" (My People First!): Nationalism, Identity, and Insurgency in the Chicano Movement in Los Angeles, 1966–1978* (Berkeley: University of California Press, 2002), 45, 49; Ian Haney López, *Racism on Trial: The Chicano Fight for Justice* (Cambridge, MA: Belknap, 2003), chapter 6.

6. Herb Cutchins interview with author, July 1, 2003.

7. Albert Broussard, *Black San Francisco: The Struggle for Racial Equality in the West* (Lawrence: University Press of Kansas, 1993), 175; *Application to the Department of Housing and Urban Development for a Grant to Plan a Comprehensive Model Cities Program* (San Francisco: Department of Housing and Urban Development, April 1968), 45–46 (hereafter Model Cities Application); Neil Eddington, "The Urban Plantation: The Ethnography of an Oral Tradition in a Negro Community" (Ph.D. dissertation: University of California, Berkeley, 1967), 16; *SFC*, February 15, 1972, 7.

8. *SFNCB*, December 5, 1951, 10. Broussard, *Black San Francisco*, 223. Eddington, "Urban Plantation," 15, 20, 21. United States Bureau of Census, *Census of Housing: 1950*, Volume 5, Part 8, Table 3, 31; *Census of Population and Housing: 1960*, Volume 1, Part 10, Table P-1, 41; *Census of Housing: 1960*, Volume 3, Part 3, Table 2, 26; *Census of Housing: 1970*, Volume 3, Part 5, Table 2, Calif. 204, 205.

9. Gerald Horne, *Fire This Time: The Watts Uprising and the 1960s* (Charlottesville: University of Virginia Press, 1995), 248; Thomas Sugrue, *Origins of the Urban Crisis: Race and Inequality in Postwar Detroit* (Princeton, NJ: Princeton University Press, 1996), 15; Daniel Crowe, *Prophets of Rage: The Black Freedom Struggle in San Francisco, 1945–1969* (New York: Garland, 2000), 57; United States Commission on Civil Rights, *Hearing before the United States*

Commission on Civil Rights, held in San Francisco, California, May 1–3, 1967 (Washington, DC: U.S. Government Printing Office, 1967), 16; *SFC,* February 14, 1972, 28.

10. *SR,* March 12, 1966, 3; July 28, 1962, 5; April 13, 1963, 2; February 2, 1963, 8; March 30, 1963, 14.

11. *SFE,* August 27, 1961, 20; Real Estate Research Corporation, *San Francisco Housing Fact Book* (San Francisco: Real Estate Research Corporation, 1962), 82, 84.

12. *TS,* February–March 1968, 7; Orville Luster interview with author, September 3, 2002; David Dodd, "The Life and Times of Albert Alexander: A Study of Identity Formation and Disintegration in Urban Afro-America" (Ph.D. dissertation: University of California, Berkeley, 1971), 80, 300–302. Also see Eddington, "Urban Plantation," 54; *TS,* September 29, 1965, 3.

13. Eric Schneider, *Vampires, Dragons, and Egyptian Kings: Youth Gangs in Postwar New York* (Princeton, NJ: Princeton University Press, 1999), chapter 4; Lawrence Ephron and Irving Piliavin, *A New Approach to Juvenile Delinquency: A Study of the Youth for Service Program in San Francisco* (Berkeley: Service Research Center, University of California, 1961), 84; *SFNCB,* August 4, 1961, 15.

14. Walter Turner interview with author, June 12, 2002; Carl Werthman and Irving Piliavin, "Gang Members and the Police," in *The Police: Six Sociological Essays,* ed. David Bordua (New York: Wiley, 1967), 83–84; *SFNCB,* August 4, 1961, 15.

15. *SFC,* May 19, 1956, 1, 2; May 20, 1956, 2. Also see *SR,* December 27, 1958, 1, 5.

16. San Francisco Committee on Crime, *A Report on the Police Department, Part II, The Ninth Report of the Committee* (San Francisco: Committee on Crime, June 17, 1971), 7. *SR,* April 7, 1951, 1; May 5, 1951, 1. *SFE,* August 25, 1961, 1. Richard Hongisto interview with author, April 8, 2002.

17. President's Commission on Law Enforcement and Administration of Justice, *Task Force Report: The Police,* 147; Werthman and Piliavin, "Gang Members and the Police," 72, 74, 87.

18. Werthman and Piliavin, "Gang Members and the Police," 88; *San Francisco Police,* October 1959, 10. Also see *SFC,* August 29, 1961, 5.

19. Werthman and Piliavin, "Gang Members and the Police," 76; *San Francisco Police,* October 1959, 10; Hongisto interview.

20. Arthur Hippler, "The Game of Black and White at Hunters Point," *Trans-Action* 7, no. 6 (1970): 57. Also see *SR,* June 17, 1961, 2.

21. *SR,* April 24, 1965, 11, 29; National Advisory Commission on Civil Disorders, *Report of the National Advisory Commission on Civil Disorders,* 161.

22. *San Francisco Police,* October 1959, 10; John Lehane interview with author, June 23, 2003; Werthman and Piliavin, "Gang Members and the Police," 78.

23. Werthman and Piliavin, "Gang Members and the Police," 66.

24. *TS,* September 17, 1966, 2; Gerald Crowley interview with author, May 20, 2003.

25. When a 1960 federal commission asked Mayor George Christopher to discuss bigotry in San Francisco, the city leader could only call to mind an episode in which juveniles painted swastikas on buildings. Christopher added, "We in San Francisco have never had any incidents that could be called 'racial incidents' as such." United States Commission on Civil Rights, *Hearings before the United States Commission on Civil Rights,* held in San Francisco, California, January 27, 28, 1960 (Washington, DC: U.S. Government Printing Office, 1960), 470, 473.

26. Civil Rights Congress, "Fact Sheets on Police Brutality, Frame-Ups, Jobs, Housing, FEP" (San Francisco: Bay Area Conference on Negro Rights, August 26, 1950), 2, San Francisco African-American Historical Society, Folder: "Negroes—San Francisco"; California State Assembly Interim Committee on Criminal Procedure, *A Public Hearing of the Assembly Interim Committee on Criminal Procedure: Laws of Arrest,* held in Sacramento, California, February 18–19, 1960 (Sacramento: State of California, 1960), 75. Also see *ACLUN,* October 1957, 4.

27. United States Commission on Civil Rights, *Hearings before the United States Commission on Civil Rights,* held in San Francisco, California, January 27, 28, 1960, 764.

28. "Adults Arrested and Charged by Sex and Race," in SFPD, *Annual Reports* (San Francisco: City of San Francisco, 1957, 1958, 1959); United States Bureau of Census, *Census of Population and Housing: 1960,* Volume 10, Table P-2, 77.

29. *SFC,* April 1, 1957, 1, 2; April 3, 1957, 1, 4; May 19, 1956, 1, 2; May 20, 1956, 2. "The Negro Crime Rate: A Failure in Integration," *Time,* April 21, 1958, 18. "Adults Arrested and Charged by Sex and Race" and "Disposition of Adult Arrests," in SFPD, *Annual Reports* (San Francisco: City of San Francisco, 1951–1959). The average of 44 percent for murder arrests does not take into account 1952, when the SFPD did not provide figures by race, and 1956, when without explanation the SFPD published conflicting homicide arrest rates. During the period from 1951 to 1959, the SFPD made arrests for roughly 70 percent of all murders and only 20 percent of all robberies. Criminologists regard murder rates as the most reliable crime index since they are the easiest figures to audit. Robbery rates were more susceptible to police manipulation, but criminologists view the crime itself as the best indicator of safety on the streets. Michael Flamm, *Law and Order: Street Crime, Civil Unrest, and the Crisis of Liberalism in the 1960s* (New York: Columbia University Press, 2005), 5.

30. "Negro Crime Rate," 18.

31. *SFC,* January 13, 1959, 10; *San Francisco Police,* November 1959, 7; President's Commission on Law Enforcement and Administration of Justice, *Task Force Report: The Police,* 149. During the late 1960s, the SFPD's handful of Latino officers attempted to bring anti-Latino police racism to mainstream attention. Mary Ellen Leary, "The Trouble with Troubleshooting," *Atlantic Monthly,* March 1969, 95.

32. *SFC,* March 9, 1964, 34; Broussard, *Black San Francisco,* 232; *SFC,* January 15, 1959, 42. Also see *SR,* May 30, 1953, 10; January 17, 1959, 10; February 17, 1962, 16; December 29, 1962, 12. Approximately two-thirds of the city's black population came from the South. Broussard, *Black San Francisco,* 138.

33. *SFNCB,* December 8, 1961, 23; December 11, 1961, 13. *SFC,* January 13, 1959, 10. *SR,* October 10, 1964, 3. Also see Charles Raudebaugh, "Juvenile Delinquency" (memorandum), September 26, 1956, 8, BL, Scott Newhall Papers, Carton 8, Folder: City Desk; *SFNCB,* December 13, 1961, 23; California State Assembly, Interim Committee on Criminal Procedure, *A Public Hearing of the Assembly Interim Committee on Criminal Procedure: Laws of Arrest,* 86.

34. *SFN,* June 26, 1956, II:13; April 2, 1958, III:21. Broussard, *Black San Francisco,* 232. Khalil Muhammad, *The Condemnation of Blackness: Race, Crime, and the Making of Black America* (Cambridge, MA: Harvard University Press, 2010), 78, 232. Also see Daryl Michael Scott, *Contempt and Pity: Social Policy and the Image of the Damaged Black Psyche, 1880–1996* (Chapel Hill: University of North Carolina Press, 1997), 140.

35. *SFNCB*, December 4, 1961, 8; *SFC*, January 13, 1959, 10.

36. *SFC*, January 13, 1959, 10.

37. *SFE*, August 27, 1961, 20.

38. *SFNCB*, December 4, 1961, 8; *SFE*, August 27, 1961, 20.

39. *SFC*, January 13, 1959, 10.

40. *SFNCB*, August 4, 1961, 15; August 6, 1961, 4; December 5, 1961, 10.

41. *SFC*, August 25, 1961, 1, 2; August 26, 1961, 4. *SFE*, August 25, 1966, 1, 21.

42. *SR*, September 9, 1961, 22; *SFC*, August 27, 1961, 1, 6.

43. *SFE*, August 28, 1961, 1, 10.

44. Steven Schlossman and Michael Sedlak, *The Chicago Area Project Revisited* (Santa Monica, CA: Rand Corporation, 1983), 8, 62–63.

45. Andrew Diamond, *Mean Streets: Chicago Youths and the Everyday Struggle for Empowerment in the Multiracial City, 1908–1969* (Berkeley: University of California Press, 2009), 205, 256; Stephen Thiermann, *Welcome to the World: Discoveries with the American Friends Service Committee on the Frontiers of Social Change* (San Francisco: American Friends Service Committee, 1968), 52; Vera Haile interview with author, September 16, 2002; *SFE*, February 4, 1959, II:3; *SFNCB*, March 21, 1960, 1; David Meyers, *Ask Me, Don't Tell Me* (film) (San Francisco: American Friends Service Committee, 1960); Youth for Service, "An Inventory of Youth for Service," 1, Orville Luster's personal papers.

46. *SFC*, September 6, 1961, 4; Ephron and Piliavin, *New Approach*, 143.

47. Thiermann, *Welcome to the World*, 58.

48. May also invited newspaper photographers to shoot pictures of interracial groups of youth conducting service projects. *SFC*, September 6, 1959, 2; *SFNCB*, September 7, 1959, 16. On Orville Luster's relations with the press, see "Interview with Percy Pinkney," 20, SFAP, Box 1, Folder: 1:2.

49. *SFNCB*, March 21, 1960, 1, 6; March 22, 1960, 31. Also see *SFEC*, November 3, 1963, TW22–24.

50. *SFNCB*, August 1, 1961, 4; August 5, 1961, 4.

51. *SFNCB*, August 1, 1961, 4; August 7, 1961, 13; August 8, 1961, 17. Throughout the nation, liberals during this period accepted short-term race-conscious programs as a means of achieving black "assimilation." Scott, *Contempt and Pity*, xiv.

52. *SFC*, September 13, 1959, 15; Cutchins interview.

53. Luster interview; Thiermann, *Welcome to the World*, 61–62; Ephron and Piliavin, *New Approach*, 29.

54. Luster recognized that the social welfare community paid "comparatively little attention" to female involvement in youth violence, but he resisted integrating young women into Youth for Service because he worried that the male youth would become too hard to control with women involved. Additionally, Luster feared that including females could lead to acts of sexual harassment or impropriety by his street workers or male participants. Nevertheless, when male jacket club members came to the Youth for Service building for meetings, women often arrived with them, and Youth for Service's administrative assistant and sole female staff member, Vera Haile, began taking the teenaged women out for Cokes. Before long she was serving a role similar to that of the male street workers. The Ford Foundation, however, showed no interest in sponsoring activities dedicated to young women and street crime. Youth for Service, *YFS: A*

Story of Juvenile Decency in San Francisco (brochure), 1962 or 1963, Luster's personal papers; Luster interview; Haile interview.

55. Luster interview; Orville Luster, "The Policy of Negotiation," presented at the California Association for Health and Welfare Conference (February 23–26, 1964), 3, Luster's personal papers; McSamuel Carr interview with author, September 6, 2002; Diamond, *Mean Streets*, 255; *SR*, January 1, 1966, 7.

56. "Interview with Zeke Singleton," 13, SFAP, Box 1, Folder 1:4; Turner interview; Haile interview; *The Present Youth for Service Program* (San Francisco: 1965–1966), 2, California State Archives, Office of Economic Opportunity Papers, Folder: Grant Applications/Project Proposals—California Counties File, San Francisco County, Youth for Service. For discussions of the range of activities street workers organized to keep the peace, see Christopher Agee, "The Streets of San Francisco: Blacks, Beats, Homosexuals, and the San Francisco Police Department, 1950–1968" (Ph.D. dissertation: University of California, Berkeley, 2005), 319–20.

57. Natalie Becker and Marjorie Myhill, *Power and Participation in the San Francisco Community Action Program, 1964–1967* (Berkeley: Institute of Urban and Regional Development, University of California, Berkeley, 1967), 4–10. *SR*, October 19, 1963, 3; October 26, 1963, 2. *SFC*, October 26, 1963, 24; October 27, 1963, 1, 20. Alison Isenberg, *Downtown America: A History of the Place and the People Who Made It* (Chicago: University of Chicago Press, 2004), 246. Also see David Wellman, "Negro Leadership in San Francisco" (master's thesis, University of California, Berkeley, 1966).

58. Flamm, *Law and Order*, 37–38, 43, 188. *SFC*, July 20, 1964, 1, 10; July 21, 1964, 3; July 22, 1964, 3; August 8, 1964, 3. For references to black community members protesting discriminatory treatment from the Chinese-American storeowner, see *SR*, August 1, 1964, 4; Werthman and Piliavin, "Gang Members and the Police," 65.

59. *SFC*, September 15, 1964, 4; September 28, 1964, 4. Also see *SFE*, September 23, 1964, 3.

60. Flamm, *Law and Order*, 42, 153. SFC, October 18, 1963, 4; August 20, 1965, 41. *SFNCB*, May 11, 1962, 17; January 21, 1964, 21. *SFE*, March 12, 1964, 1. Also see *SR*, May 19, 1962, 2.

61. Horne, *Fire This Time*, 184, 219, 299; *SFE*, September 19, 1965, 1, 27.

62. *SR*, September 2, 1961, 14. Also see *SFC*, February 15, 1972, 7.

63. *SFC*, September 6, 1961, 4; *SFNCB*, August 3, 1961, 4; *SFE*, September 1, 1961, 10.

64. "Interview with Leff, Luster, Haile, October 7, 1993? [*sic*]," 25, SFAP, Box 1, Folder: LLH; Haile interview; Becker and Myhill, *Power and Participation,* 19–20; Tom Wolfe, *Radical Chic and Mau-Mauing the Flak Catchers* (New York: Farrar, Straus, and Giroux, 1970), 98.

65. *N&V*, June 1966, 8. *SFC*, November 7, 1962, 1B; November 9, 1960, 14. "Interview with Percy Pinkney," 83, SFAP, Box 1, Folder: 1:2. For an award ceremony and testimonial dinner honoring Luster, see *SFE*, May 2, 1968, 38; *SFC*, May 17, 1969, 2.

66. *N&V*, October 1967, 3; *SFNCB*, August 1, 1961, 4; *SFC*, October 9, 1964, 1.

67. Luster interview; Youth for Service, "How Things Look to Us" (1963), 7, 9, Luster's personal papers.

68. Luster interview.

69. Nicholas Lemann, *The Promised Land: The Great Black Migration and How it Changed America* (New York: Vintage, 1992), 150–51. Luster interview. *SFC*, June 23, 1965, 42; August 30, 1965, 7; January 8, 1966, 12.

70. Ralph Kramer, *Participation of the Poor: Comparative Community Case Studies in the War on Poverty* (Englewood Cliffs, NJ: Prentice Hall, 1969), 50–51.

71. *TS*, August 6, 1966, 6; July 9, 1966, 5. Haile interview.

72. Heidi Hardin, "Senior's Notes Compiled for the Play, 'Our Part of Town,'" SFPL, Vertical File: "Districts. Bayview–Hunters Point," Folder: "SF. Districts. Bayview/Hunters Point"; *SFC*, September 29, 1966, 20B; San Francisco Committee on Crime, *Report on the Police Department, Part II*, 111.

73. Kennedy audiotape. After the first forty-eight hours of the uprising, Bruce Kennedy, a white priest working in Hunters Point's poverty program, recorded onto an audiotape what he had witnessed over the previous two days. Sources used to substantiate Bruce Kennedy's narration of the uprising include Arthur Hippler, *Hunter's Point: A Black Ghetto* (New York: Basic Books, 1974), 203–14, and F. Long and R. Trueb, *128 Hours: A Report on the Disturbance in the City and County of San Francisco* (San Francisco: San Francisco Police Department, 1966).

74. Kennedy audiotape.

75. Ibid.; "Thomas Cahill Interview," 88, SSJ, 97 026.

76. Pat O'Brien, "Willie Brown at Bayview Community Center," KPIX, September 30, 1966, San Francisco Bay Area Television Archive, https://diva.sfsu.edu/collections/sfbatv/bundles/191384; *SFC*, September 29, 1966, 20A.

77. Subcommittee on Employment, Manpower, and Poverty of the Committee on Labor and Public Welfare, United States Senate, *Examination of the War on Poverty: First Session on Examining the War on Poverty (Part 11),* held in San Francisco, California, Wednesday, May 10, 1967 (Washington, DC: U.S. Government Printing Office, 1967), 3440. *SFC*, September 30, 1966, 17; February 16, 1972, 6. Crowe, *Prophets of Rage,* 204. Kennedy audiotape.

78. Matthew Countryman, *Up South: Civil Rights and Black Power in Philadelphia* (Philadelphia: University of Pennsylvania Press, 2006), 160. *SFC*, September 29, 1966, 1, 18, 19; September 30, 1966, 1.

79. Diamond, *Mean Streets*, 275; *SFC*, September 30, 1966, 17.

80. *SFC*, October 1, 1966, 8; Comfort audiotape. For the only located reference to an organization named Young Women for Action, see Hunters Point Community Youth Park Foundation, *A Park for Hunters Point* (no date), JLAP, Box 4, Folder 16.

81. Youth for Service veterans filled the early YMA leadership positions. *TS*, September 3, 1966, 6; January 1968, 4. For Luster's attempts to place Robert Rutherford at the head of YMA, see Dodd, *Life and Times of Albert Alexander*, 66.

82. Haile interview; *TS*, September 3, 1966, 6; *SFE*, February 17, 1977, 4.

83. *SFC*, September 30, 1966, 15; February 16, 1972, 6. Kennedy audiotape.

84. Kennedy audiotape; *TS*, June 1967, 3; *SFE*, October 1, 1966, 4; *People's World*, October 22, 1966, 3; Caspar Weinberger with Gretchen Roberts, *In the Arena: A Memoir of the 20th Century* (Washington, DC: Regnery, 2001), 141–43.

85. Huey P. Newton, *Revolutionary Suicide* (New York: Harcourt Brace Jovanovich, 1973), 130–32; Gene Marine, *The Black Panthers* (New York: New American Library, 1969), 54–55; *TS*, June 1967, 3.

86. *SFC*, October 30, 1967, 3.

87. *SFC*, November 9, 1967, 16; Nicholas Pileggi, "Crime and Punishment," in *America's Mayor: John V. Lindsay and the Reinvention of New York*, ed. Sam Roberts (New York: Columbia University Press, 2010), 79; Charlayne Hunter-Gault, "Black and White," in Roberts, *America's Mayor*, 47; *SFC*, February 17, 1972, 8. Chicago's Mayor Richard J. Daley, by contrast, fought the trend toward gang politicization as a challenge to his existing machine. Diamond, *Mean Streets*, 276.

88. Frederick Wirt, *Power in the City: Decision Making in San Francisco* (Berkeley: University of California Press, 1974), 92–93.

89. *SFC*, November 9, 1967, 1. *TS*, January 1968, 4; May 1968, 1, 2. *SFE*, March 28, 1972, 1, 6. Subcommittee on Employment, Manpower, and Poverty of the Committee on Labor and Public Welfare, United States Senate, *Examination of the War on Poverty*, 3505. Mike McCone interview with author, November 6, 2002.

90. *SFC*, March 10, 1970, 16; February 14, 1972, 28. "Letter from Irving Reichert to John A. DeLuca, Executive Secretary to Mayor," October 12, 1970, JLAP, Box 2, Folder 28. Espanola Jackson interview with author, September 11, 2002.

91. "Offenses Known to Police," in SFPD, *Annual Reports* (San Francisco: City of San Francisco, 1959–1970).

92. "Adults Arrested by Race," "Adults Arrested by Age," and "Arrests by District of Occurrence," in SFPD, *Annual Reports* (San Francisco: City of San Francisco, 1959–1970).

93. *SFC*, February 17, 1972, 8; *SFE*, March 27, 1972, 4. On occasion Alioto moved beyond the young men's peacekeeping achievements and discussed their social-uplift activities. He praised those latter efforts in congressional hearings: "The world doesn't know how much work is done by young militant blacks who never get their names in the paper or their faces on television, working on remedial reading, for example, with young black students." Hearings before the Select Committee on Crime, House of Representatives, Ninety-First Congress, *The Improvement and Reform of Law Enforcement and Criminal Justice in the United States* (Washington, DC: U.S. Government Printing Office, 1969), 131 (hereafter, Improvement of Law Enforcement hearings).

94. Wolfe, *Radical Chic*, 112, 121. Also see Steve Estes, *I Am a Man! Race, Manhood, and the Civil Rights Movement* (Chapel Hill: University of North Carolina Press, 2005), 170–71.

95. Dodd, *Life and Times of Albert Alexander*, 147.

96. Alioto, "State of the City Message, October 7, 1968," 3, JLAP, Box 17, Folder 55.

97. Hunter-Gault, "Black and White," 47, 49. Alioto later recounted that he received a call from President Lyndon Johnson congratulating him for staving off a riot. *SFE Magazine*, March 17, 1996, 23.

98. "Letter from Joseph Alioto to Stanley R. Tupper, Executive Director, Urban Action Center, Inc.," April 29, 1968, 1, 2, JLAP, Box 15, Folder 18; *SFC*, February 17, 1972, 8, 9. Also see Improvement of Law Enforcement hearings, 116, 102. Alioto stated that he emphasized the young men's militancy so they would not "acquire the image of an Uncle Tom" and lose status among their peers. Improvement of Law Enforcement hearings, 131.

99. "Letter from Joseph Alioto to Stanley R. Tupper, Executive Director, Urban Action Center, Inc.," April 29, 1968, 1, JLAP, Box 15, Folder 18. Also see Improvement of Law Enforcement Hearings, 115.

100. Suleiman Osman has identified the emergence of a "hybrid" political style fostering a New Left emphasis on inclusiveness within a centralized governing arrangement. Suleiman Osman, "The Decade of the Neighborhood," in *Rightward Bound: Making America Conservative in the 1970s*, ed. Julian Zelizer and Bruce Schulman (Cambridge, MA: Harvard University Press, 2008), 119.

101. Chiou-ling Yeh, *Making an American Festival: Chinese New Year in San Francisco's Chinatown* (Berkeley: University of California Press, 2008), 98–99.

102. *SFC*, May 20, 1968, 1, 22; April 29, 1969, 8, 20; April 30, 1969, 32. Improvement of Law Enforcement hearings, 94, 102, 97. Karl Beitel, "Transforming San Francisco: Community, Capital, and the Local State in the Era of Globalization, 1956–2001" (Ph.D. dissertation, University of California, Davis, 2003), 45. *Black Panther Black Community News Service,* November 2, 1968, 1, JLAP, Box 22, Folder 1. Office of Mayor Joseph Alioto, "Untitled Public Statement" (no date), JLAP, Box 17, Folder 19.

103. Improvement of Law Enforcement hearings, 94, 102; "Meet the Press: America's Press Conference" transcript, 13:24 (June 15, 1969), 13, JLAP, Box 17, Folder 9; "Eldridge Cleaver: A Candid Conversation with the Revolutionary Leader of the Black Panthers," *Playboy,* December 1968, 91.

104. Orville Luster interview by David Dodd, David Dodd's personal papers; *SFC*, May 17, 1969, 2; *SFE*, March 29, 1972, 14; Jackson interview; Improvement of Law Enforcement hearings, 131; Ben Williams, "Youth for Service Christmas Party (1970)," KPIX, December 24, 1970, San Francisco Bay Area Television Archive, https://diva.sfsu.edu/collections/sfbatv/bundles/190204; "San Francisco Committee on Crime: Sub-Committees" (no date), JLAP, Box 2, Folder 28. Luster responded to Alioto's fixation on the Black Panthers by incorporating the specter of the Black Power group into his mau-mauing sessions. Wolfe, *Radical Chic*, 98.

105. *TS*, May 1969, 2; Paul Lockwood, "Festival in Gilman Park (Hunters Point)," KPIX, October 18, 1969, San Francisco Bay Area Television Archive, https://diva.sfsu.edu/collections/sfbatv/bundles/190077. Shortly after Alioto took office, Rogers pronounced, "Black people wake up, we are all in prison, we are all Huey Newtons. He may be doing time in jail but we are doing it in the ghetto." *TS*, March–April 1968, 1.

106. *SFC*, March 5, 1970, 1, 24; March 12, 1970, 3; April 2, 1969, 1, 4.

107. *SFE*, March 10, 1970, 18; March 12, 1970, 3. *SFC*, March 11, 1970, 3; October 13, 1972, 13. Henry Izumizaki interview with author, June 7, 2002.

108. *SFC*, March 10, 1970, 1, 16; *The Black Panther*, March 21, 1970, 7, 20; "Malcolm X Birthday (1970)," KQED, May 19, 1970, San Francisco Bay Area Television Archive, https://diva.sfsu.edu/collections/sfbatv/bundles/189475.

109. Dodd, *Life and Times of Albert Alexander*, 66; Orville Luster interview by David Dodd, David Dodd's personal papers; Luster interview with author. Also see *SFC*, February 18, 1972, 9.

110. *Los Angeles Times*, October 28, 1971, A21; October 30, 1971, B9. *SFC*, November 1, 1971, 28; November 3, 1971, 1; November 4, 1971, 26. *San Francisco Progress*, October 29, 1971, 7. *SFE*, March 29, 1972, 14.

111. *SFE*, March 29, 1972, 14; March 30, 1972, 9.

112. During the late 1960s, one investigator estimated that seventy percent of Hunters Point male residents ages 12 to 25 had faced, at a minimum, a street interrogation by the police. *Model Cities Application*, 135.

113. Izumizaki interview; Luster interview.

114. *SFC*, March 11, 1969, 2; April 2, 1969, 4; April 28, 1971, 4. Countryman, *Up South*, 290–91. In addition, the Neighborhood Legal Assistance Foundation worked through the courts by filing a civil rights suit against the SFPD for false arrests of black Hunters Point residents. *SFC*, July 11, 1969, 5.

CHAPTER 6

1. Robert Jeffrey interview with author, May 2, 2003.

2. David Alan Sklansky, *Democracy and the Police* (Stanford, CA: Stanford University Press, 2007), 77; Robert Fogelson, *Big-City Police* (Cambridge, MA: Harvard University Press, 1977), 284.

3. David Patrick Geary, *Community Relations and the Administration of Justice* (New York: Wiley, 1975), 376–77.

4. Jeffrey interview.

5. John Mindermann interview with author, March 29, 2004.

6. San Francisco Committee on Crime, *A Report on the Police Department, Part II, The Ninth Report of the Committee* (San Francisco: Committee on Crime, June 17, 1971), 158; *SF-NCB*, December 11, 1961, 13; Mindermann interview.

7. Don Kates Jr., "Police Malpractice," 15, ACLUP, Folder 744. James Richardson, *Willie Brown: A Biography* (Berkeley: University of California Press, 1996), 69. *SR*, August 18, 1951, 1; October 1, 1955, 1, 8; July 12, 1958, 1; May 19, 1956, 1. Also see *SR*, July 24, 1954, 1; August 21, 1954, 1; June 7, 1958, 3; February 27, 1960, 10; January 16, 1965, 3. And see "CORE Press Release Packet," March 10, 1965, San Francisco African American Historical Society, Folder: Congress of Racial Equality, Civil Rights Congress; and Bay Area Conference on Negro Rights, "Fact Sheets on Police Brutality, Frame-Up, Jobs, Housing, FEP," August 26, 1950, San Francisco African American Historical Society, Folder: Negroes—San Francisco.

8. San Francisco Committee on Crime, *Report on the Police Department, Part II*, 83, 87.

9. Ibid., 14; *Good Times*, October 1, 1971, 3.

10. *SR*, November 7, 1959, 1, 12. Thomas Fleming, a coeditor at the *Sun-Reporter*, connected his newspaper to the ACLU by serving on the latter's board of directors. Thomas Fleming interview with author, January 7, 2003.

11. *SR*, July 24, 1954, 8; June 7, 1958, 6. California State Assembly Interim Committee on Judiciary, Subcommittee on Constitutional Rights, *A Public Hearing of the Assembly Interim Committee on Judiciary, Subcommittee on Constitutional Rights*, held in San Francisco, California, July 28–29, 1958 (Sacramento: Interim Committee on Judiciary, 1958), 65, 69 (hereafter, Constitutional Rights hearings of 1958). On the use of cover charges elsewhere, see Paul Chevigny, *Police Power: Police Abuses in New York City* (New York: Pantheon, 1969), chapter 8.

12. *SR*, April 18, 1959, 16; July 26, 1958, 1. Richardson, *Willie Brown*, 66. Constitutional Rights hearings of 1958, 69.

13. San Francisco Committee on Crime, *Report on the Police Department, Part II*, 18. Authorized by the San Francisco city charter, a special police officer was a private citizen hired by local businesses and licensed to carry a gun and make arrests.

14. *ACLUN,* February 1947, 1; San Francisco Committee on Crime, *Report on the Police Department, Part II,* 18; *New York Times,* October 1, 1971, 3.

15. San Francisco Committee on Crime, *Report on the Police Department, Part II,* 17; *ACLUN,* February 1949, 2; Don Kates Jr., "Police Malpractice," 20; Constitutional Rights hearings of 1958, 69.

16. Fleming interview. Also see *SR,* June 2, 1951, 1; February 23, 1952, 1.

17. Don Kates Jr., "Police Malpractice," 14. *SR,* June 7, 1958, 1; February 27, 1960, 10. *SFN,* June 26, 1956, II:13.

18. Scott Tang, "Pushing at the Golden Gate: Race Relations and Racial Politics in San Francisco, 1940–1955" (Ph.D. dissertation, University of California, Berkeley, 2002), 232–33; Constitutional Rights hearings of 1958, 65.

19. Gale Wright interview with author, June 4, 2003. Also see *SFC,* February 6, 1955, 2.

20. Gerald Crowley interview with author, May 20, 2003.

21. Hevery Juris and Peter Feuille, *Police Unionism: Power and Impact in Public-Sector Bargaining* (Lexington, MA: Lexington Books, 1973), 17–18. *SFC,* April 22, 1942, 7; February 22, 1961, 16. Sol Weiner interview with author, March 2, 2003. Wright interview. William Bopp, Paul Chignell, and Charles Maddox, "San Francisco Police Strike of 1975: A Case Study," *Journal of Police Science and Administration* 5, no. 1 (1977): 33.

22. *SFE,* January 18, 1962, 28. John Thomas Delaney and Peter Feuille, "Police," in *Collective Bargaining in American Industry: Contemporary Perspectives and Future Directions,* ed. David Lipsky and Clifford Donn (Lexington, MA: D.C. Heath and Company, 1987), 277. *SFC,* December 13, 1958, 2; February 21, 1961, 1, 2; February 22, 1961, 16. Weiner interview. *Notebook,* July 1966, 3.

23. Mayor's Committee for Municipal Management, *A Report to the Blyth-Zellerbach Committee on Modern Management for San Francisco,* Vol. 2 (San Francisco: Mayor's Committee for Municipal Management, June 1961), 1, 6; San Francisco Committee on Crime, *Report on the Police Department, Part II,* 65.

24. San Francisco Committee on Crime, *Report on the Police Department, Part II,* 67–68. *Notebook,* June 1961, 1; March 1961, 1.

25. John Lehane interview with author, June 23, 2003; *SFNCB,* August 8, 1961, 17; *Notebook,* July 1961, 3.

26. *Notebook,* July 1961, 3; October 1961, 1, 3.

27. *SFC,* April 20, 1962, 1, 9; Barron Muller, *The Adventures of a San Francisco Newsman* (San Francisco: Don't Call It Frisco Press, 1990), 45. Thomas Fleming noted that Aaron's description was sketchy and questioned whether her attacker was black. *SR,* May 19, 1962, 2.

28. *SFNCB,* May 14, 1962, 1, 6; May 11, 1962, 1. *SFC,* May 9, 1962, 1, 12. Also see *SFC,* May 7, 1962, 14.

29. *SFC,* April 26, 1962, 3; May 9, 1962, 12; May 15, 1962, 1; May 19, 1962, 1, 14; October 1, 1960, 1, 2. *SFNCB,* May 11, 1962, 1. United States Commission on Civil Rights, California Advisory Committee, *Police-Minority Group Relations in Los Angeles and the San Francisco Bay Area* (Washington, DC: United States Commission on Civil Rights, 1963), 23.

30. *SR,* June 22, 1963, 22; *SFC,* May 19, 1962, 14; *SFNCB,* May 14, 1962, 6. Also see *SFC,* September 20, 1962, 3.

31. *SFC,* December 31, 1962, 1; June 24, 1962, 8.

32. *SFC*, May 23, 1962, 1, 17; May 10, 1962, 1, 16. Mayor's Committee for Municipal Management, *Report to the Blyth-Zellerbach Committee*, 4. Delaney and Feuille, "Police," 273.

33. *SFC*, August 28, 1962, 2; *Notebook*, December 1962, 1; Lehane interview. On POA resistance to hiring women, also see *SFC*, January 12, 1963, 2.

34. *Notebook*, January 1963, 1; March 1963, 4. *SFC*, February 6, 1963, 3; February 12, 1963, 1, 7; February 19, 1963, 1, 10; February 20, 1963, 38. SFPD, *Annual Report* (San Francisco: City of San Francisco, 1950), 6; *Annual Report* (San Francisco: City of San Francisco, 1970), 1–2.

35. W. Marvin Dulaney, *Black Police in America* (Bloomington: Indiana University Press, 1996), 28; *SR*, February 7, 1953, 16.

36. Dulaney, *Black Police*, 71, 76; Sklansky, *Democracy and the Police*, 83; *SFC*, May 26, 1965, 5; *SFEC*, May 9, 1971, A19.

37. Dulaney, *Black Police*, 76; Terry Link, "Black and White in Blue," *San Francisco Magazine*, June 1970, 17.

38. In the 1960s the activists' faith in SFPD integration disintegrated further when black police officers began taking part in the department's violence against black people. *SR*, January 23, 1965, 8; March 13, 1965, 3.

39. *SFC*, August 16, 1963, 16; August 19, 1963, 46. *SR*, January 16, 1965, 6; March 13, 1965, 3.

40. *SFNCB*, December 4, 1961, 8; "Report of Tri-District General Public Meeting. Potrero–Northern-Park Police-Community Relations Committees," December 11, 1963, 3, 4, BL, Joseph D. Lohman Papers, 1930–1969.

41. Mary Ellen Leary, "The Trouble with Troubleshooting," *Atlantic Monthly*, March 1969, 94; *SFE*, January 30, 1962, 7; *SR*, February 4, 1961, 3; *TS*, February–March 1968, 7. In 1947 Joseph Lohman, who served as dean of Berkeley's School of Criminology during the early 1960s, created the blueprint for the community relations concept in *The Police and Minority Groups* (Chicago: Chicago Park District, 1947). Also see Samuel Walker, *Popular Justice: A History of American Criminal Justice*, 2nd ed. (New York: Oxford University Press, 1998), 171.

42. *SFE*, January 30, 1962, 7; February 1, 1962, 32. Leary, "Trouble with Troubleshooting," 94–95.

43. Leary, "Trouble with Troubleshooting," 95. Mindermann interview. Wright interview. *SR*, January 25, 1964, 2; October 9, 1965, 8. Mayor Christopher was hostile to the PCR concept and never attended a PCR meeting. "Our War Was with the Police Department," *Fortune*, January 1968, 197.

44. Jon Shuholm, "Police and Community Relations in San Francisco" (San Francisco: 1970), 1, SFPL, Vertical Files: "S.F. Police. Community Relations"; *SFC*, August 21, 1963, 36.

45. "Follow-up Meeting Agenda for the San Francisco Police-Community Relations Institute," February 28, 1967, 2, SFPL, Vertical Files: "S.F. Police. Community Relations."

46. *SR*, June 16, 1962, 2; February 16, 1963, 2. *N&V*, July 1966, 2; June 1966, 14. Jerome Skolnick, "The Police and the Urban Ghetto," in *Ambivalent Force: Perspectives on the Police*, 2nd ed., ed. Arthur Niederhoffer and Abraham Blumberg (Hinsdale, IL: Dryden Press, 1976), 223. Dante Andreotti, "Human Relations Programs," speech delivered at the 1963 Annual Conference of the Police Chiefs' Department League of California Cities, held in San Francisco, California, 3, Institute of Governmental Studies Library, University of California, Berkeley. "Our War Was with the Police Department," 195.

47. Skolnick, "Police and the Urban Ghetto," 225, 224; Leary, "Trouble with Troubleshooting," 95; *TS*, April 16, 1966, 2.

48. "Our War Was with the Police Department," 197; Alvin Rosenfeld, "The Friendly Fuzz," *The Nation*, April 21, 1969, 506; *SFC*, August 4, 1967, 18. PCR officers held benefits to raise funds for special projects.

49. "Our War Was with the Police Department," 197. Thomas Cahill, "Training in the Interracial Picture for 1963," *The Police Yearbook, 1964* (Gaithersburg, MD: International Association of the Chiefs of Police, 1964), 355. *SR*, October 2, 1965, 2; October 9, 1965, 8. District captains used the PCR unit to avoid community complaints from liberals and conservatives alike. When merchants in the Ingleside neighborhood demanded more police officers on the street, the Ingleside District command staff directed them to file a petition with the PCR unit. *N&V*, July 1966, 3.

50. Rosenfeld, "Friendly Fuzz," 504. Also see Skolnick, "Police and the Urban Ghetto," 223.

51. William Turner, *The Police Establishment* (New York: Putnam, 1968), 142, 161; National Center on Police and Community Relations, *A National Survey of Police and Community Relations* (Washington, DC: U.S. Government Printing Office, 1967), 44, 51. Also see *SR*, January 8, 1966, 9.

52. Skolnick, "Police and the Urban Ghetto," 224; Thomas Johnson, Gordon Misner, and Lee Brown, *The Police and Society: An Environment for Collaboration and Confrontation* (Englewood Cliffs, NJ: Prentice-Hall, 1981), 382.

53. Carl Werthman and Irving Piliavin, "Gang Members and the Police," in *The Police: Six Sociological Essays,* ed. David Bordua (New York: Wiley, 1967), 91. Leary, "Trouble with Troubleshooting," 97. *TS*, August 6, 1966, 6; March–April 1968, 3. Many jobs required that employees be bonded, and a police record made this difficult. Unmarked newspaper clipping, CORE Papers, Part 1, Western Regional Office, 1962–65, Reel 3, frame 00175.

54. Leary, "Trouble with Troubleshooting," 97; Jeffrey interview; *SFEC*, October 6, 1968, 3; Rosenfeld, "Friendly Fuzz," 504.

55. Shuholm, "Police and Community Relations," 2; "Letter from Charles R. Garry and James Herndon to Marshall Krause, Esq.," December 3, 1963, ACLUP, Folder 744; *SR*, March 13, 1965, 3.

56. Mindermann interview; Crowley interview.

57. Michael Hebel interview #1 with author, May 20, 2003.

58. Leary, "Trouble with Troubleshooting," 97; Richard Hongisto interview with author, April 8, 2002; *New York Times*, September 28, 1969, 1; Rosenfeld, "Friendly Fuzz," 504; "Our War Was with the Police Department," 196.

59. Jacob Ehrlich, *A Life in My Hands: An Autobiography* (New York: Putnam, 1965), 82; Robert Jones, "Black vs. White in the Station House," *The Nation*, October 13, 1969, 370; *SFE*, October 29, 1966, 3; *TS*, November 26, 1966, 1; *Notebook*, November 1966, 5; Turner, *Police Establishment*, 166–67, 164; Skolnick, "Police and the Urban Ghetto," 225.

60. *SFC*, January 14, 1959, 5; *HAI*, July 22, 1965, 2; Rosenfeld, "Friendly Fuzz," 503; "Our War Was with the Police Department," 197. Cahill's political concerns were not entirely misplaced. Andreotti had in fact built an independent base of political support among civil rights advocates, and prominent members of this group initiated a whisper campaign suggesting that

Mayor Shelley might replace Cahill with Andreotti. Shelley quickly reaffirmed his support for Cahill. *SFE*, May 12, 1967, 1.

61. Subcommittee on Employment, Manpower, and Poverty of the Committee on Labor and Public Welfare, United States Senate, *Examination of the War on Poverty: First Session on Examining the War On Poverty* (Part 11), held in San Francisco, California, Wednesday, May 10, 1967 (Washington, DC: U.S. Government Printing Office, 1967), 3498. *SFC*, January 6, 1967, 6; August 4, 1967, 18. Skolnick, "Police and the Urban Ghetto," 225. Rosenfeld, "Friendly Fuzz," 505. Leary, "Trouble with Troubleshooting," 98. Jeffrey, who is black, expressed respect for Bruneman's leadership of the PCR unit. Jeffrey interview.

62. Suleiman Osman, *The Invention of Brownstone Brooklyn: Gentrification and the Search for Authenticity in Postwar New York* (New York: Oxford University Press, 2011), 250.

63. *SFEC*, March 24, 1968, TW5; *N&V*, March 1968, 2; Leary, "Trouble with Troubleshooting," 97. For Mayor Alioto promising to oversee the nation's best PCR unit, see *SFC*, May 1, 1968, 4.

64. *SFC*, May 4, 1968, 1; *SFEC*, May 5, 1968, 31. Shortly before retiring in 1969, Osterloh advocated ending the PCR unit's neighborhood committee meetings because they degenerated, in his opinion, into "hollering sessions." Leary, "Trouble with Troubleshooting," 98.

65. Shuholm, "Police and Community Relations in San Francisco," 2. For instance, Goodlett recommended Hongisto for a spot on the PCR unit. Hongisto interview.

66. *SFEC*, August 4, 1968, A7. Also see Joseph Alioto, "'Law and Order in San Francisco,' Joseph L. Alioto" (campaign position paper), 1967, 2, JLAP, Box 15, Folder 17. All but one of the thirty-two original tac squad members were white. *SFC*, January 24, 1969, 2.

67. *SFC*, August 4, 1968, 7; February 21, 1968, 2. *SFEC*, August 4, 1968, A7. Hearings before the Select Committee on Crime, House of Representatives, Ninety-First Congress, *The Improvement and Reform of Law Enforcement and Criminal Justice in the United States* (Washington, DC: U.S. Government Printing Office, 1969), 95 (hereafter, Improvement of Law Enforcement hearings). *Good Times*, May 8, 1970, 18. Christian Parenti, *Lockdown America: Police and Prisons in the Age of Crisis* (New York: Verso, 1999), 112. *Good Times* was an underground newspaper published in San Francisco.

68. *SFE*, January 12, 1968, 1. *SFEC*, August 4, 1968, A7; August 11, 1968, 28. *SFC*, January 14, 1969, 3.

69. *SFC*, March 7, 1969, 1, 6, 28; September 18, 1968, 3; October 6, 1968, 1; March 11, 1969, 2.

70. *SFC*, October 2, 1968, 2; October 11, 1968, 28; October 9, 1968, 1.

71. *SFC*, October 1, 1968, 1; October 3, 1968, 28. *TS*, September 1968, 2. *SFE*, October 2, 1968, 11; February 26, 1969, 3.

72. *SFC*, March 4, 1969, 5; October 1, 1968, 26.

73. *SFC*, October 1, 1968, 26; October 30, 1968, 24.

74. The *Examiner* put its sole black staff writer, Rush Greenlee, on the story.

75. *SFC*, October 10, 1968, 1, 30; October 15, 1968, 3. *Los Angeles Times*, October 20, 1968, EB1.

76. *SFE*, October 2, 1968, 1, 11. *SFC*, October 1, 1968, 26; March 11, 1969, 2. *Los Angeles Times*, October 20, 1968, EB1.

77. *SFC*, October 1, 1968, 26.

78. *SFC,* October 10, 1968, 1, 30. The POA also called on Cahill to discipline the various officers involved in investigating O'Brien. *SFC,* October 15, 1968, 3.

79. *SFC,* March 6, 1969, 2; March 11, 1969, 2.

80. *SFC,* February 4, 1969, 2.

81. *TS,* February 1969, 2; William Barlow and Peter Shapiro, *An End to Silence: The San Francisco State College Student Movement in the '60s* (New York: Pegasus, 1971), 225, 264–65, 268.

82. *SFC,* November 7, 1967, 3; October 30, 1968, 2; January 24, 1969, 1, 26. Marjorie Heins, *Strictly Ghetto Property: The Story of Los Siete de la Raza* (Berkeley, CA: Ramparts Press, 1972), 126. Barlow and Shapiro, *End to Silence,* 261–64, 273.

83. Improvement of Law Enforcement hearings, 95. *SFC,* May 23, 1968, 1; March 8, 1969, 2. "Meet the Press: America's Press Conference" (transcript), June 15, 1969, 7, JLAP, Box 17, Folder 9. *SFE,* March 14, 1969, 8.

84. "Violence, No; Dissent, Yes;—But Not the Dogs of War" (Alioto Speech at Town Hall of California, Anaheim, California, June 26, 1969), 1, 2, JLAP, Folder 78; Improvement of Law Enforcement hearings, 93. Also see Barlow and Shapiro, *End to Silence,* 277–78.

85. *SFC,* May 28, 1968, 1; *SFEC,* January 26, 1969, TW5; "Meet the Press: America's Press Conference" (transcript), June 15, 1969, 10; *SFE,* April 18, 1969, 15; Improvement of Law Enforcement hearings, 104.

86. Improvement of Law Enforcement hearings, 104.

87. *SFC,* February 4, 1969, 2; March 21, 1969, 1, 28; March 22, 1969, 3.

88. *SFC,* May 1, 1969, 50.

89. Improvement of Law Enforcement hearings, 104, 125.

CHAPTER 7

1. *SFEC,* October 1, 1972, 8.

2. Suleiman Osman, *The Invention of Brownstone Brooklyn: Gentrification and the Search for Authenticity in Postwar New York* (New York: Oxford University Press, 2011), 250.

3. United States Bureau of Census, *Census of Population: 1970,* Volume 1, Part 6, Table 24, 6–155, and Table 86, 6–523.

4. Suleiman Osman, "The Decade of the Neighborhood," in *Rightward Bound: Making America Conservative in the 1970s,* ed. Julian Zelizer and Bruce Schulman (Cambridge, MA: Harvard University Press, 2008), 107, 117; Osman, *Invention of Brownstone Brooklyn,* 87.

5. San Francisco Department of City Planning, *Housing in the Haight Ashbury: A Background Study* (San Francisco: San Francisco Department of City Planning, 1972), 4. United States Bureau of Census, *Census of Population and Housing: 1960,* Volume 10, Table P-3, 223–24; *Census of Population and Housing: 1970, Census Tracts,* Part 19, Table P-3, P-189. Department of City Planning, *Haight-Ashbury Community Services: A Background Study* (San Francisco: San Francisco Department of City Planning, 1973), 2. White-collar professional, technical, and administrative workers made up 27 percent of the neighborhood population. San Francisco Department of City Planning, *Haight Ashbury: Improvements Recommended* (San Francisco: San Francisco Department of City Planning, 1973), 3.

6. David Smith and John Luce, *Love Needs Care: A History of San Francisco's Free Medical Clinic and Its Pioneer Role in Treating Drug-Abuse Problems* (Boston, MA: Little, Brown, 1971), 75; United States Bureau of Census, *Census of Population and Housing: 1960,* Volume 10, Table P-1, 39, 40, Table H-2, 367–68; Sherri Cavan, *Hippies of the Haight* (St. Louis, MO: New Critics Press, 1972), 45.

7. United States Bureau of Census, *Census of Population and Housing: 1960,* Volume 10, Table P-1, 39, 40; *Census of Population and Housing: 1970, Census Tracts,* Part 19, Table P-2, P-117. San Francisco Department of City Planning, *Haight Ashbury: Improvements Recommended,* 3.

8. Throughout San Francisco residents identified their neighborhoods with the small commercial strips that ran through these areas. Frederick Wirt, *Power in the City: Decision Making in San Francisco* (Berkeley: University of California Press, 1974), 27.

9. Mark Harris, "The Flowering of the Hippies," *The Atlantic,* September 1967, 66.

10. Osman, "Decade of the Neighborhood," 115; Guian McKee, *The Problem of Jobs: Liberalism, Race, and Deindustrialization in Philadelphia* (Chicago: University of Chicago Press, 2008), 10. During the 1950s, for example, the neighborhood included a home for unwed mothers. Cavan, *Hippies of the Haight,* 43. Localist activists such as Susan Bierman and Connie Duskin ran the Haight-Ashbury Children's Center, a preschool child care program. *SFC,* September 29, 1970, 7. By the end of the 1960s, the radical feminist movement had produced an explosion of Haight-Ashbury institutions serving the economic, medical, and social needs of neighborhood women.

11. *HAIL,* April 1967; *SFC,* October 18, 1959, 3.

12. *SFC,* October 18, 1959, 3.

13. During the mid-1960s HANC sponsored a civil rights worker from the Student Nonviolent Coordinating Committee to help organize black poor people in the area. Cavan, *Hippies of the Haight,* 44.

14. *HAIL* insert in *HAR,* December 4, 1969, 8. Harris, "Flowering of the Hippies," 66. *HAI,* November 12, 1964, 1; August 26, 1965, 1. Similarly, a local minister enthused, "We like the Haight-Ashbury because of its diversity and find in it a potential for vigor that is typically American." *SFE,* February 9, 1967, 5.

15. Cavan, *Hippies of the Haight,* 45; Harris, "Flowering of the Hippies," 66; William Issel, "'Land Values, Human Values, and the Preservation of the City's Treasured Appearance': Environmentalism, Politics, and the San Francisco Freeway Revolt," *Pacific Historical Review* 68, no. 4 (1999): 632–33, 628; *HAI,* July 30, 1964, 1; Katherine Johnson, "Captain Blake versus the Highwayman: Or, How San Francisco Won the Freeway Revolt," *Journal of Planning History* 8, no. 1 (2009): 70, 74. For reference to a successful petition drive to stop the San Francisco Redevelopment Agency from tearing down Victorian houses in the neighborhood, see Smith and Luce, *Love Needs Care,* 76. HANC activists secured a second single-vote victory over the freeway plan in 1966.

16. Jane Jacobs, *The Death and Life of Great American Cities* (1961; reprint, New York: Vintage, 1992), 31; *SFC,* May 22, 1962, 1, 10.

17. *SFC,* May 23, 1962, 2.

18. *HAIL,* April 1967; "Distribution of Automotive Equipment," in SFPD, *Annual Reports* (San Francisco: City of San Francisco, 1961, 1962). Also see Dante Andreotti, "Human Rela-

tions Programs" (speech), 1963, 3, Institute of Governmental Studies Library, University of California, Berkeley.

19. *SFE,* November 16, 1966, 9. Michael Hebel interview #2 with author, June 11, 2012. *HAI,* February 25, 1965, 1; July 22, 1965, 1; September 2, 1965, 1.

20. *SFC,* May 23, 1962, 2.

21. Cavan, *Hippies of the Haight,* 47, 50; Harris, "Flowering of the Hippies," 66; Smith and Luce, *Love Needs Care,* 99.

22. For discussions of nuisance arrests in the Haight-Ashbury neighborhood, see *SFEC,* January 15, 1967, 1; *SFC,* July 18, 1967, 4. In January 1967 the American Civil Liberties Union sued the SFPD in federal court in an attempt to stop public nuisance arrests against hippies. William Turner, *The Police Establishment* (New York: Putnam, 1968), 160. Later that summer a Superior Court judge issued an injunction against nuisance arrests against hippies. *SFC,* August 12, 1967, 24.

23. *SFE,* November 16, 1966, 9; Allen Cohen, "Haight-Ashbury Meets Police," *The San Francisco Oracle,* September 20, 1966, 1; *SFC,* September 17, 1966, 9. Hippies also baited the SFPD. Bohemians jammed traffic with "mill ins," blocking the intersection at Haight and Ashbury streets, and an anarchist collective called the Diggers published recipes for Molotov cocktails. *SFC,* March 27, 1967, 1, 6; Leonard Wolf, *Voices from the Love Generation* (Boston, MA: Little, Brown, 1968), xxxvi.

24. *SFEC,* January 15, 1967, 3. Smith and Luce, *Love Needs Care,* 109, 139. *SFC,* March 12, 1967, 11; March 15, 1967, 3; April 19, 1967, 3; May 15, 1968, 1, 18; July 27, 1967, 1, 12; *SFBG,* August 10, 1967, 5. State lawmakers facilitated the local push against the hippies by criminalizing LSD possession in October 1966. Smith and Luce, *Love Needs Care,* 108.

25. William Hedgepeth, "Inside the Hippie Revolution," *Look,* August 22, 1967, 60. *The Atlantic* reported, "It was easy to see that the young men who were hippies on Haight Street wore beards and long hair and sometimes earrings and weird-o granny eye-glasses, and that they were generally dirty." Similarly, it noted that female hippies were "dirty from toe to head." Harris, "Flowering of the Hippies," 63.

26. *SFC,* March 28, 1967, 1, 10; April 19, 1967, 3.

27. Harris, "Flowering of the Hippies," 66; Cavan, *Hippies of the Haight,* 51–52; *HAI,* October 28, 1965, 1; *HAR,* February 15, 1968, 1. Some sexually and culturally conservative members of HANC individually protested over the explicit behavior of the hippies. Josh Sides, *Erotic City: Sexual Revolutions and the Making of Modern San Francisco* (New York: Oxford University Press, 2009), 73–74. As these conservatives were marginalized in HANC, they made their voices heard in the short-lived Haight-Ashbury Citizens Committee.

28. "The Maze: Haight/Ashbury," KPIX-TV, 1967, Bay Area Television Archive, https://diva.sfsu.edu/collections/sfbatv/bundles/189371.

29. Cavan, *Hippies of the Haight,* 47. *SFBG,* September 25, 1967, 3; August 10, 1967, 2.

30. *HAMR,* February 9, 1967, 2; *HAIL,* April 1967; *HAR,* February 29, 1968, 2.

31. In 1966 hippies complained that they were being treated as shock troops for gentrification. "We have made this community attractive, brought people here, brightened up the scene," a painter claimed. "Now it's time to make a bundle. They will roust us, just like they rousted us from Telegraph Hill, Greenwich Village, Carmel—everywhere the artists go." *SFE,*

November 17, 1966, 3. By 1967, however, the mainstream press regarded hippies as harbingers of neighborhood decline.

32. *HAMR*, August 10, 1967, 1; *SFBG*, November 1, 1968, 5; *SFC*, January 17, 1967, 3; *HAR*, October 17, 1968, 1; *HAIL*, March 1967.

33. *N&V*, October 1966, 6. *HAMR*, September 14, 1967, 6; August 31, 1967, 4. Smith and Luce, *Love Needs Care*, 140-41.

34. Smith and Luce, *Love Needs Care*, 222-24, 339. *SFBG*, August 10, 1967, 2. *SFC*, August 5, 1968, 2; August 12, 1968, 1, 22. *SFEC*, July 21, 1968, 22.

35. *SFC*, May 5, 1968, 31; May 10, 1968, 3; April 13, 1968, 2; May 15, 1968, 1, 18.

36. Hebel interview #2. *HAR*, August 15, 1968, 8; October 24, 1968, 6. For an earlier interaction between McInerney and residents involved in the PCR citizens committee, see *N&V*, May 1967, 9.

37. *HAR*, March 21, 1968, 1; *SFE*, March 14, 1968, 9. Also see *HAR*, December 19, 1968, 1.

38. *SFC*, May 1, 1968, 4.

39. Smith and Luce, *Love Needs Care*, 253-54; *SFBG*, February 28, 1968, 5, 10; *SFC*, February 21, 1968, 2.

40. *SFBG*, February 28, 1968, 10. *SFC*, July 18, 1968, 2; July 20, 1968, 12; February 21, 1968, 2; July 19, 1968, 1. For more discussions of the "peculiarly irrational character of the new Haight-Ashbury population," see *SFC*, August 5, 1968, 2.

41. *SFC*, May 15, 1968, 1, 18; April 20, 1968, 5.

42. Smith and Luce, *Love Needs Care*, 277. *SFC*, July 18, 1968, 1; July 19, 1968, 2; July 20, 1968, 12. *SFEC*, July 21, 1968, 22.

43. *SFBG*, February 28, 1968, 10. *HAR*, February 22, 1968, 1; February 29, 1968, 1. *SFC*, July 26, 1968, 2. Smith and Luce, *Love Needs Care*, 251, 325.

44. San Francisco Department of City Planning, *Haight Street Shopping Area: A Background Study* (San Francisco: Department of City of Planning, 1972), i; *HAR*, February 29, 1968, 2; *SFC*, March 14, 1969, 3. In October 1970 Sue Bierman, a HANC member who had led the fight against the Golden Gate Park Freeway, continued to implore the mayor for more "humane police protection and hard drug control, without harassment of our residents." "Telegram from Sue Bierman Constance to Honorable Joseph Alioto," October 16, 1970, JLAP, Box 4, Folder 11.

45. David Talbot, *Season of the Witch: Enchantment, Terror and Deliverance in the City of Love* (New York: Free Press, 2012), 158-59; *SFC*, March 14, 1969, 3; *HAIL* insert in *HAR*, March 6, 1969. Waller had previously served as the director of a neighborhood center serving mostly black youth. *HAR*, December 19, 1968, 1.

46. *SFC*, March 14, 1969, 3. *HAR*, February 20, 1969, 1; February 29, 1968, 2.

47. *HAR*, October 9, 1969, 1; February 29, 1968, 2; November 20, 1969, 4; October 24, 1968, 1, 6; May 15, 1969, 1. *HAIL*, April 1969. In a 1971 city-directed survey, a majority of the Haight-Ashbury residents polled indicated a need for more foot patrols and better police-community relations. San Francisco Department of City Planning, *Haight-Ashbury Community Services* (San Francisco: San Francisco Department of City Planning, 1973), 32.

48. Robert Jones, "Black vs. White in the Station House," *The Nation*, October 13, 1969, 368. Ehrlich and the POA also offered legal representation to another white officer who fatally shot a black youth in the spring of 1969. *SFC*, April 3, 1969, 3.

49. W. Marvin Dulaney, *Black Police in America* (Bloomington: Indiana University Press, 1996), 74, 78.

50. *SFC*, March 18, 1969, 18; Terry Link, "Black and White in Blue," *San Francisco Magazine,* June 1970, 18, 19.

51. Link, "Black and White," 16; Richard Hongisto interview with author, April 8, 2002.

52. Link, "Black and White," 16; Jones, "Black vs. White," 368.

53. Dulaney, *Black Police,* 74; *New York Times,* September 28, 1969, 69.

54. *SFC*, February 27, 1969, 2; March 21, 1969, 2. *SFE,* March 21, 1969, 10.

55. Jon Shuholm, "Police and Community Relations in San Francisco" (San Francisco: 1970), 11, SFPL, Vertical Files: "S.F. Police. Community Relations"; *SFC,* April 18, 1969, 13.

56. John Lehane interview with author, June 23, 2003. Also see "Letter from 'A Very Sad & Disappointed Police Officers' [*sic*] Wife' to Police Chief Al Nelder," July 1, 1971, JLAP, Box 5, Folder 31.

57. Hebel interview #2. *SFC,* March 12, 1970, 5; March 13, 1970, 38.

58. Will Cooley, "'Stones Run It': Taking Back Control of Organized Crime in Chicago, 1940–1975," *Journal of Urban History* 37, no. 6 (2011): 924; Shuholm, "Police and Community Relations," 2; *SFE,* November 14, 1967, 1; *SFC,* May 20, 1968, 1.

59. *SFC,* October 29, 1968, 1, 22.

60. SFC, February 17, 1970, 2; January 15, 1972, 2; September 3, 1970, 1. Michael Hebel interview #1 with author, May 20, 2003; Marjorie Heins, *Strictly Ghetto Property: The Story of Los Siete de la Raza* (Berkeley, CA: Ramparts Press, 1972), 187.

61. For discussions of police grumbling over the initial orders not to arrest civil rights protesters, see Jacob Ehrlich, *A Life in My Hands: An Autobiography* (New York: Putnam, 1965), 82–83.

62. Kevin Mullen interview with author, November 21, 2002; John Mindermann interview with author, March 29, 2004.

63. *SFC,* June 18, 1969, 1; June 27, 1969, 1.

64. *San Francisco Policeman,* December 1970, 4; October 1971, 7. *SFC,* June 27, 1969, 26. *Notebook,* November 1970, 4; June 1972, 4; May 1972, 3.

65. Hebel interview #2.

66. David Alan Sklansky, *Democracy and the Police* (Stanford, CA: Stanford University Press, 2007), 76–77, 171; Hevery Juris and Peter Feuille, *Police Unionism: Power and Impact in Public-Sector Bargaining* (Lexington, MA: Lexington Books, 1973), 25; Link, "Black and White," 18; Jones, "Black vs. White," 368.

67. Jones, "Black vs. White," 370.

68. *SFC,* November 14, 1970, 18; March 29, 1969, 7. Douglas Hope, "Police Are Developing New Political Muscle," in *The Police Rebellion: A Quest for Blue Power,* ed. William Bopp (Springfield, IL: Thomas, 1971), 76.

69. Alessandro Baccari and Associates, *A Report to the Officers and Members of the San Francisco Police Officers' Association* (San Francisco: A. Baccari and Associates, 1971), 7–8; Hebel interview #1; Paul Chignell interview with author, April 30, 2003.

70. Hebel interview #1.

71. Alessandro Baccari and Associates, *Report to the Officers,* 8; "Appointments and Removals," in SFPD, *Annual Reports* (San Francisco: City of San Francisco, 1967, 1968, 1969). After

hiring only 78 new officers in 1967 and 86 new officers in 1968, the department made 146 new hires in 1969.

72. Mullen interview.

73. *SFC*, January 26, 1970, 1, 20; Hebel interview #1.

74. *SFBG*, December 22, 1972, 9. Hongisto also earned endorsements from the *San Francisco Bay Guardian* and the city's liberal Council of Democratic Clubs. *SFBG*, September 27, 1971, 19; December 22, 1972, 9.

75. *SFBG*, September 27, 1971, 19; December 22, 1972, 10. Link, "Black and White," 16.

76. *SFE*, November 3, 1971, 1.

77. Nicholas Pileggi, "Crime and Punishment," in *America's Mayor: John V. Lindsay and the Reinvention of New York,* ed. Sam Roberts (New York: Columbia University Press, 2010), 75; Joshua Freeman, "Lindsay and Labor," in Roberts, *America's Mayor,* 129; Jeff Greenfield, "The Second Toughest Job," in Roberts, *America's Mayor,* 152; Charles Morris, "New York's Great Society," in Roberts, *America's Mayor,* 180. William Bopp, "Incident at Vallejo," in *The Police Rebellion: A Quest for Blue Power,* ed. William Bopp (Springfield, IL: Thomas, 1971), 186. For Alioto's efforts to forbid a police strike, see *SFC*, April 29, 1970, 2.

78. *SFE*, November 14, 1970, 4.

79. Shortly after the O'Brien trial, Alioto's Police Commission attempted to arrange direct negotiations with the POA that excluded Ehrlich. The traditional POA leadership rejected these overtures, but Alioto's offer made it clear that Ehrlich was not the rank and file's only conduit into the political sphere. *SFC*, July 11, 1969, 4.

80. *SFC*, February 5, 1970, 1.

81. *SFC*, February 17, 1970, 2; February 18, 1970, 4. The POA's policy of allowing retired members to participate in elections prevented the Blue Coats from winning an even greater number of positions. Gerald Crowley interview with author, May 20, 2003.

82. William Hemby, a Potrero Station Blue Coat, edited the *Notebook.*

83. *SFC*, December 29, 1970, 16.

84. *SFC*, July 16, 1970, 4; January 14, 1971, 1, 22; February 2, 1971, 2. *SFE*, December 29, 1970, 4.

85. Supervisor John Barbagelata, a Republican and a close runner-up to George Moscone in San Francisco's 1975 mayoral election, followed this pattern. William Bopp, Paul Chignell, and Charles Maddox, "San Francisco Police Strike of 1975: A Case Study," *Journal of Police Science and Administration* 5, no. 1 (1977): 41.

86. *SFC*, January 26, 1970, 20; Crowley interview.

87. *SFC*, February 24, 1971, 18; February 3, 1971, 1, 26; February 4, 1971, 1, 22. In 1971 the Blue Coat–led POA also sued gay activists and underground newspapers for publicly criticizing individual police officers. *Harry*, November 12, 1971, 4. *Harry* was a New Left underground newspaper published in Baltimore, Maryland.

88. *SFC*, January 11, 1971, 11.

89. Hebel interview #1.

90. *SFEC*, September 26, 1971, 1; *SFC*, April 13, 1971, 2; *Memorandum of Understanding between San Francisco Police Commission and San Francisco Police Officers' Association* (Oc-

tober 28, 1971), SFPL, Vertical Files: "S.F. Police. Associations. San Francisco Police Officers' Association."

91. "Ten Year Comparison of Reported Offenses," in SFPD, *Annual Report* (San Francisco: City of San Francisco, 1972); Wirt, *Power in the City*, 167.

92. Osman, *Invention of Brownstone Brooklyn*, 250; *SFC*, January 12, 1972, 3; *SFE*, January 22, 1972, 3; *San Francisco Progress*, March 15, 1972, 1, 27. Also see Mayor's Committee for Municipal Management, *A Report to the Blyth-Zellerbach Committee on Modern Management for San Francisco*, Vol. 2 (San Francisco: Mayor's Committee for Municipal Management, June 1961), 6. A 1971 department-wide study found "exasperatingly slow" police reactions to be "a recurring complaint by citizens from all parts of the city." San Francisco Committee on Crime, *A Report on the Police Department, Part II, The Ninth Report of the Committee* (San Francisco: Committee on Crime, June 17, 1971), 17.

93. *SFC*, January 12, 1972, 2; *SFE*, January 22, 1972, 3; *Notebook*, January 1972, 3. The SFPD's Bureau of Planning and Research and the city's Planning Commission were also caught unaware even though both were in the midst of developing capital improvement and master plans based on the district station model. *SFE*, January 19, 1972, 24.

94. Crowley interview.

95. *San Francisco Progress*, April 5, 1972, 1, 2.

96. *San Francisco Progress*, January 15, 1972, 31; *HA*, June 1972, 3; *SFE*, March 10, 1972, 16.

97. *San Francisco Progress*, March 29, 1972, 5; *SFE*, January 20, 1972, 46; *SFC*, April 13, 1972, 4. The Haight-Ashbury Merchants and Property Owners Association grew out of the earlier Haight-Ashbury Merchants and Improvement Association.

98. *HA*, June 1972, 6; May 1973, 3. On April 24, 1971, Vietnam War veterans participating in a massive antiwar demonstration alleged that the SFPD motorcycle patrol had attacked them. This incident helped critics further associate centralized policing with militarization. Alioto attended the April protest and shook hands with participants. *Good Times*, October 15, 1971, 6; *Freedom News*, December 1973, 5. *Freedom News* was a New Left organ based in Richmond, California.

99. *SFC*, July 21, 1972, 3; *HA*, July 1973, 4.

100. *HA*, May 1973, 3; *SFE*, January 22, 1972, 3; *Good Times*, October 1, 1971, 3; *SFEC*, October 1, 1972, 8.

101. *SFC*, January 20, 1972, 4; March 18, 1972, 2; April 21, 1972, 2; April 29, 1972, 2; May 5, 1972, 3; January 15, 1972, 2.

102. On the Church of the Good Earth's earlier clashes with Alioto over redevelopment and concurrent run-ins with the SFPD over drugs, see *SFC*, January 8, 1971, 8.

103. *SFC*, February 10, 1973, 6; *SFE*, May 15, 1972, 3; *HA*, June 1972, 4–5; *Takeover*, June 13, 1972, 6. *Takeover* was an underground newspaper published in Madison, Wisconsin.

104. *SFE*, May 15, 1972, 3; *HA*, April 1972, 8; *Takeover*, June 13, 1972, 6; *SFC*, May 27, 1972, 4. Just prior to the May 1972 Good Earth raid, police assaulted participants in a 2,500-person antiwar march. *SFC*, May 13, 1972, 1, 14.

105. *SFC*, May 26, 1972, 3. *SFE*, March 10, 1972, 16; January 28, 1972, 20.

106. *SFC*, May 26, 1972, 3; November 8, 1972, 5C; *SFE*, March 24, 1972, 40. Bruce Brugmann and Greggar Sletteland, eds., *The Ultimate Highrise: San Francisco's Mad Rush toward the Sky* (San Francisco: San Francisco Bay Guardian, 1971), 65; *San Francisco Policeman*, October 1972, 12.

107. Stephen Barton, "A History of the Neighborhood Movement in San Francisco," *Berkeley Planning Journal* 2, nos. 1-2 (1985), available at http://comm-org.wisc.edu/papers97/sfhist .htm; Chester Hartman, *City for Sale: The Transformation of San Francisco,* rev. and updated ed. (Berkeley: University of California Press, 2002), 228-29.

108. Sklansky, *Democracy and the Police,* 152; *The Black Panther,* May 5, 1973, 5. The NAACP, League of United Latin American Citizens, Chinese for Affirmative Action, and National Organization for Women also signed on to the lawsuit. This OFJ lawsuit and one other succeeded, and both dramatically advanced SFPD racial integration (and, inadvertently, gender integration). OFJ also spent the 1970s using its limited clout to protect the PCR unit from its political opponents and to teach new black recruits "survival tactics" for handling racism in the SFPD. Dulaney, *Black Police,* 77, 110.

109. *HA*, May 1973, 3. *SFC*, February 10, 1973, 6; March 30, 1973, 23.

110. *San Francisco Policeman,* July 1973, 1.

111. Daryl Maeda, *Chains of Babylon: The Rise of Asian America* (Minneapolis: University of Minnesota Press, 2009), 73.

CONCLUSION

1. "1984 Jeane Kirkpatrick," available at http://www.cnn.com/ALLPOLITICS/1996/conven tions/san.diego/facts/GOP.speeches.past/84.kirkpatrick.shtml.

2. "Rep. Graves (R-MO) Attacks Opponent's 'San Francisco Values' in New TV Ad," available at http://www.youtube.com/watch?v=uROhNSsi79E; "Baptist Church Becomes Target in the Culture Wars," *Christianity Today,* November 8, 1993, 57. In 2013, tapes from a campaign strategy session for Senator Mitch McConnell revealed that the Republican's staff planned to attack Ashley Judd, a potential Democratic challenger, at one point referring to San Francisco as her "American city home." "Secret Tape of McConnell Bashing Ashley Judd: Anatomy of a Smear," *Los Angeles Times,* April 9, 2013, available at http://www.latimes.com/local/lanow/ la-me-ln-mcconnell-ashley-judd-20130409,0,2216803.story.

3. Robert Fogelson, *Big-City Police* (Cambridge, MA: Harvard University Press, 1977), 245.

4. Jon Teaford, *The Rough Road to Renaissance: Urban Revitalization in America, 1940– 1985* (Baltimore, MD: Johns Hopkins University Press, 1990), 192-99.

5. Peter Dreier, John Mollenkopf, and Todd Swanstrom, *Place Matters: Metropolitics for the Twenty-First Century,* 2nd ed. (Lawrence: University Press of Kansas, 2005), 171, 177; Terry Nichols Clark, "Race and Class versus the New Political Culture," in *Urban Innovation: Creative Strategies for Turbulent Times,* ed. Terry Nichols Clark (Thousand Oaks, CA: Sage Publications, 1994), 23; Jonathan Simon, *Governing through Crime: How the War on Crime Transformed American Democracy and Created a Culture of Fear* (New York: Oxford University Press, 2007), 91, 100.

6. Fogelson, *Big-City Police,* 304.

7. Christian Parenti, *Lockdown America: Police and Prisons in the Age of Crisis* (New York: Verso, 1999), 51.

8. David Alan Sklansky, *Democracy and the Police* (Stanford, CA: Stanford University Press, 2007), 77.

9. During the new century, liberal city officials who defended tactical police actions against protesters did not follow Alioto's approach of arguing that tactical law enforcement defended democracy. Instead, they emphasized the physical threat protesters posed to policymakers. Don Mitchell, "The Liberalization of Free Speech: Or, How Protest in Public Space Is Silenced," *Stanford Agora* 4 (2003); Don Mitchell, "The Battle of Seattle Revisited: Or, Seven Views of the Protest-Zoning State," *Political Geography* 26, no. 5 (2007): 603.

10. Warren Hinckle, *Gayslayer! The Story of How Dan White Killed Harvey Milk and Got Away with Murder* (Virginia City, NV: Silver Dollar Book Publishers, 1985), 17, 25; Randy Shilts, *The Mayor of Castro Street: The Life and Times of Harvey Milk* (New York: St. Martin's, 1982), 272.

11. Robert Self, "Sex in the City: The Politics of Sexual Liberalism in Los Angeles, 1963-79," *Gender & History* 20, no. 2 (2008): 300.

12. Sklansky, *Democracy and the Police,* 77. In Detroit, the Detroit Police Officers Association teamed up with black and white liberal unionists to campaign against affirmative action programs endangering traditional seniority rights. Dennis Deslippe, "'Do Whites Have Rights?': White Detroit Policemen and 'Reverse Discrimination' Protests in the 1970s," *The Journal of American History* 91, no. 3 (2006): 954.

13. Sklansky, *Democracy and the Police,* 82-84, 87; Katherine Beckett and Steve Herbert, *Banished: The New Social Control in Urban America* (New York: Oxford University Press, 2010); Katherine Beckett and Steve Herbert, "Dealing with Disorder: Social Control in the Post-Industrial City," *Theoretical Criminology* 12, no. 1 (2008): 9.

14. Parenti, *Lockdown America,* 100-103; George Kelling and Catherine Coles, *Fixing Broken Windows: Restoring Order and Reducing Crime in Our Communities* (New York: Martin Kessler, 1996), 209; Bernard Harcourt, *Illusion of Order: The False Promise of Broken Windows Policing* (Cambridge, MA: Harvard University Press, 2001), part I; Franklin Zimring, *The Great American Crime Decline* (New York: Oxford University Press, 2008), 155.

15. Sklansky, *Democracy and the Police,* 101; David Alan Sklansky, "The Persistent Pull of Police Professionalism" (unpublished paper, courtesy of the author, 2010), 1; Steve Herbert, *Citizens, Cops, and Power: Recognizing the Limits of Community* (Chicago: University of Chicago Press, 2006), 4. The rise of community policing was one of several trends in municipal governance during the 1980s that promoted participatory democratic principles. Planning scholars have shown how progressive coalitions forced governments to institute participatory neighborhood planning models that emphasized cooperative, discretion-based relationships drawing together government planners and neighborhood residents. Susan Fainstein and Clifford Hirst, "Neighborhood Organizations and Community Planning: The Minneapolis Neighborhood Revitalization Program," in *Revitalizing Urban Neighborhoods,* ed. Dennis Keating, Norman Grumholz, and Philip Star (Lawrence: University Press of Kansas, 1996), 96-97.

16. Jerome Skolnick, "The Police and the Urban Ghetto," in *Ambivalent Force: Perspectives on the Police,* 2nd ed., ed. Arthur Niederhoffer and Abraham Blumberg (Hinsdale, IL: Dryden

Press, 1976), 223–26; Louis Radelet and Hoyt Coe Reed, *The Police and the Community* (Beverly Hills, CA: Glencoe, 1973), 642; David Patrick Geary, *Community Relations and the Administration of Justice* (New York: Wiley, 1975), 238; James Richardson, "Conflict and Differences over Police Performance: An Historical Overview," in *Police-Community Relations: Images, Roles, Realities,* ed. Alvin Cohn and Emilio Viano (Philadelphia, PA: Lippincott, 1976), 296; Thomas Johnson, Gordon Misner, and Lee Brown, *The Police and Society: An Environment for Collaboration and Confrontation* (Englewood Cliffs, NJ: Prentice-Hall, 1981), 381–82; Michael Hebel interview #2 with author, June 11, 2012.

17. Herbert, *Citizens, Cops, and Power,* 40.

INDEX

The letter f following a page number denotes a figure.

African Americans (*continued*)
  of force against, 64, 152, 161, 163, 169, 175,
  180, 181, 187, 190, 206–7, 209; preventive
  policing and Operation S and, 39, 40,
  151; reactions to K-9 unit, 167, 194; riot
  (*see* Hunters Point riot); in the SFPD, 53,
  185–86, 195–96, 202, 227–29, 296n38;
  Sun-Reporter (see *Sun-Reporter*)
Afro-American Patrolmen's League of
  Chicago, 227
Ahern, Francis "Frank": appointment as
  chief, 31; Chinatown relations, 34; commitment to SFPD's closeting approach to
  gays, 76; photo, 33*f*; police professionalism and, 31–32, 35, 90, 266n42
Alcoholic Beverage Control, Department
  of (ABC): closing of gay bars after the
  gayola scandal, 99; empowered to enforce
  moral standards, 86; establishment of, 86;
  officials' investigative tactics, 87; reliance
  on SFPD officers, 99, 107; *Vallerga* ruling,
  88–89
Alioto, Joseph: acceptance of OFJ, 227;
  appointment of a black police commissioner, 204; attitude towards homosexuality, 140–41; Blue Coats' alliance with, 235,
  238, 304n79; campaign and election in
  1967, 4, 15, 139; campaign and election in
  1971, 182; Catholic Action and, 140–41,
  176, 210; City Hall-oriented vision of
  democracy, 140, 177–78, 209, 210–11, 212,
  235, 244; common good and, 140, 176, 212,
  239; compared to Lindsay, 143, 174, 177,
  179, 204, 209–10, 213–14, 239, 293n100;
  emphasis on violence threatening whites,
  182; harm principle and, 141–42; incorpo-
  ration of racial pluralism in the concept
  of citizenship, 177–80, 292n98; introduction of cosmopolitan growth liberalism
  into City Hall, 140–42; justification of his
  use of force against demonstrators, 211;
  national reputation, 176, 210, 211, 292n97;
  negotiation-based response to rising

crime rates, 176, 292n93; opposition to
  Black Panther Party, 179–80; outreach to
  the black voting bloc, 174–76; outreach
  to young professionals, 140; PCR unit
  strengthening, 204–5; photo, 178*f*; POA
  and, 235, 304n79; political motivation for
  supporting police-community dialogue,
  223; prioritizing economic growth over
  peacekeeping, 179; punishment of discretionary use of force, 208, 211; redevelopment and, 139, 175, 176, 184, 235, 239, 242,
  305n102; response to the State College
  strike, 209–10, 211; self-branding as a cosmopolitan liberal, 139, 140; tactical squad
  and, 205–6, 209, 224–26; tolerance for
  cultural and sexual pluralism, 141, 142, 223,
  285n109; vital liberalism and, 140, 141, 176.
  See also cosmopolitan growth liberalism;
  cosmopolitan liberalism
American Bar Association (ABA), 37–38
American Friends Service Committee, 159,
  162
American Sunbather, 120
Anderson, Chester, 68–69, 273n87
Andreotti, Dante, 188, 197, 198, 203, 297n60
Ann's 440 (nightclub), 121
Armstrong, Elizabeth, 74
Asian Americans: city demographics and,
  5–6, 215; downtown press's comparisons
  of blacks and, 156–57; run-ins with police,
  116, 119, 271n64; in the SFPD, 195, 197,
  236–37. *See also* Chinatown
Atherton investigation, 20, 21, 38, 193
Atlanta, Georgia, 4, 32, 214, 251
autonomous police discretion:
  African-American fight against, 183,
  185, 188–90, 196–97; allowance for in
  order-maintenance policing, 252; challenges of curbing through top-down
  reforms, 59, 71, 273n92; in Chinatown
  (*see* Chinatown detail); city leadership's
  assumption that police would use discretion justly, 39, 40; city leadership's denial

for Service); downtown fears of gangs'
race-conscious orientation, 157, 160–61;
formation and organization of, 150; the
media and, 157; relations with police, 150,
160; relations with women, 150; YFS's
gang-tolerant, cross-neighborhood approach, 159–61
Garner, Washington, 204
gay and lesbian bars: ABC's crackdown
on, 86–89, 99–100; autonomous police
discretion and, 78–81, 95, 96, 96*f;* Board
of Equalization's interest in, 84–85;
cosmopolitan liberal attitudes toward,
97, 99–100, 101–2, 107; discrete nature
of, 77; gay and lesbian ownership of, 93,
101; legislative fight to reform liquor law
enforcement, 85–86; owners' strategies
to delay liquor agency's charges, 88, 101;
police attitudes towards, 76, 77–78; police
payoffs, 80–81; political mobilization
through the Guild, 101, 102; proliferation
of during Robinson's term, 81–82; *Stoumen v. Reilly* and, 85, 86, 88, 89; Tommy's
Place raid fallout and, 82–84; *Vallerga*
ruling and, 88–89. *See also* Black Cat Café;
gayola scandal; gays and lesbians
gayola scandal: cosmopolitan liberals' support gay-citizen rights, 97; impact of the
gayola trials on the SFPD, 96–97, 98–99,
277n65; issues of homosexuality and
discretion gayola trial, 94–96
gays and lesbians: autonomous police
discretion and, 11, 78–81, 95, 96, 96*f;*
conservatives' view of, 74, 76, 88, 89, 106,
125, 274n6; cosmopolitan liberals' attitudes
toward, 97, 99–100, 101–2, 107, 140–41,
142; cosmopolitan liberals' recognition of
a desirable gay voting bloc, 102, 279n81;
courts' biases against, 87–89, 276n39;
discriminatory underpolicing of, 79, 101;
homophile activism, 74, 90, 91, 103 (*see
also* Council on Religion and the Homosexual); homosexual perspectives and

themes in obscenity trials, 118, 119–20, 122,
124, 135; increased media attention due to
post-gayola raids, 99–100, 278n76; lewd
vagrancy and, 76, 98–99, 279n97; mask
of respectability, 74, 75, 94*f;* obscenity
detail's interest in *The Love Book,* 110; police officers' attitudes towards, 76, 77–79;
Republican Party and, 90, 247; state
high court's conflating of homosexual
status with actions, 89; Wolden's antigay
politicking, 90–91; Wolfenden Report and,
14, 142, 143. *See also* gay and lesbian bars;
gayola scandal
"general public welfare." *See* common good
Gibson, Phil, 88
Ginsberg, Allen, 46, 114–15, 118. See also
Howl and Other Poems
Gleason, Ralph, 69
Golden Cask, 89
Golden Gate Freeway, 217
Goldwater, Barry, 12, 163
Gonzales, Robert, 243
Goodlett, Carlton, 67, 200, 298n65
Good Times, 143, 241
graft. *See* gayola scandal; machine politics;
payola
Graves, Sam, 247
Grey, Cynthia, 51–52
Grosjean, Lyle, 241
Grunsky, Donald, 58
Guth, Anna, 218
Guth, Leland, 241

Haight Action, 241
Haight-Ashbury Children's Center, 300n10
Haight-Ashbury Free Medical Clinic, 222,
224
Haight-Ashbury Independent, 219
Haight-Ashbury neighborhood: Aaron
slashing in, 193, 218, 295n27; Alioto's
attempt to integrate his coalition, 223;
appeal to young professionals, 214–15,
299n5; centralized policing practices and,

Krikorian, Leo, 44, 45
Kronhausen, Phyllis, 126

LAPD. *See* Los Angeles Police Department
Latinos, 154–55; city demographics and, 215, 261n10; PCR unit and, 197, 198, 205, 212; relations with police, 154–55, 206, 230, 236, 288n31; voter suppression and, 166
Lau, Fred, 236, 237
law-and-order politics, 2, 5, 12–13, 42, 163–64, 193, 235, 251–52, 253
Laws of Arrest inquiries (1960), 57
Lazarus, Leland, 131–32
LCE News, 101
Lee, Dai-Ming, 27
Lehane, John, 79, 229, 237
Leighton, Elliot, 104
Lenn, Ernest, 36–37, 39
Lenoir, Henri, 44
Leway, Incorporated, 179
lewd vagrancy, 60, 76, 90, 98, 107, 279n97, 283n77. *See also* vagrancy laws
liberalism. *See* cosmopolitan growth liberalism; cosmopolitan liberalism; cosmopolitan liberal policing; cosmopolitan localists; traditional liberals; vital liberalism
Lindsay, John, 143, 174, 177, 239
Little City News, 133, 281n19
localists. *See* cosmopolitan localists
Los Angeles, California, 4, 10, 32, 35, 107, 122, 143, 148, 151, 164, 205, 217, 251
Los Angeles Police Department (LAPD), 10, 35, 143, 205
Los Siete, 230
Love Book, The (Kandel): arresting of the book's sellers, 133–34, 283n76; defense argument about the value of female sexual perspectives to women, 135–37; obscenity detail's interest in, 110; role of Catholic mores in the trial, 134–35, 137, 284n88; Shelley's condemnation of the poem, 134; trial's results, 137–38
Lowenthal, Morris, 85, 89

Lucas, Don, 77–78
Luster, Orville: Alioto's adopting and adapting of his negotiation model, 177, 178–79; appointment as YFS secretary, 161–62; attempts to deal with the police's disproportionate use of force, 167; decline of YFS, 182–83, 293n112; focus on negotiation, 168; focus on political integration, 147, 165–67, 180; focus on youth employment, 168; leveraging white fears of black violence to raise funds, 166, 293n104; linking of racial pluralism with violence prevention, 165–66; peacekeeping during the riot, 145–46, 171; photo, 160*f. See also* Youth for Service
Lynch, Thomas, 26, 37, 82, 93–94, 98, 119–20, 121, 128, 282n35

machine policing: autonomous discretion and, 9, 23–24, 42–43; Chinatown detail as archetype of, 23–24; federal and state opposition to, 22, 26, 31, 85; graft in, 20, 21, 24–25; weak police chief and, 21
machine politics: Christopher's campaign against, 30; conflicts with downtown growth advocates, 18–22; *Examiner's* influence over City Hall, 28, 266n33; police professionalism seen as a remedy for, 20; politicians' view of police officers, 8. *See also* Robinson, Elmer
MacPhee, Chester, 113, 114, 125
Maguire, Leo, 219
Maguire, Michael, 1, 3, 33*f,* 54
Maloney, Peter, 110, 133, 283n75
Mana, Lawrence, 134–35
managerial growth politics: advocates' faith in top-down reform, 18, 20, 32–33; advocates' promises to serve color-blind, family values, 30, 34, 37, 39, 74, 287n25; advocates' redevelopment agenda and, 13, 20, 30, 32, 36, 47, 92; advocates' tolerance for police discretion, 11, 39, 40, 74; Chinatown business leaders and, 27, 34; *Chronicle's*

111–12; criticized by cosmopolitan liberals, 65, 97; gay bars and, 95, 97; hippies and, 283n77; informal policing strategies and, 112; Juvenile Bureau's approach to, 110, 112, 115, 120, 121, 122, 133, 282n37, 283nn75–76; Lenny Bruce's arrest, 121–22; obscenity detail and, 110, 133, 283n75; political censorship, 143; presumption of adult male prerogatives and, 112, 122; professionalized law enforcement and, 112, 121, 143–44, 282n35; Vorpal Gallery raid, 122. See also *Howl and Other Poems; Love Book, The;* sexually explicit materials and performances; topless clubs controversy

Police Commission, SFPD: Christopher's commission, 17–18; control of by the mayor, 17, 20–21; first black commissioner in, 204; increased power of, 15; investigations of anti-black police violence and, 189, 190; manipulation of by the mayor, 20–21; O'Brien case and, 208, 211; OFJ and, 227; PCR unit and, 229; personnel decisions by, 21, 22; POA and, 191, 195; practice of picking Catholics for leadership positions, 53, 115; relationship with the *Examiner,* 28; station consolidation plan and, 239–40, 242; support of police-community dialogue, 223

police-community relations unit (PCR): Alioto's strengthening of the unit, 204–5; Cahill's exploitation of, 199–200; Cahill's opposition to, 197–98, 203–4; cooperative discretion between residents and officers, 198–200; efforts to check autonomous police discretion, 200–202; introduction of racial pluralism into the SFPD, 201–2; new gay community liaison position, 107; O'Brien investigation and, 207; officers taking on political roles, 199, 201–2, 223; OFJ's relationship with, 228–29, 306n108; overview of populations the unit worked with, 198–99

police professionalism: arguments for PCR unit and, 196–97; black activists' difficulty achieving professionalism reforms, 189; Christopher's message and, 30–31; civilianizing reforms and, 194–95; civilian review boards and, 185, 196; establishment of, 186, 196–98; K-9 unit and, 193–94; liberal rule-of-law arguments and, 3, 11, 56, 57, 58, 211, 248, 263n26; national movement representing a governing mindset, 20; obscenity policing and, 112, 121, 143–44, 282n35; Operation S and, 35–37; path to political integration for Chinatown business elites, 26–27; path to political integration for gay and lesbian bars, 102; politicians' use of to build electoral coalitions, 29–30; rank-and-file reactions to Christopher's speech on police reform, 18; redevelopment and, 19–20, 36–37, 267n58; station consolidation plan, 21, 192, 239, 293, 305nn92–93; tactical squad creation and, 205–6; tolerance for autonomous police discretion, 39, 40

Poole, Cecil, 165

pornography. *See* obscenity trials; police censorship; sexually explicit materials and performances

Potrero Station, 150–51, 152, 153, 232, 234, 235. *See also* Southeast Station

Potter, Gail, 118

Presidential Commission on Obscenity and Pornography, 141, 142

preventive policing. *See* Operation S; stop-and-frisk policing

professionals. *See* white-collar professionals

Proposition 3, 86

Proposition K, 243, 244

Psychedelic Shop, 110, 133–34

Quinlan, Daniel, 133, 283n76

race consciousness. *See* African Americans; racial pluralism

46, 47, 49, 57–58, 63, 65, 67–70; coverage
of the Hunters Point riot, 171; coverage
of the O'Brien case, 207, 211; coverage of
the Wolden campaign, 91; criticisms of
machine policing, 22, 29; double-standard
on vagrancy law arrests, 59; faith in top-
down reform, 36, 228; ignoring allegations of police racism, 68–69; opposition
to civilian review boards, 196; religious
allegiances of, 266n35; reporters' jabs at
censors' masculinity, 124; reporting on
issues of black crime, 193; resistance to
newspaper staff integration, 62; strategies
for undercutting the *Examiner's* power,
28–29, 266n35; support for Alioto, 141;
support for Christopher, 29; support for
the K-9 unit, 194; support of Operation
S, 36; support of police professionalism
campaign, 18, 28–29, 31; support of the
PCR concept, 197–98. *See also* newspapers
San Francisco city charter, 19
San Francisco Department of Public Health,
220, 221
San Francisco Examiner: coverage of gays
and lesbians, 76, 82, 83; coverage of
Hunters Point, 157, 158, 165; coverage of
obscenity controversies, 119, 124, 130, 131;
coverage of the beats, 46–47, 49, 58, 63,
69; coverage of the O'Brien case, 207,
298n74; coverage of the PCR unit, 197,
203; coverage of the Wolden campaign, 91;
influence over City Hall, 28, 31, 265n32,
266n33; racial integration of staff, 62;
support of Operation S, 36–37, 39. *See also*
newspapers
San Francisco Housing Authority (SFHA),
148, 152
San Francisco Mime Troupe, 283n77
San Francisco NAACP, 148, 187, 188, 189,
197, 306n108
San Francisco Police Department (SFPD):
African Americans in, 53, 185–86, 195–96,

202, 227–29, 296n38; autonomous police
discretion (*see* autonomous police discretion); beatnik patrol (*see* Bigarani, William
"Bill"); Blue Coats and (*see* Blue Coats);
Bureau of Special Services, 21, 22, 25, 26,
76, 79, 98, 103; Catholic composition of,
53; Central Station (*see* Central Station);
challenge to the discriminatory minimum
height requirement, 236–37; Chinatown
detail (*see* Chinatown detail); civilianizing program, 194–95; cooperative
discretion (*see* cooperative discretion);
corruption inquiry in 1937, 20; discretionary use of force (*see* autonomous police
discretion); failure of the post-Atherton
structural reforms, 21 22, 265nn15–16;
Juvenile Bureau (*see* Juvenile Bureau);
K-9 unit, 167, 194; lack of procedural and
policy training and instruction, 9; limited
gender and racial integration, 53, 195–96,
270n38, 296n38; Northern Station (*see*
Northern Station); obscenity detail (*see*
police censorship); OFJ and (*see* Officers
for Justice); payola and graft schemes
by officers (*see* payola); PCR unit (*see*
police-community relations unit); POA
and (*see* San Francisco Police Officers'
Association); political influence on appointments, 8, 17, 20–21, 22, 28, 53, 192,
223, 232, 238; Potrero Station (*see* Potrero
Station); power of sergeants in, 81; rank-
and-file's labor rights in, 190–91, 192–95
(*see also* Blue Coats); rank-and-file's
political rights in (*see* Blue Coats; San
Francisco Police Officers' Association);
rise in violence against police, 230; second
platoon subculture, 231; sex detail (*see* sex
detail); Southeast Station (*see* Southeast
Station); supervisory structure, 53–54;
tactical squad (*see* tactical squad); women
in, 53, 194–95. *See also* cosmopolitan
liberal policing; machine policing; police
professionalism

Making the Second Ghetto: Race and Housing in Chicago, 1940–1960
by Arnold R. Hirsch

Smoldering City: Chicagoans and the Great Fire, 1871–1874
by Karen Sawislak

Modern Housing for America: Policy Struggles in the New Deal Era
by Gail Radford

Parish Boundaries: The Catholic Encounter with Race in the Twentieth-Century Urban North
by John T. McGreevy